SERPENT IN THE CELLAR

LOVE AND DEATH IN LIFE AND MYTH

TOM STRELOW

Serpent in the Cellar—Love and Death in Life and Myth
Author: Tom Strelow
Illustrations: Tom Strelow

Credits for academic fair use quotations are cited in-line by author and publication date and then tabulated in the *Reference* subsection.

Credits for media rights and authorship for all photos and artwork are tabulated in the *Media* subsection.

Printed in the United States of America.

Library of Congress Control Number: 2022912071

Published by Xrysalus Media, Orange, California

XRYASALUS MEDIA

ISBN
Hardcover: 9798986522401
Softcover: 9798986522418
Ebook: 9798986522425

For permission and inquiries, contact: media@xrysalus.com

For additional information, reference: http://media.xrysalus.com

This book is dedicated
to the outsider and the outcast,
to the poor, the weak, and the exploited,
to the mourners and the broken-hearted,
and to those who seek truth and wholeness.

May you find hope, healing, and satisfaction.

May you grow in love and community,
and in strength and maturity,
as you in turn bring renewed life to others.

ACKNOWLEDGEMENT

There are truths, that are beyond us, transcendent truths, about beauty, truth, honor... It is only through the language of myth that we can speak of these truths. — J.R.R. Tolkien

In the Hero's Journey into the Dark Night of the movie *Donnie Darko*, the final descent is through the cellar of an elderly eccentric woman known as *Grandma Death*. This mythological event is foreshadowed by Donnie's English teacher, Ms. Pommeroy, who had earlier written "cellar door" on a chalkboard—referring to the literary alchemist J.R.R. Tolkien, she explains, "This famous linguist once said that of all the phrases in the English language, of all the endless combinations of words in all of history, that 'cellar door' is the most beautiful."

In life, teachers are the storytellers that immerse us in the deeper mysteries of beauty, truth, and honor from the collected mythos of past generations. These truths may then guide us on our own journey through life. On the subject of teachers, Tolkien himself wrote, "I wish I could now tell some of [my teachers of long ago] how I remember them and things they said, though I was (only, as it appeared) looking out of the window or giggling at my neighbour".

Likewise, in my own journey through life, I am deeply indebted to the many storytellers that have inspired me and shown me the many paths into the twisted soul of humanity. Some of these storytellers were artists, scientists, or advocates, and others were teachers and coaches. Some of these storytellers I have invoked as alchemical muses in each chapter proem, and others I have listed by name in the *Prologue*—though by no means is this list complete. Yet, I want to especially thank my first teacher, my mom, on so many levels, but in particular for her dedication to teach me phonetics and how to read when I was barely out of diapers, well before I was enrolled in school. She has inspired my love for language and writing which now has become this book.

CONTENT

FIGURES

TABLES

MODEL

ABBREVIATIONS

BCE	Before Current Era
CC	Creative Commons (for licensing)
CE	Current Era
CLV	Concordant Literal Version of the Christian Bible
KJV	King James Version of the Christian Bible
NIV	New International Version of the Christian Bible
N.p.	No place of publication listed in the book (for citation).
SME	Subject Matter Expert (for research)
Strongs	Strongs' Expanded Exhaustive Concordance of the Bible

THE CELLAR

Standing naked in the damp cellar air,
  the cold cobblestones frozen to my feet,
  I gaze into the dark moonlit shadows
  effervescing through the welled cellar vents.
Here all is quiet except for the wind
  rustling through odd cracks in the old stone walls.

Off in the distance, the clock strikes midnight—
  a slight shadow moves on the edge of sight.
Muting the silence, I cry out, "Who's there?"
A voice replies back from atop the stairs,
  "I am the Dreamer... so, who might you be?"

(Yet, what is this dream if it's not by me?
  Certainly, I am as I think I am,
  standing alone in this dark cellar pale.)

The question lingers, unsure what to say,
  watching the stranger descending this way.
"Where do you come from?" I cautiously pry.

"Beyond the new dawn," she vaguely replies,
  stepping down the last step reaching the floor,
  "I've come to continue our nightly accord."

She now seemed to know me, once she drew near—
  clothing me, she beckons, "Come here, my dear."
Enchanted, I follow. As night wears on,
  we play in the shadows 'til the break of dawn.

Then she ascended the stairs, went on her way,
  as I shed the night's wear, the dark fades away.
I lay down to sleep on the worn cellar floor
  wondering what awakens beyond dawn's door.

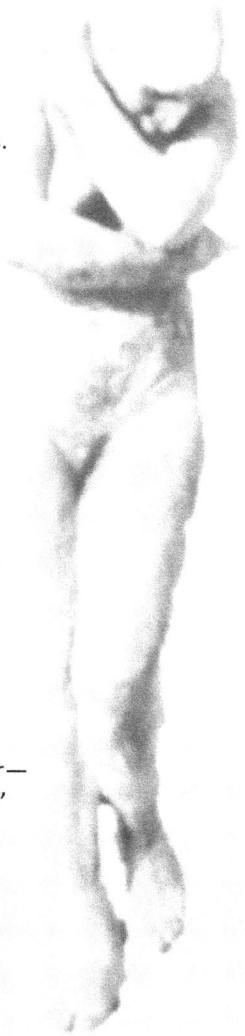

*Your visions will become clear only when
you can look into your own heart.
Who looks outside, dreams;
who looks inside, awakes.*
— C.G. Jung

PROLOGUE

Café Terraces at Night, Vincent Van Gogh, Drawing, 1888.

I enter the cafe and take a seat at my usual table in the back, nodding as the cafe owner places a presumptive cup of coffee in front of me and asks, "Usual?" I settle into my quasi-bohemian bubble with the smell of fresh coffee and an open computer, awaiting breakfast. In my quixotic imagination, I am an artist/writer/philosopher sitting in a street cafe in nineteenth-century Paris or Prague, ready to wrestle the mysteries of life.

A ping from my cellphone heralds a new message, awakening me from my pretense. Like a sorcerer conjuring forth an oracle, I reach into my pocket for my phone, only to become a jester, juggling emails and text messages in service to some mechanical god. I open the endless scroll of mischief to see what new trickery has befallen mankind, finding only dismay as the winter of mankind's hopes and dreams is once again beset by a storm of ignorance and greed. Yet, I hope—as Aristotle mused, "hope is the dream of a waking man."[1] I hope that which slumbers in the dark of winter will soon awaken. As hope springs eternal—seasons inevitably change, storms inevitably pass, and the ice begins to thaw—I hope that Mankind will dream anew. I hope...

The waiter stops by to refill my coffee cup. My mind wanders back to those nineteenth-century cafes in Paris and Prague—taking a sip from my rewarmed cup, smelling the fresh-brewed aroma—I wonder if they had good coffee in Nouveau Paris.

My bohemian fantasy began early as a child of the sixties. The year 1963 was a pivotal year for the decade—it was the year that President Kennedy was assassinated, the space race was ramping up, the beatniks had just

---

[1] Diogenes Laertius (1853) p. 187

become hippies, and the conflict in Vietnam had just become a war. The civil rights movement came into full swing with the protests in Birmingham, the March on Washington, and King's "I Have A Dream" speech. And most importantly, at least in my world, I was born—completely oblivious to all the aforementioned events. I just lay about, ate, burped, and shat my way through that year, and the next (come to think of it, that sounds a lot like this year as well). Eventually, I came to understand, appreciate, and be inspired by the *sitz im leben* of my origin story as these narrative threads unfolded into my adulthood.

One of these narrative threads unfolded in the late sixties when my clean-cut bespectacled aerospace engineer dad took an uncharacteristic predilection to a new church on the edge of the burgeoning *Jesus Freak* movement—a suburban version of a hippie commune, celebrating love, art, music, and spirituality as a way of life, embodied with greater enthusiasm and charisma than the usual staid church temperament would have approved. Over the course of a decade, I witnessed this close-knit band of a few hundred longhaired Jesus enthusiasts grow into a worldwide religious institution with a prodigy of corporate entities. This small group of free-spirited misfits living a passionate lifestyle of love for their fellow man, in a community ostensibly founded on honesty and creativity, evolved into a large group of good church-going Christians, fitted neatly in their pews by the thousands, committed to following the institutional dogma and principles of this developing denomination.

In the early eighties, I went off to college at UCLA. As an elite distance runner, I had hopes of continuing my athletic career there, but a series of injuries and unfortunate circumstances overshadowed that aspiration. My path took a different turn as I prepared to attend; I was given an ultimatum by my deeply religious father to join a Christian fraternity he had learned about, that is if I wanted any financial assistance from him. So, I did. Over the next few years, I witnessed that group, similarly, go from a more open and diverse ideological group when I pledged, to a more rigid, conservative Christian cabal, paralleling the rise of the rightwing Moral Majority and the synthesizing of the evangelical church with Reagan era politics. While I would have been a church mouse in an Animal-House style fraternity, I became a *radical* in this moralistic religious fraternity. By *radical* I mean I had a diverse interest in music, leaning towards punk rock (as was the trend in early 80's LA), I had an occasional beer or trendy wine cooler (yes, it tastes as bad as it sounds), I went to lots of concerts and dances (and DJ'd a few). In short, I was a fairly typical, mild-mannered college student in this dynamic era of Los

Angeles. However, that was enough to get me censured and secretly blacklisted by the alumni overseers.

The fraternity already had a rule that the chapter could not sponsor events having drinking (of alcohol) or dancing, which I was fine with, given the history of fraternities becoming wild moronic fetes, animated by drugs, alcohol, and a puerile sexist and racist culture. However, when I ran for chapter president in my junior year, the alumni overseers responded to my candidacy by immediately passing a new rule that any elected officer had to sign a paper stating that they would not drink or dance in their private lives as well. Not that my occasional beer or outing was a matter of utmost importance that I couldn't abstain for a year, but this sudden and deliberate moralistic directive was quite intentionally directed at me, as a matter of principle, to distinguish two entirely different worldviews. If this were a Hollywood movie, the kids would have gotten together and had a final dance-off to mystically save the town, but this wasn't *Footloose* or any other hackneyed eighties teenage morality flick. By their actions and intent, I was clearly not one of them, and, quite frankly, I agreed with them. I withdrew my candidacy. Over the years, I watched quite a few of my fraternity brothers go off to seminary to become pastors or missionaries. I can say, in all honesty, I learned a lot about religion, theology, and the inner workings of church authority from them, but not so much about authentic spirituality.

I took my time at UCLA, graduating in five and half years. As a natural polymath, I had diverse interests outside of my major, Mathematics and Computer Science—that is, beyond proving that 1+1 = 2 and figuring out how to build programs to take over the world (*ARPAnet*, partially developed at UCLA, would become the *internet* within a decade). Consequently, I took courses in a wide range of fields including philosophy, psychology, linguistics, art, architecture, history, geography, and economics—anything that fed my deep curiosity about life and the world around me. If UCLA had minors, I would have earned a minor in history, founded particularly on my interests in the history of art, architecture, and the early Jesus movement. In my freshman year, the prominent New Testament History professor, Dr. Scott Bartchy, joined the UCLA History Department—I took every course he taught over the next five years. I quickly diverged from the theological interpretation of my evangelical brethren to a more rigorous historical and philosophical exposition of the source text within its cultural framework.

By my first junior year, I was already working part-time as a Systems Analyst for a large aerospace company. Eventually, I was assigned to an information engineering project that was tasked with researching every level of the company's business operations, interviewing key subject matter experts, extrapolating their underlying narratives into process models, and then breaking them down into data models. This naturally evolved into a career in database design and development. I eventually became a consultant and spent the better part of three decades honing these skills. I became an expert at researching and deconstructing large complex systems into models and usable components. While it may sound unrelated, it is actually what I have done here in writing this book.

As my career in technology flourished, I began looking at other outlets to develop my diverse interests. I got involved in various community groups— joined and eventually led a local chapter of a human rights advocacy group, experimented with community theater, became a small group leader in a church-based support group, co-founded and facilitated a community art group, started a small production company, and immersed myself in the diversity of music and the arts in greater Los Angeles. In search of adventure, I bought a sailboat christened, *La Gitana*, "the Gypsy," with dreams of wandering around the world with my friend and boat partner, Rob. However, I finally concluded that the reality of uprooting my life and relationships for several years to become a hobo sailor was too much of a disruption to my personal and career aspirations. So, I settled for adventures sailing around and to the local Channel Islands off the coast of California. As an inchoate outsider wandering almost imperceptibly in a boundless oceanic wilderness, subordinate to the mercurial weather and the capricious wind that can change from friend to foe in a wink, bounding from trough to peak and back with each succession of waves, one's enfeebled supposition of mastery over all one surveys is challenged and hastily dissipates—there is real life and real danger in living. Sailing offshore, the familiar sights seen from afar of niggling landlubbers buzzing madly about in their infernal carriages are reduced to small pebbles in a great stream of civilized humanity, and then, are quickly lost in the swelling of a vast unfathomable sea and the enduring forces of wild life and nature.

Ultimately, the narrative thread that began with a bunch of hippies in my youth developed into a philosophical intrigue regarding *love and relationship*. I was both an observer and participant in the societal milieu. As a socially awkward computer geek, I often felt like an outsider trying to understand the mysteries of the relational universe—a scientist, clipboard in hand, wandering deep into the relational rainforest to study the ways of some remote indigenous tribe. One of these indigenous tribesmen... uhm, I mean, girlfriend, Pam, was a graduate student in Psychology. She suggested that I might study Depth Psychology, which brought many of these interests together as an academic field of inquiry. So, I applied to the Counseling Psychology program with an emphasis in Depth Tradition at Pacifica Graduate Institute, with summers overseas in Hawaii and Greece. I eventually earned my master's degree in 1997 with a thesis entitled, *Return to Eden—Apple In Hand: The Psychomythology of Genesis-Creation and the Ontogenesis of Polymorphic Consciousness*, from which some of the structural theories in this book have evolved or been derived.

During my time at Pacifica, I learned about drama and creative art therapies from another friend, Stephen. Subsequently, I also pursued and completed my studies at the Drama Therapy Institute of Los Angeles with Dr. Pam Dunne. However, having already established a successful career in Information Technology, I never pursued the required internship hours to become either a Registered Drama Therapist (RDT) or a licensed Marriage Family Therapist (MFT). Along the way, I also pursued a certificate in Experiential Psychologies with the Trees of Life Institute in Santa Barbara with Annette Guionnet (now the Guionnet Center for Expressive Art Therapies) and was a participant in the first couple of years of the *Psyche and the Sacred* program[2] with Dr. Lionel Corbett. In all, these programs taught me a great deal about psychology, psychoanatomy, and the healing arts. More than just acquiring knowledge, they immersed me in the depth and breadth of human experience, beyond the rational constructs of daily life and academics. With a personality more bent towards the philosophical, in lieu of any clinical application for my newfound knowledge, other than leading small community groups, I have pressed on with my studies in my field of interest and endeavored over the last two decades to write several versions of this treatise—finally taking three years off during the world-wide pandemic to focus my research and build this creature I call "book."

During my summer overseas in Hawaii, the local Hilo elders in our host Halau impressed upon us how opprobrious it was for western scientists, metaphorically with their white coats and clipboards, to intrude into their communities, to studiously observe and collect data about them. In reaction to this disrespectful intrusion, as a form of resistance, the Hawaiians would just make shit up about the things they inquired. In fact, that wooden ceremonial staff on display at your local museum, in actuality, is probably Auntie Healani's kitchen spoon. Many of these "resistance fables" are now in textbooks and museums, unbeknownst to the men in white coats, and to the bemusement of the native Hawaiians. On the contrary, the honorable way to

---

[2] Corbett (2019)

approach any fellow human being, to *talk story*, unsurprisingly, is to come on an equal footing, to share your own story, and then, to respectfully inquire of another's. As a scientist, explorer, and groovy therapist, I have tried to honor their guidance in writing this book by sharing my own story in the process of traversing the academic material, a product of white coats and clipboards.

The book is thusly written in multiple voices, both academic and personal. It spans diverse academic fields from psychology, mythology, history, religious studies, philosophy, information engineering, and perhaps a few others. Purposefully, I am exploring the foundational mythology that underlies the religious traditions of Christianity, Judaism, and Islam; attempting to restore the prototypical moral psychology of *love and relationship* within the Universal Family, founded on the Genesis Creation myth, expanded on in the Exodus story, and fulfilled in the Gospel narrative. I will explore the experiential purpose and intent of the original relational myth, which stands in direct opposition to the moralistic theologies that have historically claimed institutional authority over it. Given the nature of the source material, and since at heart I am still a bohemian/hippie/punk, I venture beyond a merely objective exploration of this important mythology as an academic field of inquiry to personally advocate for the *radical* moral principle it espouses, *to love one another*, as a primary objective in mature psychological development. This eclectic literary approach, of course, breaks several written and unwritten conventions on building a cohesive academic thesis and voice; whether it becomes my downfall or not, time, and my eventual critics, will surely tell.

After much hard work, this is the creature I have given life to, pouring out my passion and experience—reified in the irrepressible sentiment of the great nineteenth-century scientist, Dr. Victor Frankenstein, "It's… alive!"

INITIATION

My eyes drift inward into an apocalyptic world entranced in a battle between the sun-lion and moon-wolf; a lost people gather in a dark patch of earth on the precipice of a rocky crevasse, ether in disequilibrium, awaiting a final resolution. Substantively, I am sitting on a dislocated marble pedestal amongst the rubble of the temple of the healing god Asclepius in Epidaurus, Greece—awash in the Mediterranean sun illuminating marmoreal ruins under a cloudless blue sky—engaged in the final moments of a dreamtending ritual, honoring this mythic tableau instantiated a month

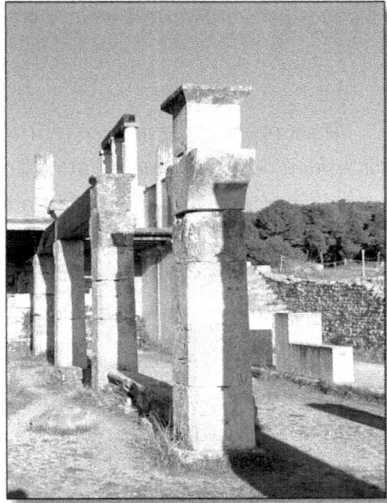

Abaton, Epidaurus. Chabe01, Photo, 2022.

prior. It is both an intimate incursion into the microcosm of my own soul, as well as, in context, an erudite expedition in the art of dreamtending as part of my summer studies in depth psychology, cloistered in the cradle of western civilization and culture, Greece and Crete.

My own journey into this mystic dreamscape of worlds colliding was born as a nocturnal fantasy several weeks ago and carefully recorded in my journal, then, faithfully engaged in an ongoing imaginal discourse threading its way to this moment, the apex of a long, ritualized process. I now sit, legs akimbo, on a marble chaise, immersed in the flux of this cataclysmic operetta, reaching out into the imaginal dreamscape in open acceptance—an invocation of sacrifice into the unknown, letting go of any entitlement to rational interpretation over its ephemeral construct, and offering tribute for this gift of the imagination.

As I make an honorific offering of a poem, eyes drifting inward, my dreamtending partner sitting askew on an adjacent pedestal as a witness, I am brought back to attention by the lightest of touches on my bare short shorn leg. Opening my eyes, before me is what I perceive to be the integration of a lifetime of self-doubt, darkness, and depression, instantiated narratively by a black butterfly marked by a concentric moon overlaying a sun—a white circle overlaying a yellow circle on the tip of a black butterfly's wings now resting on my bare leg. In this touch, immersed in the prior weeks of exploration, I experience an immediate and permanent non-rational psychic shift—the dreamworld bursting into a luminal construct of reality—subsuming a fraught personal narrative into a restorative mythic landscape.

Dreamtending was an essential part of the healing ritual conducted at this *Asklepion* in Epidaurus dating back to the classical period when these marble fragments set in their intended places on top of one another. After a period of cleansing and preparation, the sufferer would enter the *abaton*, the sacred dormitory, to descend into the dreamworld where Asclepius would come in disguise to reveal the path of healing.

The mission of Asclepius as the god of healing is personified by his staff, emblazoned with a serpent wrapping its way upward around it, representing the gift of his restorative power to humankind. The serpent commonly symbolizes healing, and sometimes eternal life, owing to its characteristic ability to renew itself by shedding its skin. It also frequently represents divine revelation by virtue of its ability to traverse between the chthonic underworld and the quotidian upperworld through holes in the ground. Snakes were often used ritually as oracles for divination and healing rites. At Epidaurus, the Asclepian Snakes roamed freely throughout the sacred dormitories of the *abaton* as divine aides in the healing process.

❖The Cellar Door

The heart of any ritual is the approach to the *temenos*, the bounds of the sacred space. The journey towards, and in preparation for, the engagement with the unknown is an essential precursor for any narrative shift within the sacred space, the crucible of the soul. It invites the dreamworld to break into a moment of reality—the elemental psyche offering wholeness and healing to a broken soul. It is a fragile space, easily disrupted by our rational drive to put our own boundaries on the unknown.

Our immediate response to a phenomenal encounter such as the one I have recounted above is to create a linear interpretation of what happened based upon our preconceptions and past experience—we are inclined to rationalize the product of the narrative. Some will look upon my story and see it as a groovy experience that reinforces a perspective of an open universe filled with exciting possibilities beyond our material constructs of reality. Others may see the narrative as a product of neurochemical formulas in the brain calculating a compensatory projection from underlying phenomenological forces instantiated by happenstance. Essentially, what I have presented is a personal myth—a narrative founded on a very real and personal experience, without embellishment, although aptly abbreviated for my own privacy as the full import of it is sacred to my own life journey. The rationalization of the metaphysical framework as to how and why and what forces are at play, while interesting as science or mystical amusement, is merely a distraction and, in the moment, a distortion of the narrative.

The process of dreamtending that is abbreviated above is founded on, and reflective of, a general theory of dreamtending presented by Depth Psychologist, Stephen Aizenstat, which is fundamentally non-interpretative, allowing the narrative of the dream to unfold on its own, discouraging rationalization and judgment.[3] This emphatically goes against most people's instincts to want to impose a rational framework on any experience or narrative based on their prior construct of reality. Substantially, the dream exists, in and of itself, as a separate construct, and must remain sacred, set apart, in order to experience the call of the psychic clarion that beckons reformation of our conscious or operative narrative.

However, not all dreams are numinous or remedial; in fact, most dreams are emotional anecdotes of one's waking experiences—a process of integration and reorientation of one's personal narrative. The deeper narrative can only emerge from the *unconscious* once one has prepared the space in the *conscious* realm. They are not separable, but a continuum of experience and meaning emerging from a pre-rational construction. Once the deeper narrative emerges, it reorients and reuses the conscious symbols and tableaus to build new narratives and patterns, in the same way that a kidnapper cuts out words from a magazine and rearranges them to construct a ransom note (at least that's what they do in the movies.)

Unfortunately, many dreamers attempt to reassess the dream using the old framework, completely negating the evolution of the narrative. In fact, most people commonly default to dream *interpretation*—the presumptive art of deconstructing and rationalizing the symbols of the dream to match some catalog of preconceived associations. Or else, they deflect from the dream narrative to their own ideological narrative, asking why this is happening to me right now, (or possibly bemoaning, why did I eat that spicy burrito before going to bed?) The sacred question is, however, *who visits now*? We must

---

[3] Aizenstat (2011) as general reference—the approach in the narrative was directly from Dr. Aizenstat lectures and assignments as instructor during our summer session in Greece and Crete.

make our waking selves available to a deeper process of discovery than how does this fit into my rational understanding of myself and the universe. There is an intuitive path inward, into the *play space* of the psyche, where all things are possible, and the nature of our authentic inner non-rational selves can speak freely to our egoic waking self. This is the starting point to discuss how we engage the non-rational.

❖The World As I See It

Our bias toward an egocentric interpretation of reality is essentially illustrated in the ill-fated foray of the iconoclastic mathematician and

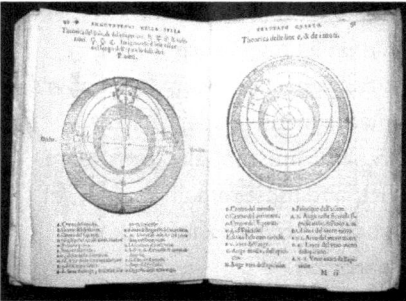

Ptolemaic System, Mauro Fiorentino, Illustration, 1550

Figure 1 - Ptolemaic Geocentric Model

astronomer, Nicolas Copernicus, early in the European Renaissance. The consensus of contemporary science and the church was that the Earth and, more importantly, Man, was the center of the universe. It was quite apparent that the sun rose in the east, flew across the sky before us, and set in the west on our opposite side from where it arose; stars revolved in the heavens, marking the seasons, and planets appeared regularly in predictable places in the sky at set intervals based upon a point of observation. From this, a complex mathematical model of epicycles was formulated showing planets spinning around the sky in smaller circles on their own, sometimes in reverse, as they, in turn, encircled the earth. This *geocentric* model was, to say the least, quite complicated, yet was still effective in predicting where the planets and stars would be in the night sky at any point in time, but not essentially, why they behaved in the manner observed.

In search of a better mathematical model, Copernicus found that if you put the sun at the center, the geometry turned out to be a lot simpler, predicting concentric circular orbits for the planets, including the earth, around the center point of the sun. This was not a new theory—the *heliocentric* model had its adherents going back to classical Greek philosophy. But Copernicus based his theory on scientific evidence using his newfangled telescope, making his observations from a fixed location on Earth but imagining a different center

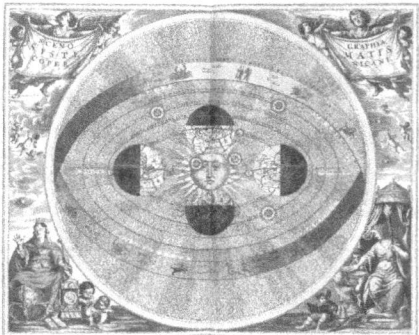

Copernican World System, Andreas Cellarius, Illustration, 1661.

Figure 2 - Scenography of the Copernican World System

point from which to extrapolate his measurements, the sun. With resistance from parochial institutions in the orbit of the Church, it took another century and another astronomer, Galileo Galilei, to readvance the heliocentric model, and eventually, it was accepted as a valid model of our planetary system in Western academia with a few minor tweaks to the circular orbits.

What is significant about this ancient dilemma is that it illustrates a primary psychological operative. The *geocentric* universe is quite literally based upon an *egocentric* observation of how the world operates—how do astronomical objects move around me standing on a specific patch of earth, in this case, Italy? From this personalized perspective, it seems apparent how things will continue to operate going across one's field of perception and we begin to imagine why it is so. But until astronomers shifted to a *heliocentric* model, they were not able to accurately explain the cause and effect of the astronomical rotation, which came in the later theories of gravitation and relativity. Likewise, a *holocentric* psychology, which emphasizes the whole of the personal and relational psychological universe, a *holomorphic* construction of known and unknown parts, gives us a better explanation of the cause and effect of human experience and development and its gravitational pull towards wholeness and healing. The *egocentric* model is inherently *exclusionary*, focusing on the authoritative experience of the ego's perspective, or else, similarly, the perspective of another as it relates to our ego; what we inherently preface with "I," "you," or "it." The *holocentric* model is inherently inclusionary incorporating the *other* as essential in relationship to our ego; what is fundamentally prefaced as "us."

❖The Nature of Modeling

A model is a representation of a physical object or set of objects, and often their behavior. In popular culture, it evokes the image of a genetically endowed female upon which clothes or make-up are modeled for the less genetically endowed females—a practice more concerned about aspiration and marketing than actually representing what the clothes will look like on the average female consumer. From a scientific perspective, this underlines a key aspect of modeling—how effective is the *model* in representing *reality*. In principle, the *model* is not *reality* but rather a representation that requires scope and definition to understand its effectiveness. A size zero fashion model wearing a size zero dress can really only effectively model what that dress will look like on a size zero consumer with similar height, proportions, skin tone, and gait—so essentially, the model's twin sister who grew up eating the other half of a cracker for dinner. The model becomes less effective as we move away from the ideal scope of the model.

The scope and definition of the geocentric model were, likewise, only effective at describing how astronomical bodies appeared to the observer in a particular place. Specific aspects of this model could vary by the geographic latitude and longitude upon which the observer set foot, or more dramatically, from what planetary body or system the observer made his observations.

In classical physics, Galileo showed that it is a relative fact that a feather and a coconut will fall from a height at the same speed and reach the ground at the same time. The simple mathematical formula that describes this behavior requires a circumstantial scope of assumed criteria that can break down in the real world—air resistance within the planetary atmosphere, the mass of the planet and proximity to the planetary gravitational forces, interference by external influences such as wind speed and curious aerobatically-adroit swallows—all can change the time it takes an object to hit the ground. As such, one can either expand the model to represent more complex assumptions or be satisfied by the predictive behavior of the model within the known parameters, being careful not to overapply the model to circumstances that do not meet those assumptions.

Humans by nature model their world. We use words and ideas to represent objects and actions. Words carefully placed together make sentences and sentences together make stories. These stories describe how we believe the world works and our relationship to that world. However, a story is not real life; it is not a real experience, in and of itself. When we read or hear a story, our imagination can interpret those stories as real experiences as we respond to artifacts in the narrative. The monster in the story may not be real, but our imagined response to the monster is very real and can become a part of our personal narrative, changing our behavior in other circumstances that represent similar artifacts. Herein lies the complexity of the personal narrative as the foundational artifacts can be distortions, and the model that they evoke can be overapplied to circumstances that do not meet the original narrative. Our personal narrative is a developmental construct; it grows with our better understanding of ourselves, the nature of the world around us, and our place in it.

❖Dawn of Consciousness

In philosophy and psychology, the term *consciousness* describes a cohesive narrative of self-awareness with the concomitant ability to self-adjust to environmental circumstances. On one level, it seems self-evident what it means to be *conscious* as we make our way through our busy day—caring for our own needs and navigating the needs and concerns of others.

We intuitively develop a simple model of what it means to be *conscious* without understanding the constraints and mechanisms for its attainment.

In ancient mythology, *Light* universally symbolizes consciousness or awareness—the illumination of daylight or lamplight allows us to see what is present, and to evaluate and respond. *Darkness*, on the other hand, is the unknown, often symbolizing ignorance, chaos, or danger lurking in the shadows. In the Greek creation myth, from the primordial Chaos is born Erebus/Darkness and Nyx/Night who then join to give birth to Hemera/Day. Night and Day are separated in Tartarus/Pit in a diurnal cycle that begins as Nyx descends across the threshold of bronze in Tartarus at dawn and Hemera ascends to begin a new day (the opposite, of course, occurring at dusk). Similarly, at the beginning of the Genesis Creation myth, the Elohim/Great Powers creates the heavens and the earth. And the earth "became a chaos and vacant, and darkness was on the surface of the submerged chaos."[4] Then the Elohim/Great Powers created light and darkness, separating them, calling the light "day" and the darkness "night."

As the Genesis Creation account unfolds, on the fourth day the Elohim create *Time*—populating the Heavens/Skies with the sun, moon, and stars to bear the celestial light that moves across the sky.

> And saying is the Elohim, "Become shall luminaries in the atmosphere of the heavens, to give light on the earth, to separate between the day and the night. And they come to be for signs and for appointments, and for days and years. And there come to be luminaries in the atmosphere of the heavens to give light on the earth."
>
> And coming is it to be so. And making is the Elohim two great luminaries, the greater luminary for ruling the day, and the smaller luminary for ruling the night, and the stars. And bestowing them is the Elohim in the atmosphere of the heavens to give light on the earth, and to rule in the day and in the night, and to separate between the light and the darkness.[5]

Likewise, in the Greek creation myth, the primordial Titan gods Hyperion/"He who goes before" and Theia/Goddess—themselves children of the first rulers of the cosmos, Uranus/Sky and Gaia/Earth—consort together to give birth to Helios/Sun, Selene/Moon, and Eos/Dawn. Helios and Selene are the bearers of the Celestial Light to the Earthly dwellers—the intersection between the Heavens and the Earth. They are fundamentally defined by their awareness, or consciousness, of the cosmos they oversee. Helios, the Sun-God, is the "eternal eye," the watcher who illuminates and reveals the workings of both

---

[4] CLV Genesis 1:2
[5] CLV Genesis 1:14-18

men and gods, as well as everything else that goes on in the cosmos. The
Orphic Hymn VIII[6] thusly proclaims:

> Hear, golden Titan, whose eternal eye
> With matchless sight illumines all the sky.
> Native, unwearied in diffusing light,
> And to all eyes the object of delight:
> Lord of the Seasons, beaming light from far,
> Sonorous, dancing in thy four-yok'd car.
> With thy right hand the source of morning light,
> And with thy left the father of the night.
> Agile and vig'rous, venerable Sun,
> Fiery and bright around the heav'ns you run,
> Foe to the wicked, but the good man's guide,
> O'er all his steps propitious you preside.
> With various-sounding golden lyre 'tis thine
> To fill the world with harmony divine.
> Father of ages, guide of prosp'rous deeds,
> The world's commander, borne by lucid steeds.
> Immortal Jove, flute-playing, bearing light,
> Source of existence, pure and fiery bright;
> Bearer of fruit, almighty lord of years,
> Agile and warm, whom ev'ry power reveres.
> Bright eye, that round the world incessant flies,
> Doom'd with fair fulgid rays to set and rise;
> Dispensing justice, lover of the stream,
> The world's great master, and o'er all supreme.
> Faithful defender, and the eye of right,
> Of steeds the ruler, and of life the light:
> With sounding whip four fiery steeds you guide,
> When in the glittering car of day you ride,
> Propitious on these mystic labours shine,
> And bless thy suppliants with a life divine.

Likewise, Selene, the Moon-Goddess is "the eye of the night"[7] and proclaimed
to be "all-seeing" in the Orphic Hymn IX[8] as follows:

> Hear, Goddess queen, diffusing silver light,
> Bull-horn'd, and wand'ring thro' the gloom of Night.
> With stars surrounded, and with circuit wide
> Night's torch extending, through the heav'ns you ride:
> Female and male with silv'ry rays you shine,
> And now full-orb'd, now tending to decline.
> Mother of ages, fruit-producing Moon,
> Whose amber orb makes Night's reflected noon:
> Lover of horses, splendid queen of night,
> All-seeing pow'r, bedeck'd with starry light,

---

[6] Orpheus (1896) p.22-24
[7] Aeschylus (1991) p.37
[8] Orpheus (1896) p.24-28

Lover of vigilance, the foe of strife,
In peace rejoicing, and a prudent life:
Fair lamp of Night, its ornament and friend,
Who giv'st to Nature's works their destin'd end.
Queen of the stars, all-wise Diana, hail!
Deck'd with a graceful robe and ample veil.
Come, blessed Goddess, prudent, starry, bright,
Come, moony-lamp, with chaste and splendid light,
Shine on these sacred rites with prosp'rous rays,
And pleas'd accept thy suppliants' mystic praise.

Selene and Helios bring Light to the Earth revealing what is true and beneficial in the cosmos.

Archetypally, the celestial lights of the Sun and Moon together represent the transcendent consciousness of the holomorphic universe of the psyche—the aspect of our psychic being that operates outside, above, and beyond our egoic awareness symbolized by the Earth, what is often referred to as the *unconscious*. Thus symbolically, Eos, the goddess of the Dawn, represents that liminal place where earth and sky meet in Tartarus, the Earthen Pit, and where Nyx/Night and Hemera/Day pass each other at dawn. It is the place where the egoic unconscious meets ego consciousness—the place of dreams and intuition.

In Greek mythology, the personal dreamworld is the domain of Morpheus, one of the greater Oneiroi, the Greek gods of the dreamworld. As a dream messenger, similar to Asclepius' role in the *abaton*, he shifts his shape into any purposeful form deemed necessary, in order to convey a deeper vision of truth to the dreamer. One of his most important roles is to listen to the gods and then to convey their message to the dreamer. As the dream messenger, he is an essential part of the non-egoic holomorphic universe of the psyche—one who transverses between the deeper world of the gods and the waking world in the manner of the serpent. But he is only a small part of this deeper cosmos.

In a simple model of human experience, there is, on one hand, how we interface with the earthen waking world, the objective *real* world, that we experience through our basic senses—sight, sound, smell, taste, and touch. Then, on the other hand, also within this earthen realm, there is how we interpret and organize those experiences by rationally evaluating and integrating them into our prior perceived framework or model of the world. However, our rational framework is incomplete and susceptible to prejudice and distortion; at times reacting quite dramatically to our fears and unfounded expectations, forming an intrinsic bias. When an experience is anomalous or counter to the way we believe the world works, or how we believe ourselves to be, we may encapsulate that experience through a brutal process of deconstruction and denial, what Sigmund Freud referred to as our *rational defenses*; creating within the individual, what he called *neuroses*. Different psychological theories reframe this in terms of informational or emotive conflicts, but the premise is still the same. In the middle of these two functions of the psyche is some form of what is often referred to as the *unconscious*. Freud saw it as a bucket in which rejected parts were thrown. Jung saw it as an archetypal and universal dimension with both personal and collective aspects. Others just see it as the unknown parts of ourselves we must discover.

In building a broader theoretical model to explain non-rational experience we do see a more dynamic function within this middle realm than just a hidden repository. In modern psychology, beginning in the late nineteenth century, Freud and Jung developed various ways to engage the *unconscious* through projective and imaginal techniques and dreamwork, focused on bypassing our rational preconceptions and defenses. By the middle part of the twentieth century, new theories were developed to engage this holomorphic realm through the arts, movement, drama, and sound. Highly effective approaches in Creative Arts and Drama Therapies openly engage the experiential dynamics of the non-rational, readily exposing aspects of this *unconscious* domain, deepening our access to symbols, archetypes, and narratives. As a product of the mythic celestial realm of deeper awareness, these approaches engage the pre-rational narratives of the holomorphic realm that formulate our authentic orientation to what we perceive as objective reality.

However, in this holomorphic perspective, there is no *unconscious*—a term born of our intrinsic egocentric bias. Rather, *consciousness* is a multidimensional construct. The psychoanatomy of our endogenous holomorphic universe functions more broadly than the mental processes of which we are aware. Egocentric consciousness is a product of a more complex psychic body that functions with much more complexity and non-egoic deliberation. In the same way that our physical body functions, most of what happens is not born of deliberate thought. In our bodies, the heart not only continuously beats, but adjusts to environmental circumstances to supply oxygen and nutrients to organs and muscles broadly distributed throughout the body. Universal stem cells are born and then modify their specificity to function together with adjacent cells, to create distinctive organs. And the nervous system communicates distress and adverse circumstances, which prompt innumerable adjustments to fix and accommodate changes in our internal environment. Most of what happens in us throughout the course of the day is not a product of deliberate thought. What is *unconscious* to the ego is not only fundamental awareness to the cells and organs that make up the body, but likewise, is most of who and what we are psychologically in the broader holomorphic dimensions of the psyche—only a small part becomes conscious to the present ego. What is often labeled as *unconscious* is actually indirectly conscious as awareness organically centered in specific domains of the whole psychoanatomic drives and functions that embody us. Once we turn this model right side up, to understand that most of who we are in being, in existing—in wisdom, truth, and functionality—is happening constantly without our egoic awareness, we can begin to engage this non-rational embodiment through the archetypal and narrative interfaces to which we have some access, but not necessarily control. We can begin to explore the underlying psychoanatomy of the holomorphic organs that create and maintain our existence apart from the narrow sliver of rational awareness of our ego.

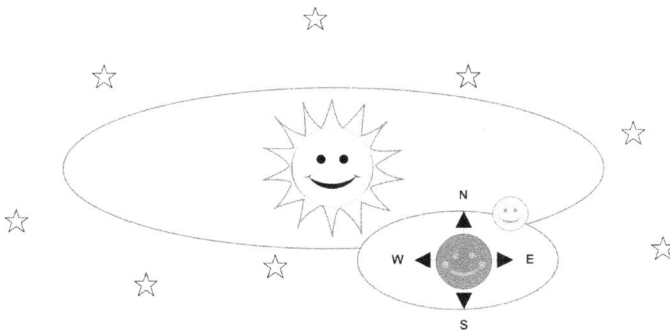

Figure 3 - Psycho-astronomical Model of Holomorphic Consciousness

As such, in a psycho-astronomical model, the Sun and Moon essentially operate in two gravitational spheres. The Moon's orbit is a function of the Earth's gravitational pull, which, in turn, is guided by the Sun's gravitational pull. The Earth represents our egocentric orientation and awareness. Selene, the Moon-Goddess, symbolizes the deeper awareness within the personal unconscious, whereas Helios, the Sun-God, symbolizes some form of universal awareness that transcends the interdimensions of personal experience, shining its light onto our earthen egoic consciousness. This universal gravity of the Sun-God is evidenced as a central pull to integration within the psyche, as well as our archetypal awareness of social and cultural elements that transcend the personal. It is also experienced in the phenomenological experience of a numinous encounter with a powerful guiding force outside ourselves. The most developed perspective on this is what Carl Jung called the *collective unconscious*, which is based on a Neo-

Platonic model of universal archetypes embedded deep within humanity laying the semantic foundation for operative psychic experience. Other more broadly promulgated but arguably less well-developed ideas in mythology are the notions of a *soul* or *essence* at the core of our humanity, or elsewise, some spiritual dimension of the gods that may also influence our personal orientation within the quotidian or waking world.

❖**Model of Humanity**

Consciousness is only one aspect of our personal psychodynamics. Beyond the emergent mythos of reactive and proscriptive stories that are directly conscious to the ego, or indirectly through the egoic unconscious, are organic operators that turn experience into story, building narrative threads out of events, relationships out of context, and meaning out of function. The psyche is essentially a storyteller built upon these functional narratives that form the core holomorphic repertoire of the psyche. The moderating dynamic agency that assigns meaning, value, trust, and virtue to these stories is what is often called the *conscience*.

Our essential personal narrative describes what we believe it means to be human, to be one part of humanity, and to be ourselves. In the Genesis Creation myth, this narrative is founded on a fundamental understanding of personal power, what it means to be *elohim*, or to be a "great power" in the likeness and community of a family of "great powers":

> *So Elohim created humanity in His image; in the image of Elohim He created it: male and female He created them. Elohim blessed them, and Elohim said to them: Be fruitful and increase; fill the earth and subdue it.*[9]

The source and pattern of humanity is the ideal image or *imago* of the Elohim. The myth continues on to describe how the first Adamite is a product of the red clay of the Earth and the sacred breath of the Imago Elohim. Our *Adamness* is what is translated in the text by the English term "humanity." As *Adamkind*, we are of one Universal Family in the image of the Imago Elohim. The word *kind* comes from the word *kin* originating in the Old English word *cynn* meaning "family." Etymologically and symbolically, the term *kindness* means to have the quality of being one's kindred, to fundamentally treat one another as family. In English, the term *humanity* has both the connotation of belonging to *humankind*, as well as to have *kindness*, the generous quality of treating others as being an active part of one human family. Thus, in both senses, the primary objective in the myth is to *cultivate our humanity*.

---

[9] CLV Genesis 1:27-28

In building a functional model of human psychological development, *Cultivate Humanity* is the primary scope I propose to define a model of the underlying Elohim mythology. It is the starting point for our exploration of the narrative that follows. Notationally, I will borrow from the field of information engineering developed for the purpose of taking complex systems and deconstructing them into useful components for further development. Process and data models are built based on narratives collected from subject matter experts (SME) of the targeted human enterprise to be described. In place of the enterprise SMEs, I will use the authentic mythological text to describe the cultivation of our humanity. I will only expose the basic aspects of the IDEF0 standard process modeling in the context of describing how an individual develops within the scope of *cultivating humanity.*

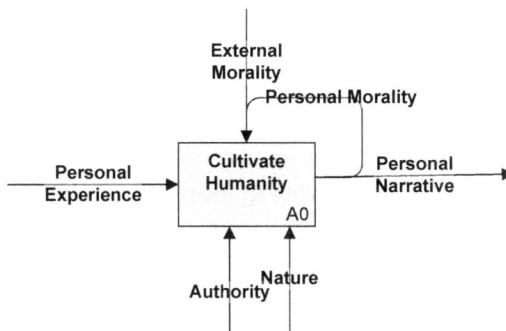

Model 1 – Cultivate Humanity (A0 Context)

In the parlance of this information modeling approach, the A0 diagram is called the *context diagram*. It establishes the scope of any further activities to be described. The *Activity* is shown as a box, which describes the inputs to the *Activity* on the left, the outputs to the right, the constraints above, and the mechanisms below. In this A0 context diagram, *Personal Experience* is transformed into an individual's *Personal Narrative* constrained by *External Morality* and a feedback loop of *Personal Morality* (a component of the prior Personal Narrative). The process is enabled by the *Nature* of who we are and the world around us as well as social narratives regarding *Authority* in culture and society. The contextual A0 *Activity* is then broken down into component narratives that describe the defined scope, the A0 deconstruction diagram. As the myth will take us on a deep dive into the relational, I have chosen to focus on the psychological interplay between the development of the personal and relational narratives. The A1 Activity thusly describes how we develop our Personal Narrative. The A2 Activity describes how we develop our relationships.

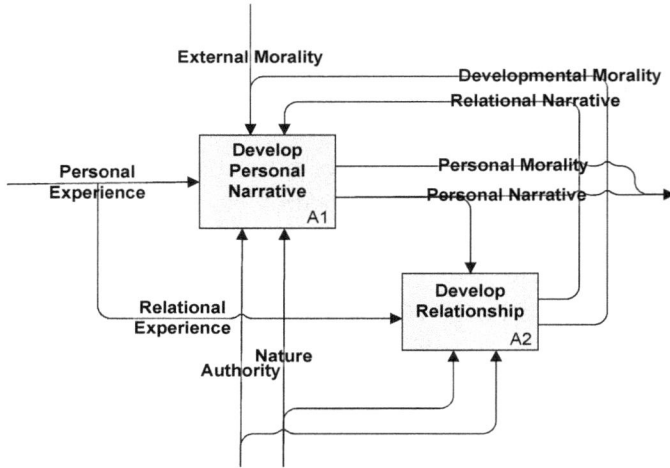

Model 2 - Cultivate Humanity (A0)

The Activity *A1: Develop Personal Narrative* describes how *Personal Experiences* are transformed into *Personal Narrative* and its component *Personal Morality*. At times, I will break out *Personal Morality* from the *Personal Narrative* to provide visibility to the process; at other times, it will be subsumed as a component of the *Personal Narrative*. The Activity is constrained by the output from the experience of *A2: Develop Relationship*. The *Relational Narrative* is developed from new *Personal Experiences*, which influence new values that comprise our *Developmental Morality*. These narratives constrain the development of the dynamic *Personal Narrative* by adding new dimensions to the semantic construction of the narrative. Much of the *Initiation* chapter in this book will focus on describing in detail how we develop our *Personal Narrative*. The subsequent chapters will focus on the mythological narrative of the unified Torah and Gospel mythology, which is fundamentally about relationship. Thus, our deeper focus will be on deconstructing the A2 Activities in support of this exploration.

The process of developing relationships within our narrative scope is the product of human development from infancy to maturity. The three levels of development I shall invoke in this exploration based on psychological theory, as well as the mythological content itself, are (1) Juvenile, (2) Adolescent, and (3) Mature Adult (with some references to Young Adult). These levels refer to the psychological and moral development of the narrative rather than the chronological development of the subject individual. A person can have developmental narratives both above and below their chronological and social development.

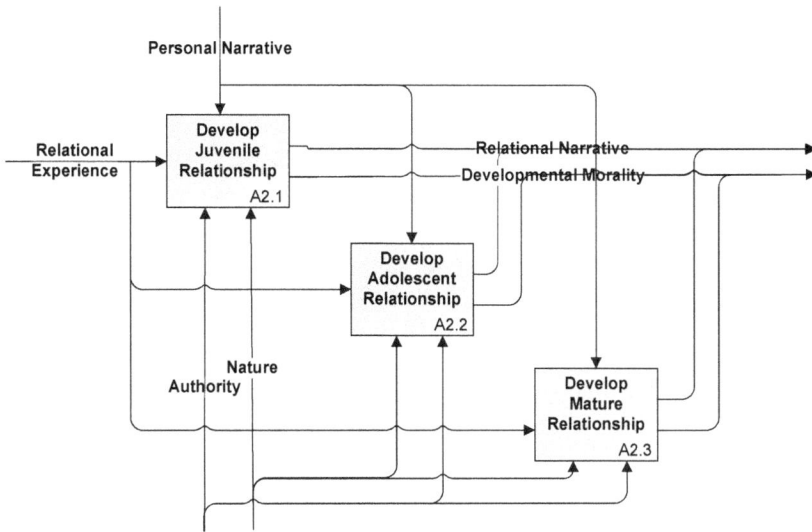

Model 3 - Develop Relationship (A2)

This dynamic is reflected by decomposing the A2 Activities into developmental processes. These activities, as noted, are not structurally linear. Some *Relational Experiences* may activate different levels of psychological maturity based on the underlying trigger in the narrative that is invoked. Some relationships may prompt one to act in a more mature manner towards one another, while others activate primitive stories from one's childhood *Personal Narrative*, often involving some type of early trauma that, unless dealt with, will continue to degrade many of one's relationships.

❖ **Phenomenological Healing**

Another key function in the holomorphic psyche that guides the development of one's Personal Narrative is the phenomenology of healing the damaged narratives, the unintegrated discontinuities, and vulnerabilities that influence our ability to personally function and have intimate relationships. On one hand, there are internal mechanisms that attempt to rebuild stories into healthy narratives. On the other, we may require assistance from others, from intuitive healers who help to facilitate our journey.

Historically, phenomenological techniques in healing are ancient going back to the twilight of human experience. As such, they are universally practiced throughout world cultures—from Shaman in Siberia and Medicine Men in the Americas to Sangoma witch doctors in Africa. There are various deep intuitive facilitators and ritualized narratives in most, if not all, traditional tribal cultures and often hidden within modern transnational societies as well. In Western transnational culture, the emotive and experiential are often allocated to the artistic realm as a form of Cartesian categorization of human experience. As such, modern psychology in its various theories has only occasionally embraced the healing power manifest in the non-rational psyche. Non-rational techniques are still viewed with suspicion in the modern medical model, given that the mechanics operate relative to the client's personal narrative, which can be difficult to formulate into a prescriptive body of knowledge—although, I would argue that it is entirely possible to develop a general theory of psychology based intrinsically on narrative and myth within a client-centered model.

In an intuitive client-centered practice, the therapist is a facilitator or vessel for the process, in the same way that tribal healers engage the sufferer in traditional modalities—helping the sufferer along their own path to healing and wholeness. As such, the healing process necessitates that the therapist has an essential deep intuition to engage the client in their journey. This can be quite disconcerting for those that hold a more concrete or authoritarian view, concomitant with the medical model, preferring rather to modify the biochemistry of the patient than openly engage the underlying dysfunctional narrative—an approach which unfortunately often distorts and masks the very nature of the dysfunction.

To be clear, there are important uses for medication in psychology, but which require a more delicate and less frequent reliance than some clinicians currently use. It is critical that the clinician understand the importance of the client's narrative in conjunction with their biological constitution. However, the framework for this distinction is out of scope for this current exploration. My intent at this juncture is simply to contrast the technological approach of modern biomedicine with the ancient modalities of traditional psychology that have been effective for most of human history. The modern reductivist ideology depreciates and deconstructs the human psyche to some set of biomechanical parts, constellating anything before the advent of modern neurochemistry as primitive superstition, using the terminology of *myth* and *placebo* to mean something falsely imagined. In contradiction, these ancient tools exist precisely because they have worked for thousands of generations across multiple cultures and societies.

❖Mythology and Empiricism

This is the framework from which we begin our deep dive into the mythological realm—letting go of our need to rationalize the narrative, to find the holomorphic construction within the experience beyond our egoic bias. *Myth* is an ancient form of storytelling that incorporates primitive constructs of human experience into intensified narratives and tableaus to illustrate deeper forms of universal truth about the nature of ourselves and the universe around us. Mythological stories were not some ancient form of entertainment to fascinate folks gathered around a campfire. They encapsulate maps and formulas of psychological and metaphysical awareness to teach and inspire moral responsibility. Their creation can be argued as divinely imagined or merely purified narrative through the crucible of generational retelling. Some myths may have greater universal application across generations and geography than others. Some stories may be found, over time, to be more culturally bound to a specific time and place. But they have in common that they emerge from the deeper well of human experience to form narratives that are larger than the personal story of one person.

It bears noting that the pejorative usage of the term *myth* to indicate a false narrative is both inaccurate and illustrative of a general bias against meta-empirical or non-rational ways of knowing in certain academic fields. Fundamentally, the term *myth* is the Greek word for "story" and as a field of study is indicative that we are intrinsically storytellers. The psyche essentially builds narrative threads out of experience—subjectively interpreting patterns, creating relationships, and formulating meaning from both physical and imaginal cues.

In philosophy, *epistemology* is the exploration of what is knowable as fact and, conversely, what is beyond certainty—how do we know that something is true. Its academic application is the *scientific method*, which is based on our tools to measure phenomena through experimentation—to validate hypotheses in ways that are reproducible by other scientists. However, *scientism* mythologizes objectivity—over-applying the vestiges of science upon things that are not inherently measurable by our material tools and methods in order to presuppose some interpretive bias. Empirically, the process of scientific study is inherently *subjective*—not that scientists are at the whim of their morning caffeine intake, but rather, science begins with the subjective interpretation of highly intelligent and educated individuals searching for deeper truths in the formulation of *hypotheses*. The subjectivity of the *hypothesis* is then subjected to the rigors of the scientific method to test whether there is an objective reality to support the hypothesis.

The study of mythology applies a heuristic approach that finds relative certainty in patterns of narrative in literature, art, culture, and personal experience, but is ultimately a soft science that cannot be accurately measured with tools like the size of an atom. The early modern mythologists, such as Joseph Campbell and Carl Jung, examined the larger body of mythological narratives to find archetypal patterns and images that recurred in relatively non-variant ways to propose underlying universal elements of the personal and cultural psyche.

❖The Semantic Universe

The great cinematic storyteller Federico Fellini once stated, "Talking about dreams is like talking about movies, since the cinema uses the language of dreams; years can pass in a second and you can hop from one place to another. It's a language made of image. And in the real cinema, every object and every light means something as in a dream."[10] This explication quite accurately describes the main aspects of the primitive semiotic psyche presented in myth, dreams, and the unconscious. First, the semiotic universe does not follow rational metaphysics—space and time are fluid, things fly, things fall, sometimes they break, sometimes they do not, some things mutate unexpectedly, things can feel familiar even when unrelated to any prior real-world experience—rational rules do not apply. It is a language of meaning and emotion; a semantic universe built into narratives and tableaus. Secondly, it is authentic based on a deeper truth-telling about our personal semiotic psychic reality, unlike the rational framework, which is founded on *acceptability* and thus can be distorted in response to our fears and confusion.

Jung posits a third axiom, a corollary to the second, that there is a gravitational force within this psychological realm that moves us towards truth, wholeness, and healing, which he called non-descriptively, the capital S, Self. Similarly, the ancient Romans, long before Jung, represented this as the goddess *Salus* whose operative domain is likewise represented by her name, which in Latin means wholeness, health, and safety. Archetypally, *Salus* is expressed as a vital agency within the transcendent psyche analogous to the synergistic construct in the body that works to fix injury to our genetic form—a cut to the hand will initiate seemingly unrelated functions in the body to stop bleeding, attack invasive pathogens, and then rebuild tissue. This happens also in the psychogenetic realm through the interaction between the sensational, semiotic, and rational domains of the psyche, reacting to ordinary and extraordinary ordeals to bring wholeness and healing in the cosmos of our intrinsic holomorphic constitution, a process of *truth-telling*. While our physical body is constructed from cells and tissue, our psychic form is built out of narrative and images that we knit together as our identity, our *truth*. Psychotherapy and other spiritualized healing modalities

---

[10] Cott (1984) interview.

are a way to engage those stories and, when necessary, transform and integrate them in beneficial ways.

❖Ancient Psychology of the Basar

As previously noted, this psychogenetic formulation for health and healing is not a uniquely modern necessity or development; it is operative throughout human history. One of the most well-developed ancient psychologies is the *Basar* tradition in Jewish mythology, which will be my focus in the following exploration. The myth is a fundamental psychological map to the restorative power of *Love* within the framework of moral development, built around the core principle of loving your fellow man—to love one another. While often misconstrued as a moralistic endeavor in the religious paradigms that borrow from it, leading to existential perplexity in the metaphysical domain, the myth is actually a consistent relational and psychological construct that evolves over the course of the narrative. Historically, the metaphysics of the mythology has been broadly debated, leading to innumerable distortions and interpretations of the myth based on the political ideologies of various religious sects within Judaism, Christianity, and Islam that recognize aspects of the myth, without embracing its fundamental relational core founded on the premise of a Universal Family.

As a psychology, I will examine the mythological narrative phenomenologically without going into the applied metaphysics necessary for developing a spiritual practice. The cosmological and ontological framework of the material existence or historicity of elements referred to in the myth are out of scope to our discussion, in the same way that a dreamscape exists separate from waking or rational reality. While the metaphysics of life and death deservedly capture much attention in religious and spiritual practice, in the mythological realm they represent aspects of the interior cosmos towards integration and disintegration, as well as existence and nonexistence. The central relationship with Yahweh as Parent Elohim will be explored in terms of the interior psychological correspondence to the archetypal role of the ideal Parent Image within the transcendent psyche as laid out in the mythscape of the narrative, leaving the externalities of determining the metaphysical existence of a supreme being to the spiritual practice of the reader.

The mythological narrative encapsulates an intensified psychological or spiritual map that stands on its own. In the same manner as dreamtending, one must first sit with the authentic construction of the narrative, without the influence of preconceived ideas, or rationalized deconstruction, as to what it should say. Then, allowing the myth to speak for itself, one can authentically apply the narrative to one's own personal psychological or spiritual practice or values. After which, the reader may choose to extrapolate and explore these ideas and their implications, personally or metaphysically, based on the countless volumes of ideological, philosophical, and religious tomes— hopefully keeping in mind what is actually in the text, which is often rationalized and distorted in the institutional commentaries.

To be clear, however, I am not positing a secret or esoteric interpretation of a classic myth from which the theologies of Traditional Christianity and Rabbinic Judaism evolved, subsequently influencing other moralistic traditions such as Islam. I am arguing that the religious interpretation intrinsically contradicts the actual myth in its simple clear form. Just as dream interpreters distort and contort a dream into preconceived inauthentic conclusions using a rationalized tableau to decode the dream narrative, the religious and political interpreters use a rationalized tableau of moralism, idolatry, and tribal affinity to force their own distorted and contorted inauthentic conclusions, ignoring and transforming sections of narrative into their opposite. An intrinsic relational myth about a Universal Family founded on love, becomes, through the secret decoder ring of religious rationalization, a moralistic myth founded variously in sin, condemnation, heaven, and hell within a framework of exclusionary tribal identity.

❖**Ancient Mythology of the Near East**

The myth, however, does exist in a historical context originating in Mesopotamia and the Levant, also referred to as the Ancient Near East. It is necessary to understand history to develop the semantic framework of the archetypes, symbols, and narratives. My approach to the text will be biased toward the internal commentary of the mythographers and myth collectors that are nearer to the source of the narrative. From a psychological perspective, this commentary is usually more consistent and explanatory in the framework of the myth than the extrapolated versions of some modern historians that view the archaeological record as a more determinative factor, sometimes ignoring, or minimizing, the description within the myth itself. While the general consensus is that most of these myths originate in oral tradition before the age of writing, and then are recorded later, the historical narratives can be biased to those who wrote it down first, pivoting to a later origination in the essential process of social and cultural evolution.

The Israelite mythology is generally believed to have been collected from various sources subsequent to the Judean Neo-Babylonian captivity in the sixth century BCE, which produced the written collection we now know as the Hebrew canon—the Torah or Pentateuch, and the subsequent books of history and poetry. Mythologically, the established Yahweh tradition is traced to an ancient prehistorical source known internally as *Abraham*, probably in the Early Bronze Age, who had many sons who distribute the Yahweh tradition throughout the Levant to many descendant tribes. The earliest written records, however, are Egyptian referring to an Arab tribe called the Shasu that worshiped Yahu in the southern Levant and a Warrior-God named Yahweh recorded in stone Steles in Moab as well as a similar warrior tradition in Phoenicia/Ugarit in the northern Levant.

The Abrahamic mythology assigns Edom in the southern Levant as descendants of Esau, the grandson of Abraham. Then, further south, in the coastal desert region, the Arab tribe of Midian, is associated with Abraham's fourth son by his second wife Keturah, which later becomes important as the center of the revival of the Yahweh tradition in the Exodus narrative. Ugarit and Phoenicia are great regional powers in the northern coastal Levant who do not have a mythological relationship to Abraham. So mythologically their references to Yahweh as a minor deity, in this context, is annotated as a separate syncretic construction from the mythology underlying the oral Abrahamic tradition. From the perspective of the Abrahamic myth, rather than an argument for an evolution of a regional deity named Yahweh originating in a specific tribe that wrote it down first, the myth argues for the devolution of the myth through the distribution of oral narrative over generations through various tribal groups in prehistory associated with a distinct patriarchal lineage. This will become more important in opening up the semiotic formulations portrayed in the narrative.

❖Ancient Israel

The tribal identity of Ancient Israel is founded on the Torah mythology that is written down in the Pentateuch, the first five books of the Judeo-Christian canon. The first book Bereshit/Genesis begins with a description of primordial creation and then follows the development of early humanity through to the establishment of the Abrahamic tribe of Israel. The remaining books of the Pentateuch describe the development of the Kingdom of Yahweh Elohim in Israel. Additional books of proto-historical mythology follow the Kingdom of Yahweh Elohim administered through his appointed Judges until Israel rejects the kingship of Yahweh under the last judge, Samuel.

The remaining books tell the story of the political kingdoms of Israel, starting with the appointment of the first political king Saul, followed by what Jews commonly consider to be the golden era of the unified kingdoms of David and Solomon. It then chronicles the divided monarchies of the Northern Kingdom of Israel in Samaria and the Southern Kingdom of Judah, centered in Jerusalem. In the annals of the prophets, the Northern Kingdom is destroyed by the Neo-Assyrians, which is historically dated to be in 722 BCE. Then, a century and a half later, the Southern Kingdom is conquered by the Neo-Babylonians in 588 BCE, who utterly destroy the ancient city of Jerusalem and the Temple of Solomon, thus ending the era of the tribal kingdoms.

The prophetic annals continue through several generations of exile in Babylon until the Judahites are released from captivity by the Persian King Cyrus the Great who conquered the Babylonians in 539 BCE. Upon their return, the Judahites establish a vassal government subject to the rule of the Persian Achaemenid Empire and then proceed to rebuild Jerusalem and a Second Temple. The last of the prophetic annals that comprise the Old Testament/Tanakh is written shortly thereafter in the mid-fifth century BCE.

Historically, the vassal era lasts from the late sixth century BCE until the early second century CE. The Achaemenid Empire is eventually overthrown by Alexander the Great in 332 BCE. Then after his death, Judea transitioned back and forth between the warring Seleucid and Ptolemaic Empires until 140 BCE when the Israelites were able to establish a greater level of autonomy under the Jewish Hasmonean dynasty as the Seleucid Kingdom declined, weakening its grip on the region. This lasted until Rome wrested control in 63 BCE. The vassal era ends with a series of three Jewish Roman wars between 66 CE and 136 CE. In the first Jewish Roman War, the Romans annihilated the city of Jerusalem and burned the Second Temple to the ground. In the last Jewish Roman War, the nation of Judah is completely destroyed. The survivors are exiled, dispersed throughout the Mediterranean world, and forbidden to return to Palestine.

The Basar mythology evolves out of the transitional period between the end of the political kingdoms and the beginning of the vassal kingdoms, as the Judahites struggle to find their identity upon returning to rebuild Jerusalem and the Second Temple. In this transitional period, the mythology of Jewish history is organized and written down, to form the Hebrew canon that we know today. In addition, as the political status quo no longer existed, the concerns of the prophets became focused on the personal lives within the community. Regarding this, scholar Lawrence Boadt in his book, *Reading the Old Testament*, writes:

> *Under the pressure of the fall of Jerusalem and the exile, Israel's prophets had to face major changes in what they preached. No longer did it make sense to hold kings responsible for national evil, nor could one warn a people that they would lose their kingdom if they did not repent. The prophets from Jeremiah to Zechariah faced new situations never before dealt with by their predecessors... The result was a profound shift in the nature of prophecy in Israel. It now addressed the people in matters of daily living and worship that were much closer to the priestly concerns..., Prophecy lost its sharp interest in the working of government and directed its attention more to rebuilding community life for the future. This made the prophetic message much more personal and inner-directed and less centered on judgment oracles against social injustices committed by the whole society.[11]*

This sets up the intimate focus of the Unified Basar and Torah mythology, which Rabbi Jeshua founds on the 61st chapter in the book of the prophet Isaiah.

❖Prophet Isaiah

The book of Isaiah is written over three distinct periods, beginning with the exile of Israel to Assyria. This early part of the book, chapters 1 through 39, is directly attributed to the prophet Isaiah. The second part, chapters 40 to 55, is written later by an anonymous prophet concerning issues that arise during the exile of Judah to Babylon. Then the third part, chapters 56 to 66, is written by another anonymous prophet regarding issues faced by Judah on their return from exile. It is this third part that forms the context for the Basar mythology. Boadt writes concerning the Third Isaiah authorship:

> *Another major source for our knowledge of conditions in the land of Palestine after the return from exile is the third and last part of the Book of Isaiah. Unlike Second Isaiah... the viewpoint of the writer is no longer that of someone in Babylon, but of one already back in the promised land. Where Second Isaiah mocks foreign idols and believes they have no power over Israel, the prophet of this last section of the book berates Israel itself for falling into idolatry (Isa 57:1–13). Where Isaiah 40–55 never accuses Israel of sin, but assures the people that their sins have been doubly forgiven, Isaiah 56–66 is full of condemnations of Israel's sin (Isa 58:1–9; 59:9–15; 65:1–7). For these reasons, scholars have identified Isaiah 56–66 as a separate collection of oracles by unknown prophets who spoke in the years immediately after the return from Babylon. This section is simply labeled Third Isaiah (or Trito-Isaiah).[12]*

---

[11] Boadt (2012) p.390
[12] Boadt (2012) p.388-389

30

Then Boadt summarizes the themes of Third Isaiah:

> *Third Isaiah does continue the major theme found in all parts of the Book of Isaiah: the love of "Holy One of Israel" for Jerusalem and Zion. And like Second Isaiah, he speaks to the people a word of comfort and hope that God will soon restore Jerusalem to its former glory and make a new home not only for the exiles but for all peoples... The prophets have a vision, but the people fail to live up to it. The Lord wants justice and not fasting (Isa 58); he wants faithfulness to the covenant and not works of violence (59); and he wants repentance and a spirit of humility (63–64). If the people will turn from their sinfulness, God will restore Jerusalem so that the just will live there in peace, and they will be the Lord's servants (65). He will dwell in their midst as ruler and lord of all the world (66:1–2). Chapters 56 to 66... reflect the tensions between the vision of a renewed Israel and the plain, hard reality that the exiles found on their return.*

Third Isaiah defines the context for the struggles throughout the arc of the vassal kingdom era out of which the mythology of the Reified Basar emerges in the apocalyptic period just prior to its conclusion in the late first and early second centuries CE. Boadt notes, in particular, how the relational themes of Isaiah are echoed in Rabbi Jeshua's teachings:

> *Third Isaiah found it necessary to oppose the one-sided value given to the temple by other prophets such as Haggai and Zechariah. For Third Isaiah, Yahweh was more interested in true inner faithfulness than in external rites and forms. He reaches a high point in his concern for justice in chapter 58... Jesus' words about feeding the hungry and clothing the naked in his judgment scene about the sheep and the goats (Matt 25:31–46) echo this passage of Third Isaiah.[13]*

The passage that Boadt references in Isaiah 58:6-8 states:

> *Is this not the fast that I choose: to break the chains of evil, to untie the bonds of the yoke, and let the oppressed go free and smash their yoke? Are you not to share your bread with the hungry, and bring the homeless into your houses? When you see someone naked, should you not clothe him, and not refuse to help your own relatives? Then light will burst upon you like the dawn, and healing cover your wounds quickly.[14]*

Third Isaiah emerges at the beginning of the vassal kingdom era of Judah upon their return from exile to rebuild Jerusalem and the Temple. Subsequently, Rabbi Jeshua reifies the relational themes of Third Isaiah as the vassal kingdom era closes, just before the final destruction of Jerusalem and its Temple by the Romans, which, according to Rabbi Jeshua, ushers in the next age of the universal Kingdom of Elohim.

---

[13] Boadt (2012) p.389-390
[14] Boadt (2012) p.390 quoting Isaiah 58:6-8

❖The Reified Basar

The anglicized Hebrew word *basar*[15] identifies good or fresh news, message, or story. The word is closely related to the later more widely used Middle English term *gospel* indicating "good news," which historically is used by Christians to refer to the collection of four pre-Christian chronicles of the ministry of the first century Jewish Rabbi Jeshua—identified as the Basar/Gospel accounts of Matthew, Mark, Luke, and John. The first three accounts are believed to be based on an earlier oral tradition historians refer to as *Q* from the German word *quelle* meaning source. However, within the Basar/Gospel narrative, the foundation of the tradition is contained in the book ascribed to the prophet Isaiah.

Accordingly, at the start of the Gospel/Basar account of Luke, Rabbi Jeshua begins his ministry in Nazareth by teaching in the synagogue on the Sabbath. The narrator of the Basar of Luke states that Rabbi Jeshua was handed the scroll of the prophet Isaiah. Upon opening the scroll, he found the place where it describes the Basar and he claimed it as his own mission or anointing, founding the principle upon which the entire myth pivots:

> *The spirit of the Lord is on me, on account of which He anoints me [mashach] to bring the evangel [basar/good story] to the [poor/weak]. He has commissioned me to heal the crushed heart, to herald to captives a pardon, and to the blind the receiving of sight; to dispatch the oppressed with a pardon, to herald an acceptable year of the Lord.*[16]

Then it states that he closed the scroll, handed it back to the deputy, and sat down while the eyes of all in the synagogue were still looking intently at him. He then stated, "Today this scripture is fulfilled in your ears." Jeshua therein claims to reify or fulfill the Basar of Isaiah in first-century Palestinian Judea. Thus, the Gospel accounts establish Jeshua's three-year mission as the *Reified Basar*.

The central tenet of the Reified Basar mythology, as we shall see develop over the course of the narrative, is that Rabbi Jeshua was anointed by Yahweh as the substitutionary firstborn son to fulfill the Basar, or Good Story, within the Universal Family of Elohim. His mission is to encourage and restore the integrity and well-being of those suffering and in need. The Reified Basar expects that those who value and identify with the Universal Family of Elohim are empowered to do likewise. As the ultimate flourishing of moral development, the students of Rabbi Jeshua are to take on the

---

[15] Strongs H1319 (ref. Glossary)
[16] CLV Luke 4:18-19 referencing Isaiah 61

responsibilities of Guardian-Caretaker in support of the Universal Family. By the end of the Reified Basar myth, they are adjured to be the mature agents of loving-kindness, compassion, and healing towards one another motivated by a dynamic moral conscience founded on an indwelling *Sacred Breath* of *ahav*/love inspired by, but independent of, the Parent Elohim and the anointed big brother Jeshua. This is the fulfillment of the Basar narrative as an expansion of the Isaiah proclamation, the Good Story—to love one another.

Rabbi Jeshua is the central protagonist within the Reified Basar myth and thus embodies its meaning. In order to understand what his role and function are within the myth, it is important to note the names and titles given to him. The main archetypal identifier is his name *Jeshua* or *Yehoshua* which means, "Yahweh brings safety."[17] In context to the Isaiah Basar, it invokes his role as an agent of healing and restoration. It is a reprisal to the dyspathic human conditions listed in the Isaiah Basar narrative, which, in turn, points to the original terror of psychological nakedness, vulnerability, and *missingness* that is instantiated by eating the fruit of the Tree of the Morality in the Garden of Eden—an essential consolation for our endemic psychological dysfunction. The titles *Prince of Peace* and *Emmanuel* are both used in Matthew's account of Jeshua's birth. The first title invokes his role as one who restores peace within the Universal Family of Elohim. And the last title, which means "the great power with us," invokes his role as the one who restores the intimacy of the Parent Elohim in his relationship with his children. The honorific title, *rabbi*, is used throughout the narrative of the Reified Basar to identify Jeshua as a "master-teacher," which recognizes a fundamental role in Jewish society for those that are exceptionally learned in the Mosaic tradition and Law.

The Hebrew word *mashach*[18] in the first sentence of the Isaiah proclamation that Jeshua claims to fulfill means "to anoint or commission." It is the root of the Hebrew word *messiah*, meaning "one who is anointed," translated directly into Greek as the more familiar Christian term, *Christ*. However, it fundamentally requires an objective "to do what." Kings and prophets were anointed to perform various political and spiritual roles in Jewish society. And, in the tradition of primogeniture, the eldest son (or exceptionally a younger son) was commissioned by a father to be guardian and caretaker of the family upon his passing. Rabbi Jeshua describes his role, in accordance with the prophecy in Isaiah 61, as the anointed son who brings

---

[17] Strongs H3091
[18] Strongs H4886

healing and restoration to those in need within the family. However, this is a major point of contention in the mythology. The dominant messianic dogma in first-century Jewish religion and culture is that a Political Messiah would be sent by Yahweh to militarily deliver the nation from foreign rule, restoring the golden age of the ancestral Davidic Kingdom. By rejecting the political interpretation of asymmetric power and, instead, instantiating the symmetric power of the familial Anointed One, Jeshua disrupts this political narrative. In a familial context, he claims the birthright of primogeniture as the anointed son within the Universal Family of Elohim. He becomes enrolled as the big brother appointed by the father who is responsible for the essential well-being of the family.

In this framework, Jeshua's proclamation to *love your enemy*, in particular, when applied to the much-hated Samaritan half-breeds and Roman overlords as inclusive in the Universal Family, makes sense of the familial interpretation of *messiah*, but did not sit well with the religious and political establishment in Jerusalem. The political interpretation of *messiah* based on struggle and conflict was a compelling outgrowth of a society embroiled in the delicate dance of pacifying their Roman overlords by nominally cooperating with them, and then simultaneously opposing them, trying to subvert their authority in order to eventually free themselves from their rule. However, the politics of struggle and domination fundamentally contradicts the unifying role of the Familial Messiah.

Essentially, the Reified Basar myth is the dream of the Familial Messiah, the Anointed Son. It is an exploration of what it means to love that reaches back to the Garden of Eden, into the wilderness of Sinai, then first-century Palestine, and once understood, can become a guiding narrative even today. Unlike the religious narratives, it is not divorced from, but a fulfillment of a prior mythological framework in the Torah regarding the Universal Family. As such, it is not a history, a scientific treatise on metaphysics, a recipe book, or a cult manual. It is a narrative about how and why to love one another. Philosophically, it is a statement that the meaning of life is to love one another, to value one another, to give to one another. Mythologically, to understand it, to embrace its veracity and force as truth, is to become it.

❖The Good Story

The Reified Basar myth is, hypothetically, what influences the *Gospel* tradition underlying Christianity. However, the Christian religion represents a moralistic rationalization of the narrative based on a selective review and a distorted conclusion of the text, deliberately divorced from the Jewish Torah tradition to which the Basar is intrinsically tied through both the Mosaic Law and the Third Prophet of Isaiah.

This, of course, is a highly sensitive thing to state and deserves a more careful explanation in the following paragraphs. But it is essential to draw a clear distinction between the historical pre-Christian Jewish mythology and the derivative religious ideologies that eclipsed it to become the institutional religions of Traditional Christianity and Pharisaic Judaism. What I am not doing is negating the Gospel myth but rather, just like in our previous discussion on dreamtending, moving it to a restorative, authentic exploration of the narrative based intrinsically on the text. If I am successful, it is the textual narrative that speaks rather than the political interpretation that we are accustomed to hearing from the institutions that claim authority over it.

Since we are fundamentally constructed out of story, narrative and image, when we inculcate a false narrative or story it becomes problematic, sometimes destructive, and possibly toxic. Similarly, when we inculcate a true narrative, a good story, it corrects those false narratives and it can intrinsically inspire us and empower us to be fully ourselves, fully *elohim*, empowered in all our possibilities and potential, shifting the non-rational construction of our psyche towards Salus—wholeness and healing. The purpose of the Reified Basar myth is to be a *truth* narrative—*the truth shall set you free*. We have also seen historically what happens when it is distorted into an instrument of fear and control, of rewards and punishments before a presumptively angry god.

The Reified Basar, or the realized Good Story, is essentially a psychology, a way of being, and is fundamentally resistant to institutional and religious encapsulation—actually forbidding it in the text. In the Basar of Matthew, Rabbi Jeshua forbids his students from being identified as Master-Teacher, Father, or Authority [down-leader]:

> On Moses' seat are seated the scribes and the Pharisees. All, then, whatever they should be saying to you, do and keep it. Yet according to their acts do not be doing, for they are saying and not doing. Now they are binding loads, heavy and hard to bear, and are placing them on men's shoulders, yet they are not willing to stir them with their finger. Now all their works are they doing to be gazed at by men... Now they are fond of the first reclining place at the dinners, and the front seats in the synagogues, and the salutations in the markets, and to be called by men "Rabbi."
>
> Now you may not be called "Rabbi," for One is your Teacher, yet you all are brethren. And "father" you should not be calling one of you on the earth, for One is your Father, the heavenly. Nor yet may you be called

[authority][19]*, for One is your [authority], the [Christ/Anointed]. Now the greatest one among you shall be your servant.*[20]

Functionally, Pharisees were religious authorities in Jewish society who believed in a particular moralistic interpretation of the Torah. The Scribes were the scholars and theologians in that religious tradition. They categorically have their equivalence in every religious system. In Christianity, for example, the titles *Pastor*, *Preacher*, and *Theologian* are used to describe Master-Teacher*s*, and the priestly titles of *Father* and *Pope* are quite literally used as variations of the term *Father*; and the titles *Cardinal*, *Deacon*, *Elder*, *Chaplain*, *Minister*, *"church leader"*—amongst dozens of other semantic cousins—are used to indicate those who wield authority in the denomination. Church hierarchy establishes the rules of the religious dogma and inclusion into the social circle of the denomination. On the contrary, the Reified Basar unifies around the equality of the *brethren/sistren* in the Universal Family, the *fatherhood/parentage* of Yahweh, and the *authority* of the Anointed Son alone as demonstrated in his moral and relational servanthood to the Universal Family.

The Reified Basar is a mythology concerned with the development of a healthy, mature conscience built on the value of others, and the power to support and change the lives of those around us. It is essentially a myth about *love*. However, it needs to be noted that the meaning of the English word *love* is considerably fragmented and bastardized beyond any essential form or meaning. In English, I can say "I *love* my mother," "I *love* ice cream," and I can also say, "I would *love* to punch you in the face." And in our commoditized world, I also can refer to "making *love*," "giving *love*," "receiving *love*," or "searching for *love*." All of these are proper uses of the English term, but it should be clear, upon reflection, that the term does not mean the same in each context. In Greek, there are many similar concepts indicating different forms of action and desire—such as *agape*, *philos*, *storgos*, and *eros*—that are all translated into English by the one term, *love*, losing a great deal of nuance, integrity, and specificity in translation. In Hebrew, the word *ahav*[21] is translated as "love" fundamentally meaning "to breathe after" indicating an act of generosity in giving life to another—a more specific definition and connotation than its English translation. Herein, I will use the compound term *act-love* to emphasize this original meaning. For now, be forewarned that it will be necessary to explain the underlying language further in other

---

[19] Strongs G2519
[20] CLV Matthew 23:2-11
[21] Strongs H157

situations to clarify the imprecision of the English translation from the Hebrew and Greek sources to which we are bound in the scope of this exploration.

The source text for the Reified Basar mythology is the four Gospel narratives, in context to, and in combination with, the Torah—the *Unified Basar and Torah*. The Middle English term *gospel* is a translation of the anglicized Hebrew word *basar* by way of the Greek word *euangelion* with a side trip to the Latinized word *evangel*. Each of these words is a reference to good tidings, news, or story. While Christianity selectively uses these good stories for their own purposes, I will look at them based on their intrinsic mythological and symbological content. I will ignore the theological lens, a distortion of the underlying myth that presupposes a rationalized moralistic framework. This distortion is founded on two thousand years of folks trying to explain "what Jesus *really* meant to say"—from the neo-apostle Paul to the neo-platonic Christian philosopher Augustine, to the ideological reformers Luther and Calvin, and then countless theological reconstructors, thereafter, up to, and including, your neighborhood pastor, priest, mullah, or rabbi expounding their favorite politic last weekend in a million pulpits, synagogues, and mosques across the globe. However, I will occasionally return to the theological to illustrate the intrinsic point the myth makes about the moralistic enterprise of the soul, and to clarify meaning against popular notions that have been propagated by theologians for centuries.

❖Jewish Basar Versus the Christian Gospel

In the Reified Basar mythology and the subsequent cultural movements, there are eyewitnesses, students, and teachers. The four Gospels are described as the eyewitness accounts containing the actual words of Rabbi Jeshua. However, the interstitial commentaries, represented in the letters or epistles that comprise the rest of the New Testament Christian canon, document the historical/mythological successes and failures of the student and teachers to proscriptively apply the Gospel myth to specific communities of students—much in the same way that the Mishnah and Gemara operate within Rabbinic Judaism. Rather than additive to the Gospel construction and narrative, they are merely interpretive biases, for better or worse, of a specific author's concerns in a specific community, wielding limited authority in relation to the actual myth, and only in as much as they reflect the core Basar/Gospel narrative.

In the subsequent moralized mythology derived from the Basar/Gospel, which evolves into the Christian religion, the deviation from the source myth Q, the oral tradition on which the four Gospel accounts are based, begins within the first generation of adherents and interpreters. The most influential revisionist of the Gospel myth is the reformed Pharisee and neo-apostle Paul, who joins the movement some seven years after the crucifixion account. Paul portrays himself as a prophet—an authoritative source of new revelation. In his various letters, he definitively states that his account is separate from the *gospel* of the oral myth Q, which has yet to be formally written down (at least not in any form in which we have any historical record), as well as any reference to the eyewitness accounts of those students of Jeshua who were still alive and active in Jerusalem, or from any direct experience by himself during the life and ministry of Jeshua. In his letter to the Galatians, he states:

> *I want you to know, brothers and sisters, that the gospel I preached is not of human origin. I did not receive it from any man, nor was I taught it; rather, I received it by revelation from Jesus Christ.*[22]

Paul's new *gospel* negates the Gospel/Basar of the oral myth Q by claiming a new revelatory origin apart from it. Although at times, Paul captures in his epistles the spirit of service within the Reified Basar, at other times, his interpretation reads more like the moralistic religious tradition of Pharisaic Judaism, the rationalized cultural interpretation of the Torah mythology with which he formerly identified. However, more often than not, his new theology mirrors the moralism of Greek philosophy, attempting to find order and control in a chaotic universe.

Subsequently, Paul's works become the basis for the fundamental deviations from the *relationalist* meaning and purpose of the original Gospel/Basar text. His moralistic theology is then built upon by the Early Christian Fathers and later religious prophets and reformers. Eventually, in the fourth century CE, his epistles are institutionalized as authoritative when they are canonized by the Nicaean Council; reinforcing the belief that they are *scripture*, signifying to many that they are the *infallible* or prophetic words of the Christian-God, cementing his moralistic theology as the foundation of what Christians refer to as the New Testament.

Nevertheless, this new revelation directly contradicts Rabbi Jeshua's proclamation that the Isaiah Basar guides his anointed mission to alleviate the suffering of the Universal Family. In his first letter to the Corinthians (and elsewhere), Paul modifies Jeshua's proclamation of *gospel* to refer instead to a moralized interpretation of the death of the Christ/Anointed as an appeasement for humanities sins against the Holy Father:

---

[22] NIV Galatians 1:11-12 compare also with Galatians 2:2 and 2 Corinthians 12:1-10

Now, brothers and sisters, I want to remind you of the gospel I preached to you, which you received and on which you have taken your stand. By this gospel you are saved, if you hold firmly to the word I preached to you. Otherwise, you have believed in vain. For what I received I passed on to you as of first importance: that Christ died for our sins according to the Scriptures, that he was buried, that he was raised on the third day according to the Scriptures[23]

Paul changes the meaning of *gospel* to be that which Christians now commonly associate with the moralized Christian Gospel throughout Church history.[24] Paul effectively transforms the Familial Anointed Son that has come to serve the Universal Family back into a cultural and political messiah that the first century Jews had wished for, but instead of purging the Jewish Nation of immorality and foreign oppressors, the Christian Christ now comes to save those adopted into a new tribe of people, which Paul refers to as the *ekklesia*, later translated as *Church*, and purging the immoral and the unfaithful outsiders from it.

In the New Testament Acts of the Apostles written by Luke, a follower of Paul, the new moralistic and tribalistic gospel proclaimed by Paul is celebrated as being more powerful and correct than the social gospel of Peter and Jacob/James, the brother of Jeshua, who together headed the Messianic community in Jerusalem. As a result of this conflict, Paul, who claims to be a prophet separate from the three-year Reified Basar of Rabbi Jeshua, effectively avoids Jerusalem for decades until later in his ministry. Peter and Jacob/James, as actual students and eyewitnesses to the three-year Reified Basar, continue Jeshua's call to actively care for the poor and weak within the Jerusalem community in fulfillment of the Universal Kingdom of Elohim. According to Luke, Peter is much more traditionally moralistic in his views of how non-Jews, referred to as Gentiles, might be included in the community, whereas Paul is shown to have a more open interpretation of the Universal Family of the Eden mythology as inclusive of the Gentiles, without the baggage of Jewish traditions in the Mosaic Law, such as circumcision and food restrictions. So, Paul thusly discards Jewish moralism as being inconsistent with his understanding of the gospel narrative, which Luke indicates that Peter does eventually accept as well. However, in his zeal to reach the broader Hellenistic world, Paul creates a new gospel that merely replaces Jewish moralism with a universal moralism that was more consistent with the Greek pursuit of order and control in a chaotic universe. Later, Peter walks a

---

[23] NIV 1 Corinthians 15:1-4
[24] Tabor (2013) general reference exploring Paul's transformation of Christianity

tenuous line referring to Paul's innovative gospel as "hard to apprehend," stating:

> *According as our beloved brother Paul also writes to you, according to the wisdom given to him, as also in all the epistles, speaking in them concerning these things, in which are some things hard to apprehend, which the unlearned and unstable are twisting, as the rest of the scriptures also, to their own destruction. You, then, beloved, knowing this before, be on your guard lest, being led away with the deception of the dissolute, you should be falling from your own steadfastness.*[25]

Peter, a modestly educated, lower-class fisherman who was one of Rabbi Jeshua's closest companions for three years, politely calls the doctrinaire gospel innovation of the erudite, upper-class Paul, incomprehensible. He then deflects from attacking Paul directly to rather blame Paul's "unlearned and unstable" students for using his epistles *deceptively*, warning others to not follow in their footsteps.

❖Authenticity and the Text

As with all myths and dreams, in order to understand the narrative dynamics, one must let the narrative authentically speak for itself. One cannot rationalize what they might think it should say or mean based on their preconceptions, or what makes them feel comfortable. Given how Christianity has claimed the Gospel/Basar text as its own domain, I will spend some time delineating a distinction between the pre-Christian Jewish Basar myth founded on Isaiah and the institutional development of Christian theology through Paul and the Early Christian Fathers within its various political and cultural constructs. At the heart of the Christian narrative is the reinterpretation of what is the *gospel*. While the Basar/Gospel text itself clearly delineates the role and centrality of the Isaiah proclamation of safety for the suffering and oppressed, Christianity in its various forms typically declares a moralized Gospel/News that Jesus' death on the cross saves you from the wrath of the Holy Father that would otherwise cause you to painfully roast in the fires of Hell for eternity, but instead purchases your potential place in Heaven if you say the right prayer, repent and change your ways, or in some theologies earn your way by being good, or else by paying the church for absolution. The specifics of conversion vary considerably and are the cause of the separation of Christianity into some thirty thousand sects throughout its history.

---

[25] CLV 2 Peter 3:15-17

The exploration of the Unified Basar and Torah mythology in its historical and mythological context creates its own hazards. The very claim of letting the myth speak for itself establishes that the only clear line of reason comes solely from reading the text and finding a deeper resonance with its narrative. I will violate this upfront by trying to bring the text out of the ancient framework into the archetypal and universal. I will fundamentally be vulnerable to the same accusations I levy against the theologians who claim authority over the text. What I hope to do differently is to use the plain text as the foundation, the starting point, instead of a convoluted theology for interpretation. I establish an archetypal interpretation based on essential representative dialogue in the text, letting the voice of Jeshua and his original students define what is the Basar/Gospel (restoration from suffering[26]), what is the meaning of the law (summarized as love[27]), what is the purpose of the cross (healing and life represented as the raised serpent of Moses[28]). Or going further back into the Torah, what is the central dilemma of human suffering (the trauma of psychological nakedness[29]) and human relationships (our core adversarial drive based on fear[30]). To honor the sacred text, the reader, in the end, must ultimately judge whether I have succeeded in this endeavor based on the text not by any correspondence with one's favorite theological interpreter.

❖Christian Moralism

Christian moralism is fundamentally an egoic interpretation of the mythology. It is a moralist manifesto that presumes to explain how *I* should live, how *I* should avoid hell, how *I* can get to heaven, how *I* should practice my religious faith or *walk*, and how *I* should judge and treat others who do not believe the *truth* of what *I* believe. It is engendered as one's testimony to the power of the Christian-God to change one's life to conform to his will. Thusly, in modern society, it is a form of magic that cures disease, makes addicts sober, and guides one's political aspirations, choice of mates, and menu selections. It keeps one on the straight and narrow path of a particular form of morality, unless, of course, it is inconvenient, or is a response to a person one does not think they should like. Often it is practiced as a form of *infantilism*, claiming that one can do nothing apart from the Christian-God upon whom one is wholly and fully dependent.

---

[26] CLV Luke 4:18-19
[27] CLV Mark 12:30-31
[28] CLV John 3:14
[29] CLV Genesis 3:7-8
[30] CLV Genesis 3:8-19

Christians tend to be the last ones to understand their own idiosyncratic divergence from the teachings of the Christian Jesus (let alone Rabbi Jeshua in the actual myth). It is a condition that is fundamentally obvious to most outside observers, often evoking the cry of "hypocrisy," which is covered over by Christian apologists stating that "no one is perfect" or "we are all sinful," rather than addressing the obvious issues. This lack of self-awareness in Christianity was the basis for the great comedic film, *Monty Python's Life of Brian*, which parodies the absurdity of religious behavior. In *"Life's a Piece of Shit": Heresy, Humanism, and Heroism in Monty Python's Life of Brian*, Kevin Schilbrack argues:

> Throughout the movie, Jesus is portrayed in a respectful and even orthodox way. The movie satirizes not what Christian believers believe, but instead the way that some believers believe. First, it mocks a certain religious eagerness to believe. Some philosophers of religion have also criticized this... Even more sharply, the film mocks a certain religious smugness. Religious belief can feed a sense of satisfaction with oneself that can lead to carelessness, hypocrisy, and even violence.[31]

Terry Jones, one of the writers of the film and a member of the iconic comedy troupe, *Monty Python*, for whom the script was written, explains:

> Well, it's not blasphemous because it accepts the Christian story; in fact, the film doesn't make sense unless you take the Christian story, but it's heretical in terms of [being] very critical of the Church, and I think that's what the joke of it is, really: to say, here is Christ saying all these wonderful things about people living together in peace and love, and then for the next two thousand years people are putting each other to death in His name because they can't agree about how He said it, or in what order He said it.[32]

The contrast between a simple reading of the actual Gospel/Basar accounts portraying the essential call to compassionate service to one's fellow man, and the political ideology of church authority and tribal conformity to religious dogma is quite stark, easily substantiating the incompatibility of Christian moralism with the actual teachings of Rabbi Jeshua. When the missionary Stanley Jones asked Mahatma Gandhi, "though you quote the words of Christ often, why is that you appear to so adamantly reject becoming his follower?" Gandhi replied:

> Oh, I don't reject Christ. I love Christ. It's just that so many of you Christians are so unlike Christ. If Christians would really live according to the

---

[31] Hardcastle (2010) p.14-15
[32] Morgan (1999) p.247

teachings of Christ, as found in the Bible, all of India would be Christian today.[33]

❖Christian Theology

Christian theology is both diverse and divisive, which is why there are so many sects. However, most Christian denominations are fundamentally moralistic, believing that "sin" and "evil" are the primary preoccupation of the Holy Father from which everything in the theology is interpreted—heaven, hell, salvation, and condemnation. Aside from the problem that there is no correlative concept in the text for *sin* or *evil*, the magic decoder ring that is used by the translators makes it so, covering up the fact that the original text does not say that the result of eating the forbidden fruit was "sin." As such, the theologian steps in to magically reconstruct a tangential narrative as if *sin* were mentioned as the foundation for the "fall of man" that introduces *sin* and *evil* into the world, resulting in humanity's deservedness to spend an eternity being tormented by the Christian-God in the Christian Hell.

Christianity rationalizes the text to conform to this moralized objective with the help of distorted translations of the text. In the English version of the Bible, translators often use an unknown foreign word, insert it into the English text, and then give it a new meaning. It is a fairly reliable rule to say that any word other than a name that is not directly and accurately translated from either Greek or Hebrew into English or is arbitrarily translated into a second language such as Latin or German, was done to reconstruct a different meaning than the original text—such as *sin, hell, blasphemy*, and *god*. It should also be noted that in mythology even names are a declaration of the intrinsic identity of a character; while they may not be translated, they should be understood.

There is no reason not to translate every word accurately and in context according to the common usage of the terminology in casual conversation. Most Hebrew can be reduced to simple heartfelt, poetic imagery, often of an agrarian origin. Any theologically laden words used in the translation are almost certainly made up, as neither the Greek nor the Hebrew language is based on theology, albeit Greek has a few more philosophically precise images and words. But then again, nearly all the actors in the text spoke Hebrew or Aramaic, so any Greek translations are merely approximate representations of Hebrew ideas and imagery—the result of multiple layers of translation.

---

[33] Stoud (2011) p.162

Accordingly, I have chosen to use the Concordant Literal Version (CLV) of the Bible as a reference throughout this book. The CLV translation is based on taking what the translators consider to be the common or concordant meaning of a word, and then consistently using that word to literally translate the text as an attempt to avoid theological manipulation by the translator. Originating in the late nineteenth century, it has some issues with using terms that are now archaic or out of fashion; and it has some readability problems. However, it avoids some of the worst English translation errors commonly found in the theological interpretations of the Bible. There is a desperate need for an accurate poetic or mythological translation of the text into modern English based on the original words and imagery as opposed to Christian or Jewish theology.

Since most commentaries and interlinear study materials are cross-referenced to the Strongs' Concordance, for ease of documentation, I have followed suit. For those who review the references to Strongs' in the footnotes, you will find a pattern of first giving the literal or linguistic translation, followed by an often ridiculously incompatible theological interpretation, which cannot in any way be reconciled to the linguistic definition they just gave. So, when I refer to Strongs, I am only indicating the actual linguistic definition included therein. I *strongly* suggest one ignore the author's attempt to theologize the language (pun intended.) Many of the key Hebraic and Greek words in this treatise, along with other important concepts, are included in a *Glossary* at the end of the book.

Concept	Basis	Definition	Hebrew Word	Hebrew Meaning	Greek Word	Greek Meaning
sin	Latin *sons*	guilty	*chatta'ah*	missing or failure	*hamartia*	missing or failure
Hell	German *hel*	the frozen underworld in Norse myth	*gehenna*	location outside of Jerusalem wall	*hades*	the benign underworld in Greek myth
blasphemy	Greek derived *blasphemos*	insult or heresy against the sacred	*naqab*	curse or pierce	*blasphemos*	slander, vilify, or misrepre-sent
god	German *god*	deity to whom one pours of-ferings; an idol	*elohim*	one who has many or great powers	*theos*	deity or supernatural overseer

Table 1 – Key Theological Mistranslations

Sin. The religious invention and usage of the term sin is defined within the theological commentary as a moral offense against the Judeo-Christian god for which one has been judged guilty, deserving of the most severe punishment. In fact, the underlying Greek word *hamartia*[34] is a more mundane concept—to miss or fail at an objective. It is an everyday Greek word, requiring a context to define what the objective is—hitting a target with an arrow, reaching an intended destination, or meeting a certain standard of conduct. The objective is not presumed but would be indicated in the context of the sentence or paragraph. Many times, the target in context does turn out to be the Mosaic Law (as opposed to some theological abstraction). However, in the Kingdom of Love narrative, Jeshua summarizes the Mosaic Law as a fundamentally relational concept—to love Yahweh wholly and deeply and to love your neighbor as yourself. When it is used in this relational context, it indicates a failure to love distinct from the moralized concept of failing to follow the rules in such a way that makes the Christian or Jewish god angry. Likewise, the Hebrew word *chatta'ah*[35], which is also translated as *sin*, is a similar concept of missing or failing an objective. It is often used within a relational context indicating one has acted towards someone in such a way as to have incurred an obligation to restore the value taken, to repay the one offended—notably, not to some divine intermediary.

On the other hand, the etymology of the English word *sin* is the Old English word *synn* based on the Latin word *sons*, which means *guilty*. It is a moralized reinterpretation and recontextualizing of the original concept and meaning to indicate a religious or moral failure for which one has been legally condemned, found guilty. It is formulated to be consistent with the preconceived theology, narrowing it to a singular presumptive domain— behavior which the Judeo-Christian god disapproves that results in one's condemnation and guilt before the law, representing the *Will of God*. In the original text, there is actually a Hebrew word that means guilty, *asham*[36], and a Greek word, *hypodikos*[37]—neither are used in the texts that are translated as "sin."

Every modern bible translation is governed by a theological board that is tasked with preserving its interpretive bias. So, to understand the Reified Basar myth, we must move beyond the distortions of the theological economy and deal with the authentic text and its inherent implications in its appropriate psychological context in the same way that one deals with a dream or any other intensified, non-rational narrative. In order to restore the integrity of the underlying myth, given the audacity of the theological

---

[34] Strongs G266
[35] Strongs H2398
[36] Strongs H816
[37] Strongs G5267

translators' creative use of the Latinized term *sin/sons* to translate the words *hamartia* and *chatta'ah*, when necessary, in the context of quotation and explanation, I will attempt to restore the literal translation as "missing" or "failure." Or else, where it implies a quality or state, I will use the literalized construct "missingness." However, if the context is clearly a failure of the Mosaic Law, I may use the interpretative modification "moral failure" or "relational failure" or "failure to love" for literary clarity to the detriment of fundamental accuracy based on the assumed validity of Jeshua's interpretation of the Torah in its cultural context.

Hell. Another bastardized term that is central to Christian theology is the term *hell*, indicating a fiery place where the Christian-God eternally tortures *sinners* for unrepented *sins*. However, it does not exist in the actual Reified Basar myth. The Germanic name, *Hel* refers to the Norse goddess of the frozen underworld as well as the place itself. The term is most often used to represent the Hellenized Aramaic word *Gehenna*, which is an actual historical geographic location outside the gates of Jerusalem known as the *Valley of Ben Hinnom* that forms the southwest boundary of the ancient city below Mount Zion. In the Basar of Matthew, Rabbi Jeshua refers to the "judging of Gehenna" in a series of woeful condemnations of the Pharisees, which is brashly transformed into "Hell" in many translations:

> *Woe to you, scribes and Pharisees, hypocrites! for you are resembling the whitewashed sepulchers which outside, indeed, are appearing beautiful, yet inside they are crammed with the bones of the dead and all uncleanness. Thus you, also, outside, indeed, are appearing to men to be just, yet inside you are distended with hypocrisy and lawlessness... Serpents! Progeny of vipers! How may you be fleeing from the judging of Gehenna?[38]*

Within the Hebrew canon, the *Judging of Gehenna* refers to a prophecy portending the destruction of Jerusalem by fire in the book of Jeremiah as a consequence of the Jews sacrificing their children to *Baal* in the Valley of Ben Hinnom,[39] followed shortly thereafter by the burning of the city by the Babylonians and the exile of the Judahites to Babylon. Thus, the desecrated valley became a symbol of filth and judgment. In this context, some claim that a portion of the valley became the town garbage dump outside the gates wherein the Jerusalemites performed their daily chore of taking out the trash. There are associated references elsewhere in the Basar/Gospel to a judgment of fire, which is both a forewarning of the destruction of Jerusalem by fire at

---

[38] CLV Matthew 23:27-33
[39] CLV Jeremiah 18:23-19:13

the end of the National Age, as well as a symbol of the desecrated town dump in Gehenna that is believed to have been kept burning with brimstone/sulfur to purge the rotting debris, invoking the visceral image of a perpetual fire. Rabbi Jeshua tells the self-righteous, hypocritical Pharisees—who considered themselves ritually clean before the Mosaic and Levitical Laws, whilst at the same time having no value for, and taking no action to assist, the poor and oppressed—that they belonged in the garbage dump. It is what we call in English, an *insult*. In the history of Christianity, *hell* is a medieval myth straight out of *Dante's Inferno* and Hieronymus Bosch's paintings. It is not a translation of the original Reified Basar myth.

Blasphemy. An important, but often overlooked term that is left untranslated, and then twisted in all sorts of ways is the Greek word *blasphemos*,[40] meaning "to slander," which is, in turn, associated with the Hebrew word *naqab*,[41] meaning "to curse or pierce." However, in Christianity and Judaism, its meaning is moralized—identifying it conceptually with the religious mandate to not speak Yahweh's name rashly or in vain, and then extended into the idea of not cursing using his name or attribute, or else a prohibition even of writing or speaking his name aloud. It also is twisted into a religious obsession concerning doctrinal *heresy*, which sanctions the attack, segregation, or judicial killing of those who go against the tenets of a religious sect.

In Greek, however, *blaspheme* means to vilify, to attribute false or harmful intentions to someone, to slander or falsely accuse of a failing. Its key usage in the Reified Basar is the statement by Rabbi Jeshua that all sins/failures will be forgiven/let go, except to blaspheme/slander/vilify the sacred spirit/breath. The *Sacred Breath*, or *ruach hakodesh*[42] in Hebrew, refers to Yahweh's expressed desire or intention that actively engages or guides the lives of humans. Rabbi Jeshua clarifies this intent, numerous times, as *ahav* or act-love. It is illustrated in the parable of the Sheep and Goats when the religious folks are condemned for not taking care of the poor and oppressed. Rabbi Jeshua states, "whatsoever you have done unto the least of these you have done unto me." These Goats who implicitly consider themselves righteous before the Mosaic Law are the ones thrown into the perpetual fire of the garbage dump as worthless trash as opposed to the so-called "sinners," or those who fail before the Mosaic Law, whom Rabbi Jeshua states will be forgiven/let go. In this context, it would be blasphemy/slander

---

[40] Strongs G989
[41] Strongs H5344
[42] Strongs H7307, H2932

to imply that the Great Father was intending to harm the so-called "sinners," such as telling them they will be cast into *Hell*.

God. If you are following the pattern here, you might not be surprised that the oft-used word *god* is not an actual translated term. The Germanic word *god* has several possible derivations that either indicate a specific Norse deity or, more likely, some primitive Norse conception of deity as one to whom you pour offerings. The problem is that the early Hebrew concept equivalent to this notion of deity that one serves through offerings is a *gillul*[43], often translated as *idol*. The Hebrew word that is often erroneously translated as *god* is the word *elohim*.[44] The root of the word *elohim* is *el*, singularly indicating one who is powerful, founded on the image of a strongly rooted tree. Depending on its context, *elohim* may be the plural of the word *el*, thus indicating *the many powerful ones,* or when used as a singular superlative of *el* in the context of a sentence, it indicates one who is functionally a very great power, or literally one with much or many powers. *Elohim* is not equivalent to deity or god, although *gillul* by construction is a type, or representation, of great power—all *gilluls* are *elohim* but not all *elohim* are *gilluls*. *Elohim* is rather a functional description that may alternately refer to various types of other-worldly beings, such as the supreme great power, angelic messengers, fantastic guardians, and adversarial entities. It may also refer to this-worldly mortal chiefs and magistrates. Or it can refer to anyone that functionally has great power over some person or domain.

In the text, theologians pointedly translate *elohim* as *god* when the subject of the word *elohim* is imagined to be of some otherworldly quality. However, when *elohim* refers to something more mundane, the translators often insert disclaimers that are not in the original text to fix their mistranslation. In the passage where Moses complains that he is not up to the task of Deliverer because he is "heavy of mouth and heavy of tongue," Yahweh replies that he will make his brother Aaron "a mouth for you, and you shall become an elohim for him."[45] In an attempt to avoid the theological burden of the mistranslation of elohim as "god," this is expanded in the KJV as "thou shalt be to him instead of God" and in the NIV "as if you were God to him."

---

[43] Strongs H1544
[44] Strongs H430
[45] CLV Exodus 4:16

This issue is compounded by various theological gymnastics that purposely privilege some portions of text while ignoring others. For example, in John 10:34, Rabbi Jeshua is asked if he is theos/overseer to which he replies that he is elohim/great power pointing to David stating in Psalms 82:6 that all humans "are elohim, and sons of the Supreme are all of you." The word *god* is typically used in each translation but is ignored or excused by theologians as poetic in Psalms and embraced as proof of Trinitarian doctrine in John's narrative, even though they are directly tied together by Rabbi Jeshua.

In various stories in the Reified Basar myth, the Greek text uses the word *theos* to represent *elohim*. The word *theos* refers to beings that either move, motivate, influence, or otherwise oversee aspects of the world. It represents a more traditional perspective of deity as an alien race separate from humans, whose powers hold sway over their fate and fortunes. The Greeks, in fact, believed that there were three races—Humans, Olympians, and Titans. In translating from Hebrew to Greek, *theos* is often used to translate *elohim* even though it does not have the same meaning. This becomes clear when *theos* is used to describe the Aramaic-speaking Jeshua in John 10:34 above, who then refers to the Hebrew word *elohim* in Psalms 82:6 creating all sorts of semantic confusion in its double translation into English as "god".

While not all *theos* are served or worshiped—*theos* become idol-gilluls when objects and images are created as substitutionary symbols for what one fears or desires, enabling the worshiper to engage and influence them. Universally, idol-gilluls are transactional by intent and nature—humans must make offerings to please them, to gain their favor, or else to appease their anger and persuade them to remove a curse. More than superstition, idolatry is an intrinsic psychological function present throughout all history and all peoples and is still prevalent in modern society as different ways to engage our fears and desires through objectification and projective empowerment or disempowerment.

Many sects of Christianity posit that the Christian-God is of a separate race represented by the *Trinity* that humans can be adopted into by a blood transaction. The Christian Jesus was both of the Trinitarian race and the Human race and thus was able to pay the blood price for human sinful behavior to pacify the anger of the Holy Father. Thus, Christian theology turns Yahweh into an idol/gillul, a god for whom a transaction must be paid in order to gain his favor and to remove a curse. As a theology, paying a transactional price for a moral failure to gain approval by the god, even if it is paid for by a god on behalf of his human servants, intrinsically contradicts the central relational premise in the Reified Basar text of forgiveness, or letting go of the same said failures—or more specifically, letting go of the legal right to judge another who has offended you. The transactional premise represents a more trenchant cultural myth of deity from other moralistic religions outside of the Unified Basar and Torah mythology.

Like the gillul in other moralistic religions, the Christian-God has a narcissistic, obsessive-compulsive, borderline personality. As such, he must be worshiped, cannot internally handle disorder, and will violently flip from acceptance to condemnation as a result of displeasing him. When he is displeased it turns his supposed great love into overt aggression, often culminating in the offender being violently dumped into the eternal fires of the Christian Hell. This does not reconcile very well with the teachings of the Christian Jesus about love and mercy, so theologians have created many convoluted theodicies to absolve the all-powerful, all-knowing Christian-God of the ramifications of these character flaws by blaming the one's being thrown into Hell for being the ones who have caused the Christian-God's horrific compulsion to torture them for eternity. In ethics, this is what is called *gaslighting*, blaming the victim, which is often used as a form of control in domestic violence: "You know you deserved it. You carelessly burned the toast, so I had to smack you. You made me do it."

In light of our understanding of love in normal psychological health and mature human relationships, the Christian-God is an abusive authority figure, a negative representation of the parental image. He is immature, unpleasant, having an inferior moral character—someone who is judgmental and uncaring when crossed, motivated by jealousy, with an underdeveloped ethos. He has more in common with the Greek gods Zeus and Cronus in needing to resolve his overbearing personality disorder through his interactions with humankind. The pervasive theodicy of the Trinity is an attempt to reconcile this fundamental contradiction in the theology of the flawed character of the Holy Father by positing that he is completed in union with the Loving Son and the Wise Spirit—a mysterious three gods in one. This perfidiously has no basis in the text other than to occasionally list their names together—Father, Son, and Holy Ghost—in the same manner as the patriarchs—Abraham, Isaac, and Jacob.

This of course is in direct opposition to the loving Good Parent of the Elohim family narrative that is actually in the Genesis Creation story and subsequently throughout, which states that from a family of ancestral Imago Elohim, humans are created in the ideal image, and are fully identified. In line with this, David, thusly states in the Psalms that "we are all elohim." Then Rabbi Jeshua, when asked if he is *theos* states that he is *elohim* just as their forefather David stated that "we are all elohim." Elohim is a familial concept in the Reified Basar, not an alien one. Jeshua declares Yahweh to be "dad" (Aramaic, *abba*) whose desire for us is beneficial, his boundaries are open and inclusive, yet whose identity is sacred, set apart from the suppositions and definitions of others. He is merciful and generous and desires his children in the Universal Family of Elohim to be the same. In the Unified Basar and Torah narrative, there is no contradiction to the openness, generosity, and forgiveness in what we understand to be *ahav*/act-love in everyday life and family relations. All humans as Adamites are inherently *elohim*, identified with the Universal Family of Elohim, rooted in relationship to the Parent Elohim as their spiritual Dad. This is the foundation for the relational architecture of the myth.

❖The Torah Myth

The Torah myth is unique in that it is fundamentally inclusive. From the beginning, humans are not alienated from, or subjugated to, the gods, but are rather Child Elohim—of the parental origin and character of Yahweh Elohim within all creation. While the tribe of Israel is declared to function as his anointed firstborn of nations, Yahweh is not a tribal god bounded by a particular region, tribe, or city-state. This claim of universality is a major distinction from many creation myths of the region, as well as many creation myths across human cultural history. It is the fundamental tenet that forms the direction and conclusion of the Reified Basar myth. It is intrinsically what makes the Reified Basar myth a psychology of human behavior constellated by the universal principle of *act-love*. Humans are not victims immersed in perpetual infantilism before a narcissistic tribal deity; nor are they conquerors, subjecting and controlling the creation under their unrestrained powers—they are *family*.

The Torah myth is the foundation of the Reified Basar mythology—it is the context and topography from which the narrative essentially evolves. The Hebrew word *torah*[46] means "guidance" and is often translated into English by the word *law*. In the Jewish tradition, it most broadly refers to the Pentateuch, the first five books of the Jewish and Christian scriptures; or else, alternatively, to a subtext of the Pentateuch described as the *Mosaic Law*—the specific list of prescribed obligations contained in the Pentateuch. However, within the broader mythology, the Mosaic Torah of Sinai is only one

---

[46] Strongs H8451

of several core *guidances*. From the perspective of the Unified Basar and Torah myth, I will focus on three major Torah/Guidances—the *Torah of Awakening* in the Genesis creation story, the *Torah of Obligation* in the Mosaic Law of Sinai, and the *Torah of Restoration* in the Messianic narrative of the Reified Basar.

❖Chronicles of Yahweh

The mythological arc of the Unified Basar and Torah narrative chronicles three distinct epochs of Yahweh's interaction with the Adamites—*Primordial*, *National*, and *Universal*. The *Primordial Age* is founded on the Torah of Awakening and chronicles the beginning of the Cosmos in the Edenic and Antediluvian Eras. The *National Age* is founded on the Torah of Obligation and chronicles the children of Israel as the favored nation of Yahweh from their birth narrative in Mesopotamia, Canaan-Levant, and Egypt, then, to the Kingdom of Elohim in Israel during the period of Moses and the Judges, and, finally, to the rejection of Yahweh as the King of Israel ushering in the era of the Political Kingdoms. The *Universal Age* is founded on the Torah of Restoration that restores the intimacy of the Kingdom of Elohim in the Universal Family after the destruction of Jerusalem and the Second Temple and the subsequent exile and dispersion of the Jewish people into other nations.

- <u>**Primordial Age of Parent Elohim**</u> **(Awakening)**
  - ○ *Edenic Era*—Birth of the Adamites (Universal Family)
  - ○ *Midbar/Nod/Antediluvian Era* (Adam, Cain, Noah)
  - ○ *Postdiluvian Era* (Noah/Babel)
- <u>**National Age of Savior Elohim**</u> **(Obligation)**
  - ○ *Prehistoric Nation/Israel* Era (Genesis/Exodus) [~400 years]
    - Patriarchal Period—Abraham/Isaac/Jacob
    - Egypt/Goshen Period—Joseph
    - Slavery/Exodus Period—Moses
  - ○ *Kingdom of Elohim in Israel* Era (Moses/Judges) [~400 years]
    - Mount Sinai Period (Moses) [~2 years]
      - Torah and Tabernacle
    - Wandering in Desert Period (Moses) [~40 years]
    - Conquest of Canaan Period (Judges)
    - Settlement of Canaan Period (Judges)
      - Rejection of Yahweh as King under Samuel
  - ○ *Political Kingdom* Era (Kings/Prophets) [~400 years]
    - Unified Kingdom Period {1000 BCE – 930 BCE}
      - Tribal Elohim/Kings (Saul/David/Solomon)
      - First Institutional Temple built by Solomon
    - Divided Kingdom Period—North/South {930 BCE – 588 CE}
      - Northern Kingdom/Israel conquered by Assyrians {722 BCE}
      - Exile of the northern tribes to Assyria and permanent dissolution of tribal identity

- Remnant intermarry with local Canaanite tribes (Samaritans)
- Judgment of Gehenna/Jerusalem (Tophet/Jeremiah)
- Southern Kingdom/Judah Conquered by Babylon {588 BCE}
- Destruction of Jerusalem and Solomonic Temple
- Exile of Judah into Babylon
  - *Vassal Kingdom Era* (Prophets/Third Isaiah) [~600 years]
    - Second Temple Period {516 BCE ~ 70 CE}
      - Return from Neo-Babylonian Captivity {516 CE}
      - Vassal nation instituted under King Cyrus of Persia
      - Colonizing of the northern territories in Samaria
      - Rebuilding of Jerusalem and Second Institutional Temple
      - Foreign Rule (Persians, Greeks, Romans)
      - Tradition of the Political Messiah
      - Second Temple demolished by Romans (Tophet) {70 CE}
    - Apocalyptic Period {3 BCE–136 CE}
      - Reified Basar (Third Isaiah) {3 BCE – 30 CE}
      - Advent of Familial Messiah (Anointed Son)
      - Persecution of Familial Messiah (Crucifixion)
      - Jewish-Roman Wars {66-136 CE}
      - Destruction Jerusalem/Temple (Judgment of Gehenna) {70 CE}
      - End of Last Jewish War (Exile/Diaspora) {136 CE}
      - Close of National Age
- **Universal Age of Beloved Elohim (Restoration)**
  - *Restored Kingdom of Elohim Era* (Universal Family)
    - Lower Kingdom Period {70 CE-present}
      - Internal realm of great power/love
    - Upper Kingdom Period {TBD}
      - Restoration of love as a universal presence

Table 2 - Outline of Mythological Ages

This describes the framework of the mythology from the perspective of Yahweh, focusing on his role as Parent/Savior Elohim moving towards his role as the Beloved Elohim. Each epoch foreshadows the next in the narrative chronology. It should be noted that the theological metaphysics of the Jewish and Christian religious systems break down the interrelated elements differently, in support of the ideological presuppositions of the theology and cultural identity. Each religious system adds its own elements into the mythology to enhance the moralistic conclusions that the narrative needs to complete the soteriological connotations of events, including the apocalyptic Revelation of John and, as a much later development, how to characterize the establishment of a modern nation of Israel in the twentieth century based on racial identity, which some religious sects presuppose is a restoration of Israel as a favored nation.

One's metaphysical outlook will certainly influence whether one interprets Rabbi Jeshua's discussion of the destruction of Jerusalem and the institutional Temple as prophetic, or, as a later revision to the text after the events occurred. As myth, I am only interested in the importance of it as a fundamental concern in the narrative that influences its outcome and conclusions. In addition, the dates suggested herein are disputed as historical markers but are not specifically relevant to the construction of the mythology, other than by defining a context and an order to the events in the narrative. My interest in the mythology is not reliant on the historical specificity or actuality of the events, but rather on the semantics that builds a developmental framework of a relational psychology founding a morality of love.

❖Gods and Archetypes

In a society's myths, the forces of nature and human activity in the cosmos are readily identifiable—their behavior is observable and patterns differentiable. The sun rises in the east and sets in the west. Storms come across the horizon from a typical geographic direction per locale, rising from the storm clouds bringing the winds, and thunder and lightning. The morning star Venus ushers in the new day just before the sun rises. Different constellations of stars position themselves in the night sky in predictable patterns during the calendar year. In the realm of human experience, the desire of humans for goodness—justice, wisdom, safety, fertility, health, and wealth—are everted in their fear of badness—lawlessness, defeat, ignorance, exposure, separation, impotence, hunger, death, disease, and poverty. The objectification and attribution of personality to the forces that encompass our existence is the foundation and advent of theology—the identification and understanding of the gods.

In Plato's *Cratylus*, written in the fourth century BCE, the character *Socrates* expounds on the etymology and semantics of the Hellenic ideation of *theos*.

> I suspect that the sun, moon, earth, stars, and heaven, which are still the Gods of many barbarians, were the only Gods known to the aboriginal Hellenes. Seeing that they were always moving and running, from their running nature they were called Gods [theos] or runners [Theous, Theontas]; and when men became acquainted with the other Gods, they proceeded to apply the same name to them all.[47]

Inherent in this idea is the power to move through nature and to influence human experience. Plato then separates the archetypal essence of an identified *theos* from the name given by man.

---

[47] Plato (1892) p.328

There is one excellent principle... that of the Gods we know nothing, either of their natures or of the names which they give themselves... [And] that we will call them by any sort or kind of names or patronymics which they like, because we do not know of any other... We are not enquiring about them; we do not presume that we are able to do so; but we are enquiring about the meaning of men in giving them these names.[48]

It is within this semantic separation that we begin to understand the individual cultural frameworks for the ideation of archetypal power in myth and life.

As a product of our psychological orientation and development, we may come to see ourselves as being either inside or outside the narrative universe of a myth. This determines whether we experience the myth as inclusive or exclusive, or else as relational or hierarchical. On a fundamental level, as Plato expounds, the myths of the gods describe the world and how it works. The myth of *Narcissus and Echo*, for example, explains the origins of the narcissus flower while interrogating the moral implications of pride and self-obsession and its downfall—what happens when empathy fails. We are included as participants in the drama, being instructed on how we should order and direct our lives in the face of enumerable forces in the cosmos, avoiding the moral consequences of disorder and chaos.

At a different level, humans have a tendency to orient themselves as aliens or victims to the forces within the drama—subject to the whims of the gods, obligated to engage in service to the gods in order to manipulate and deflect their capricious and destructive impulses. This exclusionary psychological construct is intrinsically transactional, directly affecting the outcomes of one's destiny through sacrifice and service. The idolization of these archetypal forces is reflected in the crafting of objects to represent the gods in order to serve them as a way to gain benefit from them. It is a projection of our fear and our fundamental impulse and orientation towards control.

❖Imago Mundi

As civilization evolved in the Early Bronze Age of Mesopotamia from city-states to empires, the isolated patron gods of the client cities had to be ordered into a pantheon ruled by the empire god of the subsequent ruling city-state—first, the Akkadian-Sumerian city of Akkad, and then the Assyrian city of Assur, and then, finally, the Babylonian city of Babylon. In the second millennium BCE, during the period of the Babylonian Empire, we have the documented creation myth of *Enuma Elish* elaborating the primacy of

---

[48] Plato (1892) p.335

Marduk, the patron god of Babylon, as the ruler of the pantheon of gods, while celebrating a hierarchy of primary and secondary deities placed within the cosmos. There are hundreds of gods with overlapping attributes knitted together from different regions; fifty are listed as the central council giving their names and attributes. Culturally, an overall pattern develops in the listing, showing some unique attributes combined with common concerns represented by multiple gods. However, at the heart of the myth is humanity's fundamental obligation to serve these gods; to make the gods' lives easier. Tablet VI of the *Enuma Elish*[49] describes the creation of Man, stating:

> *Once Marduk heard the words that the gods had declared,*
> *He was then determined to accomplish unparalleled deeds*
> *Directing his words to Ea, of the plan he was mulling over,*
> *"My thought is to collect blood, and construct bones also,*
> *My thought is to create a primitive human, to be called Man*
> *So thus I am well inclined to give rise to primal humanity*
> *And the work which is now done by the gods, he will do,*
> *So that the gods will not be required to labor for evermore*
> *Through this I will alter dramatically life among the gods,*
> *So that they might be viewed as one, even if in two camps."*
> ...
> *From this Ea made humankind, from out of [Kingu's] lost blood*
> *To him they gave the labor of the gods, thus freeing them*
> *Then after the knowledgeable Ea had made humankind,*
> *He had him do the labor of the gods, a deed beyond words,*
> ...
> *[Marduk] will be a shepherd to the entire people of his own making,*
> *May all his acts be spoken of in the future, never to be forsaken*
> ...
> *May his breath be as freely taken on earth as it is in heaven*
> *May he cause the entire people of earth to give him reverence,*
> *So that humankind will remember him, and call him their god*
> *May their mediating goddess give heed whenever he speaks,*
> *May these food-offerings be made to both god and goddess*
> *So that they never be forsaken! So that they abide by their god*
> *So their nation is supreme, never ceasing from erecting temples*
> *Even as the entire people each chooses his own among the gods*
> *For us, under whatever name he might be called, he is our god!*
> ...
> *May his name be declared to be 'The Son, King of the Gods!'*
> *Might they walk henceforth in the glow of his pervading aura,*
> *The humans that he made of mortal life, who must breathe,*
> *He set them to do the gods' work, that they might have leisure*
> *Both creation and obliteration, both sentence and absolution*

---

[49] Stephany (2013) Tablet VI

The gods, in response to man's labors, provide protection and provision when given the proper respect and offerings.

The Semitic cultures of the Ancient Near East have an interconnected history spreading across Mesopotamia and the Levant, as well as the Arabian Desert, through migration and conquest over several millennia. They also were influenced significantly through trade and conquest by the surrounding cultures of the earlier Sumerian civilization within Mesopotamia, the Indus Valley civilization far to the east, the Elamites, Medes, and Persians in the proximal east, the Hittites to the north, and the Egyptians to the southwest. The Great Rivers of the Tigris and Euphrates enabled agriculture to evolve in the region, which in turn allowed cities to grow and eventually empires to develop. So, the primary gods were related to fertility, storms, rivers, and war. In addition, gods that established the foundation of political power developed, both in legitimizing the ruling hierarchy and establishing principles of justice, wisdom, and charity. Some of the earliest law codes evolved from this region including the Code of Ur-Nammu (2050 BCE), the Babylonian Code of Hammurabi (1790 BCE), and then the Law of Moses/Torah (1000–600 BCE).

Map showing Assyria, Babylonia, and Armenia. FlorinCB, Photo, 2021.

Figure 4 - Imago Mundi 4000BCE

❖**The Gatekeepers**

Archetypally, gillul/idol gods are the embodiment of power—the controllers of our destiny and the gatekeepers to our fears and desires. They are the owners or lords of creation, nature, and emotive principles. They respond well to the piety of submission and sacrifice, and destructively to slander and insolence suffered against their legitimate domain. They are typically immortal until sometimes they are not due to infighting with other gods. Although, even when crushed to dust, as agents of the mythscape they will often mystically recover and reappear in later stories (such as Mot in the Ugaritic Baal Cycle). They are driven by ego and shadow impulse and are usually indifferent to human affairs unless a human offers something that gets their attention (hint: fire, food, and shiny objects are particularly effective).

The primary gods of the Levant were El, Yahweh, Baal, and Asherah— amongst a smattering of other Mesopotamian idol gods. As Plato indicates, there is a separation between the names and identities of the gods. The

Torah is fundamentally a theodicy to differentiate the idol gods Yahweh and El of the Phoenicians and Edomites from the Parent Elohim, Yahweh/El of the Edenic Torah myth. In the Ugaritic myths of ancient Phoenicia, El is a title meaning "great power/strength" given to the creator and ruler of the pantheon of all other gods, while Yahweh is the title given to a war god. The Torah mythographers argue that the Edenic Yahweh/El originates at the beginning of creation and therefore has a distinct identity. The declaration that Yahweh Elohim is One is a direct attack on and prohibition towards those that diverge from this Torah narrative.

The Hebrew tribes are fundamentally influenced by their Canaanite residency. The historiological myth of Israel chastises their propensity to worship the idol gods of the Canaan-Levant up against the priestly idealism of the Torah to call them into a parent-child relationship to Yahweh El. The invocation of the name *Yahweh* by the ancients and, for that matter, contemporary religious authorities, is clouded by Plato's prescription that the name of the god is not necessarily the identity of the god. From the outset, there is an identified path to the gillul/idol gods, as well as the Parent Elohim, which can only be resolved through the attribution and intent of the caller.

❖**The Ideal Parent**

In the Genesis Creation myth, the Guardian-Caretaker role of the Parent Elohim evolves out of the Imago Elohim who creates the Adamite Elohim in their image:

> And Elohim said: "Let Us make humanity in Our image and according to Our likeness." ...So Elohim created humanity in His image; in the image of Elohim He created it: male and female He created them. Elohim blessed them... And Elohim said: "Since I have given you all seed-yielding herbage... and every tree on which there is the fruit of a seed-yielding tree, it shall be yours for food." ...And Elohim saw all that He had made; and behold, it was very good.[50]

This is the familial foundation of the mythology. Yahweh is not a foreign entity, but rather the ideal parent-creator of the family, who provides for and blesses his children. The Parent Elohim from the very beginning values, believes in, and identifies his children as "very good." Humanity is not created to labor for the gods but rather to enjoy the sufficiency and goodness of the Garden.

The ideal qualities of Yahweh's parental character are defined in the Exodus myth episode wherein Moses ascends Mount Sinai to receive the

---

[50] CLV Genesis 1:26-2:2

Decalogue on two stone tablets. Yahweh introduces his own character to Moses as compassionate and gracious, slow to anger, and abundant with kindness and truth.[51] This declaration of character becomes a common epithet that is repeated numerous times throughout the Hebrew canon. One such invocation is the 103rd Psalm in which David invokes the paternal character of the Elohim:

> Compassionate and gracious is Yahweh, Slow to anger and with much [kindness]. He shall not contend permanently, And He shall not hold resentment for the eon. He has neither done to us according to our [failures]... For as the heavens are lofty over the earth, So is His [kindness] masterful over those [reverencing] Him. As far as the east is from the west, So He removes our [faults] far from us. As a father shows compassion over his sons, So Yahweh shows compassion over those [who reverence] Him. For He knows our formation, Remembering that we are soil... Yet the [kindness] of Yahweh is from eon unto eon over those [who reverence] Him, And His [justice] continues for the sons of sons.[52]

Similarly, in the 91st Psalm, David invokes the maternal character of the Elohim as El Shaddai,[53] meaning the "many-breasted one." However, the translators often choose a neutered form of El Shaddai, such as "him who suffices." Despite the oft-neutered translation, the image that the Psalm invokes is a mother bird protecting her children under her wings:

> He who is dwelling in the concealment of the Supreme Shall lodge in the shadow of [Her] Who Suffices [Shaddai/many breasted one]. I shall say of Yahweh: My Refuge and my Fastness, My Elohim, in Whom I trust. For [she] shall rescue you from the snare of the trapper, From the plague of woes. With [her] pinions shall [she] overshadow you, And under [her] wings shall you take refuge; A large shield and encircling-guard is [her] faithfulness... For You, O Yahweh, are my Refuge![54]

The central image of Yahweh's character throughout the Unified Basar and Torah myth is the Good Parent, or ideal Parent image, who loves his/her children and cares for them. As such, it is intended to be an essential part of the children's identity and character as well. In the Basar of Matthew, the maturity of the Good Father, whose love is not constrained by the behavior—good or bad—of his children, is invoked as a calling to all, to be thusly *mature* in character as the Good Father:

> Yet I am saying to you, Love your enemies, and pray for those who are persecuting you, so that you may become sons of your Father Who is in the heavens, for He causes His sun to rise on the wicked and the good, and

---

[51] CLV Exodus 34:6
[52] CLV Psalms 103:8-17
[53] Strongs H7706
[54] CLV Psalms 91:1-9

*makes it rain on the just and the unjust... You, then, shall be [mature]55 as
your heavenly Father is [mature].56*

The path to maturity is the central theme of the Unified Basar and Torah
myth, which will thusly be our focus in the following exposition.

Archetypally, the ideal parent image exists in opposition to its distorted
negative image that is developed through our lived experience of the family.
In her book, *The Parental Image*, Jungian psychologist, Mary Esther Harding,
introduces the archetypes of both the ideal parental image and its dissolution
into its negative aspects:

> *The image of the archetypal parents and of the home is inherent in every
> individual, having been laid down in the unconscious part of the psyche
> through the experience of generation after generation. But in addition, as
> we know full well, these images are modified by the personal experience
> each one has had of his personal home and parents. The normal archetypal
> image gives the picture of parental love and care, and of the home as a
> place of safety and a refuge in time of danger. That is, it may be called
> normal for an individual to have an experience of the positive aspect of the
> parental image. But there is also a negative aspect of this same image,
> that may at times predominate. The nurturing mother may be replaced by
> her devouring aspect; the kindly and just father may appear as tyrannical
> and vengeful. But the positive image is the normal and prevailing one.57*

The good and bad parental images are the groundwork from which our
personal narrative develops.

❖**Transcendent Relationship**

In the Torah myth, the identity and character of the Parent Elohim are
also embedded in his revealed name as *Yahweh*. While the name is used
throughout the myth, the story of the name being revealed is in the narrative
of Moses' commission to go and deliver the Israelites from slavery in Egypt.58
Moses is on the Mount of Elohim in Midian, which is in the Arabian Desert
east of the Sea of Reeds, later known as the Gulf of Aqaba at the eastern tip
of the Red Sea. This is the seat of Yahweh in the Exodus story, and the
Israelites will return here to receive the Torah Guidance/Law. The Midianites
are an Arab tribe, and thus speak Arabic, which is one of the major variations
of the Semitic languages in addition to Hebrew. While theologians debate the
meaning of the name of *Yahweh* in Hebrew, it is within the native language of
the region of the Mount of Elohim in Midian that we find consistency with the

---

55 Strongs G5046
56 CLV Matthew 5:44-48
57 Harding (1993) p.16-17
58 CLV Exodus 3:15

fullness of the Unified Basar and Torah mythology. In the Arabic dialect, *yhwh* translates as one who loves, blows, or falls[59]—all of which evoke his character as the loving parent, the spermatic breath of life, and the caretaker from whom blessings fall. The Hebrew dialect captures a narrow aspect of that as one who is self-existent, sometimes translated, as "I am that I am." In context to the Arabic, it becomes more of "I breath as I breath"—implying one who does not owe his breath or existence to another.

In the archetypal construct of the mythology, the three defining characteristics of love, breath, and provision are progressively revealed in the narrative as the *transcendent* relational roles of Yahweh as the ideal Parent Image, in correspondence with the *developmental* roles of the Adamites. Thusly, in the Genesis-Creation myth, we are first introduced to Yahweh in the role of the Parent Elohim—a manifestation of the existential and generative dependency of the one who *blows* or breathes life into the juvenile Adamites. Then, in the Exodus narrative, we are introduced to Yahweh in the role of the Savior Elohim—a manifestation of the Guide-Aide as one from whom blessings *fall* in support of the independency of the adolescent Adamites. And finally, in the Reified Basar myth, we are introduced to Yahweh in the role of the *Beloved Elohim*—a manifestation of the interdependency of the adult Adamites in relationship to Yahweh as the one who *loves*. Each of these transcendent roles builds on the previous as they develop toward a mature interdependent relationship.

❖**Relational Power**

The underlying archetypal skeleton of the Unified Basar and Torah mythology is the dynamic of relational power, which can be either *symmetric* or *asymmetric*. The *symmetric* relational power dynamic is founded on the relational archetype of the family as it develops from the juvenile *Child-Parent* relationship to the adolescent *Servant-Savior* relationship and then finally, if all goes well, to the adult *Lover-Beloved* relationship. These archetypes are rooted in a balance or symmetry of power resulting in a *liberal* psychological state based on sufficiency, love, empathy, cooperation, inclusion, and empowerment. They are systemically constructed based on equality and operate based on reciprocity and community. Leadership is familial, founded on altruism, service, and need. The archetypes operate as a relational artifact through altruistic inclusivism forming a Universal Family based on the intrinsic value of all Adamites with shared identity and responsibility as family members. Psychological development moves towards

[59] Toorn (1999), "Yahweh", p.915

maturity and responsibility; behavior is reciprocal, open, and thoughtful. Morality is based on act-love, compassion, empathy, and trust.

The symmetric relational power dynamic of the *transcendent* roles discussed previously are represented as *Parent*, *Savior*, and *Beloved*. They operate in the psyche as objective archetypes of an idealized quality or state. An actual enrolled relationship may or may not realize its full potential but is treated as embodying its full value and importance. One's relationships may not meet the potential of the ideal *Parent*, *Savior*, or *Beloved* but the permeable boundaries of the symmetric dynamic induce one to let go of perceived faults and failures—to generously embrace the enrolled potential. The mythological narrative actuates the potential of the ideal image that obligates honor and respect. The comparable symmetric dynamic instantiated as *developmental* roles are represented by the *Child*, *Servant*, and *Lover*. Each of these subjective constructs respectively correlates to a stage of juvenile, adolescent, and adult moral development; progressively moving us towards the full representation of the Mature Elohim.

The *asymmetric* relational power dynamic is represented in the politically charged archetypes of the *Victim-Villain-Victor*, the *Slave-Master*, and the *Rival-Adversary*. These archetypes are founded on an imbalance or asymmetry of power resulting in a *conservative* psychological state based on scarcity, fear, conflict, exclusion, greed, and control. They are systemically constructed based on inequality and operate based on hierarchies and transactions. Leadership is political, founded on force, obedience, and domination. The archetype operates as a cultural artifact through totemic exclusivism forming sectarian cults based on conformity to norms, dogma, and alliances. Psychological development is underdeveloped, juvenile, and proscriptive; behavior is reactionary and uncritical. Morality is highly egocentric and/or projectively focused on a totemic authoritarian construct— the self, the cult leader, the system.

The asymmetric dynamic of the dominant roles is represented by the *Villain-Victor*, *Master*, and *Adversary*. Their societal construction—defined as one who dominates, exploits, or abuses power—may be socially sanctioned, or else a corruption of some political advantage. Functionally, the archetype is expressed as some form of authoritarian role, such as Chief, King, Tyrant, Ruler, Judge, Autocrat, Despot, Lord, Master, Oligarch, Patriarch, Conqueror, Abuser, Accuser, Aggressor, Slanderer, Bigot, Bandit, Criminal, Predator, or Warrior. Historically, the control of resources or wealth enables a feedback loop that commonly gives access to the economic and political institutions that then protect the ability of the rich and powerful to dominate the poor and powerless.

The asymmetric dynamic of the submissive roles is represented by the *Victim*, *Slave*, and *Rival*. Their societal construction—defined as one who is dominated, exploited, or abused—is a counterpart to the social sanction or corruption of political advantage awarded to the dominant class. Functionally, the archetype is expressed as some form of a disadvantaged role such as Servant, Slave, Underling, Follower, Poor, Weak, Vulnerable, Powerless, Dependent, Defenseless, Disenfranchised, Immature, Exposed, or Neglected. Historically, women, children, foreigners, the poor, and the racial or ethnic outcasts, have been most often marginalized and exploited by the powerful elite.

❖**Gods of the Unconscious**

A primary example of the dominant role in the asymmetric power dynamic is the archetype of a *god/gillul* whose function is essentially to be the one who controls and rules the cosmos or some other defined domain. His power may be manifested as the *Villain-Victor*, the *Master*, or the *Adversary*. His supplicants in the submissive role are required to satisfy his appetites and desires through transactional offerings and service. This is the typical orientation to the worship of *god/gillul* encoded in the mythologies of the Ancient Near East and, archetypally, in most cultures. The *god/gillul* represents the projection of our fears and vulnerability personified by the unconscious transference of our intrinsic power and authority onto a symbolic object functioning as a *Transferent Elohim*.

In contrast, within the symmetric power dynamic of the Reified Basar mythology, Yahweh functions as the *Transcendent Elohim* in the roles of *Parent*, *Savior*, and *Beloved* of his children. This is what fundamentally sets the Unified Basar and Torah myth apart as a psychology. In the narrative, Yahweh is not a *god*, he is not of an alien race that subjugates humans into service, and he is not desirous of offerings and worship to gain his favor. He is set apart from the religious gods of the moralistic traditions. His children are born to power and called to use that power for the benefit of the family and the world in general. At times, the terms of asymmetric power are used in association with the Yahweh tradition but are contextually instantiated to transform their meaning into a symmetric power construction—terms like *king*, *worship*, and *offering* are transformed into supportive and relational concepts of servitude based on love, rather than one's indicating domination or servitude based on force or fear of violence.

The *Transferent Elohim* is a manifestation of our innate sense of vulnerability, or missingness, in the Shadow Unconscious. They are compensatory archetypal forces whose presence immures our anxiety and distrust within an asymmetric power dynamic. They allow us to engage projectively with what we fear in an objectified modality, giving us a sense of control over our instinctual powerlessness—to transfer our inabilities and insecurities onto some externalized object. The dynamic may be embodied in an actual construct, such as a statue or artifact that represents a compensatory power that counters, for example, our fear of infertility or disease, as in classic idolatry. It can also be the elevation and empowerment of an individual or group within a tribe or society to represent the identity, success, or security of the shared affiliation, such as a ruler, chieftain, or king, or else a sports team, a religious leader, or a celebrity, on which a group may collectively lavish wealth, power, and status with the only reciprocation that it makes one transferentially feel more powerful or safe in their presence. It can also be a material object that signifies power or success, like an expensive watch, a fancy car, or an extravagant house, which has no intrinsic value, other than a belief that it makes one feel special, having power over others who do not possess what one has. It can also be an ideological system that circumscribes one's fears of death, the unknown, or moral failure, such as a religion or moralistic deity. In each of these, the supplicant sacrifices time, money, or something else of value to demonstrate their worthiness to possess the objectified power.

	Transcendent *symmetric*	Transferent *asymmetric*
Juvenile *dependence*	Child-Parent	Victim-Villain-Victor
Adolescence *independence*	Servant-Savior	Slave-Master
Mature *interdependence*	Lover-Beloved	Rival-Adversary

Table 3 - Relational Archetypes by Function and Dynamic

The *Transcendent Elohim*, on the other hand, is representative of the Ideal Parent Image in the holomorphic domain of consciousness. It is a foundational archetypal force, whose presence immures our anxiety and distrust within a symmetric power dynamic. Rather than projecting our fears outward, we look to others as mutual Guardian-Caretakers for support. Power comes through community and shared responsibility. The community becomes a representative of the Ideal Parent image, providing safety and security as a function of mutual trust and accountability.

❖Dynamic Archetypes

So far, I have used the term *archetype* without a specific contextual framework. Its most common usage is in depth psychology to describe a somewhat mystical product of what Jung called the *collective unconscious*—a pattern of potential meaning and value that may instantiate into the personal unconscious in powerful and invariant ways to evoke a path towards some intrinsic calling. The epistemological foundations of this ideology are founded on Neo-Platonism and are somewhat beyond any direct provability. As such, I have generally chosen not to invoke that dimension in this discussion.

Rather, I have chosen to take a more heuristic approach in defining *archetypes* as an essential product of the collective mythscape, the common stories that evolve out of our collective experiences and cultural heritage as homo sapiens. Mythological archetypes thus evolve directly out of the semiotic construction of human behavior and experience. They exist as a higher form of language than mere words and phrases. Simplistically, it may be defined as the symbolic representation of, for example, bending one's elbow; whereas every language may have its words and phraseology to describe the experience, it is universally understood across cultures and languages as a product of the action that formulates the narrative.

One thing that is distinctive about this approach is that it allows for composite archetypes that encode multimodal semiotic patterns that evolve from the narrative. Typically, archetypes are described as embodying a singular semantic pattern such as the Good Mother, Puer Aeternis, or Trickster. But I would argue that there is an important class of archetype that varies by characteristic triggers such as position, orientation, and/or relationship within the narrative.

The Victim-Villain-Victor is one such multimodal composite archetype. It is often mistakenly portrayed as multiple archetypes, such as the *captive* and then the *monster* and then the *hero*—or classically, the damsel in distress, the dragon, and the knight in shining armor. However, there is no *captive* without the *monster* and thusly no *hero*. It is actually one composite archetype in three forms essentially tied to the narrative. Under further scrutiny, these composite archetypes are a fluid multimodal construct manifested in a dynamic narrative in which one can easily change roles within the archetype. Those who are victimized will often become victimizers, one man's hero is another man's villain, and quite often, the hero ends up saving himself from his own demons. The roles within the archetype, in actuality, depend on one's immediate orientation to power, which can shift in the narrative.

❖Moral Psychology

As a moral psychology, the Unified Basar and Torah mythology contrasts with the dominant classical and modern philosophies on morality and ethics in that it is presented in a narrative form, rather than a set of rational principles. As with all myth, it is intended to invoke, guide, and inspire a value structure in the listener rather than to delineate a theoretical construct of cognitive moral development for academicians to ponder and debate. However, the archetypal pathways and dimensions are no less profound than those espoused by the likes of Plato, Kant, Kohlberg, or Piaget. These philosophic theories in comparison and contrast are broadly debated in countless volumes of academic material, and I do not intend to address those issues.

I will briefly invoke Kohlberg's model as a representative example of a modern theory of moral development in order to bring some contrast to the Unified Basar and Torah ideation of moral development. In his model, Kohlberg posits six stages of development. While there is some correspondence between the two systems, a key difference is that the ancient Torah system has an intrinsic relational framework, whereas the modern theory has an intrinsic personal or individual frame of reference. Each of Kohlberg's stages[60] depicted in Figure 5 is a response by the individual to how an action will affect them or the system. In contrast, the Torah framework is based on the relational value of the Other as a mutual family member. The principle of mutuality places oneself as a participant in a value-laden system. To harm another is essentially to harm oneself as a member of the same family. The Universal Ethical Principle at Stage 6 in Kohlberg's model is founded on ideology as opposed to relationship. In the Torah system,

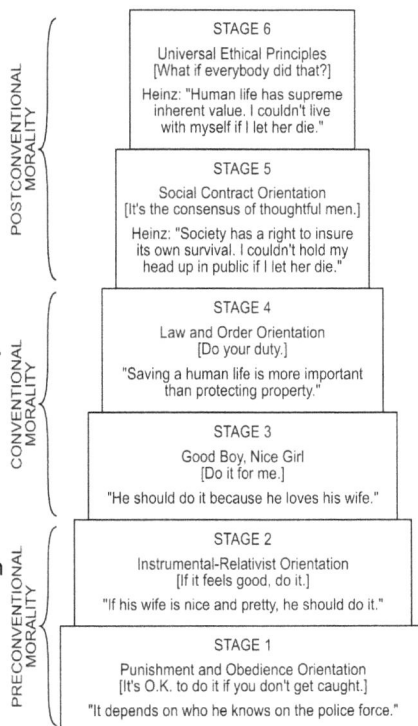

POSTCONVENTIONAL MORALITY

STAGE 6
Universal Ethical Principles
[What if everybody did that?]
Heinz: "Human life has supreme inherent value. I couldn't live with myself if I let her die."

STAGE 5
Social Contract Orientation
[It's the consensus of thoughtful men.]
Heinz: "Society has a right to insure its own survival. I couldn't hold my head up in public if I let her die."

CONVENTIONAL MORALITY

STAGE 4
Law and Order Orientation
[Do your duty.]
"Saving a human life is more important than protecting property."

STAGE 3
Good Boy, Nice Girl
[Do it for me.]
"He should do it because he loves his wife."

PRECONVENTIONAL MORALITY

STAGE 2
Instrumental-Relativist Orientation
[If it feels good, do it.]
"If his wife is nice and pretty, he should do it."

STAGE 1
Punishment and Obedience Orientation
[It's O.K. to do it if you don't get caught.]
"It depends on who he knows on the police force."

Figure 5 - Kohlberg Model of Moral

---

[60] Kohlberg (2012) illustration

rather than rule-based logic, moral action is based on empathy within an open relational system. Altruism is the highest expression of love in the Torah system, giving to another based on sharing the same breath, identifying as children of the same parent.

While I will spend time illuminating the underlying maps in the Torah value system, the intent of the myth is to stand on its own; to resonate on a psychic level with the personal life of the listener, to replicate and inspire moral values out of the narrative of the Good Story. However, in this formulation, over centuries and in the manner of presentation, the semantics and symbology of these myths are prone to be rationalized and, thusly, have been reinterpreted to support the self-serving narrative of the asymmetric political and religious institutions that claim authority over them. So, the first objective of this exploration is to restore the semantics and symbology of the underlying symmetric mythscape.

Functionally, *morality* is a belief system regarding the effectiveness or correctness of thoughts, feelings, and behavior—whether a response to a situation may be beneficial or adverse towards some objective. It may be identified and codified through custom, tradition, or law associated with a particular perspective of some authority. Enforcement is a function of the authority that defines it. It can be as simple as a personal ethic on how to conduct oneself amongst family and friends, or as complex as a society's laws and their supporting legal system.

The scope, objective, obligation, authority, and code of a moral system are critical to understanding its construction. The old adage regarding "honor among thieves" implies a *scope* of a particular community of artisans skilled at emancipating property from the control of the materially advantaged. The moral *objective* is to instantiate ordered relationship, thus avoiding conflict within that said community. The *obligation* is to show honor to each member of the community. The *authority* originates and is enforced within the dynamics and control of the community, which, since they exist outside of societal norms, is self-motivated, or by some hierarchy within the group. Violation of the moral *code* is indicated as dishonoring a member of the group.

Likewise, in the Unified Basar and Torah mythology, the *scope* of the moral system is the Universal Family of Adamites, inclusive of the Parent Elohim. The *objective* is to instantiate the value of each and every member of the family, and their right to comfort, respect, and survival—to be whole and healthy. The *obligation* is for each member to act in love towards one another, especially, those who suffer and struggle, in order to restore them to wholeness and healthiness. The *authority* evolves throughout the myth from an external motivation enforced by the parent to a societal artifice enforced by the legal system, and then to an internal conscience of a mature adult member founded on a value system of loving action. Violation of the moral *code* is defined as the failure to love, the failure to support those in need, and most emphatically, actually causing the suffering and oppression of another. The primary focus is on how one chooses to use their intrinsic power as *Familial Elohim* to maintain functional relationships rather than on any specific error in judgment.

Moreover, the Unified Basar and Torah myth, which I will dive deeply into, is a psychological map that developmentally moves us from the asymmetric archetypal power of *Victim-Villain-Victor* to the symmetric archetypal power of *Lover-Beloved*. The myth is fundamentally a moral psychology but diverges from the traditional philosophical exploration of ethics, law, and values as external artifacts and systems. It begins by recognizing the essential form of the external value systems in various Torah proclamations, most notably in the Mosaic Law, but becomes an internal psychological construct in the Reified Basar of Rabbi Jeshua. Love is not a code but an intrinsic narrative of belonging to the family. It is embodied in the Jeshuaic proclamation of the Kingdom of Yahweh's Love as an internalized realm of power nurtured by the dynamic of the *Sacred Breath* that inseminates the psyche with the Basar, so that it is no longer law, but life itself. Ultimately, it is not merely a moral psychology, but rather a relational psychology of love.

❖The Sacred Midst

In the Genesis Creation myth, the Parent Elohim plants a Garden as a safe place for the juvenile Adamites to learn and grow. He places two sacred trees, the Tree of Morality and the Tree of Life, which are specifically identified as being in the *midst* of the Garden.

> So Yahweh Elohim made sprout from the ground every tree desirable to the sight and good for food, with the tree of life in the midst of the garden, and also the tree of the knowledge of good and [bad].[61]

The Hebrew word *tavek*,[62] meaning midst, middle, or between, is used to describe the placement of the trees. It begins to develop a theme of the

---

[61] CLV Genesis 2:9
[62] Strongs H8432

sacred presence of the Parent Elohim in the midst of his children, the *tavek hakodesh*[63], or Sacred Midst:

> Thus I will hallow [kodesh] the tent of appointment and the altar; and Aaron and his sons shall I hallow to serve as priests for Me. I will tabernacle in the midst [tavek] of the sons of Israel and will become their Elohim. Then they will realize that I am Yahweh their Elohim Who brought them forth from the land of Egypt that I may tabernacle in their midst.[64]

Archetypally, the Sacred Midst describes an essential dynamic, not only in the mythic Child-Parent relationship of the Torah, but in any and all relationships, representing the sacred place between two people where they meet in mutual respect, intimacy, and honor.

As such, the Sacred Midst is the heart of the *Lover-Beloved* archetype, the *Us* in between the *I* and *Thou*—the relationship personified, in and of itself, as *Love*. It exists as a corporate entity, a sacred other, cultivated between the Lover and the Beloved—nurtured by trust and care, imbued by the ardor of both parties in the present moment, guarded by a mutual commitment to the value of the other, and the responsibility to continual care for the relationship. And, subsequently, without attention and fidelity, it dies of starvation, betrayal, or neglect.

The Jewish philosopher Martin Buber, in his book, *I and Thou*, explores the essential integrity of Love in the Sacred Midst between Lover and Beloved, stating:

> Feelings dwell in man, but man dwells in his love. This is no metaphor but actuality: love does not cling to an I, as if the You were merely its "content" or object; it is between I and You... now one can act, help, heal, educate, raise, redeem. Love is responsibility of an I for a You: in this consists of what cannot consist in any feeling—the equality of all lovers, from the smallest to the greatest... to love man.[65]

Elsewhere, in his book *On Judaism*, Buber expands this to the sacredness of community as a function of *Us* that emerges in the *Between* of the Sacred Midst:

> God may be seen seminally within all things, but He must be realized between them. Just as the sun's substance has its being among the stars yet beams its light into the earthly realm, so it is granted to human creatures to behold in their midst the radiance of the ineffable's glory. It glows dimly in all human beings, every one of them; but it does not shine in its full brightness within them—only between them. In every human being there is present the beginning of universal being (Allsein); but it can unfold

---

[63] Strongs H8432, H2932
[64] CLV Exodus 29:44-46
[65] Buber (1970), p.55

only in his relatedness to universal being, in the pure immediacy of his giving and taking, which surrounds him like a sphere of light, merging him with the oneness of the world. The Divine may come to life in individual man, may reveal itself from within individual man; but it attains its earthly fullness only where, having awakened to an awareness of their universal being, individual beings open themselves to one another, disclose themselves to one another, help one another; where immediacy is established between one human being and another; where the sublime stronghold of the individual is unbolted, and man breaks free to meet other man. Where this takes place, where the eternal rises in the Between, the seemingly empty space: that true place of realization is community, and true community is that relationship in which the Divine comes to its realization between man and man.[66]

This fundamental quality of relationship that develops in the Between is the foundation of peace, love, and understanding within the Community, "between man and man."

The Sacred Midst is the central relational archetype of the Unified Basar and Torah mythology. As a moral psychology, it is an exploration of how to nurture *goodness*, the fulfillment of purpose, and avoid *badness*, the failure of purpose, often viewed as toxic or venomous. The serpent on the Tree of the Knowledge of Goodness and Badness symbolizes the conscience, as it bends towards the higher quality of love and community, or towards the lower quality of exploitation, selfishness, and greed—nurturing or destroying the relationship embodied in the Sacred Midst. Within the morality of the myth, the death represented by eating the fruit of the Tree of Morality is not their imminent demise, but rather the dying of the Sacred Midst of the *Us* between the Juvenile Elohim and their parent, which consequently results in their immediately feeling naked, terrified, and alone. Most of the myth then is about rebuilding and resurrecting the Sacred Midst, the relationship that was damaged between the Juvenile Elohim and the Parent Elohim, and between one another—learning how to value and love one another.

❖The Nachash

It is within the context of the Sacred Midst that the crux of the Reified Basar narrative must be interpreted. The crucifixion of the Familial Messiah is given its meaning in the Basar of John, identifying Rabbi Jeshua as the serpent, or in Hebrew, the *nachash*[67] that is lifted up by Moses in the Exodus narrative.[68] The *Higher Nachash* reveals the healing power of Yahweh to the

[66] Buber (1996), p.111-112
[67] Strongs H5175
[68] CLV Numbers 21:4-8

afflicted Israelites under the judgment of venomous *Ground Nachash*, the Vipers sent to represent the toxicity of their slander, their vilification, or misrepresentation, of Yahweh and his Judges. The *Higher Nachash* restores the Sacred Midst of the Israelites' relationship with the Parent Elohim by letting go of their slander.

The *Nachash* is another example of a multimodal composite archetype defined through position, orientation, and association. The Hebrew word *nachash* fundamentally evokes a sense of whispering or hidden knowledge. In mystical traditions of the region, and near-universally, snakes are often used as oracles, a conduit giving voice to the divine; traversing between the underworld and the ordinary world to convey some hidden knowledge. In this, their functional identity is manifest in the context of what power they are attached to—Elohim, Human, Egypt, Tree of Morality, Sky-God, or Earth-God. Then, throughout the narrative, the position of the *nachash* represents its function and maturity—High/Sky, Low/Ground, and Middle/Between. And then its orientation defines whether its power is intrinsic or extrinsic to the personal experience of the subject.

	Intrinsic	Extrinsic
High Sky	*Lover/Advocate*	*Healing/Life*
Mid Between	*Conscience/Guide*	*Oracle/Prophet*
Low Ground	*Accuser/Critic*	*Viper/Death*

Table 4 - Composite Archetype of the Nachash

In the Genesis myth, the proverbial Edenic Nachash is attached to the Tree of Morality, instantiating its initial identity as the one who reveals the Knowledge of Goodness and Badness. Symbolically, it represents the *conscience*, the inner guide that weighs one's possible responses to circumstances based on some moral standard or narrative. Mythologically, the revelation of the *nachash* begins with the awareness of goodness and badness in Eden, then, encapsulates healing and punishment in the Exodus narrative, and finally embodies the Basar/Goodness on the Cross.

This is the crux of the myth that guides our descent into the depths of this ancient psychology. The tree serpent sets the dynamics of the mythology in motion declaring that the fruit of the Tree of Morality will bring power, knowledge, and life. As such, the Adamites will (1) develop moral power in their knowledge and experience of goodness and badness, (2) become identified with the capabilities and characteristics of the Parent Elohim, and (3) produce the value and prospect of a mature life. I will explore these qualities as a search for them within the *Torah of Awakening*, then the loss of them within the *Torah of Obligation*, and then, finally, the restoration of them within the *Torah of Restoration*.

❖**Historical Reprisal**

Foundationally, it is important to note that the Reified Basar myth of Rabbi Jeshua is intrinsically Jewish in content, acted out in Jewish society, primarily by Jewish people, as a struggle to reconcile the social and political meaning of *messiah*. Much of it occurs within the context of the Jewish Temple and Synagogues. Rabbi Jeshua is wholeheartedly committed to the Torah mythology, but not its moralistic or tribalistic religious construction according to the Scribes and Pharisees. While he does not support moralistic Judaism, his mission was not to create a new religion, a new moralistic enterprise, to oppose it, or to replace it. Throughout the Reified Basar account, Jeshua is routinely anti-moralistic and anti-religious, proclaiming rather a message of an intimate encounter with the Kingdom/Realm of Yahweh's love in the Universal Family of Elohim and the restoration of those who are suffering. He resolutely challenges the moralistic interpretation of the Torah, bringing criticism from the religious establishment. In the Reified Basar myth, we see the political struggle of the religious leaders to preserve their asymmetric authority over the people, and the perception that Jeshua's message of Love and Service, which includes one's enemies, is a threat to the power and authority of the ruling class, as well as the rebel cause of overthrowing the Roman rule of Palestine.

In the historical narrative, the early Jewish followers in Jerusalem, after the death of Rabbi Jeshua, continued to follow Jewish customs and laws, and go to Jewish Synagogue, under the guidance of Peter, the apostle, and Jacob/James, the brother of Jeshua. But the tensions festered, until the Pharisees under Rabbi Gamaliel II, in around 80 CE, declared that the Synagogue cult should begin with a prayer indicating that the Messiah had not yet come, cursing those who believed otherwise as heretics, thus building a wall to the continued participation of the Messianic Jews. After the destruction of Jerusalem and the Temple in 70 CE, the political tension grew more as the decades rolled on, often framed in a struggle for recognition by Rome who, during their more tolerant times, deemed ancient religions as acceptable alternatives to the worship of the polytheistic Roman gods. Beginning with the Hellenized theology of the neo-apostle Paul in 37 CE, some seven or so years after the death of Jeshua, the Christian moralists attempted to show that they were the real branch of Judaism going back centuries. The battle between Messianic and Rabbinic Jews to delegitimize the opposing side was palpable, leading to bouts of bloodshed between the groups. Much of Christian theology is formulated out of this political struggle, founded on vilifying traditional Pharisaic Judaism as a false religion, which, in turn, as Christianity grew and became more Hellenized, resulted in centuries of anti-Semitism.

By the fourth century CE, the Christians gained the upper hand politically, becoming the state religion of Rome, and eventually leading to the founding of the Holy Roman Empire upon which the authority of the Christian religion in its many forms is, in large part, formulated and built upon. The Good Story of Yahweh's Love for his children was stripped down to a political narrative and, to various degrees, combined with Greek Philosophy, and syncretized with Gnosticism and Hellenistic Mystery Religions, leading to continuous fragmentation and strife between sects for the next two millennia.

In modern church history, the New Deal social program in the United States, with the support of many American churches, attempted to revive the original Gospel mandate to alleviate poverty and distress in the wake of the devastating Great Depression of the 1930s. The economic collapse had turned the prevailing attitudes, as well as church sermons, against the greed and abuses of the upper class. This eventually led to a severe backlash from wealthy industrialists who grew tired of being portrayed as the villains in the Gospel narrative and, over the next few decades, poured millions of dollars into the Spiritual Mobilization[69] campaign of libertarian pastor James Fifield. The sole purpose of this propaganda campaign was to proselytize American pastors through meetings and pamphlets in order to undermine what was often derisively called the "Social Gospel," supplanting it with a new church dogma that syncretized political conservatism with a divisive libertarian gospel that was critical of the poor and favorable to wealth and privilege. Then, from the mid-seventies to the end of the millennium, the leaders of the new Religious Right, in particular Republican operative Paul Weyrich and Moral Majority founder Jerry Falwell, built on the success of the midcentury economic campaign, adding a newly defined conservative social agenda that manipulated historically and theologically benign social issues into passionate moralistic ones, complete with falsified doctrinal support. It continued the original political mandate to undermine the social policies instituted under the New Deal by consolidating political authority into the hands of those who were resolutely anti-Gospel.

---

[69] Kruse (2015) general reference on subject for more in-depth analysis

By the early twenty-first century, mainstream American Christianity in large part had become synonymous with the Religious Right as the most dedicated wing of the Republican Party. American Christian religious culture had been permanently changed—mainstream church dogma and attitudes became fully aligned with conservative political and economic ideology. The nominally accepted Gospel of the Christ was fundamentally dead. Beyond even traditional moralism, the American church became predominantly a sociopolitical entity based on the relativistic ethics of conservative political ideology of wealth and privilege, theo-fascist social policies, gun rights and white nationalism built from the ashes of Southern racist ideology, and right-libertarian morality closely aligned with Ayn Rand's pseudo-philosophy of Objectivism and the Virtue of Selfishness.

This hyperbolic religious interpretation, by what can only be described contextually within the myth as overachieving Goats, takes the political and economic deviations of Jeshua's prohibition in the parable of the Sheep and Goats, "whatsoever you do unto the least of these," as an outright challenge. Mainstream American Christianity invented a new gospel of selfishness and greed—represented in the various contemporary teachings of the Prosperity Gospel, Christian Libertarianism, and Christofascism—espousing that the Christian-God's blessing is the privilege of comfort, wealth, and Eurocentric identity; and consequently, his punishment for the lazy and undeserving, the takers of society, is poverty. The Gospel message of compassion and justice for the poor and oppressed was successfully rebranded as a form of "socialism" for lazy poor people, often couched in racist dog-whistles. Likewise, immigrants, the "strangers" mentioned in the Gospel, were characterized as trespassers, deserving to be apprehended and abused for their inferiority and perceived crimes. The infirm were rejected and ignored, only deserving of whatever care their wealth, or lack thereof, could afford. And the minority poor were racially characterized as inferior, undisciplined, and indecent creatures, who should be separated from decent society, violently apprehended and caged, undeserving of fundamental protections under civil law.

Manifestly, the modern American church is not, however, a new ideology. In the same way that the Pharisees in the first century Reified Basar myth perceived themselves as the Jewish-God's chosen people but ignored the plight of the poor, the American church represents a reprisal, a modern version of the same attitudes and actions of conservative social and religious cultures of the past. Even going back further into Jewish history, the prophet

Ezekiel warns dire consequences to Israel for being like Sodom who was prideful and ignored the plight of the poor:

> Behold, this was the depravity of Sodom, your sister: For herself and her daughters there was pomp, [overindulging] with bread and quiet ease, yet she did not hold fast the hand of the humble and needy. They were haughty and committed abhorrences before Me; so I put them away just as you see.[70]

Rabbi Jeshua, likewise, lays out his anger and judgment against his contemporary religious counterparts and their conservative ideological descendants, identifying them as Goats in the parable of the Sheep and Goats:

> Now, whenever the Son of Mankind... shall He be seated on the throne of His glory, and in front of Him shall be gathered all the nations. And He shall be severing them from one another even as a shepherd is severing the sheep from the [goats]... Then shall He be declaring to [the goats] "Go from Me, you cursed, into the fire eonian made ready for the Adversary and his messengers. For I hunger and you do not give Me to eat; I thirst, and you do not give Me drink; a stranger was I and you did not take Me in; naked and you did not clothe Me; infirm and in jail and you did not visit Me." Then shall they also be answering, saying, "Lord, when did we perceive you hungering or thirsting, or a stranger, or naked, or infirm, or in jail, and we did not serve you?" Then shall He be answering them, saying, "Verily, I am saying to you, In as much as you do it not to one of these, the least, neither do you it to Me." And these shall be coming away into chastening eonian, yet the just into life eonian.[71]

While the judgment of *sinners* is a religious fabrication in moralistic Christianity, the judgment of the *Goats*, those who ignore the plight of the poor, the weak, and oppressed, is clearly stated: as was the fate of Sodom, they are to be perpetually chastened, thrown into the burning garbage dump as worthless trash. The Goats, who elsewhere are inferred in the narrative as being the religious and political conservatives by Rabbi Jeshua, are fundamentally anti-gospel and anti-christ despite their pretense of having the Jewish and/or Christian god's approval. Not only is act-love portrayed as the fulfillment of the Kingdom of Yahweh, but lack of act-love is also portrayed as untenable, having dire consequences to one's relationship to one another, and to the spiritual Father, resulting in the death of the Sacred Midst. In summary, don't be a Goat.

---

[70] CLV Ezekiel 16:49-50
[71] CLV Matthew 25:31-46 Compare to Isaiah 58:6-8.

❖Religious Encounter

At the heart of the Exodus myth is the Israelites' direct numinous encounter with Yahweh at the foot of the fiery Mount of Elohim in Horeb/Sinai. Here Yahweh gives his formal Torah/ Guidance en masse to all the Israelites gathered before him. Uncomfortable with this intimate, albeit dramatic, numinous encounter, the Israelites implore Moses to go up the mount alone to face Yahweh and then subsequently return to tell them what to do. Hence, Moses ascends the fiery mount by himself and spends weeks face to face with Yahweh, who consequently gives him the *Decalogue* as a souvenir to bring back to the Israelites commemorating this meeting on Mount Sinai, which, in turn, will guide the Israelites on the rest of their journey to, and settlement in, the Promised Land. Meanwhile, when Moses does not return from the fiery mount as quickly as expected, fearing his demise, the Israelites become anxious and decide to take matters into their own hands, creating a substitutionary symbolic object, a *gillul* in the form and image of a Golden Calf in order to guide them and protect them on their journey to the Promised Land. It is an intentional act that effectively reduced the active presence of Yahweh as Parent/Savior to a handmade idol/*gillul*, which was more comfortable for them to directly deal with, allowing them to influence the Great Power by their dramatic service and offerings to consequently assuage their fear of the direct numinous encounter.

The Exodus from Egypt, after many generations under slavery, presented a great opportunity for a life of freedom and hope. It was also fraught with unknown dangers and circumstances no longer in their control as they wandered across a hostile desert and amongst hostile tribes. Under the circumstances, the Golden Calf was a product of an Egyptian mythology that they were intimately familiar with—invoking a moralistic god/*gillul* that would be a powerful ally to guide and protect them. As such, the creation of the Golden Calf was not so much an act of rebellion as it was a regression to the familiar in the face of fear and loss of control. It represents the transformation and transference of their relationship to the Parent/Savior Elohim into a symbolic form that they could then influence and control through offerings to pacify their fears and conjure their desires.

The cultural and historical context of the Israelite mythology exists within a greater mythological narrative. It is founded on the crosscurrent of regional religious schemas—from the Egyptian religious tradition originating on the southern borders of Canaan to the Mesopotamian and Ugaritic religious traditions in the north and east. The various Canaanite tribes of the Levant drew from both directions, syncretizing aspects of these elemental myths into their local religious practices. The Yahweh mythology is in constant dialogue with these cultural myths, describing how the Israelites engaged the boundaries and prohibitions against following other elohim, such as the transactional worship of *gillul*. The mythology consistently draws a line between the path of familial *relationalism*, following the Parent Elohim to a place of peace and plentitude, and the path of idol *moralism*, following an alien power born of their fears who would favor them if given the proper sacrifice. The mythology is a continual compare and contrast between these two paths, more often than not, describing the failure of the children of Israel to accept the parental intimacy of Yahweh, which, in the end, results in their removal as the favored nation of Yahweh at the close of the National Age.

Similarly, in the first and subsequent centuries, the Reified Basar myth engages the dominant Greco-Roman mythologies of the region and time. The relational psychology of the original pre-Christian/Jewish Basar myth is recast, beginning with the Prophet Paul and the Early Christian Fathers, into the form of the Greek myth as a path to find order and control within the hostility and uncertainty of a fallen uncivilized world. The moralized Christian myth syncretized Hellenistic mythology with Jewish moralism, and then, reframed it as an idolized Gospel text; turning Rabbi Jeshua as the Anointed Son who is murdered by the conservative religious/political establishment into a Golden Calf that acts as a substitutionary sacrificial *gillul* to appease an angry authoritarian *gillul*. This innovative marketing strategy asserted that a *gillul* is sacrificed to a *gillul*—an ultimate offering on the cross by the Christ Son *gillul* to save humanity from the wrath of the Holy Father *gillul*. Hypocritically, this distortion of the relational mythology of the Reified Basar is equivalent to reframing the exemplary life of someone like the great anti-imperialist Mahatma Gandhi, insidiously claiming that he was a champion of British rule over India, rather than opposing it—an utter contradiction of the history and character of Gandhi. But after two thousand years of religious interpretation of the Christ story, we are so deep in the weeds of theology that no one notices that the Christ is not the champion of the religious or the conservative moralistic establishment, but rather is its opponent and was murdered by it.

In this light, I will examine how the relational mythology of the Unified Basar and Torah is influenced by the moralistic mythologies of the Greeks, Canaanites, and Egyptians. While the relational myth is intrinsically a guide to the development of a mature conscience that leads one to love others, the moralistic mythologies are intrinsically motivated by a compulsion for order and control within the uncertainty of the powers of nature, compelling Man to perpetually reach out in service to the gods for protection and provision.

Each of these mythologies illustrates the psychological drives within us to encounter our own vulnerability in the midst of uncertainty. This dynamic is often easier to see within the pure moralistic mythologies, rather than trying to separate the inglorious amalgam of the moralistic theology of Christianity and Judaism from the underlying relational imperatives of the Unified Basar and Torah myth. The dynamic of each story within the moralistic traditions, however, is not intrinsically black or white, moralistic versus relationalistic. The Greek myths, in particular, while founded on a moralistic worldview, have their personal saviors in relationship to humankind such as Dionysus, Prometheus, and Asclepius. However, what each one of these personal saviors had in common was that they were punished by the moralistic gods for acts that disturbed their control of the natural order.

Structurally, a moralistic impulse born of our fears and vulnerability is what drives culture towards institutionalized religion with all its embedded control structures and hierarchical authorities to protect the cult narrative. This is exemplified in the story of the Golden Calf, wherein this moralistic impulse born of fear drives the Israelite's discomfort in an actual numinous encounter with the Parent/Savior Elohim, which requires a personal response. So, the Israelites appoint Moses as a priestly intermediary to handle the numinous encounter with Yahweh. Next, they further distance themselves from the personal narrative by creating a projective object that they can control to represent the numinous encounter at a safe distance. In the process, they create a system to manage that encounter and an ecstatic dissociative ritual that provides an emotional intensity devoid of content or real intimacy with the numinous. When offered an authentic intimate encounter based on the parent as direct Guardian-Caretaker and Guide-Aide, they chose something they can manufacture and control.

Likewise, in the Basar of Mark, Jeshua brings Peter, James, and John up to a high mountain to witness a numinous encounter with Moses and Elijah. The narrator states:

And [Jeshua] was transformed in front of them. And His garments became glistening, very white, as snow, such as not fuller on earth is able thus to whiten. And Elijah, together with Moses, was seen by them, and they were conferring with [Jeshua].

And... Peter is saying to [Jeshua], "Rabbi, it is ideal for us to be here! And we should be making three [dwellings]: for Thee one, and for Moses one, and for Elijah one." For he was not aware what he may answer, for they became terrified. And there came a cloud overshadowing them. And a voice came out of the cloud, saying, "This is My Son, the Beloved. Hear

Him!" And suddenly, looking about, they no longer perceived anyone,
except [Jeshua] only, with themselves.[72]

Again, we see this response to build something to preserve and
institutionalize the moment, while also attempting to distract and distance
themselves from the terrifying numinous encounter that was actually
happening in front of them.

This demonstrates the archetypal framework that separates the
personal intimate encounter from the impersonal institutional structure,
which we call in English, *religion*, from the Latin *religare* meaning to restrain
or tie back.[73] Religion defines a codified system of moralized attitudes,
beliefs, and practices that are packaged and institutionalized into an
authoritative framework such as in Judaism, Christianity, Islam, or Buddhism.
Ironically, each of these exemplified religious systems began with an essential
relational narrative, a personal encounter. Judaism began with a Parent
Elohim trying to connect with his children—it develops into a set of rules
placed on top of more rules in the rabbinic literature until eventually
Orthodox Jews are left debating whether it is an offense against the Jewish G-
d to push an elevator button on the Sabbath. Christianity began similarly with
a Parent Elohim and his Anointed Son also trying to connect with his family—
it is reduced to a moralistic system of dogmas debated by thirty thousand
sects regarding what salvation means while trying to eliminate the opposing
groups and ideas. Islam began with a prophet encouraging compassion and
mercy towards the poor and oppressed, whilst elevating women in society
and bringing peace amongst warring tribes—it has been reduced over its
history to tribes perpetually at war, both within and without the religion, and
a fundamentalist framework known for its subjugation and control of women.
Buddhism began with a note of compassion, as the Buddha, having reached
his intended unification in Nirvana, chooses to return to help others—it
evolves into a bunch of folks on a quest for "enlightenment" by separating
themselves out from society in monasteries, or else wise by themselves,
pondering the mystery of one hand clapping. Adherence to the institutional
dogma helps to insulate the follower from responsibility for their actions, as
long as it conforms to the system. Real personal transformation towards act-
love within a universal community of suffering humans becomes an exception
rather than the rule.

The institutionalization of the personal and experiential is a function of
our need to hold on to, and control, what in the moment feels valuable, but

---

[72] CLV Mark 9:2-8
[73] Merriam-Webster (2014) "Religion"

which then loses its value in our stranglehold. As the psychologist, Carl Jung, observed in *Psychology and Religion* (CW11), one of the main functions of organized religion is to protect people against a direct experience of the numen or god:

> It is true that an overwhelming majority of educated people are fragmentary personalities and have a lot of substitutes instead of the genuine goods. But being like that meant a neurosis for this man [a previously mentioned client], and it means the same for a great many other people too. What is ordinarily called "religion" is a substitute to such an amazing degree that I ask myself seriously whether this kind of "religion," which I prefer to call a creed, may not after all have an important function in human society. The substitute has the obvious purpose of replacing immediate experience by a choice of suitable symbols tricked out with an organized dogma and ritual. The Catholic Church maintains them by her indisputable authority, the Protestant "church" (if this term is still applicable) by insistence on belief in the evangelical message. So long as these two principles work, people are effectively protected against immediate religious experience.[74]

Jung was known as a founding father of modern psychology whose ideas were institutionalized as Analytical/Jungian Psychology. He was a deeply intuitive explorer examining the depths of human psychoanatomy and experience. He inspired a great following of admirers and students even while he was alive. Programs and schools have been created to replicate what Jung sought to define. In response, Jung was known, on occasion, to proclaim, "Thank God I am Jung and not a Jungian."[75] The distinction was fundamentally clear to him that his own intuition and experience were not the same as the institution and dogma.

Likewise, religion is not the same as an active relationship with one another and some transcendent presence based on numinous experience. Dogma imprisons us into some past experience, which at the time may have been relevant, but by definition, has nothing to do with the present, the here and now. Myth and narrative provide a road map without prescribing a path. The experience of the Imago Elohim, the Authentic Self, Sacred Breath/Spirit, Moral Intuition, or Conscience, is what actively guides us on our personal path through this mythological universe.

❖Modus Operandi

The next stage of this treatise is to examine the Unified Basar and Torah mythology within its own context as it builds an ancient psychology of human

---

[74] Jung (2014) p. 43
[75] Hannah (1997) p.87

relationship. The philosophical framework for this evolving study and exploration is founded on several reasoned assumptions in epistemology, ethics, logic, and metaphysics.

Epistemology. The epistemological framework of this exploration builds on research in the fields of history, archaeology, religious studies, moral philosophy, mythological studies, as well as depth and experiential psychologies. Based on prior inquiry in these fields, it is reasonably observed that the morality of human relationships and psychology is a consistent archetypal construct, at least over the last eight or so millennia for which we have a sense of the sociological narratives—human history is inherently recursive, repetitive stories within stories. However, this notably contrasts with the traditional western ethnocentric bias, which posits that older and, in particular, non-western cultures were less intelligent, less sophisticated, and less civilized. They were prone to be wild, superstitious, and disorderly—the Greeks called them *barbarians*; early Christians called them *pagans*; colonial explorers called them *savages*. Academia, up through the twentieth century, commonly asserted humanity was evolving from primitive tribal cultures to modern enlightenment. Even in the early psychological tradition of Carl Jung, in the late nineteenth and early twentieth centuries, he identifies tribal cultures as existing in an undifferentiated, unconscious dream-like state evolving towards the consciousness of civilization.

In actuality, as historians and archaeologists have dusted off the past, it has become more apparent how consistent is human nature. Every society has had their *Albert Einsteins* and their *Forrest Gumps*, as they struggled with the questions of how to organize, cooperate, and get along. Technology and methods may have changed, evolved, become more sophisticated, and, in many cases, just more lethal, but, morally and emotionally, even with contextual deviations, we have not really changed. The constancy of a mother's love for her child, the transcendence of standing on a high mountain, the peace of sitting in a fertile oasis by a stream, the disorientation of a dark moonless night, the sense of danger when we perceive a predator is about—what constitutes human nature has not fundamentally mutated or evolved.

In the Unified Basar and Torah myth, we find a recursive story within a story as subsequent generations struggle with the same issues—and more often fail. The same social and ideological classes emerge in each society. There is a thread that leads from today's religious fundamentalists, back through ancient narratives of the early Christian Moralists, to the first century Pharisees of the Reified Basar, going further back to the burgeoning Hasidic movement of the Neo-Babylonian captivity that instantiated Judaism. And mythologically, going back to the Israelites before Mount Sinai worshiping the Golden Calf, and the builders of the Tower of Babel attempting to reach the heavens, to Cain's ill-considered offering, and ultimately, to Eve's "do not touch" the Tree of Morality. They are all built from the same ideological cloth—a fundamental desire to control our world, to protect our deep-seated sense of vulnerability, and to master our fate.

Ethics. At its heart, this treatise is a depth-oriented exploration of moral psychology underlying one of the central mythologies of Western Asian and Eurocentric civilizations. The *prima materia* of the mythology is *love*—the value inherent in the Universal Family. The value system underlying the myth is reasoned to be authentic and universal. The mythscape is essentially an aggregated form of the personal dreamscape—a product of the same non-rational dynamics of semantic formation from deep within the associative core of human perception constructed from symbols, archetypes, stories, and tableaus. The same tools and approaches are required to experience their meaning as a universal truth of the collective psyche in order to understand the moral development that flows and forms our human nature. Rationalizing the narrative disrupts and dissolves its meaning. We find the authenticity of the value-oriented narrative by locating it within ourselves, finding resonance between the narrative elements in the myth with our own inner story world.

Logic. The semiotic structure of the myth evolves from the narrative through symbols and archetypes, founded on a shared construct of humanity, built out of experiences tied to a historical framework of a specific time and place. Semantic maps identify universal psychological dynamics that transcend the ancient narrative. As such, an important assumption is that *meaning* derives from *context*. A hat in one story is not the same hat in another story, even when evoking some archetypal quality of hats. It requires a story in order to understand what it means within a context. As Plato points out, we only know them by the names given, and they tell us only about those that give them those names. The Sesame Street approach of trying to connect analogous detritus by which names sound like the other is suspect at best. The Yahweh of the Edomites as a Warrior-God is not the same as the Yahweh of the Israelites as a Parent Elohim. The usage of titles, like *Lord*, requires a specifier to indicate of what. The *Baal* or *Lord* of the Phoenicians is not necessarily the same as the *Baal/Lord* of the Israelites, or for that matter, the *Baal/Lord* of the Philistines. *Baal* is not the name of a god, but a function that takes form within the context of those societies given specific narratives, attributions, and relationships to those that are owned by that *Lord*. The same is true for *El* or *Elohim* meaning a great power.

It also applies to the development of ideas. Some historical theories derive from who wrote it down first. At the dawn of writing, when everything begins as an oral tradition, being the first to carve an idea in clay or stone does not mean that it is the origin point of that idea or meaning within that culture, let alone between different cultures. In the same way that a dream is informed by an individual personal history and associations but does not directly chronicle a person's actual history, a myth is informed by the contextual history and archaeology of the incipient culture, providing a semantic context for the myth; but the myth does not necessarily correlate to historical events. A myth is the psychological impression of history made on the culture, woven from its hopes, fears, and foibles.

The nature of deconstructing myth to formulate these archetypal themes, symbols, and maps is somewhat simpler than for the historian; the mythological narratives do not need to be connected to verifiable archaeological or historical facts. The mythscape is a rich psychological artifact that is informed by history and culture but is not constrained by it. This, however, begets the question, whose psychological construct defines the semantics of the myth, given that the mythscape develops over two millennia including elements that are prehistoric?

The mythological material itself is broadly constructed, having many subplots and themes. One subplot that is most often the interest to Jewish scholars is the ethnological origin story for the identity of "Israel" and the moral system that is set up to define it. Historians and archaeologists, on the other hand, may be more interested in the development of that identity as it interplayed with the religions and cultures of the Levant, or within the context of the political dynamics of conquest and settlement. There is certainly much narrative content that specifically traverses and elucidates these avenues of inquiry, although some might say unsatisfactorily when compared to verifiable records associated with these times.

My interest, on the other hand, is in how the context of archaeology and history builds the semantics of the mythology, in particular, the universal themes of human relationship and development that encompass the broad arc of the narrative evolving from the Adamic Universal Family through the Jeshuaic proclamation of a Universal Kingdom of Yahweh's love. Thusly, the limited scope of material that will be covered focuses on this psychological framework underlying the Reified Basar, going backward to the essential narratives that develop the archetypal themes, ignoring many subplots that are of interest to other scholars. Thus, I cover the core narrative of the Torah fairly extensively, but only brush through the books of History, Poetry, and Prophets to review several ethnographic narratives in the canon that are mentioned in the Reified Basar—more specifically the Isaiah text, which defines the purpose and mission, and the narrative of Elijah and King Ahab in the Book of Kings, which establishes the archetypal topography. The possible avenues that diverge from this narrower path are innumerable and have filled volumes of both speculative and academic material over the centuries.

Ultimately, the scope of the myth that defines the psychological construct I will examine is closely defined as the cultural framework that existed in first-century Palestine. Much of the mythography and myth collection of the Hebrew canon was settled centuries prior between the sixth and fourth centuries BCE. Consequently, the written canon is quite stable by the first century CE as the myth of the Reified Basar is developing.

Fundamentally, my approach to the mythology is a post-postmodern reconstruction of the narrative. As postmodernism is defined by the deconstruction of the narrative, in the end, one inevitably ends up with a series of deconstructed parts that no longer work together. If one imagines the narrative to be a carefully crafted watch, in the deconstruction you might end up with a bunch of parts, including perhaps a few dust bunnies and broken springs, and the knowledge of how it might have worked, but no working watch. What I have tried to do is deconstruct the myth, symbolically throwing out the dust bunnies, replacing the broken springs, and then rebuilding the myth to how it was originally presented as a fully functional "watch," which then can be used in the present moment to orient oneself in time and place.

Metaphysics. The mythscape is the collective form of the personal dreamscape and has its own internal metaphysics that does not rely on rational constructions in history and science. As such, it is assumed that the internal metaphysics is not deterministic. Just as with the dreamscape, the mythscape exists outside of the extrinsic metaphysical determinants. Although it may suggest a path to them, our journey through the myth is not predicated on the reader's personal metaphysical outlook or any specific academic construction. The cosmology invoking the existence of an alternatural world inhabited by supernatural entities that become a destination after life is beyond epistemological testing or certainty.

The external metaphysics of the myth is out of the scope of this exploration; that is left to the personal experience and spiritual practice of the reader. The narrative provides a framework for personal exploration of those dimensions but does not necessitate a conclusion. Similarly, Jung studied religious experience, not the religious metaphysics itself. He did not posit the existence or non-existence of a god, but rather described the experience of an internal god-image as a dynamic in the unconscious that moves us towards wholeness and healing. The mythscape is a container for the numinous—the transcendent experience. It leads us in our development as moral beings. In the Basar myth, it leads us to love.

PART I

DA'ATH – THE TORAH OF AWAKENING

Redwood Trees, Julia Rodgers, Photo, 1920.

Standing in front of a giant redwood tree as a young boy, in awe of its massive presence and grandeur, bathed in the invigorating fragrance of a forest in continuous renewal, the cool mountain air framing this otherworldly experience, I was seized by a feeling that I was home—I was in a place I belonged. My family had scaled the Sierra Nevada Mountains in the family Buick to explore the wonders of this forest of giants ensconcing the heavens, spread amongst vast meadows, inhabited by wandering bears, squirrels, and other manner of woodland creatures, watched over by the towering granite protrusion of Moro rock, teetering over a vast crevasse a mile deep, and hiding the gaping mystery of Crystal Cave, framed by giant stalactites and stalagmites deep in the granite earth.

In this moment, I was awakened to my interconnectedness to life and nature in this magnificent world, eclipsing the concreted suburban maze of cinderblock walls that framed my childhood upbringing. It was a world, even at a young age, in which I found peace, joy, and inspiration. It anchored me to an ancient reality and truth about the makeup of the universe I had been living in, but unaware. It was a world that made me smaller in stature and yet grander in spirit.

The awakening to a deeper understanding of ourselves as a part of the greater world around us is a profound experience. While much is written in the annals of depth psychology exploring how we differentiate and individuate from the key relationships in our world, our core identity begins with how we see ourselves in connection to our surroundings; how we relate to what we see, touch, smell, taste, and hear. We develop a sense of whether the world is safe—providing sufficient support and sustenance. At a primitive or infantile level, we are compelled to explore what is the meaning of each object in our purview—is it good, does it bring satisfaction, is it pleasant; or is it bad, harmful, or unpleasant. Humans are explorers, intrinsically curious, we build catalogs and maps of the things in our environs, growing in knowledge and wisdom as we define our relationship to the fuzzy and spikey, loud and soft, sweet and sour world within our reach.

As social creatures, we also learn from each other, owing a great debt of gratitude to those who went before and found which plants made our tummies hurt, which made us permanently go to sleep, and which made a pleasant afternoon tea. One of the earliest scientific studies of note was by paleobiologist Thag Simmons who discovered that certain large slow-moving herbivores with spikey tails (now called a *Thagomizer* in his honor) can move much more quickly when studied up close (may he rest in peace).[76] We often take for granted the amount of knowledge that has been passed down to us over the centuries—how to eat soup with a spoon, how to pull a chair up to the table so that we can reach the bowl of soup while sitting down, and how a simple spoon can serve as a catapult when an adult human is not around (an early exploration in adaptive reuse).

❖Da'ath of Tov and Ra

In the beginning of the Genesis Creation myth, we are introduced to the nature of the world we live in. At each stage and focus of creation, the Creator Elohim declares that it is *tov*[77], meaning good, pleasant, and agreeable. The experience of the goodness and interconnectedness of all things is the foundation of *da'ath*[78], meaning knowledge, understanding, or wisdom. It is an initiation into an elemental awareness that all things are created with purpose and beauty, which instantiates the *Torah of Awakening*. The Adamites are given a responsibility to develop an essential knowledge of the creatures of this new world, to serve and care for the plants and animals, as well as one another, and, finally, to create new life.

The second aspect of the *Torah of Awakening* is *ra*[79], meaning bad, unpleasant, or hurtful. It is rooted in the sense of brokenness or spoilage. It is often translated into the nebulous English term *evil*; but it does not carry the baggage of this term, which implies some essential or intrinsic quality of failed moral character, or else having an insatiable appetite for destruction

---

[76] Larson (1992) p.137
[77] Strongs H2896
[78] Strongs H1847
[79] Strongs H7451

that we associate with monsters and villains. *Ra* is more evocative of a rotting piece of fruit that is no longer good for consumption. It is the awareness of becoming lifeless and purposeless, separated from that which brings wholeness and healing.

The Tree embodying the Da'ath of Tov and Ra—the Knowledge of Goodness and Badness, or morality—is a central archetype of the Torah of Awakening. It is a companion to the Tree of Life that brings wholeness and healing; both Trees are growing in the midst of the Garden. The mythological narrative posits that the fruit of morality must mature into love—a fundamental value for all within community, the Universal Family of Adamites. Yet, the immature fruit of morality elicits an egocentric moral code focused on fear and vulnerability, leading to separation and death of the Sacred Midst in the Between.

❖**Serpent of Tov and Ra**

On the Tree of Morality sits the Edenic Nachash. In the beginning, this prototypical lizard-serpent is an essential part of the goodness of creation. It is highly intelligent and functionally neutral, despite later rationalizations of its intent. It is inferred that it has legs, given that as a result of the Exile Narrative, it will be caused to crawl on its belly in the dust. Mythologically, it was probably imagined as the snake-eyed or Lebanon lizard found in the region, which has the appearance of a snake with legs. The Edenic Nachash is the revealer of hidden knowledge. It is described as *aw-ram*[80], which is often translated as crafty, prudent, or cautious, but is rooted in a deeper sense of being made naked or uncovered, to reveal. Thus, the primary mythological characteristic of the *nachash* is to be the Revealer. In the Genesis Creation story, the Edenic Nachash is intrinsically bonded with the Tree of Morality for the purpose of uncovering or revealing that which is hidden on the path of moral development. It operates as a guide or *conscience*.

As the central archetype of the *conscience*, the Nachash is presented in three different manifestations based on association and position: (1) *Middle Nachash*, (2) *Ground Nachash*, and (3) *Higher Nachash*. In the beginning, the Edenic Nachash represents the Middle Nachash, which internally functions as Conscience and Guide, the dynamic force of moral guidance; and then, externally functions as Oracle and Prophet, a representative messenger for a moral authority from another realm. As an Oracle for some extrinsic power, the Middle Nachash appears in various roles throughout the Unified Basar

---

[80] Strongs H6175

and Torah myth. In context to the political power of the Kingdom of Matsor/Egypt, the Oracular Nachash is represented by Joseph as Vizier, the Priests of Pharaoh, and Prince Moses. And then as the Oracular Nachash of Elohim, it is represented by Noah, Joseph as Interpreter of Dreams, Moses, Elijah, Johanan the Baptist, and initially, Rabbi Jeshua, who is later raised up to embody the *Higher Nachash.*

Secondly, the *Ground Nachash* is introduced in the Exile myth as the lowered, ordinary legless serpent that crawls in the dust after Yahweh's judgment. It represents a base level of *conscience.* Internally, its function is twisted into an immature, egocentric role of the Accuser or Critic, the one who reveals our vulnerabilities to attack and punishes our failures. Externally, it is represented as the Viper or Death, often associated with one who slanders, falsely identifies, or accuses another, causing separation and harm. The Viper is invoked in various forms in the Exile, Exodus, and the Basar wilderness narratives.

Thirdly, the *Higher Nachash* represents the mature conscience, founded on an internalized morality of love. Externally, it embodies the healing power that guides humans to the ideal of Love within the Universal Family, advocating for mutuality and altruism. In mythological terms, the Higher Nachash is represented as the *Sacred Breath*, or similarly, manifested as the *arche logos* and the *paraclete*/helper in the Basar of John. It reveals Yahweh's intimate desire and intent as a personal encounter with the Child Elohim. The Higher Nachash is invoked in multiple forms in both the Exodus and crucifixion narratives.

Given the prominence of the moralized interpretation of the *nachash* in the Judeo-Christian text, it is important to acknowledge that the serpent on the Tree is traditionally associated with the Judeo-Christian *Satan* as Adversary or Accuser. In Christian and Jewish moralism, Satan as the serpent maliciously tempts Eve and Adam to their destruction by lying to them, purely as an act of malevolence; instantiating the moralistic narrative of the serpent as an evil force that brings the Fall of Man. But the actual mythological narrative does not identify the serpent on the Tree as *evil*, it merely states that it is capable or crafty, and, at that point in the narrative, everything in creation has been declared to be good. It is also internally inconsistent with the later invocation of the bronze serpent raised by Moses on the staff, and the Familial Messiah, as representatives of this same raised serpent. Later, as an archetypal construct in the Exile narrative, the defiled and dislimbed *Ground Nachash*, which crawls in the dust on its belly, in some specific cases, is represented in the form and characteristics of the Accuser or *saw-tan*, the revealer and judge of our failures. But the *Ground Nachash* has many other internal and external manifestations as well. Nowhere in the text is there a powerful evil force called *Satan* that is in an existential conflict with the powerful good of the Supreme-God, vying for ultimate control of the universe. The *saw-tan* in the actual myth represents the asymmetric political dynamic that dominates our sense of scarcity and fear of the unknown. It occasionally is portrayed in the narrative as an archetypal essence of the egoistic conscience that probes a novitiate, revealing their true moral character. However, essentially, it is an interior dynamic of an immature conscience that must be engaged and overthrown by the symmetric dynamic of Love.

❖**The Revealer**

As the representation of the Adamites' juvenile conscience, the Edenic Nachash reveals the doubts and desires that already exist. The Edenic Nachash does not, in fact, lie to the Adamites. It reveals the truth that by internalizing the Fruit of Morality, the Adamites' eyes will be unclosed, knowing goodness and badness, they will become like the Parent Elohim, and they will persist in having life, that is, they will not be struck dead by a presumptive Angry Father. However, the Edenic Nachash's guidance, as a form of primitive conscience, does not comprehend, or in any way recognize, the relational impact of eating the fruit. The immature Adamites ignore the warning that the fruit is detrimental to their well-being and that it is not theirs to take; focusing instead on what they impulsively desire and consider to be good in the moment. In addition, the promise that they will become like the Parent Elohim due to eating the fruit is misguided. The Adamites are already a juvenile form of the Imago Elohim; the fruit does not give them their great power. The mature power of the Imago Elohim was always their identity and birthright as they grew and developed towards adulthood. A core aspect of the failure of conscience is the lack of recognizing one's intrinsic power, the power to do good and to act upon it, becoming the brokenness of *ra*, the failure of purpose. This failure leads to the death of intimacy, the Sacred Midst, between the juvenile and parent Elohim, and one another.

The Edenic Nachash reveals the knowledge of goodness and badness—a projection of the unconscious that guides the quester through the moral evaluation and choices they encounter, representing our *conscience*. The *conscience* itself is neither good nor bad, nor is it omniscient, but, rather, is subject to the perils of an undeveloped scope of awareness; operating from either an egocentric guidance that is focused on a morality of pride, selfishness, and greed or a holocentric guidance that is relationally motivated and aware leading to loving action. When the conscience narrows in scope to just "what is good for me," excluding the impact on others, it is prone to causing harm. The mature conscience considers the whole of the moral impact and strives to choose that which is beneficial both to oneself and to others.

Morality without love is *moralism*—a morality of love is *relationalism*. Moralism is the product of an undeveloped or juvenile conscience. It is based on dogma and conformity to some code of conduct that absolves one of responsibility for their impact on others. The code may be institutional such as a religion or internally generated as a product of a rationalized sentiment. It is motivated in the course of human interaction by the knowledge that I will suffer consequences or punishment if I cross a certain boundary, violating a code. To avoid punishment, I will conform to the code. Developmentally, it is considered to be at the normative level of ontogeny of a five-year-old that sees a world of "shall" and "shall-not" without comprehending the relational impact of their choices. Unfortunately, it is a level of development that many people never grow beyond.

On the other hand, *relationalism* is the developed conscience motivated by the value of another, as well as oneself. I may not wish to cross the same said boundary because I am aware that I will cause harm to someone who I recognize as having great value. I may potentially even endanger myself in the process of avoiding causing harm, to protect another. This is the concept of giving of oneself in the Hebrew *ahav* and the Greek *agape*.

❖**Nature of Experience**

Beyond and beneath the development of the conscience, the *Torah of Awakening* is fundamentally about the nature of experience. The primordial ontology of Genesis Creation is the foundation of space and time, the most elemental building block of consciousness. Human experience is essentially defined by our orientation to the *future*, to the *present*, and to the *past*. It is reflected in the fact that most languages are built on these verb tenses reflecting the innate function of space-time within our conscious experience. Our *future* orientation moves us forward as we approach the intentional space, defined by motivation, volition, and passion in the personal realm, and by bonding in the relational realm.

Figure 7 - Future Orientation

Our *present* orientation is founded within the empiric moment as we engage the intentional space, defined by observation, belief, understanding, and rationality in the personal realm, and by identity in the relational realm.

Observation
Belief
Identity

Figure 6 - Present Orientation

Our *past* orientation is a reaction to the moment of the intentional space defined by emotion, evaluation, and feeling in the personal realm, and by boundaries in the relational realm.

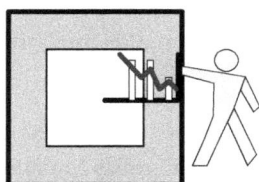

Emotion
Evaluation
Boundary

Figure 8 - Past Orientation

These formulate the archetypal spatiotemporal primitives that underlie the dynamics of all experience. They represent an elemental organic function within the holomorphic psychoanatomy that orient us to the moment of experience.

Symbolically, these spatiotemporal primitives—future, present, past— bracket several essential ranges of concepts in the narrative, such as "heart, mind, and soul" and "way, truth, and life" in the Reified Basar, with some similar variations in the Torah indicating the totality or summation of human experience.

The Adamites as Imago Elohim are essentially defined by their great power. Within this ontological framework, *power* is a function of our future orientation. It defines our potential—our essential capability to initiate actions and cause change focused by our motivations and passions. *Authority*, then, is the present orientation of power that is instantiated by our beliefs and understanding; evoked as a function of our identity as the source of power. *Impact*, consequently, is the past orientation of power, the dynamic response to the imposition of power by an authority. It is the result of power, whether intentional or not, on the emerging narrative. The *Torah of Awakening* is the process of developing awareness of our identity as great powers. It is our search for power, authority, and impact founded on purpose, meaning, and value.

❖**Archetypal Topography of Genesis**

The archetypal topography of the Genesis-Creation myth outlines a set of essential psychological primitives that formulate how we fundamentally orient ourselves to what exists or does not exist in the world—whether we experience the resources of the world as sufficient for our needs or not. The myth initially outlines two topographies—the Garden of Eden and the Wilderness of Midbar-Nod. The Garden of Eden represents an archetypal stasis of sufficiency and safety. In its primitive form, it represents a womb-like existence that intrinsically sustains and satisfies the needs of the juvenile Adamites. Later representations of the Eden archetype are (1) Salem, the city of peace in the Abraham narrative and later symbolic representations of Jerusalem and Mount Zion, (2) Canaan, the promised land of milk and honey in the Exodus narrative, and (3) the Kingdom of Elohim, the realm of Yahweh's power and love in the Reified Basar narrative.

The *Wilderness of Midbar-Nod* represents the disequilibrium of scarcity and vulnerability. *Midbar* is a habitable wilderness suitable for pastures and some degree of settlement. *Nod* means to wander—it is an inhospitable wilderness of exile and homelessness, which is introduced in the myth as the place where Cain is sent after he murders his brother Abel. Wandering due to exile and homelessness is a recurring theme throughout the Unified Basar and Torah myth. Initially, the wilderness represents moving out of the womb into the world where the Adamites must contend for their own provision and protection, working the fields to bring forth fruit. Later representations of Midbar-Nod are numerous, including the antediluvian landscape of Noah, the cities of Sodom and Gomorrah of the Abraham narrative, Egypt and the Desert in the Exodus myth, and the Crucifixion narrative in the Basar/Gospel myth.

The archetypal Garden is a fenced area that provides protection and provision apart from the surrounding world. The Garden of Eden is not the total cosmos of the Genesis Creation myth, it is only a small part that is intended for the protection and provision of the juvenile Adamites. It is a place of peace and safety, symmetric power, and intimate relationship.

On the other hand, Egypt in the mythology represents the everted image of Eden in the wilderness. One of the primary names for "Egypt" in the Hebrew text is *Matsor*, which indicates a boundary or fortress. Matsor is a fenced or bordered area like Eden, but where the Adamites must cultivate their own place of sustenance in exile. It is one of several Great River cultures in the ancient world—including Mesopotamia and the Indus Valley—that enabled the development of agriculture. Matsor is the place where Abraham, and then Jacob, go during times of famine. It is where Joseph is exiled due to his brothers' attempt to murder him, and where the family of Jeshua is exiled to escape Herod's attempt to kill the baby Jeshua. Unlike the *Garden of Elohim*, the Fortress of Matsor is founded on asymmetric or hierarchical power. It is the place of gilluls and kings, and a place of slaves and servitude. Man has mastered the technology of agriculture, forcing his will upon the earth to bring forth fruit. He has created great works of art and architecture that are overshadowed by Death—expressed in the art of mummification and the technology to build great monuments that lead their final inhabitants from this side of life to the land of Duat.

The Edenic Nachash on the Tree of Morality stands at the gateway between the two worlds of the Garden and the Wilderness. This gateway is subsequently guarded by the flaming swords of two Guardian Cherubim after the Exile, symbolizing the resulting psychological separation of the Adamites from the integrative power of the Tree of Life. Thus, psychologically, it represents the separation between the Transcendent Consciousness and the Egoic Consciousness.

The crux of the Edenic Nachash myth is the promise that the Adamites' eyes will be unclosed, knowing Goodness and Badness, they will be like the Parent Elohim, and they will not die. It is this awakening to this burgeoning need within the Adamites for the guidance of moral conscience, the identification with the adult Elohim, and the preservation of life that ushers them into the journey from the Garden to the Wilderness. In turn, it will create a map back to the Garden from the Wilderness in the Reified Basar myth, past the Guardian Cherubim through the Higher Nachash to the restore the Tree of Life.

❖The Hero's Journey

The *Hero's Journey* is an archetypal pattern of world transformation in mythology that was originally described by the mythologist Joseph Campbell. It is a metamyth of the hero's journey into the underworld to confront the dark forces that guard some mystery or treasure, which is somehow inhibiting the mythic cosmos. While Campbell attempted to define this archetypal construct as a *monomyth* that underlies all myth, a more reasonable evaluation is that what he is describing is a powerful variant of human experience found throughout human culture and experience, not the summation of all narrative paths. In fact, even in the annals of *heroes*, the *journey* serves as a specific function within a developmental narrative. Campbell's metamyth does a great job at describing the transformational hero who challenges the dysfunction of the status quo to bring balance, truth, and authentic value into the world. However, another common hero myth is the egoic or moralistic hero who affirms the social good of order and conformity to the tribal narrative. The moralistic hero is the linchpin in the battle between good and evil in the simplistic narrative of black hats and white hats. He is the enduring, white-hatted savior who comes to save the day, defeating evil and restoring order.

Even within the archetype of the transformational hero, there is the powerful variant of this metamyth often described as *the dark night of the soul*, in which the hero must face his own darkness, fear, and limitations in order to bring about authentic transformation. It is a narrative arc found throughout history and across cultures, delineating a search for some ultimate value or truth, guarded by some dark destructive force. It begins with the calling out of a potential champion from ordinary life, the descent into the underworld to face the guardian monster in the dark night of the soul, and the defeat of the heroic champion resulting in some form of death, deep loss, or deconstruction of their former self, and then the rebirth of the hero as some truer, authentic representation as he reemerges into the waking world. At the heart of the dark night is the death of the juvenile ego, letting go of the false ideations and rationalized preconceptions of identity and purpose that are internalized in ordinary development.

The original archetypal formulation of the *Dark Night of the Soul* emerges in a poem by that name and its ensuing exposition by its author, the sixteenth-century Spanish mystic monk, St. John of the Cross. St. John describes the Dark Night as dealing "with the way a soul must conduct itself along the road leading to union with God through love."[81] In his subsequent commentary, the author characterizes the soul's path as "trials and conflicts" on the way to the "perfection of love." The archetypic poem thusly narrates:

> *One dark night, fired with love's urgent longings (ah, the sheer grace!) I went out unseen, my house being now all stilled.*

---

[81] John of the Cross (1991) p.360

In darkness, and secure, by the secret ladder, disguised (ah, the sheer grace!) in darkness and concealment, my house being now all stilled.

On that glad night, in secret, for no one saw me, nor did I look at anything, with no other light or guide than the one that burned in my heart.

This guided me more surely than the light of noon to where he was awaiting me—him I knew so well—there in a place where no one appeared.

O guiding night!
O night more lovely than the dawn!
O night that has united the Lover with his beloved, transforming the beloved in her Lover.

Upon my flowering breast which I kept wholly for him alone, there he lay sleeping, and I caressing him there in a breeze from the fanning cedars.

When the breeze blew from the turret, as I parted his hair, it wounded my neck with its gentle hand, suspending all my senses.

I abandoned and forgot myself, laying my face on my Beloved; all things ceased; I went out from myself, leaving my cares forgotten among the lilies.[82]

The Dark Night eventually develops into a universal archetype of the human struggle for love and authenticity. It is the dream of the soul as it journeys into the presence of the beloved—the restoration of the Sacred Midst between lover and beloved.

In her exploration of the Parental Image, Mary Esther Harding describes the Dark Night of Soul as the path towards the "healing of the soul" in the purgation of the injured archetypal image of the mother or father:

It is not enough for many people that they can live a competent outer life. Questions as to the meaning of it all begin to press for answers. And once again ostracism from the paradise in which the Tree of Life grows becomes an urgent problem... There are [those] who have not been seriously deprived in childhood and have made a satisfactory life adjustment but in later life have found themselves cast out, as it were, into outer darkness, ostracized not from the actual parents but from communion with their deepest value, that is, from God. Others again, experience what St. John of the Cross called "the dark night of the soul" and are compelled to embark on a journey of the soul whose goal is so frequently expressed by the image of Paradise, where a man may be renewed, reborn from the womb of the Great Mother...

[In case studies, the act of individuation] involves an injury to the archetypal image of Mother or Father that can no longer exist in unbroken

---

[82] John of the Cross (1991) p.358-359

> *wholeness, and no longer remains the sole ruler of the individual's psyche. The power of the parents had been broken but their functions had now to be fulfilled in some new way. The individuals had to go through a "dark night of the soul" and as a result of their ordeal they were blessed with a "healing of the soul." For the injury to the archetypal image of the parents was healed and the individuals found that the unconscious no longer appeared to them in a frightening and destructive form. Instead it showed itself as the very source of life and creativity.[83]*

Harding threads St. John's narrative of the path to the Beloved, to the healing of the Ideal Parent image.

In the Unified Basar and Torah mythology, the archetypal descent from the Garden into the Wilderness, and then back to the Kingdom of Yahweh's Love, framed by the Reified Basar, gestated in the Torah, broadly outlines the Hero's Journey of the Dark Night as the arc of human development. Initiated in the Edenic protection of the womb, the Adamites are called to explore their innate power with the choice of doing it in relationship to the parent, or else, on their own. In this dream narrative, humankind is destined to follow the juvenile path of self-discovery alone, born into a wilderness world that requires their best efforts to survive without direct parental protection. However, even within this journey, they are given a choice to continue following a path of juvenile egocentric individuation or else adjust to a path of mature relational differentiation. On one hand, they can embody the individualistic path towards selfishness and greed, competition and conquest, instantiated in the asymmetric power dynamic of the *Victim-Villain-Victor*; or, on the other, embrace the relational path towards cooperation and community, instantiated in the symmetric power dynamic of the *Child-Parent*. The individualistic path is an abortion of the Hero's Journey into the Dark Night, immuring us within the walls of our juvenile doubts and apprehensions. The relational path, however, requires us to confront our fears and vulnerabilities in the depths of the long night, to engage the world of darkness while letting go of our fear of scarcity and need for control—to die to that juvenile distortion of our self and thus to become mature Elohim as we reengage the world from a new perspective and value system.

---

[83] Harding (1993), p.29-30

❖Cycles of the Hero's Journey

The Unified Basar and Torah myth is a series of developmental journeys from Juvenile morality to Adolescence, then Young Adult, and, finally, to Mature Adult morality. As such, it is comprised of four cycles that define the narrative arc of each developmental stage as its own cycle of the Hero's Journey of disintegration and then reintegration, leading to greater heights of maturity, or more severe depths of psychopathy.

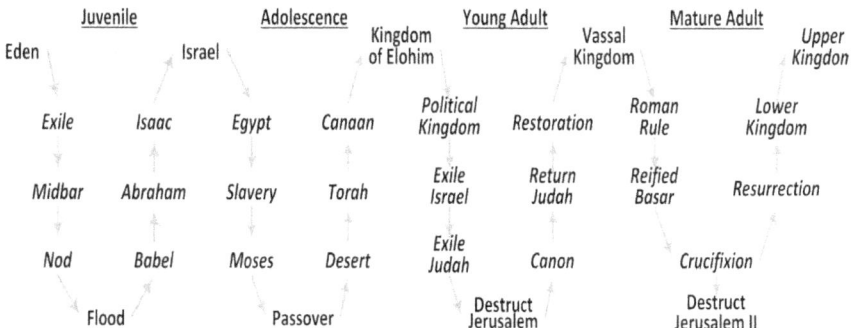

Juvenile		Adolescence		Young Adult		Mature Adult	
Eden		Israel	Kingdom of Elohim		Vassal Kingdom		Upper Kingdon
Exile	Isaac	Egypt	Canaan	Political Kingdom	Restoration	Roman Rule	Lower Kingdom
Midbar	Abraham	Slavery	Torah	Exile Israel	Return Judah	Reified Basar	Resurrection
Nod	Babel	Moses	Desert	Exile Judah	Canon		Crucifixion
	Flood		Passover	Destruct Jerusalem		Destruct Jerusalem II	

Figure 9 - Deconstructive Cycles in the Developmental Arc

The first stage of the Heroic Cycle is the *Juvenile* developmental arc starting in Eden, which then disintegrates through the Exile narrative to the flood of Noah, which wipes out the primal violence of the antediluvian world. Then, it reintegrates through the rebuilding of the prehistorical world of Mesopotamia, leading to the establishment of the Semitic tribe of Israel as the anointed nation of Yahweh.

The second stage of the Heroic Cycle is the *Adolescent* developmental arc beginning with the children of Israel whose circumstance subsequently disintegrates into slavery in Egypt. Then the story continues through the calling of Moses as the anointed savior into the Dark Night of the Passover narrative where the Israelites are freed from slavery. The reintegration begins with the rebuilding of a new identity in the deserts of Arabia, through the guidance of the Torah, before occupying Canaan and establishing the Kingdom of Elohim in Israel.

The third stage of the Heroic Cycle is the *Young Adult* developmental arc, beginning with the Kingdom of Elohim in Israel, which, then, disintegrates into the political kingdoms, starting with the tumultuous wars of Saul, then, the short-lived unified kingdoms of David and Solomon, and the building of the first institutional Temple. It then disintegrates into the divided kingdoms of Israel in the north and Judah in the south. The northern kingdom of Israel is then conquered by Assyria and taken into captivity. It ceases to exist as a nation, leaving only a disorganized remnant in Samaria that intermarries with the local tribes. Judah is then conquered by Babylon and the Temple of Solomon is destroyed. The reintegration begins after decades in exile as the Judahites/Jews are allowed to return after the Persians conquered Babylon. However, before they return, the Hebrew canon is established and, then upon return, it is used to revive the communal mandates of the Mosaic Law, leading to the rebuilding of the second institutional Temple.

The final stage of the deconstructive Heroic Cycle is the Mature Adult developmental arc beginning with the Vassal Kingdom of the Second Temple descending through the political chaos of the foreign occupation by Persia, Greece, and Rome, then to the advent of the Reified Basar leading to the crucifixion of Rabbi Jeshua and the destruction of the Second Temple. The reintegration begins with the resurrection of Jeshua, which establishes the Lower Kingdom of Yahweh through the guidance of the Sacred Spirit of Love, and then, points to a future Higher Kingdom in which Love finally fully rules. In this model, we are currently in the period of the Lower Kingdom of Elohim.

❖**The Good Parent**

The Good Parent is the archetypal image of the Ideal Parent, a representation of the Guardian-Caretaker role in response to the dependent Child within the mythic Child-Parent relationship. However, in patriarchal societies, the parental role, by definition of the patriarchy, is fragmented into opposing gender constructs. The disintegrated traits of the *Guardian* are projected onto the male gender as *masculine* characteristics, and the disintegrated traits of the *Caretaker* are projected onto the female gender as *feminine* characteristics. This abdication of intrinsic functionality by individuals based on sexual organs has dire consequences for personal development. The divestiture of the so-called *feminine* traits of the *Caretaker* by men cripples their capability to engage their interior or domestic life. Likewise, the divestiture of the so-called *masculine* traits of the *Guardian* by women cripples their capability to engage the exterior or heroic sphere.

In the Exile narrative, this dysfunctional projectivity is indicated to be a response to Adam's newfound inclination towards asymmetric power, causing his relationship with Eve to become fractured. He thusly regards Eve to be someone to rule over rather than to relate to, and to love, which devolves into asymmetric roles that fragment primary developmental characteristics into the masculine and feminine stereotypes that instantiates traditional patriarchal gender mythology. Not only do humans not fit these categories in real life by exhibiting a wide range of *guardian* and *caretaker* traits regardless of sexual organs, but the attempt to force them into traditional dogmatic roles is deeply dysfunctional in the family structure, ultimately harming a child's development as they are acculturated to divest intrinsic aspects of their own personal power. To the contrary, mature development requires the full embrace and inculcation of the integrated role of Guardian-Caretaker by both parents and child reflecting the Ideal Parent Image, becoming the magnetic point towards wholeness, healing, and relational maturity.

However, throughout history, in patriarchal culture and myth, narrowly devised assumptions about sexual characteristics become stereotypically applied in societal roles, privileges, and assumed traits to the disadvantage of women. In human biology, sexual anatomy only defines one's functional capability in procreation—the male sex provides sperm to the egg of the female sex who, when impregnated, nurtures the gestating embryo to full term. Anthropologically, in order to facilitate sexual pairing, cultures have created elaborate signaling rituals through behavior, manner of dress, and hairstyles to distinguish males and females for that purpose. Beyond this pairing ritual, however, sexual characteristics are meaningless in determining one's essential character, intelligence, skills, capabilities, and worth within the family unit or society. Across the whole spectrum of human experiences, few traits actually correlate directly to one's "naughty bits." One common argument is that "Men are stronger than Women." However, in the real world the strongest human with ovaries can outperform all but 0.1% of humans with testes—by the aforementioned rule, 99.9% of males are *weaker* than this female, so therefore by definition they are not *real* Men. To the contrary, any difference beyond procreation in characterizing humans by sex is merely social convention or a reaction to the dominant gender mythology.

In the dominant gender mythology of Greece, Zeus' magical penis is the foundation of the majority of Greek tragedies. Zeus often asserts his dominance and lack of restraint by seducing or raping mortal and immortal women alike, siring gods and demigods who have the same penchant for trouble as their father, to the dismay of his wife Hera. This contrasts with the Torah mythology in which the Imago Elohim create the Adamites in their image, both male and female. Then the prototypic relationship between the Adamites is founded on the unified declaration "flesh of my flesh." The Adamites' sexual characteristics do not essentially define them—they are each Elohim.

Likewise, throughout the Unified Basar and Torah, when Yahweh is referred to as *Father*, it is not because he has a giant cosmic penis; nor is it because he supports the asymmetric power dynamic of male domination in patriarchal society. At times, the term *Father* is used to signal a spermatic function of imparting Yahweh's characteristics, desires, or image into his children. At other times, Yahweh is portrayed as a *Mother*, nurturing her infantile young under her wing in the role of *El Shaddai*, the *powerful many-breasted one*. Then, in other situations, the relationship is more appropriately translated as *Parent* in the unified non-genderized role of Guardian-Caretaker.

In the Reified Basar, Yahweh's parental role is to impart the adult power and value system of the kingdom of love to his children. Rabbi Jeshua extensively refers to Yahweh as Father to infer affinity and love, the fullness of the parental Guardian-Caretaker, rather than the literal sperm donor or disintegrated masculinized *Guardian*. He sometimes refers to Yahweh intimately as "dad," using the more informal Aramaic word *abba*. In the Basar of Matthew, Jeshua describes the Good Father's generous spirit, stating that this should serves as a model for all to follow:

> Look at the flying creatures of heaven, that they are not sowing, neither are they reaping, nor are they gathering into barns, and your heavenly Father is nourishing them. Are not you of more consequence than they?
>
> ...Request and it shall be given you. Seek and you shall find. Knock and it shall be opened to you. For everyone who is requesting is obtaining, and who is seeking is finding, and to him who is knocking it shall be opened. Or what man is there among you, from whom his son will be requesting bread—no stone will he be handing him! Or he will be requesting a fish also—no serpent will he be handing him!
>
> If you, then, being [hurtful], have perceived how to be giving good gifts to your children, how much rather shall your Father Who is in the heavens be giving good things to those requesting Him? All, then, whatever you should be wanting that men should be doing to you, thus you, also, be doing to them, for this is the law and the prophets.[84]

The sacred relationship between the Good Parent and his children is intended to be model of loving-kindness and generosity to inspire the same in relationship with one another.

❖The Bad Parent

Unlike the symmetric dynamic of the parental Guardian-Caretaker, the Villain-Victor is a manifestation of asymmetric power, the force that wedges its way between mother and child, lover and beloved, threatening their well-being and disrupting the safety of their intimacy and home life. The Villain is the classic monster, driven by a hunger that cannot be satisfied. It feeds off of its Victim, indulging its appetite for power, wealth, domination, or

---

[84] CLV Matthew 6:26, 7:7-12

gratification. In actuality, it is a projection of a drive founded on fear, vulnerability, or missingness that inhabits the dark recesses of our unconscious.

The Victor is the egoistic Hero—the force that keeps the Villain at bay, defending the rational domain of the conscience, what is deemed appropriate and acceptable. However, in doing so, it actually creates the monster as a reciprocal function of rejecting and encapsulating what is deemed a threat to egoistic morality. The Victor and Villain are tied intrinsically together as a mirror response to some vulnerability.

A classic tale of want and desire in response to a cache of treasure possible for the taking, the egoistic conscience begins to separate around the hunger for possession of the treasure. In the context of a moral society that identifies *greed* as a sin/failure, the egoistic hero pushes the desire for acquisition deeper into the dark underworld of the unconscious, out of sight, but giving power to the desire through the same resistance used to suppress it, thus creating the monster. Societal virtue and implicit greed pushing against one another—the underlying vulnerability is real, the fear of scarcity and want, and the possibility of harm—so the response is equally real without resolving the underlying issue. The ego will either attach to the egoistic Hero or else become consumed by the ravenous *gillul*, which ultimately demands payment from the Victim. This is the internal construct of the asymmetric dynamic of the Victim-Villain-Victor operating as a composite archetype.

Jungian psychologist, Mary Esther Harding, describes this in terms of a pathological injury to the ideal parent image:

> *A normal injury to the archetypal image of parent and of child occurs in everyone, of necessity. For there is inborn in everyone an ideal picture of what the mother and father ought to be like, as well as an archetypal picture of the child as the center of the parents' attention, the cherished uninhibited one, full of promise and nascent possibilities. But the unconscious also contains an opposite picture of parent and child. "Parent" can mean tyranny, unlimited power, and so forth, while "child" can mean helplessness, limitedness, restriction. These negative aspects of the archetype come into undue prominence in the inner experience of certain people... an injury to the archetypal image of both parent and child.*[85]

Injury to the image of the Ideal Parent exposes the vulnerability of the archetypal Child, constellating their narrative experience around this

---

[85] Harding (1993) p.137-138

exposure. Harding relates this pathological injury of the ideal parent image to the developmental formation of one's archetypal sense of safety:

> *In some cases... this normal aspect of the parent world has been seriously modified and distorted, and the inner image the child carries of the parent consequently suffers a "pathological" injury. Where, for instance, the actual man and woman, his father and mother, who carry for him the role of the primal parents—that is, of the parental archetype—have not fulfilled their part in a positive sense, but have been, perhaps, neglectful or even cruel and have thus left an imprint on the child's psyche of a destructive and wrathful parental image, a serious psychic trauma results. To such children God is not a heavenly Father, but a vengeful, demanding and punitive Yahweh. In consequence they are cast out of the inner Paradise and find themselves in the wilderness... Experiences of this sort lie at the root of many of the problems of modern man, and may lead to unhappiness, neurosis, even despair.[86]*

On the developmental path towards a mature identification of self in relationship to the ideal Parent, the wayfaring soul must sacrifice their egoic attachment to the damaged inner narrative. Harding thusly writes:

> *Whichever form the childhood experience [of developmental separation from the parent] has taken, the individual is cut off from his true self, and from the most important values of life. In effect he is cut off from God. The realization of his state of alienation from Self and from God may not dawn on him till middle life, when the major tasks of the outer life have been fulfilled... The problem can only be resolved by a search for the deeper meaning, the deeper values of life—that is, by an increase of self-consciousness. This has to be undertaken as a task, one that will involve a difficult inner journey, which often proves to be a veritable "dark night of the soul." In it the ego will have to be sacrificed so that a new relation can be established with the inner "not-I" whose accomplishment is invariably accompanied by an experience of grace.[87]*

As such, the Dark Night of the Soul leads to the mature identification of one's true self in relationship to the ideal Parent.

❖Awakening of Juvenile Morality

Our awakening to the natural world is the marrow of consciousness, the soul of our essential being. We are formed of the clay of the earth—the material substance of trees and stars saturating every cell of our bodies. As the great naturalist John Muir proclaimed, "There is a love of wild nature in everybody, an ancient mother-love showing itself whether recognized or no, and however covered by cares and duties."[88] It is what grounds our feet to the earth while we reach for the sky, wandering through boundless curiosities.

---

[86] Harding (1993) p.134-135
[87] Harding (1993) p.140
[88] Muir (1938) p.315

The material construct of our bodies is what defines our sense of self, of personhood; the *I* lost amongst the *we* in space and time. Inside, we are a myriad of actors in an athenaeum of stories, tentatively enacted on one vital stage, breathed into a single insular frame that nimbly proclaims, "I am." Our developmental journey begins in the personal, grounded in the familial of the Child-Parent relationship, woven into a small coterie of *dramatis personae* performing supporting roles in our household drama—family, teachers, merchants, neighbors, and confederates. The Parent is a transcendent presence in the symmetric dynamic of the juvenile cosmos functioning as the Guardian-Caretaker of the Child.

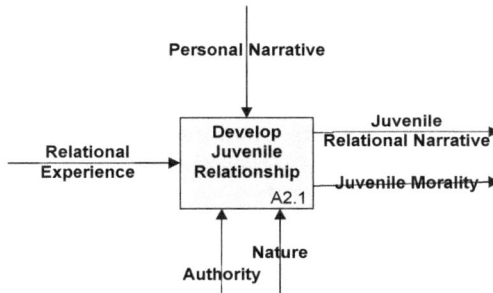

Model 4 - Develop Juvenile Relationship (A2.1 Context)

In the Torah of Awakening, the juvenile stage of moral development is the *search* for purpose, meaning, and value. The mythology of *Da'ath*, the knowledge of goodness and badness, explores the archetypal topography of scarcity and sufficiency as the foundation of juvenile conscience, portraying psychological nakedness as the failure of conscience. Our deep-seated awareness of our vulnerability in the face of scarcity distorts our view of the world and our relationships. At this stage, the Parent Elohim operates as Guardian-Caretaker with direct authority and discipline over the Child Elohim; setting boundaries and meting out punishment when the boundaries are violated. The Children are transitioning from dependency upon the Parent for their well-being. They are beginning to individuate from their environment— learning who they are, and what is their place, in the search for purpose, meaning, and value.

Sociologically, the *Torah of Awakening* describes our drive to explore the world around us, subject to the limits imposed on us by familial authorities that govern our interactions. The direct external authority may be embodied in our parents or other tribal caretakers. The rules of family life or tribal participation are plentiful and often unwritten, inculcated into our routines and expressed intuitively, until we reach their boundary, when we must consciously navigate around or through them.

Psychologically, the *Torah of Awakening* describes our inherent curiosity and imagination, moderated by the internal representation of negative parental authority—the critical or judgmental moderator within us that limits our exploration of the world, exaggerating our fears and innate sense of vulnerability. This Juvenile awareness helps us to navigate the world, telling us not to put our hand in the fire, or to be cautious climbing the stairs. But then it may also prompt us to overreact to social and environmental signals, to lash out and attack imaginary enemies, or hide from unreal dangers that we project onto very real objects in our environment; at times, causing us or another great harm. This may lead us to project or transfer our fears onto symbolic objects that allow us to transact our anxieties, giving us a sense of control over our vulnerabilities. These neurotic *gilluls* represent the scarcity we most fear and struggle to avoid, devolving into the asymmetric power dynamic of the transferent Victim-Villain-Victor relationship.

Symbolically, the primordial Eve and Adam represent the ontogenic core within us, embodying a relational morality that struggles to develop over the course of our lifetime. The juvenile Eve and Adam represent the awakening to the existence of relationship, the awareness of another, beyond one's ego-centered world. The archetypal Eve and Adam together are actors on the stage of the psyche, present in each one of us. They represent a composite archetype of relationship in response to our innate sense of missingness and vulnerability as firstborn/secondborn, older/younger, as well as friend, sibling, lover, and rival. At this stage of development, we see the world in terms of *advantage* and *disadvantage* in a world of scarcity, orienting ourselves according to hierarchical roles that we identify with most strongly. The relational dynamic often disintegrates asymmetrically as the advantage of the politically dominant forces pushes the circumstantially weaker forces into submissive roles in our inner narratives, which then begin to be projected outward to objects and people in the real world.

Archetypally, the awakening of juvenile morality unfolds, as a search, initially, for purpose and connection, then, meaning and identity, and finally, value and boundaries. There is an ideal path of discovery, which leads to the next level of development, and then, there is a broken path in the process of discovery, which distorts juvenile development. Practically, the journey is not a linear path—one will alternately find success and suffer failure along the way. For some the path to safety and maturity is straightforward, and for others, long and tortuous. Without a map, some will never reach their destination, becoming irreconcilably lost along the way. The mythology of the Unified Basar and Torah provides a map, but not a path to one's destination; ultimately, that is what each venturer must find for themselves.

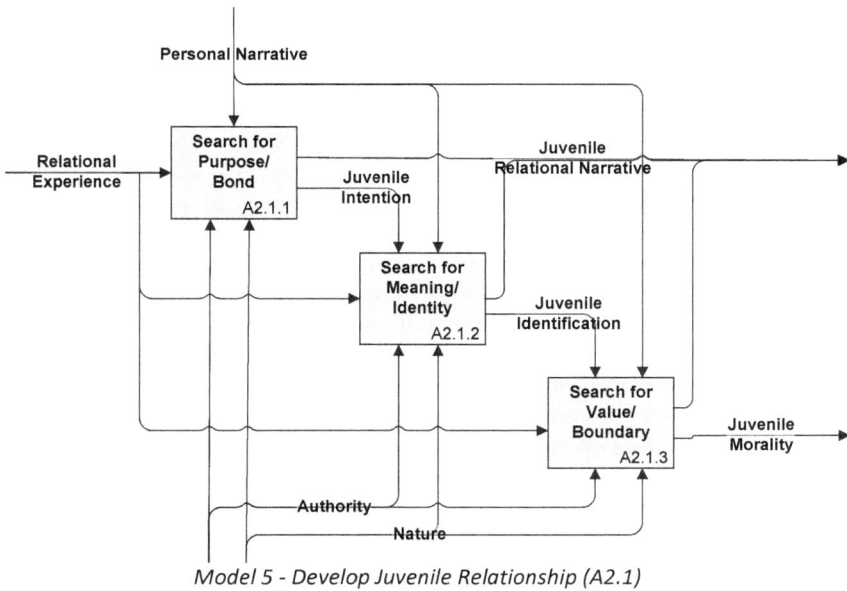

Model 5 - Develop Juvenile Relationship (A2.1)

CHAPTER [1/I]

IN THE I OF THE BEHOLDER

> O serpent heart hid with a flowering face! Did ever dragon keep so fair a cave? Beautiful tyrant, fiend angelical, dove-feathered raven, wolvish-ravening lamb, despised substance of divinest show, just opposite to what thou justly seemest, a damned saint, an honourable villain.
> —*William Shakespeare*, "Romeo and Juliet"

The first revelation of the Edenic Nachash is that the Adamites' eyes will be unclosed by eating the Fruit of Morality, knowing goodness and badness. It is an awakening to power and a promise of moral guidance—arousing awareness of one's relationship to nature, to one another, to all that exists. Intrinsically, it reveals the Adamites' inherent limitations and their need for one another as the foundation of love. However, having ignored the relational impact of their course of action, the Adamite's journey now is framed by a Wilderness of scarcity and vulnerability, a place they essentially experience as unsafe and insufficient. In the displacement from the Garden to the Wilderness, the struggle for moral guidance is intensified, and the potential for meaningful moral choice is given, whether to operate from a place of juvenile egotism or move towards a more inclusive awareness of mutuality. The journey to adulthood is not a simple path; it is not achieved by an elementary awareness or rational assent to a principle. It involves challenges to one's very core to discover truth and authenticity, to decide who and what has value—to commit to a value system—and, ultimately, to decide who and what is *family*.

The beginning of the Adamites' journey is the calling out from the ordinary—the undifferentiated state of conformity to the social and moral groundwork that is uncritically accepted as what should be, what must be, and what keeps one from fully being. The *calling* is a fundamental existential declaration, "I am," independent of judgment or causality; instigating a search for purpose and a place in life as a primary existential imperative— "Why am I here?" It directs the Adamites' energies toward some ultimate outcome somewhere down the road of their journey through life; guiding their choices to clarify what is important, and what is not, awakening them to the possibilities of their existence, and building bonds that bring them into relationship. It guides their way through the plots and perils of daily existence to some narrative of ultimate destiny.

In the Genesis Creation myth, the *Knowledge of Goodness and Badness* is the foundation of ego development—the awareness of who I am and who I am not. The Garden of Eden exists as a unified womb-like experience of the *Lover-Beloved*, the unbroken gaze of the Mother and Child, characterized by safety and sufficiency. In the beginning, Yahweh is introduced in the role of the Guardian-Caretaker who constructs a guarded world to care for the juvenile Adamites in developing their awareness of their own powers. As juvenile Elohim, the children are then given the responsibility of being the Guardian-Caretakers over Eden—to develop an essential knowledge of the world around them, to care for it and one another, as well as to create new life. This foundational responsibility will underlie the dynamic of the entire narrative arc. It is initially embodied in the symmetric relational power archetype of the *Lover-Beloved* in the context of the intimacy between Yahweh and Adam, and then develops as humanity's responsibility towards all life on this planet, in the archetypal roles of Gardener, Shepherd, Parent, and Spouse. In this, the Adamites are called to engage the vulnerable cohorts in their lives with compassion, empathy, and responsibility as Guardian-Caretakers.

❖The Birth of I

Initially, Adam is given a task to discover the characteristics and traits of all the creatures of Eden, and to intimate a name for each:

> *So the human was calling the names of every domestic beast, of every flyer of the heavens and of every animal of the field; yet for the human no helper was available as his complement.*[89]

In his task of getting to know the creatures around him, he found no reciprocity, no intimate companion to whom he can relate. So, Yahweh causes Adam to fall asleep, and fashions a second Adamite, a female, from his side. On awakening to this new creature, Adam declares, "This time, it is bone of my bones and flesh of my flesh. This shall be called woman, for this was taken from her man." Then the narrator states that the two Adamites "will be one flesh" and "both of them were *naked*... yet they were not *ashamed*."[90]

There is an intrinsic sense of safety and unselfconsciousness in the symmetric relationship between the juvenile Adamites and the Parent Elohim—no sense of vulnerability in their nakedness. The word for nakedness

---

[89] CLV Genesis 2:20
[90] CLV Genesis 2:24-25

in Hebrew, *aw-rome*[91] is rooted in the word *aw-ram*[92] used to describe the Edenic Nachash in the next paragraph, meaning to *uncover* or *make naked* but often translated as *crafty* signifying skillfulness or intelligence. As indicated earlier, the role of the Edenic Nachash in the narrative is to be the Revealer, to strip away any pretense, to reveal some level of naked truth. When the Adamites eat the fruit of the Knowledge of Goodness and Badness, the narrator states:

> Then the eyes of both of them were unclosed, and they realized that they were naked. So they sewed fig leaves together and made girdle skirts for themselves. Then they heard the sound of Yahweh Elohim walking about in the garden … and the human hid himself with his wife from the face of Yahweh Elohim among the trees of the garden.[93]

The word *buwsh*[94], which is translated as *ashamed* in the preceding paragraph, is more accurately interpreted as "to grow pale as from terror." So, as the Adamites' eyes are unclosed, they come to realize their vulnerability, they "grow pale as from terror" and cover themselves and go into hiding. The Knowledge of Goodness and Badness opens their eyes to their inherent vulnerability, seeing danger in others, evoking an egoistic state of separateness and self-consciousness—arousing existential terror and the awareness of the asymmetric power of the *Victim-Villain-Victor*.

The psychological state of nakedness in the face of adverse exposure is the hinge upon which our psychological defenses turn. We hide our vulnerabilities from others, and often from ourselves, as we push anomalous constructs deeper into the egoic unconscious, creating the groundwork for inauthentic and unprincipled behavior. These unintegrated neurotic constructs evoke what the myth calls *saw-tan*[95]; the degraded conscience in the form of the internal Adversary, Accuser, or Slanderer—also referred to in a broader psychology as the Censor or Critic, or else functionally as crippling self-doubt or hyperactive judgment.

The Exile narrative is an intensified description of the necessary process of individuation, how we become differentiated from the expectations of our juvenile support environment—the people and things in the primordial world of juvenile development. Trauma is not an essential trigger, but it is certainly an effective one. Fear is the great differentiator—it forces us to see things in black and white, to identify as quickly as possible what is safe and what is

---

91 Strongs H6174
92 Strongs H6175
93 CLV Genesis 3:7-8
94 Strongs H954
95 Strongs H7853

dangerous. Childhood trauma, whether emotional, physical, or sexual in nature, forces the child to engage the world more directly and deliberately—adultifying the child. It also tends to split the developing psyche between a regressive child persona and a hyper-vigilant caretaker persona. In severe childhood trauma, the child will often develop deep intuitive capabilities as a way to monitor the environment for danger—the ability to see beneath the surface into the deeper narrative structures present, to find what is missing or unsafe. And, in the worst types of manipulative trauma, it may even cause the identity to dissociate or split. The premature acquisition of the knowledge of goodness and badness forces the child into narratives that they are not developed or experienced enough to handle. The juvenile Adamites must now enter a transitional pre-adolescence in the Wilderness of Midbar-Nod unprepared for the next stage of their journey.

❖Experience of Tov and Ra

The fruit of the *Da'ath* of *Tov* and *Ra* is instantiated as the idiosyncratic *experience* of Goodness and Badness—knowledge becomes experience—which delineates the developmental arc of the Unified Basar and Torah mythology. *Goodness* is rooted in the image of ripened fruit—symbolizing the fulfillment of purpose. *Badness*, on the other hand, is rooted in the image of fruit that is rotten and decaying—symbolizing the loss of purpose. It is invoked variously as Life versus Death, Vitality versus Vulnerability, Wholeness versus Missingness, Home versus Wandering, or Health versus Disease. It delineates a core qualitative state of the psyche.

Goodness/Tov	Badness/Ra
Integration	Disintegration
Fulfillment	Purposelessness
Home	Wandering
Nurture	Nakedness
Life	Death
Pleasure	Pain
Healing	Brokenness
Growth/Ripen	Decay/Rottenness
Wholeness	Missingness
Joy-Life	Despair
Health	Disease
Vitality	Vulnerability
Safety	Subjugation
Love	Control/Conflict
Altruism	Alienation

Table 5 - Experience of Tov and Ra

The dynamic of the psyche integrates toward the qualitative state of *Goodness* and disintegrates toward the qualitative state of *Badness*. The Adamites are characterized as being in a shifting torrent between these forces. Ultimately, the dyspathic dynamic between *Goodness* and *Badness* defines the scope and characteristic of the restorative Basar myth founded on Isaiah that is reified in the life of the Anointed Son.

❖**Wilderness Exile**

As a consequence of the Adamites' internalizing the immature fruit of moral development devoid of the guiding principle of Love, their relationship with the Parent Elohim and to one another is injured and they are subsequently exiled from Eden. The adultified juvenile Adamites must take on new responsibilities for their own care and safety in the Wilderness of Midbar-Nod.

The story of the Wilderness begins with the establishment of the first family. Soon after Eve and Adam are expelled from the Garden of Eden, they become parents themselves, begetting two sons, Cain and Abel. Cain is the firstborn son. He is a farmer working hard in the hot sun to cultivate the crops that will sustain the lives of the Adamite family exiled in Midbar. Abel is the secondborn. He is a shepherd caring for the flocks that will also sustain the lives of the Adamite family in exile.

Cain is introduced in the narrative as one who *serves the ground*. While farming is a necessity for the survival of the family, it is also symbolic of the demotion of the Adamites and the *Ground Nachash* to the Wilderness of struggle, suffering, and destiny. While Adam is created from the red earth and the *Sacred Breath*, he becomes alienated from this intrinsic ontology in the Exile narrative, as the earthen part of his nature is accursed. The *Ground Nachash* represents this lower nature with which he must now struggle. Yahweh Elohim declares to the serpent:

> Because you have done this, Cursed shall you be away from every domestic beast And from every animal of the field! On your torso shall you go crawl, And soil shall you eat all the days of your life.[96]

And to Adam he proclaims:

> Cursed is the ground on your account; In grief shall you eat of it all the days of your life. Thorn and weed shall it sprout for you, And you will eat the herbage of the field. By the sweat of your brow shall you eat your bread, Until you return to the ground, for from it were you taken. For soil you are, and to soil you shall return.[97]

This estrangement of *ground* from the *breath/sky* is emblematic of our inner brokenness—our predominant tendency towards exclusionary experience. It underlies our persistent alienation from one another due to egocentrism, selfishness, and greed.

---

[96] CLV Genesis 3:14
[97] CLV Genesis 3:17-19

Cain, however, is *proud* of his accomplishments as a groundworker and demonstrates this by offering an approach present to Yahweh from his harvest, some of the fruit of that ground, with the expectation of a favored response. In the Yahweh narrative, this is the first demonstrated act of idolatry, an offering given as a transaction to gain the favor of an *elohim*. While the offering of *firstfruits* becomes a part of Jewish tradition as an expression of gratitude, for Cain, his offering represents pride in his hard work. It is this fundamental egocentric motivation that causes Cain to expect his work must be rewarded by the Parent Elohim.

Abel also makes an offering to Yahweh as an approach present from the "firstlings of his flock and their fat portions" which, in the cultural framework of the narrative, indicates he gave what was most valuable and preferred, the best of what he had. In contrast to the curse of toiling to make the ground productive in the act of cultivation and agricultural development, the shepherd becomes the primary recurring archetype of the Guardian-Caretaker throughout the arc of the narrative. Cultivation, on the other hand, as the act of Man forcing his will upon the earth to bring forth fruit, becomes a symbol of human achievement, the culture of asymmetric power, of Master over Servant.

The story continues in this vein, drawing out the underlying destructive rot of Cain's egocentric endeavor and its consequence, stating:

> Yahweh gave heed to Abel and his approach present but to Cain and his approach present He did not give heed; so Cain's anger grew very hot, and his face fell.[98]

Cain's pride and jealousy are born out of his egocentric morality that demands recognition for his hard work. His anger is the resulting force of this moral conviction, enforcing the boundaries he has built around his personal moral system. Psychologically, anger is a driving force of our conscience, which provides the energy to defend against anything that illicitly intrudes into the sacred domain of the psyche. This domain, however, is dynamic; its boundaries are developed as an outgrowth of the value stories that define it. When the value stories are asymmetric, based on exclusion and competition embodied in the *Victim-Villain-Victor* archetype, anyone or anything that intrudes becomes a Villain, a monster, and must be attacked, driven out, or destroyed.

---

[98] CLV Genesis 4:4-5

Cain said to his brother Abel: "Let us go into the field." Now it came to pass while they were in the field that Cain rose up against his brother Abel and killed him.[99]

As an act of egocentric morality, Cain kills Abel to calm his own self-righteous indignation; in the same way that Eve's actions were morally constructed in attaining what she believed was good for her, without considering the goodness or badness of her action towards another. But when confronted Cain does not try to defend his actions; knowing goodness and badness, he instead tries to hide the harm he has done.

So Yahweh said to Cain: "Where is your brother Abel?"

And he replied: "I do not know. Am I my brother's keeper?"

Then He said: "What have you done? The voice of your brother's blood is crying out to Me from the ground. Now you are cursed, away from the ground which has opened wide its mouth to take your brother's blood from your hand. When you serve the ground, it shall not continue to give its vigor to you. A rover and a wanderer shall you become on earth."[100]

In context to the *Torah of Awakening*, the answer to the question "Am I my brother's keeper?" is, of course, *yes*—our primary role is to be the Guardian-Caretakers of one another. As the Da'ath of Ra inculcates Cain as the archetypal groundworker, he moves further from this calling. As such, Cain is exiled to the land of *Nod*[101]—which in Hebrew means, *wander, flight,* or *exile*—to embody the *missingness* of his psychological and moral state. Throughout the mythology, the experience of drought and famine represent quite literally an intensified state of scarcity and want, which leads to a state of exile, homelessness, and wandering in a desperate act of survival. This comes to represent an inherent quality of vulnerability and missingness in the human condition.

However, Cain is not represented as a monster, an irreconcilable criminal, or an outcast, rather he becomes the primordial archetype of *Adamkind*—the firstborn of Adam. Cain is the father of human culture and civilization. He builds the first city. His grandson Jabal becomes the father of tent dwellers and cattlemen. Jabal's brother Jubal becomes the father of all who handle the harp and the shepherd's pipe. And their half-brother Tubal-Cain is the one who forges every artifact of copper and iron.

Here it is important to remind the reader that myth is not linear—one must follow the symbols and archetypes within the given mythscape and not

---

[99] CLV Genesis 4:8
[100] CLV Genesis 4:9-12
[101] Strongs H5113

rationalize the storyline. Cain is both a wanderer in exile and the builder of the first city, which intrinsically symbolizes the city-dwellers detachment from the land. He is the father of culture and civilization and exists separate from the narrative of the impending flood, where only Cain's brother Seth's descendant Noah and his family survive. Cain's archetypal legacy transcends the flood. The Kingdom of Cain represents human endeavor at its best and its worst—order and chaos, creation and destruction, safety and violence. At the end of the book of Genesis, the Fortress of Matsor/Egypt becomes the primary representation of this archetypal topography of Cain. And then later, in the Basar narrative, Cain's killing of Abel will be reprised in the conflict between the Pharisees and Rabbi Jeshua, representing the struggle between the asymmetric power of the political groundworker and the symmetric power of the spiritual shepherd.

❖ **Wandering Between**

The theme of becoming exiled from one's home or previous dwelling place due to an egocentric moral state of pride and arrogance is a major motif in the Unified Basar and Torah mythology. It is the cause of much uprooting and boundary setting throughout the myth's development—beginning with the initial egoistic act of the Adamites eating the forbidden fruit and continuing with Cain's embittered fratricidal murder of Abel. The resulting judgment was to be exiled from their homes. And then in the case of Cain, he was to wander as a nomad in the Wilderness of Nod. Later, Noah flees his antediluvian home to escape the judgment levied against humankind for their unquenchable violence and, consequently, wanders forty days on the seas before finding a new home. After several generations, the Noahites arrogantly attempt to build a tower to reach the Sky-God, and subsequently, they are exiled from Babel, separated by different languages that put a barrier of confusion between them.

Abraham is described as a nomad throughout his journey from Ur of the Chaldeans (referring to a group of nomadic western Semites that settled amongst the natives of Babylon). His descendants are promised a home in Canaan; however, Abraham's story is framed by his continual wandering from place to place, or more often, from well to well, as a nomadic herdsman in Mesopotamia, the Levant, and Egypt. Abraham's nephew Lot flees from his home in the city of Sodom to escape the judgment upon its people for their arrogance and strife. Abraham's grandson Jacob/Israel ends up fleeing to Egypt to escape famine. And then, over generations, his descendants become enslaved there.

In the Exodus narrative, the Israelites end up wandering in the desert for forty years because of the arrogance of idolatry, before making their home in Canaan. Later, the Northern Kingdom of Israel is exiled to Assyria, and then, the Southern Kingdom of Judah is exiled to Babylon, due to their lack of caring for the poor and oppressed according to the narrative of the prophets.

Likewise, in the Reified Basar account, Jeshua and his family flee to Egypt after his birth to escape the violence of Herod. And then, Jeshua begins his ministry by wandering for forty days in the Wilderness. And that is just the shortlist—there are numerous other stories involving Isaac, Joseph, David, Ester, Job, the sons of Ishmael, and many of the prophets.

A psychological state of homelessness and purposelessness underlies these stories of flight, exile, and wandering. Sometimes the subject is homeless or directionless due to their own actions. And, at other times, it is to escape the consequences of other people's actions. And then, still other times, it is a symbolic representation of an internal nomadic state of *missingness*. At the heart of the overall narrative is the search or journey to find purpose and a home—a place of provision, peace, and safety—to return to Eden. It represents a fundamental driving principle in human psychological development.

❖Missing the Mark

Wandering is the primary etymological sense underlying the Hebrew word *chatta'ah*, meaning to miss or wander from a target or mark. Wandering or *missingness* represents a primitive psychological characteristic of human nature—the quality or state of missing the mark, the failure to live up to an *Empiric Ideal*. It is initially described as the terror of nakedness in the Edenic Exile narrative; a deep-felt sense of vulnerability, of being unprotected. The *Empiric Ideal* is anchored in the conception of Eden as the protected, safe place, the womb, or home; and then is inspirited in the Sacred Midst as the place of intimacy and love, founded on the archetypal relationship of the *Lover-Beloved* nurtured by the *Higher Nachash*.

Missingness is objectified as the law, a standard of moral behavior and values reflecting the *Empiric Ideal* of the Sacred Midst, cataloging what behavior specifically misses the mark and the obligation to restore what is missed when one behaves beneath the ideal. In addition to the direct obligation to which one's behavior has failed, a ritual theater is created to enact the taking of value, and the sacrifice that is obliged to bring restoration. *Missingness* is often directly symbolized in the narrative as wandering and exile, the embodiment of homelessness and purposelessness. At the heart of "missing the mark" is the ordeal of straying or wandering from the ideal of love and protection.

Missingness is experienced as fear, vulnerability, inadequacy, failure, carelessness, deficiency, and defeat. It is represented by the *Ground Nachash* in the Exile narrative of Eden and is resolved in the Reified Basar as a product of relationship. *Missingness* is not overcome as an egocentric endeavor of domination, or conquering one's fears, but, rather, is completed in love, in relationship with others who stand with us in the Sacred Midst, supporting and enabling each other, where we alone are deficient.

❖**Calling Out**

The initiating role of Guardian-Caretaker in Eden describes our obligation to one another, to support and care for each other. It also defines the broader framework of humanity's functioning on the Earth. However, it does not instantiate, necessarily, a personal path or constitution for one's separate individualized existence in a particular time and place. Not all of us will become explorers, scientists, or academics discovering the mysteries of how the world works; although it is still necessary to have a basic education to navigate our daily lives. Not all of us will become farmers, gardeners, environmentalists, or even pet owners taking care of the plants and animals with which we share this planet; although we all must contribute to the health and well-being of our environment, in intrinsic ways protecting the resources and condition for our homes and communities. Not all of us will become doctors, nurses, social workers, or public servants to care for the health and well-being of specific personal or societal needs; but we all have a responsibility to care for each other, helping and serving our families and communities with whom we come in contact in our daily lives. Not all of us even will have children, but we still have a responsibility to create a healthy sustainable world that is supportive of our youth's health and development and is suitable for the well-being of generations that come after us.

These basic essential purposes are not sufficiently, or necessarily, evocative to define one's individual talents and purpose. There is something unique to each individual that inspires them to create and live a vibrant life— the momentum that calls them forward to go beyond the ordinary, to the extraordinary, in great or small ways. This calling is a non-rational evocation to *authenticity*—the full and complete expression of our innate power and authority as *elohim*.

❖**Staying Put**

The Unified Basar and Torah myth is a formulation of several heroic journeys. Each is broadly demarcated by a calling out from the ordinary, the descent into the unknown, an engagement with the monster in the dark night of the soul, the death of one's former self, and then rising back to the ordinary world fundamentally changed. At the heart of the hero's journey is the dying, or letting go, of the false or inhibited self, the expectations and limitations imposed from without by society and others that we have incorporated as our *truth*.

The deconstruction of the soul from this rationalized self, followed by the reconstruction into the authentic self, is typically a painful process. Many, if not most, people abandon the journey, turning back to the safety of the limited but known world. There is a fine line between breaking through the barriers that incoherently define us, versus hitting the barrier head-on without breaking it, suffering the full force of the inauthentic self, pulling us back to specious familiarity, or else the bend towards self-destruction to escape suffering without completing the journey. One must have just enough strength to tolerate the ambiguity of letting go of one's identity, expectations, and goals, to the point of chaos, without trying to control or resist the process.

As such, it is the abandonment of the hero's journey that is far more common in the personal narrative due to one's fear and perceived need to be in constant control of one's life. The failure to complete the journey leads to what Henry David Thoreau called "lives of quiet desperation." We short-circuit our search for purpose by creating diversions to avoid and pacify the demons within. "Sex, drugs, and rock and roll" conjure a path of sensations without substance—deflection and digression that stunt our development from becoming the greater powers we are intended to be. We instead look to idol powers to give us a sense of control when the chaos around us seems overwhelming. We purchase our sanity by giving up our soul.

❖**I in Idolatry**

Psychologically, gillul/idols are totems we construct to represent our shadow drives. They externalize what we struggle to control and give us the perception of agency in connection with what represents chaos to us—an attempt to control the uncontrollable. They require us to give up something of ourselves, to attempt to satisfy their hunger, which can never be quenched, at least not in this form. In ancient times, one might have had a Fertility-Goddess to externalize one's fear that their lands or their womb may lay barren. The fear is real and founded on circumstance—barren land brings starvation, a barren womb means no heir, no one to carry on the family, and no one to care for the elderly. Superstition does not beget idolatry—it is born of a deep-seated sense of vulnerability in the face of what we experience as a cruel and unsafe world.

Modern idolatry is no different. We have our status symbols and totems that represent our control over the unfathomable. Addiction, obsession, objectification, and greed are all symptomatic of our survival strategies. We project our fears and insecurity onto objects that represent celebrity, wealth, materialism, and institutional authority. When our totemic inspiration does well or inculcates success, we feel secure.

The objects of our personal idolatry vary with our individual narrative and the compensatory strategies we develop for survival that formulate what, intrinsically, can be called our *personality*. An ancient formulation of personality theory that embodies this narrative approach, providing a useful map of these survival strategies, has recently been systematized as the *Enneagram* typology of personality, positing nine personal strategies for survival and success. Unlike many other systems, the Enneagram model is dynamic, describing flows and directions of integration and disintegration. These flows are founded on the primitive spatiotemporal archetypes—our orientation to future, present, and past—represented by the *gut* as the center of passion, the *head* as the center of thought, and the *heart* as the center of emotion. The flow in each of these centers can be either broad/wide open, they can be shutdown/closed off, or they can be focused/constrained. Thus, 3x3 traits yield nine personal strategies for dealing with our fear and woundedness. It would be too big an undertaking to go into the full typological system here, to detail each personality type, but what is germane to this discussion is that we are not all the same. The fears and foibles that generate our coping strategy are broadly distinct to the wounding that motivates our strategic type. The path to our destruction or redemption follows this wounding, and conditions how we are present in the world.

On the other hand, most psychological theories, spiritual systems, and self-help programs are formulated based on the limited exposure of an author's or theoretician's strategic orientation. If you happen to be in the scope of their investigation and experience, you *might* find a reasonable path to well-being. If not, a false path or narrative will overlay one's genuine calling and inevitably worsen one's dysfunction by taking one to new places of inauthenticity, which, in practice, is quite common. As the great mythologist, Joseph Campbell astutely noted:

> *Follow your bliss. The heroic life is living the individual adventure. There is no security in following the call to adventure. Nothing is exciting if you know what the outcome is going to be. To refuse the call means stagnation. What you don't experience positively you will experience negatively. You enter the forest at the darkest point, where there is no path. Where there is a way or path, it is someone else's path. You are not on your own path. If you follow someone else's way, you are not going to realize your potential.[102]*

No solution solves every problem but is resolved if we engage our own calling—our own dynamic path as opposed to another's.

The strategic idols that we invoke are the forces and foibles we seek out to pacify our fears and vulnerabilities, giving us a fleeting sense of security. Like a castle with high walls that keep our enemies out, we fail to realize that the walls also keep us in. We become prisoners of our own devices. The *gillul* become our keeper as we circle our walls, time and time again, never arriving anywhere new, never becoming what we are called to be in an authentic construct of power and identity.

❖**Subpersonal Gods**

A general theory of psychology must be founded on the essential nature of the psyche as *storyteller*. We are not simply a singular egoic "I." The psyche is a stage upon which many *I*'s exist within many stories, at different times, and with different triggers that bring them back to center stage. These stories are inculcated through formative experiences, both real and imagined. Together these narratives form our identity. However, they are not a consistent narrative construct that can be integrated. The narrative core of the psyche, the rational interface, can be viewed as a council table. Many I's or subpersonalities are readily and easily adopted into the narrative core. They can seem seamless to our everyday experience. However, there are I's or subpersonalities that are scary or strange that we do not fully accept. In the most extreme personality constructs, they can even develop into multiple, separated subpersonalities that do not engage with one another, what is diagnostically categorized as *dissociative identity disorder*.

Within a normative functional psyche, these strange subpersonalities are still within the realm of the core communicative universe, just pushed out from the center, deeper into the egoic unconscious, the realm of the archetypal Moon-Goddess. While the core subpersonalities are experienced as safe and familiar, the strangers are experienced as dangerous, as foreign outsiders. The more psychic energy that is expended to keep them out of

---

[102] Campbell (1991) p.16

awareness, out from the familiar core where we build our sense of identity, the more powerful they become. These are the monsters in mythology—the rejected and feared elements of the egoic unconscious that inhabit the shadows of our narrative universe. In the hero's journey, this is what must be confronted in the underworld. What feels foreign and savage is, in truth, a construct of our own nocturnal world, requiring us to let go—to offer respect and acceptance rather than control or destruction in order to bring them out into the moonlight.

❖Conscience Put Asunder

In the Unified Basar and Torah myth, the elemental Edenic Nachash of the Tree of Morality is the embodiment of the Conscience, which reveals what is hidden in the unconscious and gives moral guidance. It is the mediator between our raw impulse and our moral evaluation of matters that confront us. In relationship to Eve, the *nachash* is a projection of her internal conscientious dialogue, her wonderment at the possibilities of the forbidden Fruit of Morality, and what powers it might bear. It reveals her distrust of the Parent Elohim, whom she feels is withholding a powerful mystery that she wishes to possess. The Edenic Nachash does not create the narrative of distrust, but rather reveals it—that is the function of the *nachash,* to reflect what already exists within the unconscious and bring it forward to be weighed and considered as to a course of action. The *nachash* is not the embodiment of a particular moral code, but rather mediates between the moral codes and value systems that are already developed within both the rational and unconscious value systems—fluxing between what is beneficial to ourselves, to others, to the future, to the past—whatever is called forth from within the narrative. It feeds our rational dynamics, weighing the outcomes within the framework of perceptual reality until we deduce a course of action.

The Edenic Nachash reveals Eve's egocentric impulse to acquire the power represented by the Fruit of Morality. In an act of juvenile impulsivity, she devalues the relational impact of the insult to the Parent Elohim in favor of what power she might acquire. The consequence of this relational insult is that the Edenic Nachash is separated from the Tree, its limbs amputated, and it now crawls on its belly in the dust. The conscience is split between the *Higher Nachash*, which guides us towards the power of love, and the *Ground Nachash,* which guides us towards egocentricity—pride, selfishness, and greed. The lower adversarial *Ground Nachash* that crawls on the ground embodies the asymmetric power dynamic of an egoistic morality.

In its most villainous form, the *Ground Nachash* is described as the *Viper*—a venomous snake who strikes out to injure or destroy its victim. It is the most toxic form of the *Ground Nachash* embodied in the archetypal narratives; although even the lesser forms of the *Ground Nachash*, such as the internal Critic or Judge, have some level of toxicity or destructiveness. In several stories in the mythology, the adversarial *Viper* is referred to as *saw-tan*, the Adversary or Accuser in Hebrew, and *diabolos*, the False Accuser in Greek, such as in the story of Job's trials, or Rabbi Jeshua's testing in the wilderness. In this personified form, the *saw-tan* is the one who tests the moral character of a novitiate, revealing what is authentic and what is false, by forcing the respondent to apply their declared morality to a substantive circumstance, to choose whether to embody their values, potentially at some cost to their well-being.

❖Pharaohs and Pharisees

The adversarial *Viper* is a recurring archetype in the arc of the Unified Basar and Torah myth. In the Exodus narrative, the Pharaohs are portrayed as archetypal *Vipers* that continually strike out at the Israelites causing them great harm. In the Reified Basar, the Pharisees are openly called *Vipers* numerous times due to their slanderous ways, and their continual attack on Rabbi Jeshua and the mission of the Reified Basar. In some *Viper* stories, the victim is killed by the archetypal *Viper*, often a prophet killed by an authority figure, such as Jezebel or Herodias. However, in many other *Viper* stories, it is the victim's reputation that suffers, such as in the Exodus story where the Israelites slander the character of both Moses and Yahweh, negating the generosity of their intentions, which is then, in turn, represented externally by the venomous serpents that physically attack the Israelites. Slander is considered one of the most heinous acts in the Torah moral system and is central to two of the Ten Commandments, and then, stated to be the only unforgivable moral failure in the Reified Basar narrative.

In the Genesis Exile narrative, Yahweh Elohim prophesies that the descendants of Eve will confront the power of the adversarial *Viper*, but he will in turn attack back, deeply wounding them. Yahweh thusly declares to the serpent:

> *I shall set enmity between you and the woman and between your seed and her Seed. He shall hurt you in the head, and you shall hurt Him in the heel.*[103]

---

[103] CLV Genesis 3:15

The seed or offspring of Eve, as we shall see as the narrative develops, archetypally refers specifically to the tradition of the firstborn son that bursts forth from the womb as the paragon and vanguard of the whole family.

In the Exodus narrative, the Israelites are the representative firstborn seed of Eve. They are blessed in the land of Goshen, becoming a prosperous people. Their success, however, is perceived as a threat to the power of the Pharaoh, which rouses suspicion and enmity in the mind of Pharaoh, personifying the archetypal seed of the adversarial Viper. This incites the Pharaoh to subjugate the Israelites into servitude to Egypt, inflicting great suffering upon them, and impeding their progress towards the promised land of Canaan.

In the Reified Basar, Rabbi Jeshua is the anointed firstborn seed of Eve, proclaiming the value of, and necessity to care for, the Universal Family of Elohim, including one's enemies and the poor and afflicted. This is perceived as a challenge to the hierarchical authority of the social, political, and religious establishment; arousing suspicion and enmity in the minds of the Pharisees, and other religious and political elites, whom Jeshua calls children, or seed, of the saw-tan, the Accuser, representing the adversarial *Ground Nachash*. This provokes the Pharisees to plot his murder, culminating in Jeshua's arrest and punishment as a "false prophet" and "traitor to the state" by crucifixion on a cross, inflicting great suffering upon him and temporarily impeding his progress in establishing the kingdom of Yahweh's love.

These two examples represent the enmity between the asymmetric and symmetric power dynamics. Throughout history, the wealthy and powerful are most often the archetypal *Vipers* that subjugate the poor and afflicted. They are invested in maintaining the status quo from which they profit and have always reacted with great enmity towards any threat to the system upon which their power is based. The firstborn seed becomes a threat to the seed of the adversarial *Ground Nachash* when the firstborn as Guardian-Caretaker challenges the authority of the *Viper*, or otherwise stands up to the inequities in the system that oppresses the Universal Family. This, in turn, causes the adversarial *Ground Nachash* to strike back at the firstborn's heel, which harms the support of the system and disables the progress of the Universal Family towards health and well-being.

The Viper is the monster in the Dark Night of the Soul, the alchemical element that inculcates the false identity. In the nadir of the Dark Night, its venom causes death or great harm, successfully stopping the hero for a time. However, in the broader mythology, the battle between the asymmetric political system of the adversarial *Ground Nachash* and the symmetric familial system of the firstborn, each time is won by the anointed firstborn in the rebirth of the true or authentic identity.

❖Awakening Mission

At the awakening of Rabbi Jeshua's mission, the purpose of his anointing is both revealed and challenged. Initially, Rabbi Jeshua is baptized by Johanan the Baptist. The sacred breath of *ahav* descends upon Jeshua as a dove, enunciating Father Yahweh's approval of his Anointed Son. Johanan declares Jeshua to be the Lamb of Elohim—a theme that Jeshua develops further in the Passion narrative of the Last Supper identifying himself with the Lamb that is ritually sacrificed and eaten during the Exodus Passover story. In the Passover narrative, the protective blood of the lamb is placed on the doorpost and allows the Messenger of Death to pass over the household, preserving the life of the firstborn child therein. Unlike the second and subsequent born children, the firstborn is anointed to care for the family as the Guardian-Caretaker. He represents the vitality of the family structure—embodying compassion, concern, and responsibility for its well-being. He controlled the larger share of the family inheritance for the purpose of taking care of the clan and carrying on its name. He represented love and sacrifice for the family. If he failed to embody this role because of his own selfishness and greed, the whole family suffered harm. Jeshua is claiming a fundamental responsibility for the well-being of the Universal Family as the anointed firstborn son.

Immediately following his baptismal identification as the Anointed Son, Jeshua wanders out into the wilderness for forty days, where he eventually encounters the Accuser. Operating as the stranger within the unconscious, the Accuser is represented as external to the struggle of Jeshua, but in fact, as with Eve, is a projection of the conflicts lurking within his own conscience that he must face in order to proceed with his journey. As the adversarial Viper/Ground Nachash, the Accuser works to uncover what is hidden in the unconscious of Jeshua, to reveal what is true in context to his egoistic impulse for self-promotion and preservation. Jeshua is faced with his own doubts, desires, and motives to either avoid or else reach his external objective in the easiest and most direct way. He is given the opportunity to take a shortcut to his goal, aborting the Hero's Journey of transformation.

> Then [Jeshua] was led up into the wilderness by the spirit to be tried by the [False Accuser]. And, fasting forty days and forty nights, subsequently He hungers. And, approaching, the trier said to Him, "If you are [Elohim's] Son, say that these stones may be becoming cakes of bread."

Yet He, answering, said, "It is written, `Not on bread alone shall man be living, but on every declaration going out through the mouth of [Elohim].'"

Then the [False Accuser] is taking Him along into the holy city and stands Him on the wing of the sanctuary. And he is saying to Him. "If you are [Elohim's] Son, cast yourself down, for it is written that `His messengers shall be directed concerning Thee' and `On their hands shall they be lifting Thee, Lest at some time Thou shouldst be dashing Thy foot against a stone.'"

[Jeshua] [answering] him, "Again it is written, `You shall not be putting on trial the Lord your [Elohim].'"

Again the [False Accuser] takes Him along into a very high mountain, and is showing Him all the kingdoms of the world and their glory. And he said to Him, "All these to you will I be giving, if ever, falling down, you should be worshiping me."

Then [Jeshua] is saying to him, "Go away, [Accuser], for it is written, The Lord your [Elohim] shall you be worshiping, and to Him only shall you be offering divine service."

Then the [False Accuser] is leaving Him.[104]

Jeshua is faced with his essential hunger, vulnerability, and powerlessness, and challenged to satisfy those needs within the egocentric dynamic of the asymmetric system, to react out of pride, selfishness, and greed. In contrast to Eve and Adam's encounter with the Edenic Nachash, when given a direct path to easily fulfill his personal objective and purpose, Jeshua weighs his choices in context to his relationship with the Father and the manner of his appointment and then chooses to follow the higher path as the Anointed Son, fulfilling his responsibility to the Universal Family. The lower path only accomplishes what was true and beneficial for Jeshua personally, while alienating him from his Spiritual Father and the Universal Family. The higher path will require sacrifice in order to benefit the Family but will transform the mission of the Basar into reality. From this awakening of his purpose, Jeshua starts his journey to fulfill the Basar. His calling is complete. The next leg of his journey is set to begin.

❖Between Earth and Sky

In many moralistic mythologies, the battle is not between the two different types of archetypal power dynamics, but rather between two asymmetric forces vying for control of the one hierarchical system, often between earth and sky. The *Viper* represents a violent chthonic force of the underworld, of the ground, and what lies beneath. The *Viper* either is in a

---

[104] CLV Matthew 4:1-11

continual struggle or is enlisted in a single final cataclysmic battle to overthrow the Sky-God—two cosmic forces of the asymmetric universe vying for supremacy over the cosmos.

In Egyptian mythology, the serpent Apep is in a continual battle with the Sun-God Re, the chief god of the Egyptians. Re must defeat Apep every morning so that the sun may rise from out of the earth and find its proper place in the sky.

In Greek mythology, the great Viper Typhon enters into a final cataclysmic struggle to overthrow the tempestuous Olympian Sky-God Zeus. Typhon is one of the last and most powerful Titans, the son of the primordial Earth Mother Gaia. He matches Zeus in strength and initially defeats him, imprisoning Zeus underground in a cave in Cilicia. Zeus, having had his tendons torn from his limbs and hidden in a bearskin, is left a helpless captive. Two other Olympic gods, Hermes and Aigipan (Goat-Pan) manage to retrieve the tendons and restore them to Zeus, who then is able to continue the epic battle. Zeus finally prevails, burying Typhon under Mount Etna; thus, restoring the order of the Olympic gods over the cosmos.

Likewise, in Christian moralistic mythology, the Christian Satan is imagined to be the second most powerful being that exists. With much broader powers than stated in the text, he acts in fundamental opposition to the Christian-God, the Heavenly Father as Sky-God. The *saw-tan* from the narrative is distorted and expanded significantly as the derivative adversarial entity *Satan*, which, of course, is traditionally identified as the Great Viper in Eden. He is principally the embodiment of evil in contradiction to the goodness of the heavenly Sky-God. In the battle between evil and good, earth and sky, he is the ruler of Hell, typically imagined as under the earth. He is the leader of an army of demons who are attempting to overthrow the Christian-God from his heavenly sky throne. As the serpent in the Garden, he is the primary force behind the fall of Eve and Adam, bringing sin, death, and destruction.

The Christian Satan is a necessity in the moralistic framework of Christianity to embody evil in opposition to good, on which all moralistic mythologies, by definition, are founded. However, as we already have seen with the concept of Hell, this narrative is simply part of the medieval myth that instantiates Christian moralism—it is not a part of the text. It likely, directly or indirectly, evolves from other moralistic mythologies similar to the ones mentioned. It is, in fact, an embellishment of the Judeo-Christian text, filling in and extrapolating ideas from fragments of poetic references and theological imperatives, projecting them into a religious framework.

In the actual Unified Basar and Torah narrative, *saw-tan* represents the failed system of asymmetric power, which is destined to be replaced. *Saw-tan* does not represent a great power in perpetual combat with the Sky-God. It does, however, embody a deeper psychological struggle in the conscience of the Adamites that needs to be engaged in order to transcend the asymmetric power dynamic.

❖Search for Purpose/Bond

In the prefatory chapter proem from the play "Romeo and Juliet"[105] by William Shakespeare, Juliet responds to Romeo's banishment, searching for some way to reconcile her romantic obsession for her beloved Romeo with his deadly insult to her kinsman, Tybalt. In her struggle, she frames the duality of purpose and failure, goodness and badness, in her connection with Romeo, identifying him as a "damned saint" and an "honourable villain."

Psychologically, juvenile moral development begins as a search for purpose and a connection to others—to find a fundamental sense of belonging; a place in a world that supports and challenges us. Initially, this is done for us and to us; learning how the world works through the rules set down by the parental authorities and tribal institutions in our life. Moral awareness develops as we model our behavior based on the knowledge and expectations of our tribal system—what is good and what is bad, what is right and what is wrong, what is safe and what is harmful, what is and what is not. We become reliant on our immediate tribal support system to provide for us; discovering its capabilities and limitations to meet our needs. We explore the world set before us, searching for something that calls to us that makes sense to our sensibilities.

We face our fears and vulnerability through our family and tribal narratives, which we may or may not find adequate to our circumstances. Some will find safety in a form of symmetric relationship within their tribal system, and others will find vulnerability founded on an asymmetric system of abuse and exploitation. We often wander from one moment to the next searching for power and protection; projecting those needs onto objects and people that may or may not be capable of holding those expectations.

In the asymmetric psyche, the villainous *Viper* is at enmity with the healing dynamics that essentially expose our weaker or more vulnerable aspects in the process of moving us towards the symmetric power of the *Lover-Beloved*. The *Viper* attempts to preserve and protect the status quo of

---

[105] Shakespeare (2004) p.111

the egocentric system by destroying the emergent possibilities. The enmity is often experienced in the psyche as an overtly critical or judgmental presence or voice, or else counter-intuitively converted into self-destructive behavior. The negative protective force can be directed towards one's own actions, or as a projective deconstruction of another person's action, evoking anger towards, and attacks on, the person that exhibits the weakness one perceives in oneself. The Ground Nachash fundamentally protects the equilibrium of the internal asymmetric value system, providing the energy to maintain stasis by squashing the mechanics that move us towards wholeness, healing, and mature relationship.

Symbolically, in the juvenile narrative, the immature bond between Eve and Adam is based on vulnerability and missingness, resulting in a puerile attempt to control their circumstances. Their search for purpose is primarily an egocentric endeavor as the archetypal Adamites search for what will make them "happy" or satisfied in context to the societal framework, which defines their value and worth. In the psychology of scarcity, they encounter their own limitations and the fear of want, the awareness of badness that results in competition and conflict between them.

Archetypally, we develop self-awareness through relational experiences that reveal our strengths and weaknesses. As we come to understand our vulnerabilities in relationship, we begin to fence in that which exposes us to attack by others. As we develop our knowledge of goodness and badness, we inculcate a moral value system that guides how we respond to our vulnerabilities in either good or bad ways, building the narrative of our juvenile identity.

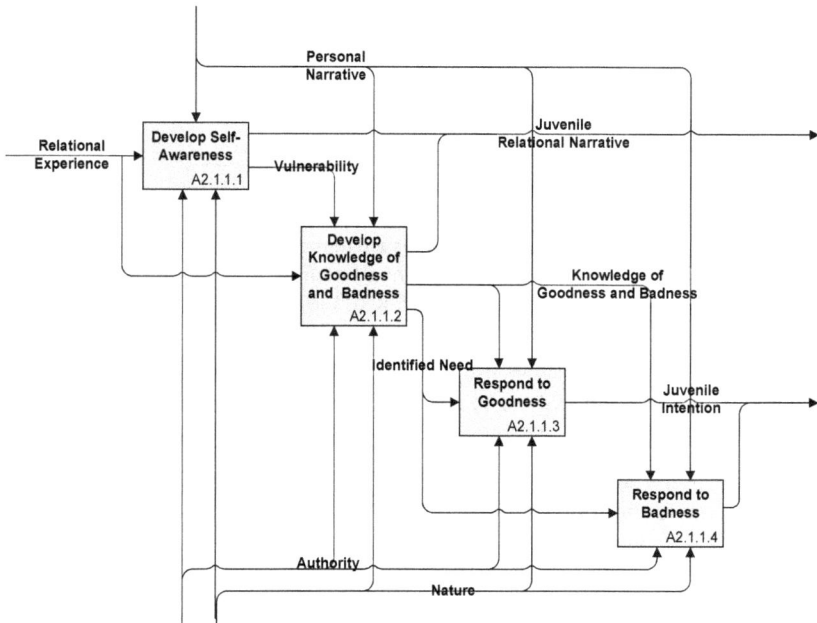

Model 6 - Search for Purpose/Bond (A2.1.1)

CHAPTER [2/1]

IN THE BEGINNING

> In the beginning the Universe was created.
> This has made a lot of people very angry and
> been widely regarded as a bad move.
> —*Douglas Adams*, "The Restaurant at the
> End of the Universe"

The second revelation of the Edenic Nachash is that the Adamites will become like the Imago Elohim by eating the Fruit of Morality—the promise of becoming identified with the greater power of the Creator and Parent Elohim. It is the Awakening to an identity within the framework of the Great Powers, establishing a foundation for personal and relational authority within the developing narrative. In the beginning, the Adamites were already Juvenile Elohim with a limited understanding of their place in the Edenic cosmos and, consequently, had limited access to that intrinsic power represented by the Tree of Knowledge of Goodness and Badness and the Tree of Life. Within Eden, they were under the parental supervision of Yahweh as the archetypal Good Parent. Thus, the pattern of interaction can be surmised to be one of appropriate developmental access to greater levels of power and authority. The implication is that, ultimately, the Knowledge of Goodness and Badness was an adult power to be used within a mature understanding of relationship—within the Reified Basar narrative that develops as the mature understanding of the symmetric power of the Lover-Beloved. In contrast, the Wilderness narrative posits that the Juvenile Elohim gained access to, and responsibility for, the moral awareness prematurely, lacking the understanding of mutuality and love; subsequently leading to the asymmetric development of moralistic hierarchical systems of religion and politics.

At the beginning of the Genesis Creation myth, the Creator Elohim creates the heavens and the earth and everything within and between and declares that it is *tov*/good. The Creator Elohim then fashions the red clay, *adamah*, into the form of Adam and breathes life into him. A guarded place is created for the juvenile Adam to develop and grow in peace and safety in the Garden of Eden. Then, a second Adamite, a sister companion, Eve, is created from the rib of Adam, establishing the opportunity for a mutually beneficial relationship as a family. The Garden of Eden is essentially identified as a place of symmetric relational power, where the Adamites are in a direct, open relationship with the Parent Elohim and one another.

In the mythic narrative, Eve is the second born, the origin and representation of humanity as an inheritance of collective experience and learning. It is important to note that in context to the symmetric relational dynamics of Eden, Eve's identity has nothing to do with the later dysfunctional religious fixation on sexual organs or asymmetric hierarchical gender roles. Whereas Adam, as the firstborn child, goes through several developmental challenges under the direct supervision of the Good Parent to discover his own identity in a test of his curiosity, creativity, and relational needs, Eve's personal narrative is framed as an inheritance, searching for her own meaning and purpose in life through the guidance of her big brother, Adam, to find the source and nature of her own authority and identity.

The role of the firstborn is well developed in the cultural narrative, enough to fill in the enrolled expectations based on the authority of his experience. As the eldest, the family is Adam's responsibility to provide for and protect as the representative of the father in the role of the Guardian-Caretaker. Eve, as the second Juvenile Elohim, is enrolled as the little sister (later as wife) under the immature Guardian-Caretaker supervision of Adam as the firstborn. It is his role to impart his initial experiences to Eve, including the prohibition of eating the fruit of the Tree of Morality. The narrative implies that Adam distorts the initial prohibition, adding his own prohibition to that which the Parent Elohim gave him, telling Eve that she should not even touch the tree, as she, in turn, repeats when she encounters the Edenic Nachash.

There is no narrative of Eve having direct formative experiences in her relationship with the Parent Elohim. Thus, there is an implied dissociation in her understanding of the Parent Elohim, which is filtered through Adam's initial experience. This induces her misunderstanding and distrust of the Parent Elohim's intentions. This distrust is implied to be a pivotal motive in her discussion with the Edenic Nachash. As the big brother, Adam initially misrepresents the Parent Elohim intentions, and then, fails to care for the family, even blaming Eve and the Edenic Nachash for his own failure.

❖**Family Elohim**

At the heart of the Genesis Creation myth is the proclamation that the Adamites are intrinsically identified with the Parent Elohim as his children, created in his ideal image or imago, imbued with his power as Guardian-Caretakers over Creation.

> *And Elohim said: "Let Us make humanity in Our image and according to Our likeness. Let them hold sway over the fish of the sea and over the flyer*

of the heavens, over the domestic beast, over every land animal and over every creeper that is creeping on the earth." So Elohim created humanity in His image; in the image of Elohim He created it: male and female He created them.[106]

The Hebrew term *elohim* literally means "one with great or many powers," but in this context serves as a fundamental trait defining the character and function of a grouping or family of Great Powers. The Adamites, both male and female, are members of this family of ancestral Imago Elohim.

The form of that Great Power is embodied in the two trees at the center of the Garden—the Tree of Morality and the Tree of Life. In its mature form, the Fruit of Morality is act-love—a theme that is developed extensively in the arc of the narrative. The immature Fruit of Morality, conversely, is egotistic pride, selfishness, and greed. The Tree of Life represents the creative life-giving character of the Elohim as Guardian-Caretakers—the giving and supporting of life in each of the animal, plant, and human spheres as an act of Love.

❖Breath of Life

The Genesis Creation myth is the beginning of life, *chay[107]*, which is founded on the word or idea for breathing.[108]

Yahweh Elohim formed the human out of soil from the ground, and He blew into his nostrils the breath of life; and the human became a living soul.[109]

Thus, the compound "breath of life," *chay nesh-aw-maw*, [110] implies "breathing of breath;" in its redundancy, it emphasizes the point that the archetypal breath is the core of our existence—it animates us and inspires our character and actions. Life is the atomic component of our identity—we breathe, we are alive. We have intrinsic value because of this essential awareness and power—to be human, to be *elohim*, is to have this Sacred Breath of the Elohim. Thus, to live is to have the power to interact and influence the world around us. And to be alive is inherently to have value and purpose. The Tree of Life/Breath at the center of the Garden represents the power of the Sacred Breath of Yahweh to instantiate healing and support life perpetually.

---

[106] CLV Genesis 1:26-27
[107] Strongs H2416
[108] Gesenius' Hebrew-Chaldee Lexicon for chaya Strongs H2421
[109] CLV Genesis 2:7
[110] Strongs H5397

The Basar of John starts, "In the beginning was the Word," the *arche logos*—the original word or idea, the breathed purpose and intention for all that exists. The Breath of Life is the essential spermatic component from which all things germinate—the genetic imprint. The Sacred Breath embodies the essential qualities of the *Higher Nachash*—healing, perpetual life, guidance, and judgment. It is a symbol of both fertility and wisdom. It inspires the creation of Adam and spermatically impregnates Mary with the Anointed Child. Rabbi Jeshua describes the Sacred Breath as the *Paraclete*—the helper, or one who comes alongside—that guides humanity towards love as a form of the mature conscience of the *Higher Nachash*.

The Breath of Life infuses all of humanity. An adult is no more or less alive or valuable than a child. A man is no more or less alive or valuable than a woman. A rich man is no more or less alive or valuable than a poor man. A man who has limbs is no more or less alive or valuable than one who has none. A person of one tribal ancestry is no more or less alive or valuable than a person of any other ancestry. And a person of mature moral character is no more or less alive or valuable than a person of immature moral character. Whatever has the Breath of Life has value.

Life is. We all are of one breath—the Sacred Breath of Yahweh. It is our essential identity and value. This shared value of all Elohim, great or small, is the foundation of the Universal Family based on *ahav*, act-love. The underlying meaning of *ahav*[111], is to breathe-after, to breathe in the direction of, and to give life to, another.

❖The Living Soul

This vital impulse of Life is the basis of the power of the Elohim—our ability to influence and be aware of the world around us, to be sentient. The soul of humankind is inherently immeasurable; it is certainly more than the sum of its material parts of cells and tissue, of electrical and magnetic waves pulsing through our nervous system. It has been suggested that it may be some quantum artifact yet to be understood. Thoughts and intentions, emotions and ideations of reality flow seamlessly through physiological pathways we do not fully understand. At best, we can interpret physiognomic constructs through expressed narrative and archetypal forms.

This is not to negate the progress science has made in understanding the neurology and physiology of the brain. We have some sense of loci in the cerebral pathways that generally influence memory and primitive impulses.

---

[111] Strongs H157

The materialists or monists argue that if we poke around enough in the cranium, we can put together an explanation for even complex thought and creative expression. But the epistemological foundations of that are no more reliable than the opposing dualist hypothesis that there is some quantum or alter-dimensional aspect of consciousness, often referred to poetically as the *soul*.

While the metaphysics of consciousness may not be measurable, and therefore provable, the concept of the *psyche* is a narrative artifact. Its construction is understood phenomenologically through the evidentiary patterns it produces in the cultural and personal enterprise of everyday life. The psyche represents the expression of the underlying operational mechanics. It is the product of our experiences in relationship to some immaterial psychogenetic form that operates in predictable patterns, analogous to discerning that there is a joint in our elbow without having the ability to peer beneath the skin. Even without understanding the muscles and connective tissue, I can surmise how the elbow joint bends, and what it is capable of doing. I can also determine what its limitations are by attempting to bend it in the opposite direction, inevitably evincing screams of pain from my unfortunate experimental subject. Modern psychology is founded on applying experimental and observational studies of human behavior to find the patterns that give us evidence of the underlying psychogenetic form hidden behind the veil of our physiological, neurological, or quantum-mechanic self.

❖Sacred Breath

However, the truth of who I am is more than just my existence as a living, breathing being. In the same way that Adam finds no reciprocity in the animal kingdom as he explores each creature's identity and characteristics in the act of naming them, the beginning of self-awareness is just as importantly, who I am not. While I may find a level of companionship with a canine comrade, I will inevitably find that there are limits to that relationship in sharing my hopes and dreams—those things that make me vulnerable in failure and success, disappointment and contentment, sorrow and joy.

There is a sacred dimension to our identity that can only be revealed by our own choice, and to those whom our trust is well-founded; what is called *intimacy*—to know and be known. As such, it is just as important to know that we do not know. We have an obligation to refrain from making attributions of another's identity and character based on assumptions or false attributions; to treat every person's identity and character as sacred and valuable. This is the key foundation of love at the heart of a healthy relationship. It is the core principle that knits together the Unified Basar and Torah mythology.

The Sacred Breath, or *ruach hakodesh*[112] in Hebrew, reveals the identity and purpose of the Parent Elohim. It is portrayed as sexual in nature by its spermatic function of imparting some psychogenetic characteristic of the Parent to the Child. There is a fundamental intimacy to its procreation, inspiring the innate potential of the Imago Elohim into a new life. The slander or vilification of this sacred identity and purpose fundamentally destroys the Sacred Midst between the parent and child Elohim. As Rabbi Jeshua states:

> Therefore I am saying to you, Every [failure] and [slander] shall be [let go of] men, yet the [slander] of the spirit shall not be [let go]. And whosoever may be saying a word against the Son of Mankind, it will be [let go of] him, yet whoever may be saying aught against the [Sacred Breath], it shall not be [let go of] him, neither in this [eon/age] nor in that which is impending.[113]

Once a person distorts and devalues the core truth of another's identity and character, there is no possibility of relationship in the Sacred Midst; whether in regard to the Parent Elohim or another in the Universal Family, the Sacred Midst is dead.

❖Love and Death in Between

In the Genesis Exile story, the death of the Sacred Midst is represented by the separation of the Adamites from the Tree of Life/Breath in the midst of the Garden:

> Then Yahweh Elohim said: "Behold, man has become like one of Us in knowing good and [bad]. Now lest he should stretch out his hand and take also of the tree of life and eat and live for the eon." So Yahweh Elohim sent him out of the garden of Eden to serve the ground from where he was taken. After He drove the human out, He made him [dwell] at the east of the garden of Eden, and He set the cherubim and the flame of the revolving sword to guard the way to the tree of life.[114]

The passage equates eating the fruit of the Tree of Life/Breath with "living for the eon," which becomes a core theme in the narrative arc as the phrase "life eonian," in Hebrew, *chay olam*,[115] and then later in Greek, *zoe aionios*,[116] often translated into English as eternal or perpetual life. However, as

---

[112] Strongs H7307, H2932
[113] CLV Matthew 12:32-33
[114] CLV Genesis 3:22-24
[115] Strongs H2425, H5769
[116] Strongs G2222, G166

previously discussed, the Hebrew concept of life rooted in *chay* is the image of breathing. Thus, the extended image of *chay olam* is the paradigm of continually breathing. Rather than a state of existence, it is a process of a continual activity, the act of breathing as an indication of being alive. The implication is that the eating of the fruit of the Tree of Life/Breath is not a singular event but a continual process. Being separated from the Tree of Life/Breath in the midst of the Garden symbolizes the cessation of breathing, that is, suffocation or dying.

Mythologically and physiologically, life begins when we take our first breath, our breath day, and ends when we breathe our last. Conceptually, that amounts to around six hundred million breaths on average for a person that lives 80 years taking fourteen breaths every minute—the vast majority of these breaths, we are not aware of taking. There is an essential rhythm to breathing—inhale, exhale, repeat. If that rhythm is interrupted, it can be uncomfortable, if not deadly. If you stop breathing for more than 3 to 5 minutes, your brain will begin to cease its functioning, and you will begin to die. Life is a delicate balance, one that we are mostly unaware of sustaining.

The quantity of breaths over our lifetime is irrelevant, other than staying in sync with our body's oxygen requirements. On the other hand, the continuation of breathing is essential, minute by minute, day in, day out. What is buried in the imagery of *chay olam* is that the quantity of breaths, perpetual breathing, is not the point of our existence. The quality of our breathing, embedded in the Hebrew word, *ahav*, to breath-after, breathing life into the Sacred Midst, is what is considered of utmost importance. This is a central theme both in the development of the Torah myth, but also later, in the Reified Basar mythology as demonstrated in the life and ministry of Rabbi Jeshua.

❖Who Am I

In life, who we are, begins with our parents. If our parents are *fish*, then we are *fish*. If our parents are *rocks*, then we are *rocks*. On the sixth day of the Genesis Creation myth, the narrator states:

> And Elohim said: "Let the earth bring forth the living soul, each according to its kind: domestic beast, creeper and land animal, each according to its kind." And it came to be so... And Elohim saw that it was good. And Elohim said: "Let Us make humanity in Our image and according to Our likeness."[117]

---

[117] CLV Genesis 1:24-26

Thus, if our parents are *elohim*, then we are *elohim*, and our siblings and our children will also be *elohim*. Our nature is a product or image of our parent's genetic identity. And yet, we also are essentially distinct from them and unique in our own identity, becoming more so through our own individual experiences and determination—the advent of nature and nurture.

Our individual beliefs and values develop over time, establishing a realization of our existence in a time and a place. They build an operative morality that defines an approach and value for what is realized to be true—a personal knowledge of goodness and badness.

❖**Topography of Moral Development**

Our conscience essentially evolves from a substantive topography of resourcefulness—we either experience the world as sufficient or insufficient to our needs. Our morality emerges in compensation to this judgment. It influences how we see power, both in ourselves and in others. *Authority* within the Genesis Creation myth is founded on the two prominent topographical archetypes: Eden and Midbar-Nod. *Eden* is a place of safety and sufficiency where the Adamites are protected and nourished. They in turn have the responsibility to take care of the plants and animals that inhabit the Garden. There is a womb-like quality to Eden that is supportive of the development of the Juvenile Elohim. On the other hand, *Midbar-Nod* is the wilderness beyond the boundaries of Eden. It is a place of struggle and scarcity where the Adamites must work the ground to feed themselves. It is the domain of the fruit of the Tree of Morality. It can be a place of competition and conflict when led by the lower conscience of selfishness and greed into a deeper state of scarcity, or it also can be a place of cooperation and industry when led by the higher conscience of love and service into a lesser state of scarcity, or even sufficiency.

Scarcity and sufficiency demarcate primitive psychological states that constellate the direction of all other psychic activity. The *scarcity* disposition invokes a sense of fear and vulnerability. It entrenches the psyche into a conservative psychological orientation that promotes the needs of the self over others. It stimulates a narrative of exclusionary authority, of domination and competition. On the other hand, the *sufficiency* disposition invokes a sense of power and competency. It opens the psyche to a liberal psychological orientation that promotes charity and responsibility towards others. It stimulates a narrative of inclusionary authority, of support and cooperation.

There is a recurring narrative of returning to Eden or the place of sufficiency. The central Exodus narrative of the Pentateuch begins in Canaan with the semi-nomadic existence of Abraham, Isaac, and Jacob in a pastoral landscape where the patriarchal economy of the tribe is pretty well self-sufficient due to the nominal wealth of the family and the fertility of the land to sustain them as they move from place to place. Then, the stability of the family of Jacob/Israel is disrupted through a series of circumstances, including the attempted murder of Joseph, a devastating period of famine prompting them to travel to Egypt, where they end up, over generations, becoming enslaved by the Egyptians. Eventually, Moses is called to deliver the Israelites from slavery, and they hightail it out of Egypt, but end up in the desert wilderness for forty years, before finally making it back to Canaan, the land of milk and honey.

The essential power and authority to meet one's basic needs is an important psychological principle. One may be victimized by another who may take what is not theirs to take. However, when one becomes identified as the Victim, that role becomes a fundamental construct of one's identity and personality. It then, formulates how one essentially interacts with the world, enslaved to that role from which there seems to be no escape. "I am a Victim," "I am a Slave," "I am not worthy or capable or powerful enough to handle my needs or to survive on my own." It is the voice of the Master echoing in the identity of the Slave.

In the asymmetric power archetype of the *Victim-Villain-Victor,* our enrollment often becomes compulsory to a greater construction that requires our service to feed its hunger. The Israelites' enslavement in Egypt was not a matter of *convenience* for the parties involved; rather, it served the political narrative of the ruling hierarchy in maintaining their version of civilized order. The patriarchal servitude of women in compulsory roles serves the needs of a ruling class of men. Racist institutions of slavery and subjugation serve the needs of the wealthy and the racial identity of a dominant culture. For those in power, there is no need to change. The roles of Master and Servant are well defined and institutional. The system perpetuates itself through coercion and investment by a conservative authoritarian class.

❖Journey through Scarcity

In the Reified Basar myth, there is a broader universal narrative going from Eden through the scarcity and struggles of human history to return to the sufficiency of the Kingdom of Elohim—the realm of Great Power founded on Love, as defined by Rabbi Jeshua. In the Isaiah Basar, the Anointed/Messiah is empowered to bring the oppressed out of scarcity.

Scarcity is represented in the Reified Basar as evolving out of the oppressive actions of the religious and political establishment of the day. The Pharisees and other religious and political authorities are identified as the Accusers or *Vipers* in the narrative, who use their power and privilege in society to attack the poor and oppressed, marginalizing and disempowering them. In this context, the religious authorities labeled the poor as *Am Ha'aretz,* which literally meant "people of the land" but, at the time, was equivalent to *country bumpkin* or *redneck* with a pejorative overtone of being morally unclean. It is a predominant attitude within moralistic religious sects to label outside groups as *sinful, evil,* or *worthless*; denigrating them as congenital failures that are inherently powerless to please the moral gods. The degenerate class is declared to be the imminent cause of the downfall of society, which justifies their continual marginalization and oppression by the dominant group.

Antithetically, Rabbi Jeshua tells the moralistic Pharisees and religious authorities that they are basically full of shit; they are refuse destined for Gehenna, the town garbage dump. On the contrary, the poor and oppressed are identified as valuable in the eyes of the Father Elohim, who, rather, is seeking to bring them out of their suffering to a place of purposefulness and safety.

❖**Path to Safety**

The psychological state of peace and safety is essential to our sense of wholeness, well-being, and health. Initially, Eden represents a place of peace and safety. As the narrative unfolds other symbols of peace and safety emerge—Canaan, the land of milk and honey; Jerusalem, the city of peace; Messiah, the one anointed to restore peace and safety; and the Kingdom of Yahweh, the realm of peace and safety under the rule of Yahweh's Love.

The Reified Basar narrative is essentially built out of stories evoking a renewed state of peace and safety. The miraculous reparations of Rabbi Jeshua's ministry each demonstrate a path or map into the realm of peace and safety—healing of the sick, comfort and empowerment of the poor and oppressed, the letting go of guilt and condemnation, and the permission to celebrate life and hope. The translation of Rabbi Jeshua's Hebrew name, *Yehoshua,* means "Yahweh brings us to safety"—an invocation of his core mission and identity. This is the heart of the Reified Basar myth. It is a journey from Eden, our descent into Chaos, and then a call to return back to Eden transformed into mature Elohim with a conscience founded on Love.

❖Institutionalizing Scarcity

In contrast to the Unified Basar and Torah proposition that purpose and relationship underlie all life, the moralistic tradition of Greek myth proposes that in the beginning was Chaos or *nothingness*. Aristophanes brings together Hesiod and the Orphic narrations of creation accounts in his play *Birds*:

> At the beginning there was only Chaos [Emptiness], Night, dark Erebus [Darkness], and deep Tartarus [Pit]. Earth, the air and heaven had no existence. Firstly, black-winged Night laid a germless egg in the bosom of the infinite deeps of Erebus, and from this, after the revolution of long ages, sprang the graceful Eros [Love-Attraction] with his glittering golden wings, swift as the whirlwinds of the tempest. He mated in deep Tartarus with dark Chaos, winged like himself, and thus hatched forth our race, which was the first to see the light. That of the Immortals did not exist until Eros had brought together all the ingredients of the world, and from their marriage Heaven, Ocean, Earth and the imperishable race of blessed gods sprang into being.[118]

Darkness generates Eros/Love-Attraction who then mates with Chaos/Emptiness to bring all that is into existence. It is a subtle but important delineation from the Genesis Creation narrative. In moralistic psychology, there is no purpose at the beginning, other than the possibility of an evolving order. It is the foundational psychology of scarcity that necessitates control to instantiate and nurture existence. Disorder, emptiness, and chaos motivate all that evolves from it. It underlines our vulnerability and evokes fear. Eros or Love-Attraction exists but is subject to Chaos, thus all that is to be evolves from nothingness into an order that holds all things together. It is founded on a morality without love that evokes existential terror in the unconscious. Avoidance of Chaos drives humanity into great feats of organization and building, as well as tragic acts of destructiveness and warfare.

The Hesiod/Orphic myth is essentially founded on the topographic archetype of the wilderness narrative but with no pretext, no promise of salvation from its rigor, other than to bring order through control. It inspires the conservative impulse to institutionalize cultural and religious systems dedicated to conformity, predictability, and the appearance of safety.

❖Search for Meaning/Identity

In the beginning chapter proem from the novel "The Restaurant at the End of the Universe"[119] by Douglas Adams, the narrator reframes the creation of the Universe as a botched endeavor, which leads to a search for the conclusive answer to the "Ultimate Question of Life, the Universe, and

---

[118] Aristophanes (2013) Birds p.291
[119] Adams (2008) p.1-2

Everything." As such, a race of hyperintelligent beings build for themselves a gigantic supercomputer named Deep Thought that, after 7.5 million years, finally announces that the answer is, in fact, 42, which promptly impels a new search to figure out what exactly is the Ultimate Question.

Psychologically, juvenile moral development continues as we search for meaning and identity—understanding who we are in the universe around us, and what entities influence us. It develops as we begin to recognize our authority to engage the world and transform it. In Juvenile development our identity is founded on our relationship with our Guardian-Caretaker, the ideal Parent expressed however competently through our real Parents. Our awareness of the world is deeply influenced by the capacity and character of those in our support environment.

Symbolically, the identity of the two Adamites is not fully formed. As a result, there is uncertainty and distrust between them. The search for identity is not satisfied in mirroring the imperfections of the other. The suggestion of a common humanity between the juvenile Eve and Adam based on scarcity and vulnerability is untenable as the archetypal Adamites reach for moral perfection according to some conceptual ideal of what another should be in relationship, an expectation to which they cannot measure up.

Archetypally, at this stage of development, either we come to recognize our creative power and authority, or else we collapse into abject infantilism. Our identity becomes a reflection of the parental image that establishes our personal mythology of who we are. When our experience of our parents is adequate and sufficient to our needs for protection and survival, we begin to identify ourselves as capable and competent. When our experience of our parents is inadequate and insufficient, in diminution we suppose that we are eternally dependent on an egocentric parental entity for all our needs, incapable of any independent identity apart from their control.

Model 7 - Search for Meaning/Identity (A2.1.2)

Chapter [3/I]

In The Name of the Father

> Let me take you to the hurting ground
> where all good men are trampled down
> just to settle a bet that could not be won
> between a prideful father and his son.
> —Bad Religion, "Sorrow"

The last revelation of the Edenic Nachash is that the Adamites will not die from eating the Fruit of Morality, nor will they be struck down or destroyed by the Parent Elohim—their lives will be preserved. The myth evolves out of a dialectic tension between a direct warning by Yahweh Elohim stating, "from the tree of the knowledge of good and [bad], you must not eat from it; for on the day you eat from it... you shall be dying"[120], followed by the Nachash revealing that, "Not... shall you be dying; for Elohim knows that on the day you eat of it your eyes will be unclosed, and you will become like Elohim, knowing good and [bad]."[121] The paradox is resolved as the narrative unfolds subsequent to eating the fruit:

> Then the eyes of both of them were unclosed, and they realized that they were naked. So they sewed fig leaves together and made girdle skirts for themselves. Then they heard the sound of Yahweh Elohim walking about in the garden in the windy part of the day, and the human hid himself with his wife from the face of Yahweh Elohim among the trees of the garden... Yahweh Elohim called to the human and said to him: "Adam, where are you?" He replied to Him: "I heard the sound of You walking in the garden, and I was fearful because I was naked; so I hid." Then He asked: "Who told you that you are naked unless you have eaten from the only tree that I instructed you by no means to eat from it?"[122]

The Edenic Nachash's statement is correct, the fruit is not toxic, and they do not die as a result of eating the fruit, nor are they struck dead by an angry, vengeful god. However, the unclosing of their eyes brings an immature critical awareness of their frailty and fragility—a sudden realization of separateness and aloneness. The experience of communion, trust, and safety within the Sacred Midst of the intimate relationship between the children and their

---

[120] CLV Genesis 2:17
[121] CLV Genesis 3:4-5
[122] CLV Genesis 3:7-11

parent dies. The children immediately feel naked and vulnerable, hiding themselves in fear when the Parent Elohim comes to visit.

At the beginning of the Genesis myth, the Juvenile Elohim are born of the spermatic breath of life and the maternal red clay of the earth. As the narrative unfolds, we discover that the breath, *ruach,* or spirit, is permanent, it cannot be destroyed, but the clay of the body is not. In the Edenic cosmos, physical death is not addressed directly; however, it is inferred by the existence of the Tree of Life/Breath that must be present to bring vitality to the Adamites. In the Exile narrative, the Parent Elohim indicates that their immature morality cannot be allowed to persist indefinitely and thus the Adamites are removed from the Tree of Life/Breath in the Sacred Midst of the Garden. As a result of this separation, they are told their bodies will not be renewed, but instead will eventually return to the dust from which they came. This is the Dark Night of ego death in the narrative represented as the dying of the Sacred Midst.

In the mythologies of the Ancient Near East, death is universally presented as the journey of the soul to a different land, to some form of chthonic underworld such as *Mot, Duat, Sheol,* or *Hades.* As noted in *A Dictionary of Ancient Near Eastern Mythology*:

> *Death as a complete annihilation is a modern concept and that all ancient and 'primitive' peoples believe in the continued existence of the 'soul' (in Egypt ka). As a 'spirit' or 'shade' it will live on in the Underworld. The communication between the two spheres was unilateral; whoever entered the underworld had to stay in it for ever ('The Land of No Return').*[123]

Similarly, in the Torah, death is described as being gathered to one's forefathers, to rejoin the ancestral family going back through time. Thus, the metaphysics of permanence within the mythology is defined in context to the family. As such, it is also expanded as one moves forward through time in the family inheritance of the firstborn, whose responsibility it is to carry on the tribal lineage of the father. Thus, the life of the Adamites will continue on in perpetuity through the subsequent generations of the family—the promise of an immortal bloodline grounded in the continuity and bond of the family heritage within the boundary of the Universal Family under the care of the Parent Elohim.

At the heart of the myth, life is lived in relationship to the family, embodied in the Sacred Midst between its members. In the Genesis Exile myth, the Sacred Midst between parent and child does die due to the

[123] Leick (2002) p.35 "Dying Gods"

children's act of hubris, unforeseen by the Adamites or the Edenic Nachash, evoking the terror of nakedness within the Juvenile Elohim. Yet, the Sacred Midst can, and is resurrected back to life, nurtured to wholeness and well-being in the subsequent Exodus and Basar mythologies.

Eventually, the form and condition of the permanence of *ruach* evolve further within the narrative arc of the Unified Basar and Torah mythology. An unusual premise of a resurrection from the Land of the Dead is described, initially within the poetry of David and the prophecies of Isaiah and Daniel, and then more extensively in the teachings of Rabbi Jeshua, in which a metaphysical resurrection of the *ruach* becomes a central theme.

❖Mark of Cain

Conversely, at the heart of all moralistic religious systems is the course and justification of divine retribution—the punishment of the serving class for breaking the divine codes of behavior and servitude. The curse of the gods may involve famine, conquest, enslavement, torture, infertility, or death. An entire family may be wiped out for the *sins*/guilt of the father.

This, however, is conspicuously not the case in the familial moral system of the Unified Basar and Torah—the Parent Elohim is not obligated or interested in enforcing a hierarchical code of submission. The Adamites are not struck down for stealing the fruit. Cain is not killed for killing his brother. When faced with the overwhelming violence of the antediluvian society, Yahweh still preserves the Adamic heritage through Noah in the ark, and then makes a promise never to enact such severe judgment ever again.

The Parent Elohim disciplines his children out of compassion and love, not some form of narcissistic vengeance. The Good Father desires for his children to mature into the fullness of their potential and, as such, his primary trait is founded on mercy, not vengeance. In the Exile of Cain, the mark that is placed on Cain is, in fact, a mark of protection and mercy, not one of shame as it is often portrayed.

> Cain replied to Yahweh: *"Too great is my depravity to bear. Since You drive me out today, off the surface of the ground, and since I shall be concealed from Your presence and will become a rover and a wanderer on earth, it will come to be that anyone finding me shall kill me."*
>
> Yet Yahweh said to him: *"Not so; anyone killing Cain, sevenfold shall he be avenged."* So Yahweh placed a sign for Cain, by no means to smite him, should anyone find him.[124]

---

[124] CLV Genesis 4:13-15

The Mark of Cain is a visible anointing—a powerful symbol of the Parent Elohim's protection of his children even in the midst of sorrow and judgment. Cain lives a full life and embodies many great things, thereafter, becoming the archetypal founder of civilization and human achievement. The Parent Elohim disciplines his children within the context of a loving family relationship, not as an egocentric tyrant who cannot tolerate disorder as in Zeus' punishment of Asclepius and Prometheus, or the Christian Holy Father who brutally tortures anyone who fails his law in the fiery pit of the Christian Hell.

❖**Ancient Family**

In ancient psychology, the *family* was the root of well-being, safety, and continuity. In modern western philosophy and psychology, the *individual* is often reimagined as the root construct from which we get our core principles of life, liberty, and happiness as a product of individualism and self-determination. In order to understand the Unified Basar and Torah myth, the reader must reconsider these modern preconceptions that found our operative bias. The family or tribe was essential to survival. without which there was no salvation. Banishment from family or tribe often meant death, as exemplified by Cain's protestation in the mythic narrative.

While the principle of *family* was sacred, it still could operate as a construct under the moral authority of either the inclusive symmetric *Lover-Beloved* archetype of the Good Parent and the Anointed Firstborn, or the exclusive asymmetric *Victim-Villain-Victor* archetype of the Chief, King, or Tyrant of the Clan. The tradition of primogeniture proscribes that the firstborn son inherited the responsibility to take care of the clan, once the father died, to carry on his name. The Anointed Son was given a larger portion of the inheritance, not as a matter of privilege, but rather, in order to maintain the core identity, property, and relationships of the tribe, including the father's surviving wives and unmarried sons and daughters. The subsequent-born males, once they married would get a lesser inheritance, and could either form a new clan or stay in the Father's clan, under the authority of the anointed firstborn son. These traditions were generally applied throughout the cultures of ancient Mesopotamia and the Levant but had local variations. While the responsibility of the Anointed Firstborn as Guardian-Caretaker of the family originates in the symmetric family unit, it also is abstracted in the right of the ascension of kingship in the asymmetric political model, where the firstborn inherits the throne.

❖**Who Beget Whom**

The primordial origin myth of the Torah begins with the first-generation family of the ancestral Imago Elohim, headed by Yahweh, begetting his children, Eve and Adam, in the Garden of Eden. Then, it tells the story of the second-generation family headed by Yahweh's firstborn, Adam, begetting his children Cain, Abel, and Seth in the wilderness of Midbar-Nod. And then, it ends that section of myth, with the story of the family of Noah begetting his children, Shem, Ham, and Japheth, in the antediluvian world, where, after the world is wiped out in the flood, they originate the new world order of ancient tribes known to the Mesopotamians.

Interspersed between these stories, and also prefacing the patriarchal myth of Abraham, and later, at the beginning of the myth of the Reified Basar, are long lists of who beget whom, detailing in elaborate particularity the concourse of ancestral lineage going back to the beginning of mythological time. It was requisite to know the origins and history of your family clan as it formed your essential identity and authority. As a mythology, it also connects all humanity into one Universal Family originating in the spermatic breath of a singular Parent Elohim.

❖Father Abraham

The story of Abraham is at the heart of the Yahweh myth in the Torah. Abraham is a descendent of Shem, also referred to as Shemites, or alternately, Semites, based on the Genesis genealogy of nations. According to the postdiluvian Noah myth, the Semites are the indigenous peoples of Mesopotamia. The Early Bronze Age myth of Father Abraham provides a structural narrative for various Semitic tribes that migrate to the Levant and the Arabian Desert as descendants of the patriarch Abraham, which inherit some, or all, of the Yahweh tradition. This includes, of course, the tribe of Israel, which is identified as Yahweh's favored Shemite nation and, later, as the functional firstborn of nations.

The mythological identity of Abraham begins with his given name *Abram*, which means "exalted father."[125] Later, after the birth of his firstborn, Ishmael, Yahweh changes Abram's name to *Abraham* meaning "father of a multitude,"[126] declaring:

> *I am El Who-Suffices [Shaddai/The Many Breasted One]; walk before Me and become flawless. I am determined to give My covenant between Me and you. I shall increase you exceedingly... You will become the father of a throng of nations. So your name shall no longer be called Abram; but your name will become Abraham.*[127]

---

[125] Strongs H87
[126] Strongs H85
[127] CLV Genesis 17:1-5

This becomes his core mythological identity throughout the arc of the narrative.

The story, however, begins, if we assume the most obvious locations with the ascribed names, in the ancient Mesopotamian city of Ur at the bottom of the River Euphrates. Abram along with his father, Terah, and family migrate upriver to Harran at the top of the Euphrates River valley, in the plains of the upper crescent, ostensibly on their way to the land of Canaan-Levant. They stay in Harran until after Terah's death of old age when Yahweh calls Abram to continue his journey to Canaan. Harran becomes the tribal homeland throughout the Patriarchal narrative of Abraham, Isaac, and Jacob, which draws Abraham's grandson, Jacob, back to Harran to find a wife (or two). By the time Abram, "the exalted father," arrives in Canaan, he and his wife Sara are older, without an heir, and despairing. Yahweh comes to Abram in a vision saying:

> You must not be fearing, "Abram! I am your Shield, your exceedingly increased Reward." Abram replied: "My Lord Yahweh, what shall You give to me? I am going heirless, and the successor to my house—he will be Damascus Eliezer... Behold, You have given no seed to me; and now a son of my household will take over from me." Yet here the word of Yahweh came to him saying: "Not this one shall take over from you, but rather the one who shall come forth from your internal parts, he shall take over from you." Then He brought him forth outside and said: "Now look up toward the heavens and count off the stars if you can number them... Thus shall become your seed."[128]

This is the foundation of the origin myth of several nations in the Levant and the Arabian Desert and the original promise that Abraham's descendants will have a broader, universal impact on humankind.

The land of Canaan becomes the promised land of Abraham's favored children. In the earlier Noahic myth, Ham and his son Canaan are cursed when Ham fails to respect his father's dignity during a bout of naked drunkenness. Thus, the mythological tribes of Canaan, descendants of Ham, are cursed to serve the descendants of Shem and Japheth. According to the ascribed genealogy, Abraham is a descendant of Shem, which sets up his inheritance of the lands of Canaan in the Patriarchal narrative. The narrative portrays the blessed Shemite/Semite civilizations of Mesopotamia—Babylon, Assur, and Akkad—as the forbearers of Abraham and thus Israel, up and against the cursed Hamite civilizations of Canaan and Egypt. A recurring theme in the Torah myth is the admonishment that Israel remembers that

---

[128] CLV Genesis 15:1- 5

they were once strangers in the land, and to always treat immigrants with loving-kindness and courteous generosity. However, as outsiders in the land, they were also admonished not to worship the idol gods of the Canaanites whose lands they occupied, or with whom they became neighbors.

Abraham is an immigrant throughout the myth. He is a nomadic herdsman, living alongside other nomadic tribesmen and previously settled cities in the region. His firstborn son is Ishmael, conceived with his wife Sara's Egyptian handmaid Hagar. Ishmael becomes the father of many nomadic desert tribes known in the narrative as the Twelve Princes, which mirror the Twelve Tribes of Abraham's grandson Jacob/Israel (by his secondborn Isaac), who were also nomadic herdsmen. According to the Exodus myth, it is not until much later, after returning to Canaan from slavery in Egypt that the Israelite tribes colonize the lands of Canaan—driving out the Hamite tribes to build cities, develop agriculture, and establish a relatively permanent presence in the lands. Based on the timeline given within the myth, the National Age of Israel covers a period of two millennia from the early Bronze Age through the Iron Age into Classical Antiquity, nominally indicated as 1800 BCE to 136 CE.

❖Scorned Birthright

The cultural tradition of primogeniture allowed the patriarch, in exceptional situations, to scorn the birthright of the firstborn *bakar* who had lost favor in his sight, to anoint a subsequently birthed son as the family caretaker. However, in the Torah, this exceptional practice of scorning the primacy of the birthed firstborn is the not-so-subtle predominating pattern. Adam's firstborn son, Cain, is hereditarily scorned and replaced by the thirdborn son Seth as an act of punishment, although archetypally Cain retained his functional designation as the prototypic firstborn of Adam founding the asymmetric cultural heritage of humanity. Abraham's firstborn son Ishmael is scorned and functionally replaced by the secondborn son Isaac as a matter of favoritism and prophesy. Isaac's firstborn son Esau is scorned and functionally replaced by the secondborn son Jacob as a matter of rashness and deception. Jacob's firstborn son Reuben is scorned and functionally replaced by Joseph as a matter of favoritism and punishment.

Likewise, the premise of the Reified Basar myth is that Jeshua is the anointed firstborn son and Guardian-Caretaker of Creation who replaces Adam, the scorned firstborn of Creation. Consequently, Jeshua reestablishes the favor of the Universal Adamic Family, superseding Israel as the scorned firstborn of nations, which had already been declared by the prophets

Jeremiah and Isaiah centuries prior, foreshadowing the end of the National Age brought about by the destruction of Jerusalem and the Second Temple.

A more archetypic depiction of the scorned firstborn is Matsor/Egypt, the fortress of civilization and human achievement throughout the narrative arc. Cain, the firstborn of Adam, is the idiosyncratic progenitor of Matsor, epitomized as the masters of agriculture, city building, metallurgy, and the arts. In the Passover narrative, this comes into sharp focus when the firstborn of Matsor/Egypt are contrasted with the anointed firstborn of Yahweh/Israel. The Israelite firstborn under the anointing of the blood of the firstling lamb on the doorpost are protected, characteristically marking them as the favored nation of Yahweh throughout the National Age. The firstborn of the land of Matsor, not under that marking, are subsequently left to the judgment of the Messenger of Death, removed from the blessing of primogeniture.

❖**Jealousy and Conflict**

Often within the moralistic mythologies, the familial relationship between father and son is denigrated as an asymmetric political struggle, punctuated by the son eventually overthrowing the control of the father. In Greek mythology, the origin story of the family of gods describes a dysfunctional family that is driven by pride, jealousy, and conflict—a generational struggle over power and status to control the order of the universe. The central familial characters are Uranus, Cronus, and Zeus—the successive generations of the rulers of the cosmos, each begat by the previous generation. Each child is as vicious and power-hungry as the parent that came before. Yet in each transition, there is also a conflated sense of justice in the demise of the preceding parent based on an egoistic morality, as the fears and sins of the father are met with retribution by the son, ostensibly done in protection of their siblings and mother, only then, to be reenacted by the next generation.

In the Hesiod tradition, after Chaos bore Gaia/Earth, she, in turn, bore Uranus/Heaven "equal to herself, so he could cover her around, and she might serve the deathless gods as firm, eternal ground."[129] Then, in union with Uranus, Gaia bore many children, which became known as the race of Titans. But Uranus despised his children:

And [Uranus] hid [his children] all away, as soon as they were born, deep in the earth; he took delight in doing this wicked deed and did not let them reach the light. But Gaia, thronging inwardly, prodigious, gave a groan, and she devised a crafty piece of cunning of her own. She made a kind of metal that was gray and very hard, fashioned a scythe and showed her

---

[129] Hesiod (2006) p.27

children what she had prepared; and though she grieved in her own heart, to make them bold she said: "O children, born to me and of a father who is bad, we'll take an evil vengeance on him, if you should agree: If anyone was first to do things shameful, it was he."

She spoke thus, but fear gripped them; not a single word resounded till great and wily [Cronus/Control], taking courage, thus responded In speech addressing his dear mother: "Mother, I promise you, I'll take this task upon myself and do what I must do. I do not scruple about our ill-named father; for as you see, if anyone was first to do things shameful, it was he." He finished, and gigantic Gaia's heart with joy expands. She hides him in an ambush and she places in his hands a saw-toothed sickle and explains the cunning stratagem.

Great [Uranus] came bringing on the night, and as he came he lay outstretched on Gaia in his longing to make love and then his son in ambush reached his left hand out and drove the sickle with his right hand (it was toothed and of great length), and hacked his father's genitalia off with all his strength. [130]

Cronus/Control having castrated his father, Uranus/Heaven, then releases his siblings from their imprisonment and becomes the ruler of the Titans and the whole of the universe. But in turn, Cronus turns on his own children having been told by his parents Gaia and Uranus that his destiny was to be overthrown by one of them:

When Rhea had been subdued by [Cronus], she bore a glorious brood: Hestia and Demeter and then Hera, …Hades, …the Shaker-of-Earth, …and cunning Zeus, the father of the gods and mortals too... But these the mighty [Cronus] swallowed up as soon as from out of their mother's holy womb each toward her knees would come, deeming that no one else but he, of those who dwell on high, should hold the rank of king among the gods who never die... giving Rhea endless sorrow.

Now when [Rhea] was about to bear …Zeus, she begged her own… dear parents then, Gaia and starry Ouranos, to help her make a plan so that she might give birth unseen... They… gave heed, and showed her what had been foretold to happen... So when she was about to bear great Zeus… they sent her off to… Crete. Gaia took [the newborn] child… hid him underground [in a cave]... But to [Cronus]… a huge rock wrapped in swaddling clothes she gave to be devoured... Not knowing that he'd swallowed rock… his son was left behind unconquered and unharmed— that very soon he would be overwhelmed by force, abandoned, overthrown, deprived of status and his son made ruler in his place. [131]

Zeus, eventually, overthrows his father Cronus, sets free his siblings, and then sets free his father's siblings, the Titans, who had been imprisoned earlier by Cronus. In gratitude, the Titans gave him thunder and lightning, the glowing

---

[130] Hesiod (2006) p.27-28
[131] Hesiod (2006) p.37-38

thunderbolt which he uses as a Sky-God to oversee both mortals and immortals alike.

Zeus becomes the final ruler of the cosmos for the rest of the Olympic mythology. However, he continually needs to defend his status, thwarting any challenge to his authority. The Titans eventually rebel, and Zeus must fight them. After finally conquering them, he sends them into exile in the great pit, Tartarus. Then within the realm of Mount Olympus, in order to maintain his place of supremacy, he devours his competition.

> Now Zeus, as king of gods, took Metis first to wife: she knew the most and was the wisest of the gods and death-born men. But when she was about to bear gray-eyed Athena, then he craftily deceived her with a guileful speech, and down his belly thrust her to the very bowels—this was done on Gaia's shrewd advice and that of starry Ouranos; for they two had made known to him that no one else but Zeus among the deathless gods should have the kingly privilege; for otherwise there would have come a crafty lineage from her by fate: the gray-eyed Tritogeneia [Athena] first, whose force was equal to her father's and whose wisdom was not worse; and next she would have borne a king of gods and men, a child having a proud and mighty spirit, passionate, strong-willed; but Zeus, before that happened, thrust her in his belly, so the goddess might advise him if a thing were good or no.[132]

So, Zeus continues to rule supreme over mortal and immortal alike, with the power of his thunderbolt (and the immensity of his stomach).

Under the discontinuous influence of Chaos without Love, the characters compositely are identified with Jealousy and Conflict. The *Child-Parent* bond fails as each successive generation tries to avert the challenge of the next generation. Threat and distrust transform the symmetry of the loving family bond of *Child-Parent* into the asymmetric power-conflict relationship of *Victim-Villain-Victor*. Order is established by the hierarchy of authoritarian rule in which only one power can be victorious, subjugating all others—favored Light defeats wily Control which previously defeated starry Heaven. Ultimately, the order of the Olympian cosmos is governed by the Thunderbolt, symbolizing Zeus, and his wrath towards, and control over, any who would challenge this Order.

❖The Ultimate Sacrifice

In the myth of Uranus, Cronus, and Zeus, there is an archetypal theme of the controlling Father victimizing and devouring his children. In the Phoenician city of Carthage, the worship of Cronus was a ritual reenactment

---

[132] Hesiod (2006) p.50-51

of his brutal devouring of his children. The first century BCE Sicilian historian Diodorus Siculus (20.14) wrote concerning the sacrifice of children to Cronus:

> *Therefore the Carthaginians, believing that the misfortune had come to them from the gods, betook themselves to every manner of supplication of the divine powers... They... alleged that Cronus had turned against them inasmuch as in former times they had been accustomed to sacrifice to this god the noblest of their sons, but more recently, secretly buying and nurturing children, they had sent these to the sacrifice; and when an investigation was made, some of those who had been sacrificed were discovered to have been supposititious. When they had given thought to these things and saw their enemy encamped before their walls, they were filled with superstitious dread, for they believed that they had neglected the honours of the gods that had been established by their fathers. In their zeal to make amends for their omission, they selected two hundred of the noblest children and sacrificed them publicly; and others who were under suspicion sacrificed themselves voluntarily, in number not less than three hundred.*

> *There was in their city a bronze image of Cronus, extending its hands, palms up and sloping toward the ground, so that each of the children when placed thereon rolled down and fell into a sort of gaping pit filled with fire... Also the story passed down among the Greeks from ancient myth that Cronus did away with his own children appears to have been kept in mind among the Carthaginians through this observance.* [133]

The earliest version of the Cronus myth has been connected archetypally, if not historically, to the Phoenician worship of *Baal Hammon*, which was sometimes referred to as *Cronus*. The fourth-century bishop, Eusebius claims to quote the now lost works of an ancient historian Sanchoniatho as describing the Phoenician practice:

> *It was the custom among the ancients, in times of great calamity, in order to prevent the ruin of all, for the rulers of the city or nation to sacrifice to the avenging deities the most beloved of their children as the price of redemption: they who were devoted this purpose were offered mystically. For Cronus, whom the Phoenicians call Il [El]... [as king before he was deified] when great dangers from war beset the land he adorned the altar, and invested [his only] son with the emblems of royalty, and sacrificed him.* [134]

A similar practice of child sacrifice is adopted by the Phoenician's southern neighbors in the Kingdom of Judah.

The Chronicles of the Jewish Histories indicate that the Judahites of the kingdoms of Ahaz and Manasseh began sacrificing their children to Baal/Lord

---

[133] Siculus (2011) Book XX sec. 20.14
[134] Sanchoniatho (1828) p.15

just outside the southwestern walls of Jerusalem in the Valley of Ben Hinnom (later known as Gehenna). In the resulting judgment of the Judahites in the book of Jeremiah, Yahweh Elohim portends the destruction of Jerusalem and the First Temple by a future conquering army, saying to the kings of Judah and the inhabitants of Jerusalem:

> Lo, I am bringing in [brokenness] on this place... because that they have forsaken Me, and make known this place, and make perfume in it to other elohims [Great Powers], that they knew not, they and their fathers, and the kings of Judah, and they have filled this place [with] innocent blood, and have built the high places of Baal [the Lord] to burn their sons with fire, burnt-offerings to Baal [the Lord], that I commanded not, nor spoke of, nor did it come up on My heart. Therefore, lo, days are coming... and this place is not called any more, Tophet [the place of burning[135]], and Valley of the son of Hinnom, but, Valley of slaughter.

> And I have made void the counsel of Judah and Jerusalem in this place, and have caused them to fall by the sword before their enemies, and by the hand of those seeking their life, and I have given their carcass for food to the fowl of the heavens, and to the beast of the earth, and I have made this city for a desolation, and for a hissing, every passer by it is astonished, and does hiss for all its plagues. And I have caused them to eat the flesh of their sons, and the flesh of their daughters, and each the flesh of his friend they do eat, in the siege and in the straitness with which straiten them do their enemies, and those seeking their life...

> Thus do I break this people and this city, as one breaks the potter's vessel, that is not able to be repaired again... so I do to this place... and to its inhabitants, so as to make this city as Tophet; and the houses of Jerusalem, and the houses of the kings of Judah, have been... defiled, even all the houses on whose roofs they have made perfume to all the host of the heavens, so as to pour out oblations to other elohims [Great Powers].[136]

Shortly thereafter Jerusalem is destroyed by the Neo-Babylonians and the defeated Judahites are exiled to Babylon, which closes the Political Kingdom Age and ushers in the Vassal Kingdom Age.

Mythologically, the Valley of Ben Hinnom beneath Mount Zion becomes synonymous with the place of murder, betrayal, and subsequent judgment of the Jerusalemites' desolate child-sacrificing idolatry and moralistic worshipping of other elohims, which Rabbi Jeshua will later refer to as the "judgment of Gehenna." Thereafter, it has been proposed that the fires of Baal were symbolically turned into a perpetually burning garbage dump by later generations. The fire would have been fed by throwing brimstone (sulfur), which was plentiful in the area of the Dead Sea, onto the heap to stoke the flames in order to consume the stench of the rotting garbage. In the

---

[135] Either "the place of drums" or "the place of burning"
[136] CLV Jeremiah 18:23-19:13

framework of the Gospel/Basar mythology, the subsequent destruction of Jerusalem and the Second Temple during the First Jewish War is portrayed as a secondary fulfillment of the "judgment of Gehenna" by fire, which closes the National Age and ushers in the Universal Kingdom Age.

Similarly, a pietistic doctrine of child sacrifice will evolve out of the neo-apostle Paul's moralized gospel as a central tenet in many Christian theologies, claiming that the Holy Father sacrificed his only son on the cross to demonstrate his love in order to save humanity from the penalty of Sin. This conspicuously ignores the aforementioned interdiction in Jeremiah wherein Yahweh proclaims his anger at the spilling of "innocent blood" that led to the utter destruction of Jerusalem and both institutional Temples. It is, of course, an utter contradiction to both Jeremiah's Judgment of Gehenna and the relationalistic mythos of the Basar/Gospel of Rabbi Jeshua.

❖Search for Value/Boundary

The preceding chapter proem is a stanza from the song "Sorrow"[137] by the punk band, Bad Religion, which probes the valuelessness of the suffering of the Biblical patriarch Job, prefaced in the first stanza of the song, "Father, can you hear me? How have I let you down?" Instigated by a senseless "bet that could not be won between a prideful father and his son," Job is a "good man" who is victimized by the Adversarial Elohim, Saw-Tan, representing the asymmetric power dynamic of the world system. Job's personal boundaries are "trampled down," fomenting his desolation and ruin. Archetypally, the Father in the song evokes the moralized family relationships of the Olympic mythology based in pride and conflict. Yet principally, the Job myth shows that there is no moralistic relationship between human behavior and the blessings or trials of the Supreme El (and essentially depicting a mythic truism that it never bodes well when one discovers oneself the star in the opening scene of a morality play, a lesson the Israelites will subsequently learn in the later mythography leading up to the Jewish Exiles and Apocalypse.) The ancient myth of Job predates the Torah myth and certainly does not follow the loving Parent Elohim paradigm of the Yahweh tradition. Rather than a relational myth, the primitive construct of the Job myth is functionally a repudiation of the traditional moralistic narratives of transactional idolatry, which advocates that the idol god's blessing is a result of the supplicant's deservedness. On the contrary, in the Job myth, value and boundaries are not defined by status or power, instead the myth crassly argues that *shit happens,*

---

[137] Bad Religion (2002)

deal with it, don't blame the gods—scarcity and sufficiency are not obligatory outcomes based on meritocratic system of behavior. Later in the Reified Basar myth, this meritocratic idolatry is reprised in the cultural views of the wealthy elite, the Pharisees and Sadducees, whose social and economic status is touted to be a blessing from the Jewish God. In the pivot of the song, the main author, Brett Gurewitz, proposes that "if every living soul could be upright and strong… Well then, I do imagine… there will be sorrow no more"—humanity's ultimate salvation is our acceptance of the value we have in community to ultimately bring us to safety, to love one another.

Psychologically, juvenile moral development progresses as we search for our values and boundaries in response to the world around us and those entities that influence our well-being. It develops as we begin to impact the world and discover value in it. In juvenile morality, our boundaries are founded on our perception of our relationship with our Guardian Caregiver. We are a reflection of the values we discover in the character of those that influence us, that represent authority to us. At this stage of development, we either come to recognize our own value reflected back at us from the world we inhabit, or we experience rejection and devaluation from the villainous forces that prey upon us, or likely, some combination of both.

Symbolically, the boundaries of the juvenile Eve and Adam are broken; the relationship between them is founded on an asymmetric power dynamic based on advantage and disadvantage. The immature valuation is established by the usefulness of the other to the evaluator's egocentric objectives and ideals.

Archetypally, as we differentiate our place and role within our tribal and familial groups, our hierarchical rank and status are established based on our relationship to the existing power structure, which becomes internalized as our belief in our own self-worth. In this asymmetric power dynamic, we are forced to contend with our vulnerability to the value system of the dominant culture and we order our lives accordingly.

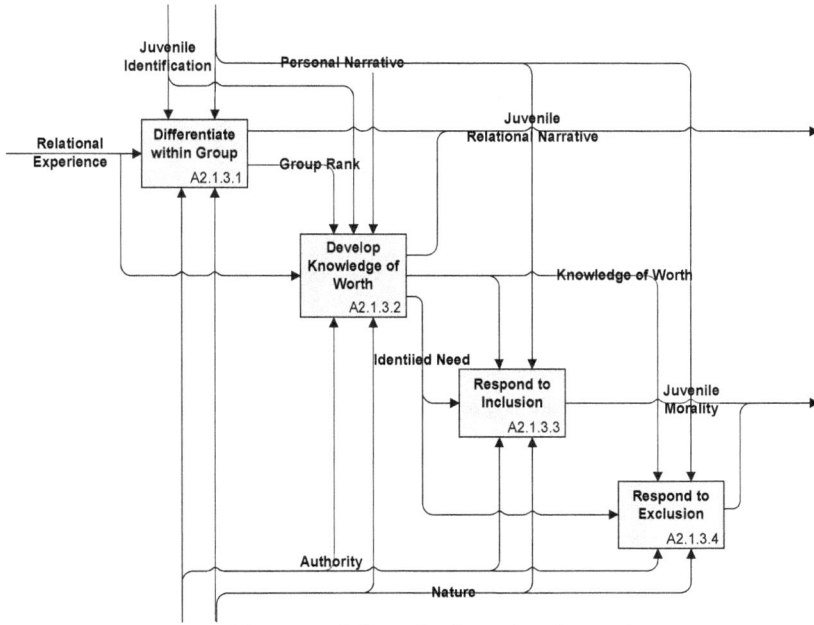

Model 8 - Search for Value/Boundary (A2.1.3)

156

Part II

Ahav – The Torah of Obligation

Sitting alone next to my father, holding his hand as the warmth drained from his arm, growing colder with each second. Only a few minutes have passed since he exhaled his last breath. The nurse had struggled for the past half hour to calm the rattle of his labored breathing as he stared incoherently off into the corner, as best as I could tell, unaware of my presence. He had deteriorated rapidly over the last couple of weeks retreating into a liminal state between worlds, becoming less responsive with each day; a crumpled shell of his former self as his mortal coil came

The Kiss of Death. Ferran Pestaña. Photo. 2010.

unwound. His heart had finally worn out—a peculiar thought as I sat there wondering about his pacemaker trying to perform its intrepid task against a lifeless heart. It mirrored the emptiness and futility I felt sitting beside his lifeless body, searching for quiescence in the utter frustration of death.

My Dad was born in the throes of the Great Depression, in the tent camps of itinerant and unemployed laborers. The shadow of those early years followed him his entire life and was the specter that haunted his family relationships—scarcity and want, fear and anger, reaching out to grasp what sanity and sense of control he could find, until eventually, in his later years, he found himself living alone in a large partially remodeled suburban house. I had my wounds from this relationship, but I did love him, and always kept my obligation to be there for him, albeit in small doses at a time, including on our birthdays, which were one day apart, and always on holidays, and then periodically checking in on him to make sure he was okay.

At one impromptu check-in, I found him collapsed and barely conscious on the floor after nearly a day trapped between his bed and some boxes, his pinned leg necrotizing under the weight of his own weakened body, an hour or two until the poisons from the decaying flesh would have killed him. Thanks to what spirit implored me to make an unexpected turn and stop to check in on him, he survived, spending months in the hospital and convalescent care. His lower leg would be permanently disabled and, as a result, he would have trouble walking for the rest of his life. He did, however, live many more years thereafter.

In life, the clock ticks persistently forward. We can never drag back the hands of time to reclaim what falls in the shadows. Then, once the mortal coil unwinds, the clock stops. Each breath before our last is a note in a vital symphony, an unbroken chain of breaths from the day we are born to the day we die. Ultimately, it is the breath we choose to give to one another—to bring hope, life, and comfort to our families, our friends, and even those we casually encounter in the course of our day—that brings meaning and purpose to our next breath. Each breath before our last presents a choice, an opportunity to give or to take, to bring harmony or dissonance, to an everlasting chorus of humanity sustained from the fount of creation, life immemorial.

The esteemed anthropologist Margaret Mead, during a lecture, once asked the question, "What is the earliest sign of civilization?" She suggested several possible answers—a clay pot, iron tools, agriculture. "No," she said, as she held up a femur, a leg bone that showed evidence of a healed fracture, "This is the evidence of the earliest true civilization."

> *Mead explained that the skeletal remains of competitive, savage societies never showed such signs of recovery. Clues of violence abound: ribs pierced by arrows, skulls crushed by clubs. But the healed femur shows that someone must have cared for the injured person—hunted on his behalf, brought him food, and served him at personal sacrifice.*[138]

Compassion, empathy, and community—our obligation to look after one another is the foundation of our civilized humanity. However, *civilization* does not follow a linear moral progression. Every generation faces the same moral choice between a "competitive, savage society" and a civilized society that values altruism, empathy, and personal sacrifice.

What is perhaps unique in modern society is the level of commitment to embrace egocentric moralism, the philosophical justification for selfishness and greed, as a modern *gillul*. A key figure in the institutionalization of egocentric moralism is the libertarian novelist and self-proclaimed

---

[138] Yancey (2019) p. 121

philosopher, Ayn Rand, who gained a cult following during the Reagan "Greed is Good" era. The aptly named *Me Generation* of the 1980s subsequently became the movers and shakers in conservative politics and religion, touting Rand's pseudo-philosophy of the virtues of selfishness and greed[139] as the ultimate "objective" good. Rand's non sequitur and strawman arguments, her lack of understanding of philosophy and psychology, and her sociopathic lack of comprehension of empathy and altruism should have made it easy to dismiss her as a crackpot. However, since the late twentieth century, she has become a major ideological force within religious and political discourse, taking on the function of a modern prophet, justifying the baser instincts of her followers. As with any extant framework that establishes an institutional level of followers with a degree of religious fervor, the movement that developed became increasingly bold in service to her sacred ideology. The libertarian social and political ideology based on her amoral/immoral code of conduct provided justification to exploit the poor and vulnerable, to attack those who oppose her egocentric ideology as *socialist* heresy, and to dismiss any contradictions in her fragile philosophy as disenlightenment.

Few societies have ever discarded the basic ethical foundation of mutuality with such abandon, primarily because throughout history one would not have survived alone as a *radical individualist.*

> *Day One: Joe proclaims he is a self-reliant individualist and runs off into the woods.*
> *Day Two: Joe is beaten up and robbed by a roving warlord, then left broken and alone on the side of the road.*
> *Day Three: Helpless, Joe is attacked and eaten by wolves.*
> *Day Four... no Joe.*

Such is life (and death) in a competitive, savage society—not everyone has what it takes to be a roving warlord, sorry Joe! While Rand's celebrity ideology is excessive by academic and basic moral standards, selfishness and greed have had a good go of it throughout history without her pedantry.

Nevertheless, it is not fundamental self-interest that motivates the usual behavior of non-sociopathic individuals in civilized society and healthy human relationships, but rather, *empathy*, the normative human capacity and tendency to feel the joys and pains of others, as well as the willingness to act and respond to suffering with altruistic intent. When we value the well-being of others, we act to preserve that value—that is the foundation of love.

---

[139] Rand (1964) as general reference

❖Love One Another

The obligation to love one another is the *prima materia* out of which the Reified Basar mythology is constructed; it is the basis of the Mosaic Law. Rabbi Jeshua, when asked, what is the greatest precept of the Mosaic Law, replied:

> *"You shall be loving the Lord your God with your whole heart, and with your whole soul, and with your whole comprehension." This is the great and foremost precept. Yet the second is like it: "You shall be loving your associate as yourself." On these two precepts is hanging the whole law and the prophets.*[140]

The *Torah of Obligation* is *ahav*—the actions we take to guard and care for one another in the Universal Family in honor of our spiritual Father. The Torah begins as a story of the Adamites' responsibility as Guardian-Caretakers in Creation, building on the specific narrative of their juvenile dependency on the Parent Elohim as Guardian-Caretaker of the family. As they develop further towards adolescent morality, the relationship with the Parent Elohim transitions from a *Child-Parent* relationship to a *Servant-Savior* relationship. The Parent Elohim's responsibility of Guardian and Caretaker evolves into a Savior's responsibility to Guide and Aide. The archetypal role of Yahweh becomes the Savior Elohim who, after delivering the Israelites from slavery, guides them through the challenges of the wilderness, giving aid for their basic sustenance and support, while requiring them, within community, to begin to arbitrate their moral values and obligations through a Law of Love.

At the heart of the narrative of the Sinai Law of Love is the story of Moses—a three-act play, each act covering forty years in the life of Moses. The myth explores the disintegration of the asymmetric power archetype of the *Victim-Villain-Victor* into the archetypal relationship of *Slave-Master* in the mythscape of the Fortress of Matsor/Egypt, representing the height of political power, culture, and civilization. It then continues into the sparse wilderness outside Egypt in Midian, the Arabian Desert, and the Negev. The story of Moses finishes forty years later as the Israelites approach their destination, the land of Canaan, punctuated by the death of Moses. It is not a simplistic morality play, with guys in black hats and white hats, but rather, it is a complex exploration of the dynamics of human nature in all its frailty and contradictions. It takes us on a path from mastery to slavery, and then, on a transformational journey to freedom.

---

[140] CLV Matthew 22:37-40

❖Epilogue to Exodus

The book of Bereshit/Genesis, as a complete mythological construction, also operates as the prologue to the Mosaic Exodus narrative, setting the framework for the entire journey. The Genesis myth explores the nature of the human condition and behavior, from infancy to adolescence, from Eden to Egypt. The Joseph myth is the epilogue, the culmination of the Genesis narrative arc, bringing all its elements together. The Middle Nachash that is introduced at the beginning of the book of Genesis is revived at the end in the identification of Joseph as both the Nachash of Elohim and Egypt. Joseph embodies the central traits of the *nachash* as perpetually shedding its coat, representing the renewal and preservation of life, and then as the one who moves between worlds, representing the oracular interpreter of both the Elohim and Egypt.

The final episode of the book of Genesis begins with the patriarch Jacob/Israel as a nomadic herdsman in the land of Canaan, centuries before Moses—or more specifically with his favorite son Joseph born of his favorite wife Rachel.

> Now Israel, he loved Joseph more than any of his other sons, because he was the son of his old age; and he had made him a distinctive tunic. When his brothers saw that their father loved him more than any of his other sons, they hated him so they could not speak peaceably with him. [141]

In all, Jacob had twelve sons by four women (two wives and two servants). Auspiciously, the story begins with pride and jealousy, and a callous plot to murder Joseph by his older brothers. From the onset, the narrative does not bode well for Joseph, except for two prophetic dreams, which only exacerbate Joseph's reputation.

> Once Joseph dreamed a dream; when he told it to his brothers... "Do hear this dream that I have dreamed. Behold, we were binding together grain-sheaves in the midst of the field, and behold, my grain-sheaf got up and stood upright. And behold, your grain-sheaves gathered around and bowed down to my grain-sheaf." His brothers replied to him: "Are you going to... reign over us?" ... And they hated him still more on account of his dreams and on his words.

> Then he dreamed still another dream...: "Behold, I have again dreamed a dream. Behold, the sun and the moon and eleven stars were bowing down to me." When he related it to his father and to his brothers, his father rebuked him... "What is this dream that you have dreamed? Shall we come... I and your mother and your brothers, to bow down to the earth

---

[141] CLV Genesis 37:3-4

before you?" So his brothers were jealous of him; yet his father, he observed the word. [142]

The brothers' hatred comes to a head one day while out in the pastures. After abducting Joseph and then some debate as to whether to kill him, they decide that, rather than have blood on their hands, they will profit from Joseph's demise by selling him as a slave to a caravan of Midianite merchants passing nearby on their way to Egypt. Afterward, they show their father the coat of Joseph that they have dipped in sheep's blood and tell him that a wild animal has killed him, torn him to pieces, and devoured him. In Egypt, Joseph is sold to a high-ranking Egyptian official by the name of Potiphar.

❖To Serve Man

While it is clear that Joseph is placed into involuntary servitude, the Hebrew verb form *abad*, which means "to serve," actually does not make a distinction as to the condition of one's service. Translators routinely interpret *abad*[143] and its noun form *ebed*[144], meaning *servant*, based on the context, into English as "servant, slave, or bondservant" or in verb form "to serve, work, labor, or till." The archetypal root in the narrative goes back to the Genesis Exile narrative, which curses the ground and declares Cain to be one who is "serving [abad] the ground." Then, in the Noah myth, Ham's son Canaan is cursed to be a "servant of servants [ebed] to his brothers."[145] The Abraham story mentions various servants and maidservants; most importantly the servant Eliezer of Damascus, whom Abraham initially believes will be his heir since he has no children. However, the story of Joseph is the first to develop a personal narrative of being placed into the service of another.

In the cultural context, servitude could be founded on a number of circumstances—economic, political, moral, or relational. In the asymmetric hierarchical power dynamic of the *Slave-Master,* the narratives of economic and political servitude are founded on the relationship between Master and Servant. Economic servitude typically occurs voluntarily as a matter of commerce, as a way to initiate and secure a debt, or merely, to survive famine or poverty, providing food and a place to sleep in exchange for service. There were typically legal and contractual externalities that governed the relationship and how it might end. Commonly, the alternative to

---

[142] CLV Genesis 37:5-11
[143] Strongs H5647
[144] Strongs H5650
[145] CLV Genesis 9:25

servitude for one incurring a debt and then failing to repay it would be debtor prison, or else starvation. In Jewish tradition, Jews could not become perpetually indentured and were absolved of their servitude at specified intervals, although the interpretation of those intervals specified in the Torah, seven versus forty-nine years, varied at different times and, eventually, developed numerous caveats in favor of the wealthy. Economic servitude is founded on competition and scarcity—it is directly educed from the curse of the groundworker in the Genesis Exile narrative.

Politically instituted servitude was predominately an act of the state as a privilege of the victor after a battle. In this manner, it was mostly ethnocentric and by force; it also had no limits to its length, and was typically for life, often including the next generation as well. While founded on an act of the state, it was typically carried out as a personal form of servitude by the soldiers who would divide up the spoils of war amongst themselves, including slaves. Foreign slaves had few rights, although often masters were required by tradition, and sometimes by law, to act justly and humanely. Subsequently, one could also buy and sell these slaves once they were conscripted. The curse of Ham's son Canaan is the archetypal institution of political servitude, both in general as well as specifically with regards to the justification for the Israelite's conquest of the lands of Canaan. Similar reasoning was applied later by American and European Christians for the brutal enslavement of African slaves by identifying Africans as the sons of Ham (or alternately as descendants of Cain).

Morally obligated servitude begins to straddle the line between asymmetric and symmetric power dynamics, depending on the authority under which one serves. Duty, obligation, and honor for moral servitude could be compelled by tradition, law, or a personal ethic. Women were morally obligated in patriarchal society to serve their husbands. Men were morally obligated to give their wives children—under levirate tradition, the brother of a deceased husband was obligated to impregnate his brother's wife in order to carry on his brother's lineage. Service to a king or ruler was obligated in the matters of statecraft to build political or religious structures, or to go to war. Service to a gillul/idol was obligated to assert one's deservedness for the gillul's blessing. The obligation of the Guardian-Caretaker established in the Eden narrative is the founding of moral servitude and, as such, may straddle the institution of relational servitude.

Relationally obligated servitude is founded on the symmetric power dynamic of the *Lover-Beloved*. This is service motivated by love—to guard and care for a family member or another person of value. This is the service of a mother to her child, or a parent's efforts to train a child up to be a mature adult. It is the service one ideally gives to one's spouse as an act of compassion and generosity or a friend as a gesture of care and concern. It can be an offering of appreciation to an *elohim,* or a gift of support to one in need. The recognition of the Universal Family, *flesh of my flesh*, in the Eden narrative is the endowment of relational servitude.

One form of servitude that crosses all the above categories was sexual servitude, which could be economic, political, moral, or relational. The economic service of prostitution was commonly embedded throughout most societies as unmarried, divorced, and widowed women had few options to support themselves in a traditionally patriarchal society. One way to survive was to sell their bodies to men for their sexual gratification as a means to put food on the table for themselves and their children. Political slaves—male, female, and children—could be compelled into service as sexual slaves to satisfy the appetites of their masters. Temple prostitution was a morally founded obligation in many societies to channel the power of a god, usually a fertility god, through the act of sex. And then relationally founded sexual servitude to one's spouse or spouses was idealized as a form of care and an act of love.

❖Joseph in Egypt

In the story of Joseph, he is illicitly sold by his brothers into political servitude. And then, we briefly see Potiphar's wife attempt to force him into sexual servitude, which leads to his imprisonment when he rejects her overtures. In prison, Joseph encounters two functionaries from Pharaoh's court who have fallen out of favor—the Chief Cupbearer and the Chief Baker. Each of them has a dream, which Joseph, acting as the Oracle of Elohim, interprets—the Baker to his demise and the Cupbearer to his restoration to the court. Years later Pharaoh has a troubling dream of his own.

> It came about at the end of two full years that Pharaoh was dreaming. And behold, he was standing by the waterway, when, behold, seven young cows, lovely in appearance and plump of flesh, were coming up from the waterway and grazed in the marsh grass. And behold, seven other young cows, ugly in appearance and thin of flesh, were coming up after them from the waterway; and they stood beside the other young cows on the ridge of the waterway. Then the seven young cows, ugly in appearance and thin of flesh, ate the seven young cows that were lovely in appearance and plump.
>
> At this Pharaoh awoke. He fell asleep again and dreamed a second time. And behold, seven ears of grain, plump and good, were coming up on one stalk. And behold, seven other ears of grain, thin and blasted by the east

wind, were sprouting after them. Then the seven thin ears of grain swallowed up the seven plump and full ears of grain.

At this Pharaoh awoke; and behold, it had been a dream. It occurred in the morning when his spirit was agitated, that he sent and called all the sacred scribes of Egypt and all her wise men. And Pharaoh related his dream to them; but there was no one to interpret them for Pharaoh.[146]

At that point, the Cupbearer recollects his previous encounter with Joseph's oracular endowment to Pharaoh. Joseph, who is still in prison, is then summoned to the court, and, of course, given a new set of clothes. He tells Pharaoh that Yahweh Elohim is warning him that seven years of plenty will come followed by seven years of famine. He then advises Pharaoh to appoint a Vizier to oversee the plentiful years and to set aside a fifth of all the grain harvest so that there will be food to eat during the famine. This impresses Pharaoh and he proclaims that there could be no one wiser than Joseph, and he appoints him Vizier, second only to Pharaoh.

The story develops just as Joseph has interpreted, and eventually, his family in Canaan, who are also suffering from the famine, make their way to Egypt where, after some subterfuge, Joseph is reconciled to his brothers and then reunited with his father—after, of course, his family bowing down to him as the second most powerful man in Egypt, in fulfillment of the earlier dream. With the blessing of Pharaoh, the entire family of Jacob/Israel moves from Canaan to northeastern Egypt. They are well cared for in the fertile land of Goshen in the Nile delta throughout the famine and, the narrative states, they were "fruitful and increased more and more in number."[147]

As the famine progresses, however, Joseph brings all of Egypt into economic servitude to Pharaoh. Everything that the Egyptians own, money, land, and livestock, are all given up to Pharaoh in exchange for bread. By the seventh year of the famine, Pharaoh owns everything under the shrewd oversight of Joseph as Nachash of Egypt/Pharaoh. The Egyptians become mere vassal tenants.

So Joseph took in all the money that was found in the land of Egypt and in the land of Canaan in payment for the grain rations which they were purchasing. And Joseph brought the money to Pharaoh's house. When all the money from the land of Egypt and from the land of Canaan was spent, all Egypt came to Joseph, saying, "Grant us bread; why should we die in front of you since our money is expended?" Joseph replied, "Grant me your cattle, and I will supply you in exchange for your cattle since your money is expended."

---

[146] CLV Genesis 41:1-8
[147] CLV Genesis 47:27

So they brought their cattle to Joseph, and Joseph gave them bread in exchange for their horses, their stock of flocks, their stock of herds and their donkeys. In that year he got them through the famine with bread in exchange for all their livestock. When that year came to end, they came to him in the second year and said to him, "We should not suppress the fact from my lord that, since our money is spent and the stock of our domestic beasts belongs to my lord, there is nothing left before my lord barring if our body and our ground. Why should we die before your eyes, both we and our ground? Buy us and our ground for bread; and we and our ground shall become serfs to Pharaoh. Give us seed that we may sow and may live and not die, and the ground may not be desolate."

So Joseph bought all the ground of Egypt for Pharaoh, for all Egypt sold to Pharaoh, each man his field, because the famine held a fast grip on them. So the land became Pharaoh's. As for the people, he made them pass over to the cities, from one end of Egypt's territory unto its other end...

Then Joseph said to the people: "Behold, I have bought you today with your ground for Pharaoh. Lo Here is seed for you, and you must sow the ground with it. Yet this will apply to the harvest yields: You must give a fifth to Pharaoh, and four fifths shall be for you as seed for your fields and as food for yourselves and for all those in your households, and as food for your little ones." They answered, "You have preserved our lives. May we find grace in the eyes of my lord; we will be serfs to Pharaoh."[148]

Notably, the one exception to the servitude of the Egyptian people to Pharaoh was with regards to the Priest who acted as an extension to, and in support of, the political power of the Pharaoh.

But the ground of the priests he did not buy, for the priests had a statutory allowance from Pharaoh. So they lived off their statutory allowance... they did not sell their ground... And Joseph made it a statute concerning the ground of Egypt, still valid to this day: Pharaoh must have a fifth; but the ground of the priests, theirs alone, did not become Pharaoh's.[149]

By the end of the famine, Joseph as Vizier and Nachash of Egypt had brought all of Egypt under the control of the religious and political establishment of Pharaoh and the Priests of Egypt.

❖Nachash of Egypt

The story of Joseph is the conclusion of the Genesis mythology, bringing the archetypes, themes, and symbols of the Genesis Exile narrative to completion. Matsor/Egypt is the Kingdom of Cain, invoking the scarcity of the wilderness and the architectural, artistic, and metallurgic achievement of Cain's archetypal legacy in both the hierarchical political and religious

---

[148] CLV Genesis 47:14-25
[149] CLV Genesis 47:22,26

institutions that embody its asymmetric power and the economic servitude that evolves from that power.

While it never specifically mentions the *nachash* in the Joseph narrative, the earlier symbolism from the beginning of the Genesis myth is carried through into the story of Joseph at the end of the Genesis myth. Joseph is conspicuously introduced and identified with the "distinctive tunic" or coat his father gives him. The narrative arc is demarcated by his putting on, and then, shedding his coat or vestment. The first layer of vestment invokes Joseph's juvenile egocentrism and arrogance in light of his father's favoritism. The tunic is shed and dipped in sheep's blood as he is abducted and sold into slavery, mirroring the fleece that is dipped in blood and wiped on the doorposts during the Passover narrative, marking the end of slavery in Egypt, as the Israelites, likewise, transition from juvenile egocentrism to adolescent moral development. Joseph then puts on the second layer of vestment as a captive/slave and for a period manages the household of Potiphar, a high-ranking Egyptian official. When the official's wife attempts to subjugate him into sexual servitude, he flees leaving his coat behind. She uses the coat to falsely accuse him of attempted rape. He is then put in prison with the next sublayer of vestment instantiating him as a captive/prisoner. For the next several years, he becomes the manager of the prison. He then sheds this vestment and puts on his last layer of vestment to enter the court of Pharaoh, where he then becomes the second most powerful ruler in Egypt.

Each layer (if we combine his slavery and imprisonment as sublayers) is punctuated by two dreams in which Joseph acts as the Oracle of Elohim. Each dream is a foretelling of some future dilemma as a sign of Yahweh Elohim's guidance in the narrative. Each of these is demarcated by some judgment, or consequence that leads to the next.

As an oracle and moral actor in continual renewal, Joseph operates as both the Nachash of Elohim and the Nachash of Egypt—this dual identification is essential to the narrative. The Middle Nachash is fundamentally an instrument of moral servitude and becomes an actor for whatever authority it is identified. On the one level, as the Nachash of Elohim, Joseph, the son of Israel, is fulfilling the first prophetic dream that leads to preserving the health and well-being of his family during a period of scarcity and famine. He subsequently becomes the Oracle of Elohim through several dreams given to guide his Egyptian cohorts.

Then as the Nachash of Egypt, Joseph represents the power of each of his masters. In context to his higher connection to Yahweh Elohim, whatsoever Joseph did "Yahweh was with him, and all that he was doing,

Yahweh would cause to prosper."¹⁵⁰ So in each of his servant roles, he rises to master, subject only to his Egyptian masters—Potiphar, the jailer, and then only to Pharaoh himself. Joseph serves their power and intention making each domain realize its fullest potential as household, institution, and then kingdom. In the last, we see the full realization of the kingdom instituted by Cain in the subjugation of a populace to their *elohim* as a function of the scarcity that afflicts them, dissociating them from the land to become mere vassals of the ruling powers. Egypt represents both the height of civilized achievement and the depths of competitive, savage society.

❖Spiritual Authority

The Middle Nachash, as conscience and agent of moral servitude, becomes what it serves, founding the operative narrative within the psyche. In essence, the human psyche is a stage on which specific inculcated narratives are enacted, triggered by internal or external events that threaten or promote one's safety or well-being. All stories have authors and are developed under their authority. These spiritual or psychological authorities drive our narrative, our personal mythology that defines who we are and what we value. Our underlying narrative of nakedness, vulnerability, or *missingness*, formulates our individual repertoire of stories we favor and repeat over and over; it defines our personality strategy.

This central archetypal construct we encounter as "who is the author of our story"—our authority. It is a cross-function of *experience* and *relationship*. The *experiential* dimension is defined by the ontological primitives of space-time—*future, present, past*—embodied personally in passion, understanding, and valuation; and delimited relationally as bond, identity, and boundaries. On the other hand, the *relational* dimension is defined either *exclusively* as *I, You*, or *It*; or *inclusively* as *Us*.

In our previous discussion, we had only identified the egoic *I* and relational *Us* as phenomenologically distinct perspectives. However, there are two complicated deferential psychological states that invocate external influencers and patterns as drivers in the psyche—the *You* and *It*. Expanding the familiar model, which uses the Latin word *ego* for *I*, to similarly use the Latin terms for *You, It, and Us—Vos, Id, and Nos*—we can begin to explore the *voscentric* and *idcentric* psychological states that defer authority to externalized egoic or systemic construction. The egocentric model only acknowledges the dominant perspective of the individual. The *voscentric*

---

perspective is the deferential state of inculcating the egoic dominance of another into one's own egoic narrative. Historically, women's culture, in particular, has been *voscentric*—operating in deference to the dominant patriarchal influencers (*You*) creating damaging false narratives that have distanced women from the power of their own potential narratives. Similarly, and just as damaging, are the *idcentric* perspectives of traditional and religious narratives (*It*) that inculcate false personal narratives through dogmatic indoctrination.

Like our personality strategy, our *authority* construct becomes fixated on one or more narrative scripts represented in the cross-product of these dimensions. Our narratives will tend to be dominated by some form or forms of perceived archetypal authority. Some personalities are characterized by a *future* orientation that forms comfort and empowerment through passion, motive, and movement forward through space and time towards some faceted ideation of reality or wonderment. Within that movement, one might become biased to an egocentric perspective (Ego/*I*) or become submissive to another egoic perspective (Vos/*You*) or an abstraction of one (Id/*It*). A future-oriented *egocentric* personality [EF] builds their narrative based on their own egoic drive constellating around such broader scripts as narcissism or authoritarianism. However, some futurists are *voscentric* [VF]—more *reactive* to egoic narratives; prone to define their motivation and authority from another egoic perspective that they inculcate as their own. Their narratives might be driven by self-denial, asceticism, or submissivism providing a projective framework to guide one to an externalized outcome. Still, other futurists are *idcentric* [IF]—prone to abstract their prime authoritative relationships and submit their motive drive to cultural or ideological systems—tradition, religion, or ethical codes—that guide their actions. Likewise, there are similar dynamics in the *present* and *past*-oriented authority scripts, as I have outlined in Table 6.

	Exclusionary		Inclusionary	
	Ego/I *(E)*	Vos/You *(V)*	Id/It *(I)*	Nos/Us *(N)*
FUTURE *(F)* {*Volitional, Passion, Bond}*	*EF* Narcissism Authoritarianism {Ruler}	*VF* Asceticism Submissivism {Servant}	*IF* Moralism Traditionalism Perfectionism	*NF* Love Altruism {Way}
	e8	e9	e1	
PRESENT *(P)* {*Rational, Belief, Identity}*	*EP* Intellectualism Conservatism Individualism	*VP* Fanaticism Conformism Tribalism	*IP* Rationalism Optimism Occultism	*NP* Understanding Mutualism {Truth}
	e5	e6	e7	
PAST *(X)* {*Emotional, Feeling, Boundary}*	*EX* Romanticism Sensationalism Hedonism	*VX* Opportunism Materialism Stoicism	*IX* Emotionalism Pessimism Libertarianism	*NX* Peace Relationalism {Life}
	e2	e3	e4	

Table 6 - Theory of Spiritual Authority

These authority scripts become the building block of our personal narratives and our sense of continuity across narratives. The scripts presented above are not precise but are meant as possible examples of our authoritative narratives; some may bleed into other quadrants based on how they are defined or what role one takes. But the broad patterns are illustrative of how our narratives constellate around a core sense of authorship. It presents how the individual uniquely experiences them, but also how they bring one into broader narratives across quadrants in relationship to others.

The exclusionary authority scripts operate within the asymmetric power dynamic. They correlate to immature and dysfunctional psychological development. They are constructs that are not integrable in the operative psyche, which pushes them into our unconscious shadow narratives. The exclusionary relational operatives (I, You, It) have a similar but non-determinative relationship to the flow operatives (on, off, restrained) of the Enneagram personality model, which is also based on the ontological spatiotemporal primitives (future, present, past) expanding the narrative patterns by suggesting additional pathways for integration and shadow work. This may help to reveal how these exclusionary authority scripts influence personality strategies. However, the clinical applications are much broader and require a deeper investigation than is possible here. Our focus here is on moral development. Maturity is defined by our movement from an *exclusionary* experience of authority, seated in the *I, You,* and *It* orientation, to become more *inclusionary*—the experience of ourselves in relationship to others, the experience of *Us*. While being fixated on a spatiotemporal orientation is not ideal, it is not as constitutional as our relational orientation—developing a fundamental *noscentric* value of Us.

These exclusionary authority archetypes allow us to explore the nature of gillul, the *Transferent Elohim* in the psyche. There is an intrinsic hunger of the *Transferent Elohim* manifested in the egoic unconscious that requires servitude from the operative psyche. Whether or not the gillul are symbolized as external objects, as material idols, or operate as naked psychological states, they have a distinct correlation to, and are a fundamental embodiment of, these exclusionary authority archetypes. The egocentric gillul is easily identified as an inflation of personal authority, but the model also helps to define how *fanaticism* [VP] makes a gillul of celebrity, or *emotionalism* [IX] makes a gillul of reactionary emotionally charged systems such as ecstatic or charismatic religious experience.

Whichever gillul one comes to serve out of their shadow narrative, the gillul operates the same. These *Transferent Elohim* embody our fears and vulnerability. We project our nakedness upon them, and then, try to dress them up so that they appear more powerful and secure than we actually are. We feed them with our time, energy, and resources so that they, in turn, make us feel like their power is ours to take. But their hunger and our fears can never be satisfied. Unless we build a relationship to our underlying authentic self, in all its weakness and pain, we are just endlessly projecting our power out into the void. Our relationship to spiritual authority is a central theme in the Unified Basar and Torah mythology, which is developed over the course of the Mosaic Exodus myth.

❖**Obligation of Adolescent Morality**

Our obligation to support and care for one another is the understructure of family and society. Without this obligation, there are no laws, no family, no community, no cooperation—only competition, chaos, and societal collapse. Humans have survived and thrived throughout history precisely because they formed cooperative groups—put bluntly, those that did not cooperate did not survive. Individualism is a modern fiction born out of an increasingly complex society that seems to function effortlessly on its own—until it does not. Selfishness and greed appear to lead to success—until one reaches the limits of an exploited resource, or else a catastrophe occurs, and the individual is suddenly faced with their aloneness, reminded of their need for others to survive.

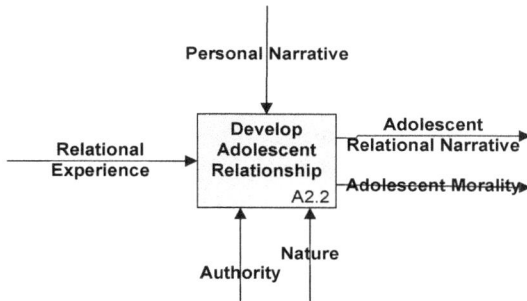

Model 9 – Develop Adolescent Relationship (A2.2 Context)

Our developmental journey takes us from juvenile awareness, the personal mythology of Da'ath/Knowledge grounded in the family or clan, to adolescent obligation, the group mythology of Ahav/Love grounded in the larger tribal Servant-Savior relationship. The Savior Elohim is a transcendent presence in the symmetric dynamic of the adolescent cosmos functioning as a Guide and Aide in support of the independent growth of the Adolescent Elohim.

In the Torah of Obligation, the adolescent stage of moral development is a reaction to the loss of juvenile purpose, meaning, and value. The mythology of *Ahav*, the essential experience of act-love, continues the exploration of the archetypal topography of scarcity and sufficiency as the basis for the knowledge of goodness and badness by expanding beyond an egocentric morality of causality and consequence, to develop an understanding of the value of others and one's obligation to support and satisfy those in need. Our deep-seated awareness of our vulnerability in the face of scarcity and *missingness* becomes the foundation for empathy towards others—unless, of course, the shadow of our psychological nakedness overwhelms us. With a greater sense of our own power, empathy can lead us to compassionate action; however, fear and lack of empathy will lead us to exploitation and abuse.

Adolescent morality fluctuates readily between the underdeveloped conscience of the juvenile *Ground Nachash* and the burgeoning potential of the adult *Higher Nachash*. At this stage, the Parent Elohim begins to fade from direct guardianship into the role of the Savior Elohim as Guide-Aide in support of the external societal systems of governance. These societal systems become more prevalent, exercising broader authority and discipline over the *Adolescent Elohim*, setting boundaries, and meting out punishment when the boundaries are violated. The abuses of the societal authorities also become more relevant as some *Adolescent Elohim* become identified with the *Viper*, striking out to exploit and exercise control over others. The *Adolescent*

Elohim are individuating from the parental environment, losing their juvenile purpose, meaning, and value.

Sociologically, the *Torah of Obligation* describes our engagement with the world around us, subject to the limits imposed on us by societal authorities that govern our actions. The societal authority may be embodied in the governmental hierarchy, religious and cultural authorities, employers, or group leaders. We now are responsible for creating either a symmetric or an asymmetric power dynamic in the communities in which we live.

Psychologically, the *Torah of Obligation* describes our inherent capacity for empathy and responsive action, moderated by the internal representation of societal authority. However, we may become conditioned into submission to another authority, bound to serve through an economic or political obligation to it, operating out of fear and an innate sense of vulnerability. Adolescent awareness helps us to differentiate between appropriate and inappropriate authority; seeking to right the wrongs we encounter and protect those victimized by the asymmetric power hierarchies.

Symbolically, the adolescent Adamites must operate outside of their original family dynamic incorporating the value of others into a broader moral framework. The juvenile schema of parental authority is no longer effective in the diverse marketplace of social convention. The Adamites must contend with others who may have different interests and values than the ones experienced in the household drama. In the community, there is no longer a singular arbiter of correctness and each Adamite must open up their indigenous boundaries to include diverse perspectives.

Archetypally, the obligation of adolescent morality unfolds, initially as a reaction to the loss of our juvenile purpose and connection, then meaning and identity, and finally, value and boundaries. The path leads us from the personal and familial to a greater identifying group, the tribe or nation. However, the mythology of *Ahav* emphasizes that identification in the group is based on contribution to the well-being of the group; those that merely take from the group, exploiting others within the group, are not authentically considered a part of the group, and in the mythology, are separated from the group for the benefit and survival of the group. This is what the political and religious elite in the myth continuously and conspicuously run afoul in the mythology of Ahav.

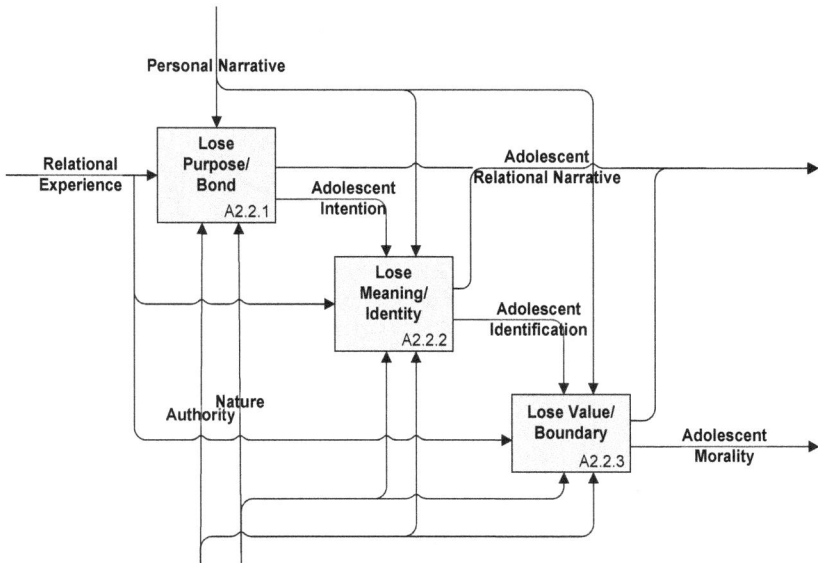

Model 10 – Develop Adolescent Relationship (A2.2)

CHAPTER [1/II]

NIGHT FALLS BEFORE DAY BREAKS

> Listlessness to everything, but brooding sorrow, was the night that fell on my undisciplined heart. Let me look up from it— as at last I did, thank Heaven! —and from its long, sad, wretched dream, to dawn.
> —*Charles Dickens*, "David Copperfield"

The Torah of Obligation begins in the heart of civilization, the Fortress of Matsor, the kingdom of Egypt under the authority and rule of the great Pharaoh. It is a story of hardship and servitude for the Israelites and power and glory for Egypt, at least, as the Exodus myth begins. The Genesis myth ended with the subjugation of Egyptian people to the Pharaoh under the oversight of Joseph during the scarcity and deprivation of a seven-year drought, whilst the Israelites settled at ease in the fertile lands of Goshen in the Nile delta. The Exodus myth expands the hierarchical asymmetric power narrative from the Victim-Villain-Victor to the Slave-Master archetype through the life of Moses, divided into three acts, each spanning forty years of his life. Each act arises metaphorically from the Sea of Reeds, in Hebrew, *Yam Suph*. It weaves the narrative of the archetypal spiritual authority of the future-egocentric Pharaoh as Villain/Master with the future-voscentric Israelites as Victim/Slave within the future-idcentric context of the Egyptian religious ideology and power. Moses' character begins as the asymmetric Victor/Hero archetype and develops, later, into the symmetric tribal Deliverer/Savior.

The first forty-year Act of the story of Moses chronicles the loss of the Israelites' juvenile purpose and bond. The Israelites no longer have the same function or role in the Egyptian social structure that they did under Joseph. Rather than a people through whom salvation is brought to Egypt through Joseph, they are perceived to be a threat to the political hierarchy. The story unfolds from this ignoble construct. Likewise, at the beginning of the First Act, as a child, Moses loses the integrity of his primary association with his tribe and family, and then, by the end, he loses his privilege and identity as a prince of Egypt.

❖Obligation to Serve

After the death of the Pharaoh for whom Joseph had served as Vizier, "a new king arose over Egypt who knew nothing about Joseph."[151] The new Pharaoh sees the growing population of Israelites as a threat to Egyptian security.

> He said to his people: "Behold, the people of the sons of Israel are more numerous and staunch than we. Do grant attention! Let us show ourselves wise as to them lest they increase, and it come to be if war should befall us, and they are added, even they, onto those hating us, that they fight against us and ascend from the land."
>
> Hence they placed over them chiefs of tributary service that they might humiliate them with their burdens. So they were building as provision cities for Pharaoh, Pithom and Raamses. Yet just as they were humiliating them so they multiplied and so they breached forth.
>
> Hence they were irritated in view of the sons of Israel. So the Egyptians made the sons of Israel serve with rigor, and they embittered their lives with hard service in clay and in bricks, and with all service in the field, all their service which they served among them with rigor.[152]

Over the course of a few generations, the Israelites are inducted into moral servitude to king and state, the archetypal representation of the Kingdom of Cain. It is important to note that, initially, they are not slaves, the English word that is often used to describe political servitude—Israel is not a conquered people. When the narrative mentions the *chiefs of tributary*, it is invoking the moral obligation of all the subjects of Pharaoh to serve in matters of state in helping to build Egypt. The Israelites are enlisted, according to that obligation, to build the cities of Pithom and Raamses. Albeit, the narrative states, for political reasons, this obligation is made especially rigorous in an attempt to subdue their numbers. Eventually, as time passes, the Israelites do indeed come to lose their identity as the moral servants of Pharaoh, becoming enslaved as victims of his political paranoia.

As a moral psychology, it is within the broader framework of the Tree of Morality that the Egyptian narrative takes place. The Laws of a Nation embody the temporal Knowledge of Goodness and Badness—defining the obligation of its subjects to one another, to its rulers, to its religious authorities, and to the political state. Control is a primary characteristic of an asymmetric system of power. The ruling class, as the ultimate authority within the system, attempts to self-perpetuate its existence and its power

---

[151] CLV Exodus 1:8
[152] CLV Exodus 1:9-14

over those that it controls. As such, it may waiver between supporting its subjects, and exploiting or suppressing them as it sees fit. While the Egyptian people are brought into economic servitude to the dominant political system as a matter of necessity due to the drought, the Israelites are brought into servitude as a matter of their moral obligation, to serve the power of the state under Pharaoh.

❖Out of the Reeds

Moses' role as Middle Nachash is founded on his identity as the one who travels between worlds as an oracle for the *Elohim*, his progressive shedding of identities in each Act, his anointing as Deliverer to preserve the life of Israel, and his appointment as Revealer of the law, and Judge over Israel. However, Moses' role is a gradual development across each Act—beginning in the first Act as an outcast floating in a reed ark, then being adopted by the Egyptian princess, thus becoming identified with the ruling hierarchy of Egypt; and then in the second Act, losing his regal powers after killing a man, becoming a shepherd, being called by Yahweh Elohim to deliver his anointed firstborn from Egypt; and finally, in the last Act, leading them to the promised land. Thus, Moses is transformed from an initial agent of the asymmetric hierarchy to an agent of Yahweh Elohim, albeit insecure and *thick of tongue*, and then finally as lawgiver, judge, and leader of the tribal family.

If it were not for these primary characteristics of the *nachash*, it might be easy to dismiss his association with water and reeds as whimsical. However, in myth, nothing exists without meaning. In context, the water/reeds are symbolic of his association with the *nachash* who inhabit the reeds of the Nile, which in turn, is a slender stalk that is ideogrammatic of the snake. The First Act begins with Moses being drawn from the reeds of the Nile, the Second Act begins with him journeying beyond the Sea of Reeds to Midian, and the Third Act begins with Moses and the Israelites dramatically passing through the Sea of Reeds to freedom from servitude. Moses is given his name by Pharaoh's daughter, which literally means "son" in Egyptian and is usually combined with the father's name (e.g., Thutmose). But with the princess' attribution "because I have removed him from the water,"[153] the name infers that he is the son of no one, born of the Sea of Reeds.

In composite, from an Israelite perspective, these characteristics encompass Moses' role and identity within the mythology as the Nachash of Elohim. Yet, from an Egyptian perspective, they paint a portrait of the sea snake Apep, the archetypal enemy of Egypt. In Egyptian mythology, Apep is in

---

[153] CLV Exodus 2:10

a continuous battle with Re, the Sun-God and symbol of the nation of Egypt. Apep, in one myth, is killed by Re, but then is brought back to life. He is a dark force that is fundamentally at odds with the Egyptian way of life. To the Egyptians, he is the ultimate monster, the enemy of all they value. Yet, in the asymmetry of the *Victim-Villain-Victor* archetype, one man's monster is another man's hero.

❖**Between Worlds**

In Campbell's metamyth of the Hero's Journey, the Hero exists in a state of otherness, out of the ordinary, called to the extraordinary. The narrative typically begins in a familiar world that is slightly out of kilter. Often the Hero is orphaned, setting him or her apart from the typical obligations of family and society. The choice is given to the potential Hero either to push away from the hero's calling, so as to remain in the confines of the ordinary, in continual conformity to this skewed world, or else, to step out of it, to begin the journey of transformation. Of course, epics are only written of those who heed the call, not those that sit on the proverbial tree stump making up reasons not to go. Early in the narrative arc, the potential Hero will begin to feel the nag towards something different; the system reinforces that they do not fit into the ordinary, the commonplace narrative.

Moses' life begins as an ordinary Hebrew in a Levite family—the tribe that will eventually become the priests of Yahweh Elohim once the temple is built. But no temple exists and Pharaoh, wishing to diminish the threat he feels from the large population of Israelites in Goshen, has decreed: "Every son born to the Hebrews, into the waterway shall you fling him, yet every daughter you shall keep alive."[154] After his birth, Moses' mother secludes him for his first three months, and then she does indeed *fling* her child into the waterway—except she places him in a reed ark that he might survive, fulfilling her obligation to the law and to her child:

> *When she could no longer seclude him, then she took for him an ark of papyrus, daubed it with asphalt and with pitch and placed the boy in it; then she placed it in the weeds on the ridge of the waterway. And his sister stationed herself afar, to know what might be done to him.*

> *Then Pharaoh's daughter descended to bathe at the waterway, while her maidens were walking on the side of the waterway. When she saw the ark in the midst of the weeds she sent her maidservant and took it; she opened it and saw him, the boy; and behold, the lad was lamenting. She spared him and said: "This is one of the boys of the Hebrews."*

---

[154] CLV Exodus 1:22

Then his sister said to the daughter of Pharaoh: "Shall I go and call for you a woman, a wetnurse from the Hebrews that she may nurse the boy for you?" And Pharaoh's daughter said to her: "Go!" So the damsel went and called the boy's mother.

Then Pharaoh's daughter said to her: "Have this boy go, and nurse him for me, and I shall give you your hire." So the woman took the boy and nursed him. When the boy was growing up she brought him to Pharaoh's daughter, and he became her son. She called his name Moses and said: "Because I have removed him from the water."[155]

Moses now exists as both a child of Israel and a prince of Egypt—inhabiting both worlds but identified most significantly, at this juncture, with Egypt as the adopted son of Pharaoh's daughter. He is educated in the ways and privileges of nobility to fulfill his obligation to the state. Yet, he is aware that he exists between the worlds of privilege as an Egyptian and servitude as a Hebrew.

❖**Power of Pharaoh**

Historically, the role of kings and chiefs evolve out of the patriarchal obligation of the head of the family and tribe, enrolled as the anointed firstborn son of the nation, but established in a broader asymmetric power dynamic. Pharaoh, as the political firstborn of Egypt, is the embodiment of its asymmetric political power. On one hand, he is obligated to act to preserve the tribal state; on the other, he has the power to act according to his own authoritarian self-interest. In the narrative, he acts out of paranoia, threatened in his imagination by a group of foreigners, non-Egyptian, Canaanite Hebrews, inhabiting Goshen that he simply does not trust. While the Israelites are under his rule, they are obligated to serve him, and, as ceremonial patriarch, Pharaoh is obligated to protect them, as long as they are committed to him as members of his political household. But in this asymmetric political system, the moral obligation is biased toward the one in power, the one who controls how the law is instituted. Fear, based on an unfounded sense of vulnerability, gives birth to paranoia, leading Pharaoh to violate his obligation as ruler; he lashes out at his own subjects. It is an immoral act embodied by the state. However, the powerful elite at the top of this hierarchical system exist outside of any repercussions, unless by the judgment of the gods.

Pharaoh has become the Villain in the myth, the archetypal Viper, and Israel has become his Victim. The asymmetric Villain or monster in myth is driven by fear or hunger, or both. They lash out to protect or to gain

---

[155] CLV Exodus 2:1-10

something they value. They are the embodiment of unbridled power lacking any accountability unless or until someone stands up to them. This is the function of the asymmetric Hero—to do battle with the monster.

❖Hero's Calling

In the archetype of the *Victim-Villain-Victor*, the Victor/Hero is two dimensional—an agent in the battle between good and evil. His role is simply to affirm what is good, defeat the bad guy, and restore order. On the contrary, in the myth of the Hero's Journey, the Hero embodies the transformational dynamic between the asymmetric and symmetric political systems. The metamorphic Hero is the philosophers' stone, turning the failure of the ordinary into the richness of its underlying potential.

In Act One, Moses is the asymmetric Victor/Hero caught between two worlds. He embodies the law of Egypt as a prince—the knowledge of goodness and badness of Cain's Kingdom. As with Cain, who epitomizes egocentric morality, Moses is provoked into action one day by an internal ethic when he sees an Egyptian taskmaster beating an Israelite servant.

> It came to be in those days when Moses had grown up that he went forth to his brothers and saw their burdens. He also saw an Egyptian man smiting a Hebrew man, one of his brothers. He faced this way and that and saw that there was no one else; then he smote the Egyptian and buried him in the sand. [156]

In anger, Moses murders a lawful representative of Pharaoh, fully knowing that he is breaking the law, thus burying his Victim, whom he sees as the Villain, in the sand. The asymmetric Hero's role is to confront evil, to represent good, which in the reality of the asymmetric power system is relative—one man's hero is another man's monster. It is both true that Moses defends one who is being abused and that he commits murder. He knows that and attempts to hide it. But Moses does not succeed in hiding it.

> When he went forth on the second day, behold, two men, Hebrews, were striving with each other. So he said to the wicked one: "Why are you smiting your associate?" Yet he said: "Who appointed you as foreman and judge over us? Are you meaning to kill me just as you killed the Egyptian?" Then Moses became fearful and said: "Surely the matter is known." When Pharaoh heard of this matter, he sought to kill Moses. So Moses ran away from the face of Pharaoh and dwelt in the land of Midian.[157]

The simplistic narrative of the Victor/Hero comes unwound against the realities of the larger asymmetric narrative. Confronting one element of the

---

[156] CLV Exodus 2:11-12
[157] CLV Exodus 2:13-15

system, as an aspect within the system, does not change the system. Moses only becomes another example of oppression within the system. He leaves Egypt defeated. However, in the broader narrative arc, Moses is just beginning the journey of the metamorphic Hero in which he will be called to transform the reality of the asymmetric political system that has entangled the tribe of Israel into the symmetric Kingdom of Elohim.

❖Failure of Empathy

The hero's journey begins with the calling out of an unchallenged soul into a relationship with something constitutionally reformative—to discover an authentic purpose and connection in the world. In Greek mythology, the story of Narcissus and Echo investigates the loss of purpose and connection engendered by the failure of empathy—the failure to heed the call to the life Between in the Sacred Midst of the relationship of *Lover-Beloved*. In the myth, Narcissus' name descriptively is derived from the Greek *narke*, meaning *sleep* or *numbness*. It is emblematic of his inability to engage or respond to the calling out by the Sacred Midst in the context of Love and Chaos.

In Ovid's version of the myth, Narcissus is the offspring of Liriope, the Naiad, the loveliest of nymphs, who was raped by the River-God Cephisus. Tiresias, the seer, prophesies at his birth that Narcissus would live a long life, but only "if he does not discover himself," thus accentuating his eponymic character as one who is incapable of seeing beyond his inauthentic self.

> [Narcissus] had reached sixteen and might seem both boy and youth. Many youths, and many young girls desired him. But there was such intense pride in that delicate form that none of the youths or young girls affected him...
>
> One day the nymph Echo saw him... she of the echoing voice, who cannot be silent when others have spoken... and returns the words she hears. Now when she saw Narcissus... she was inflamed, following him secretly... she wants to get close to him with seductive words, and call him with soft entreaties! Her nature denies it, and will not let her begin, but she is ready... to wait for sounds, to which she can return words. By chance, the boy, separated from his faithful band of followers, had called out "Is anyone here?" and "Here" Echo replied. He is astonished, and glances everywhere, and shouts in a loud voice "Come to me!" She calls as he calls. He looks back, and no one appearing behind... says "Here, let us meet together." And... Echo replies "Together", and... comes out of the woods to put her arms around his neck, in longing. He runs from her, and... cries, "Away with these encircling hands! May I die before what's mine is yours." She answers, only "What's mine is yours!"
>
> Scorned, she wanders in the woods and hides her face in shame... But still her love endures, increased by the sadness of rejection. Her sleepless thoughts waste her sad form, and her body's strength vanishes into the

air... Her voice remains... no longer to be seen on the hills, but to be heard by everyone...

As Narcissus had scorned her, so he had scorned the other nymphs... [and] the companies of young men. Then one of those who had been mocked, lifting hands to the skies, said "So may he himself love, and so may he fail to command what he loves!" ...the goddess Nemesis, heard this just request.[158]

In the first part of this myth, Narcissus is incapable of connecting to, or even echoing, the love of any of his admirers. Emotionally numb, Narcissus' identity is the *one who is asleep and has not discovered himself*. The story becomes a counterpoint to the Edenic narrative in which Adam discovers his own emptiness and is awakened to his need for reciprocity and relationship in the process of exploring the various creatures in Eden. In Echo, Narcissus refuses to look outside himself, to have compassion, or even to hear the Love in his own inner voice—"Here," "Come to me," "Together," "What's mine is yours." Narcissus is the embodiment of the emptiness of Chaos in contrast to Echo's disembodied Love. The discontinuous influence of Chaos is expressed as pride and contempt for those whose Love falls beneath him, finding no place to rest in his empty soul.

In the second part of the myth, Nemesis, the goddess of divine retribution, brings poetic justice for Narcissus' unnatural pride and scorn by allowing the pattern he has set in the first part to develop further and take its natural course to separation and death. Narcissus is allowed to discover a shallow but empty reflection of himself.

There was an unclouded fountain, with silver-bright water... Here, the boy, tired by the heat and his enthusiasm for the chase, lies down, drawn to it by its look and by the fountain. While he desires to quench his thirst, a different thirst is created. While he drinks he is seized by the vision of his reflected form. He loves a bodiless dream... astonished by himself, and hangs there motionless, with a fixed expression... he contemplates... everything for which he is himself admired. Unknowingly he desires himself, and the one who praises is himself praised... "I am he. I sense it... I am burning with love for myself..." He spoke, and returned madly to the same reflection, and his tears stirred the water, and the image became obscured in the rippling pool...

As he sees all this reflected in the dissolving waves, he can bear it no longer, but... is weakened and melted by love, and worn away little by little by the hidden fire. He no longer retains his colour... nor has he that body which Echo loved. Still, when she saw this, though angered and remembering, she pitied him, and as often as the poor boy said "Alas!" she repeated with her echoing voice "Alas!" and when his hands strike at his

---

158 Ovid (2000) p.91-93 excerpted

shoulders, she returns the same sounds of pain. His last words as he looked into the familiar pool were "Alas, in vain, beloved boy!" and the place echoed every word, and when he said "Goodbye!" Echo also said "Goodbye!"

He laid down his weary head in the green grass, death closing those eyes that had marveled at their lord's beauty. And even when he had been received into the house of shadows, he gazed into the Stygian waters. His sisters the Naiads... and the Dryads lamented. Echo returned their laments. And now they were preparing the funeral pyre, the quivering torches and the bier, but there was no body. They came upon a flower, instead of his body, with white petals surrounding a yellow heart.[159]

Narcissus discovers his own value and beauty; however, he fails to understand its purpose and potential. Rather than become a platform for relationship in service to others, his value and beauty become the central authority of his existence, rendering him incapable of any meaningful bond, even with himself. He is a product of his celebrity status that fuels his pride and arrogance while broadening the chasm between him and his admirers, who can never measure up to his worth. They believe he is better than them, and he believes that he is better than them. He becomes an unattainable icon to be worshiped, but not touched. Cut off from any meaningful relationship, or honest love, he succumbs to his own idolatry, withers away, and dies.

The story of Narcissus is the story of Love bent inwards. Narcissus never truly awakens—he reaches inward partway to observe the beauty that is there but fails to find its meaning and purpose. Without realizing its true worth, a precious gem becomes just a shiny bauble for one's amusement. Naturally, the bonding process in a relationship begins with the discovery, or the projection, of something of value in the Other. As the identity of the individual is revealed and becomes clearer, many of these assumptions and projections are challenged, and either the relationship fails through disillusionment, or it deepens to find a connection beneath the projection— to love just because one shares a basic humanity, flawed as it may be, to love in spite of our differences.

Echo, in the second part of the myth, represents this love-in-spite-of demeanor. Although still deeply wounded, she continues to reach out in pity to Narcissus to the very end. Even after the scorn, she suffers and the temporal loss of the beauty that originally attracted her to Narcissus, she moves deeper, to find a place of compassion. She finds meaning and purpose beneath the shiny exterior that incited her desire to be "together" with Narcissus—despite her invitation for him to "come to me" and share "what's

---

[159] Ovid (2000) p.93-95 excerpted

mine is yours"—beyond her hope that he would stay "here" forever. Finally, she pushes through her great disappointment and disillusionment, giving birth to a truer, deeper form of Love.

But it is not merely her ability to Love that is significant in the story. In her relationship with Narcissus, she represents the part of the psyche that can echo the vulnerability or suffering of another—to have empathy. The inner dynamic that fails in Narcissus is his ability to empathize, to delicately hold the psychic well-being of another within himself. It is his *unawareness*, his inability to internalize or have concern for another, that ultimately defines his dysfunction. Narcissus' failure to bond with Echo is ultimately his failure to bond with himself, the part of himself that hopes and suffers just the same.

Even when the roles are reversed, and he becomes the one who hopes and suffers, the intrapsychic wall that numbs the connection between the inner parts is never pierced. He is doomed by Nemesis to live a life of unrequited love. Chaos marginalizes the power and effect of Love. Narcissus struggles and dies, numb to the beauty and love outside of himself, whereas Echo transcends her projection, to find the depths of true empathy and compassion.

❖Lose Purpose/Bond

In the initiatory chapter proem from the novel "David Copperfield"[160] by Charles Dickens, David is in the depths of the Dark Night, wandering listlessly in brooding sorrow over an amalgam of misfortune, including the loss of Dora, the wife of his youth, due to a calamitous childbirth. "Haunted by the ghosts of many hopes, of many dear remembrances, many errors, many unavailing sorrows and regrets," he searches abroad for consolation and grounding of purpose and connection. The novel initially opens with David rudimentarily inquiring, "whether I shall turn out to be the hero of my own life." The story unwinds over the course of his life as he puts on and takes off different identities, different names, and different purposes—attempting to find his own voice. At the point of this invocation, David is nearing the nadir of his Dark Nightmare, having been stripped of his prior immature identity and purpose, he is preparing to move on.

Psychologically, adolescent moral development begins as the externalized power of our juvenile morality unravels; deconstructing the *voscentric* and *idcentric* purpose that has been inculcated in us through our

---

[160] Dickens (1997) p.793

family, education, and cultural narratives. Our fundamental sense of belonging, established by the bonds of our juvenile associations, is disrupted.

A call to authentic power is invoked in us, to which we can either respond or ignore. The fear of letting go of our familiar ways entrenches us into a dysfunctional juvenile morality. We become slaves to an overpowering system that uses our fears to control and abuse us. However, if we do let go, we initiate a new journey to find our authentic power—to individuate from the juvenile domain we have outgrown, reorienting ourselves to a new home and relationship to others.

Archetypally, as we grow, our social stature changes, and we are faced with a new role and function in the community. Our relational experience within the broader social construction calls us into a more mature service to the social good, using our power and skills to benefit others. Or else, we choose to ignore the identified needs of our community, focusing on our own needs, born of our fears and sense of inadequacy, to exploit others for our own gain.

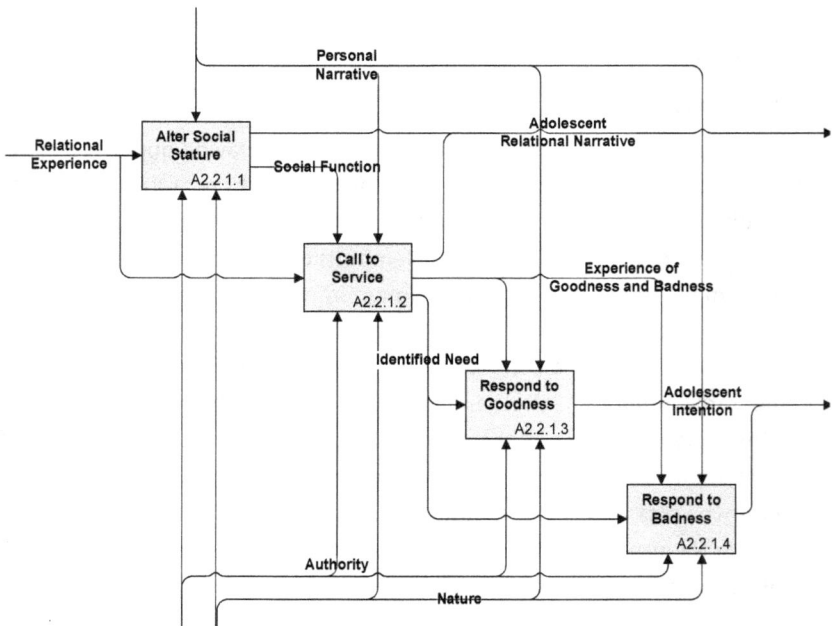

Model 11 - Lose Purpose/Bond (A2.2.1)

CHAPTER [2/II]

MIDNIGHT STRIKES

> I was born in chains, but I was taken out of Egypt. I was bound to a burden, but the burden it was raised… I fled to the edge of the mighty sea of sorrow, pursued by the riders of a cruel and dark regime. But the waters parted, and my soul crossed over—out of Egypt, out of Pharaoh's dream
> —*Leonard Cohen*, "Born In Chains"

The Torah of Obligation fully develops in the Wilderness of Midian and the surrounding desert in both the second and third Acts. But the final confrontation with the oppressive forces that hold the Israelites captive will occur back in Egypt as they descend into the Dark Night of the Passover plague. The Israelites have lost their privileged identity in Goshen over the course of four centuries to eventually become slave laborers—victims of the growing paranoia of several generations of Pharaohs. And Moses, our presumptive Hero, has become a victim of his own egotistic moral impulsivity, attacking and killing an Egyptian official. He has now escaped under the threat of death into the wilderness.

The second forty-year Act of the story of Moses chronicles how the Israelites engage the loss of their juvenile meaning and identity. It begins with Moses wandering beyond the Sea of Reeds into the desert of Midian. He now faces the loss of his prior identity as either Israelite or Egyptian, servant or ruler. By the end of the Act, the Israelites will face the loss of their identity as a part of Egyptian society—albeit as slaves, and yet their bond with their Egyptian masters is strong, representing a condition to which they are habituated after so many generations. And subsequently, the last Pharaoh of the story will face the loss of his identity as master over the Israelites and supreme power in Egypt.

❖Dark Night of Moses

The Heroic Dark Night of the Soul explores the human condition in which one's expectations and identity fail. It is the deconstruction of *truth* in the life of a soul—the breaking down and dissolution of one's juvenile perceptions of self to create the possibility of a more authentic conception of identity. In the Dark Night, the Hero encounters the gillul, representing his greatest fear or limitation, as some violent adversarial force or monster. The gillul is the manifestation of the strategic orientation one takes in compensation for what cannot be integrated into one's identity, what is not acceptable or controllable in the waking world, which is intrinsically experienced as the monster in the egoic unconscious. Ultimately the Dark Night represents loss of control in the pit of chaos—the place of existential terror, confusion, and dysfunction. However, it is also the place of opportunity—the place in the metamorphic Hero's journey that leads to authenticity and maturity in the reconstruction and restoration of the soul— but only if one lets go, to make it through to the other side.

Act Two is Moses' Dark Night of the Soul in which he is progressively transformed from an agent of the asymmetric power structure to the symmetric agency of the Nachash of Elohim, restorer of the family and revealer of the Savior Elohim. In the Moses story, the Night at issue is forty years long, culminating in the collective Dark Night for the Israelites where Yahweh passes over Egypt as the Messenger of Death. This, in turn, will take another forty years of wandering in the wilderness in Act Three to complete.

❖Land of Yahweh

In the Moses story, Midian is the land of Elohim—the place of the Mount of Elohim and the priest of Elohim. It is the place where the Parent Elohim reveals himself to Moses as *Yahweh*. Midian is the land beyond Yam Suph, the Sea of Reeds, often interpreted as the Red Sea in the English translations of the Torah. It later becomes known as the Gulf of Aqaba, the upper eastern tribute of the Red Sea south of the desert of Negev. It is the northwestern portion of the Desert of Arabia on the coast of Yam Suph, the land of the Midianites, descendants of Midian, the fourth son of Abraham and his second wife Keturah.

After being exiled from Egypt, Moses crosses beyond the bounds of the Sea of Reeds and is found sitting at a well in Midian at such a time as the daughters of the priest of Midian come to draw water for their father's flock. But other shepherds come and drive the daughters out. Moses, then, rescues them, allowing their flock to drink.

> When [the daughters] came to Reuel, their father, he said: "For what reason did you hasten to come in today?"
>
> They said: "An Egyptian man, he rescued us from the hand of the shepherds, and, moreover, he drew… out water for us and let the flock drink."
>
> Then he said to his daughters: "And where is he? Why is this that you have forsaken the man? Call him that he may eat bread."[161]

---

[161] CLV Exodus 2:18-20

Moses' first act in exile embodies the prior Victor/Hero who stands up to those who victimize and oppress, as in the former narrative of the Egyptian taskmaster that he kills. This time, however, Moses acts out of compassion rather than anger; notably, no one is killed. Moses, having been stripped of his old identity, is now accepted into a new family under the generosity of Reuel/Jethro, the priest of Midian.

> *Hence Moses was disposed to dwell with the man. He gave Zipporah, his daughter, to Moses for a wife. When she bore a son, he called his name Gershom, for he said: "A sojourner have I become in a foreign land."*[162]

Moses becomes a shepherd, the guardian and caretaker of the flocks of Reuel/Jethro, his father-in-law, the priest of Midian. Having lost his prior identity as a prince of the Fortress of Matsor/Egypt, he finds a new identity as Guardian-Caretaker, a humble shepherd in the wilderness of Midian, the land of Yahweh. However, his transformation as the Nachash of Elohim is yet to come.

❖Nachash of Elohim

After many decades, the Pharaoh, who had sought to punish Moses for the murder of his overseer, dies and a new Pharaoh rises up who likewise continues to oppress the Israelites. The Elohim of Israel hears their moaning and pledges to bring them out of captivity. He calls out to Moses as he is tending his flocks at the Mount of Elohim, commissioning Moses to go and deliver the children of Israel from Egypt. Thusly, appearing in the midst of a burning thornbush that is not consumed by fire, he declares:

> *I am the Elohim of your fathers, the Elohim of Abraham, the Elohim of Isaac and the Elohim of Jacob... I see the humiliation of My people who are in Egypt. And I hear their crying because of the presence of their taskmasters; for I know their pains. I have descended to rescue them from the hand of Egypt and to bring them up from that land to a land good and wide, to a land gushing with milk and honey, to the place of the Canaanite, the Hittite, the Amorite, the Perizzite, the Girgashite, the Hivite and the Jebusite. And now, behold, the cry of the sons of Israel, it has come to Me, and indeed, I have seen the oppression with which Egypt has been oppressing them. Now do go; I am sending you to Pharaoh. Bring forth My people, the sons of Israel, from Egypt.*[163]

This instantiates Yahweh as the Savior Elohim and Moses' identity as the Nachash of the Savior Elohim, the one who will serve as Yahweh's moral agent to deliver his children from servitude in the Fortress of Matsor/Egypt.

---

[162] CLV Exodus 2: 21-22
[163] CLV Exodus 3: 2-10

But Moses still sees himself as a humble shepherd of his father-in-law's flocks in the wilderness, far from his previous life in the land of Matsor/Egypt, proclaiming, "Who am I that I should go to Pharaoh?" The Savior Elohim assures Moses that he will be with him and bids Moses to bring the sons of Israel back to serve him on this mountain.

Moses then asks how he should identify the Savior Elohim of the burning thornbush to the sons of Israel, to which the Savior Elohim responds that his name is *Yahweh*, which in the Arabic dialect of Midian means "the one who loves, blows, and falls" indicating his intrinsic character as the one who loves his children, breathes life into them, and from whom blessings fall. In the accompanying elucidation of his name, however, Yahweh focuses on his character as the one who breathes life and who does not owe his breath or existence to another.

> *I shall come to be just as I am coming to be...Thus shall you say to the sons of Israel, I-Shall-Come-to-Be, He has sent me to you... Yahweh, the Elohim of your fathers, the Elohim of Abraham, the Elohim of Isaac and the Elohim of Jacob, He has sent me to you. This is My Name for the eon, And this the Remembrance of Me for generation after generation.*[164]

While the mythographers have referred to the Parent/Savior Elohim as Yahweh previously in the myth, this is considered to be the origin story of his revelation as Yahweh on the Mount of Elohim; specifically stating that it shall now be a remembrance for generations to come.

Yahweh Elohim then further lays out his plan, but Moses quite perceptively is still filled with doubt that anyone would believe that the Savior Elohim had spoken to him out in the middle of the desert on such grave matters. So, Yahweh tells Moses to throw his shepherd's rod that he is carrying to the ground, and it becomes a serpent/nachash. He is then told to take a hold of the nachash by the tail and it is restored to a rod. Yahweh then tells Moses to put his hand to his bosom, and when he brings it forth, it has become leprous. Returning his hand to his bosom, his hand is restored. Yahweh states:

> *Hence it will come to be should they not believe you nor hearken to the voice of the first sign, they may believe the voice of the latter sign. Yet it will come to be even should they not believe these two signs, nor hearken to your voice, then you will take some of the water of the waterway and pour it out on the dry ground. And the waters... will come to be... blood on the dry ground.*[165]

---

[164] CLV Exodus 3:13-15
[165] CLV Exodus 4:8-9

The Rod of Elohim symbolizes the power of the Nachash of Elohim and becomes an ongoing symbol of Yahweh's authority throughout the Exodus journey. The restoration of the leprous hand, a condition where the skin sloughs off the bone, is an invocation to the nachash that renews itself by the shedding of its skin. The water from the waterway can be interpreted as an allusion to Apep who is continually at odds with, seeking to destroy, the state of Egypt under the authority and protection of Re (a tangential theme that begins to develop more completely in the Plague narrative.)

Still reluctant, Moses complains that he is an inadequate speaker, heavy of mouth and tongue, and thus Yahweh should send another. Yahweh becomes angry with Moses, replying:

> *Is there not Aaron, the Levite, your brother? I know that he can speak...*
> *You will speak to him and place the words in his mouth. And I shall come to*
> *be with your mouth and with his mouth, and I will direct both of you as to*
> *what you shall do. So he will speak for you to the people; it will come to be*
> *that he shall become a mouth for you, and you shall become an elohim for*
> *him. And this rod shall you take in your hand with which you shall do the*
> *signs.*[166]

Moses ceases to strive with the Savior Elohim, his identity as the Oracle of Elohim and Deliverer is complete. He will now be the Nachash of Elohim in the approaching Dark Night.

❖Countdown to Midnight

In the Torah, the Pharaohs are never identified, nor given names. They essentially personify the power of the Fortress of Matsor/Egypt. In the Joseph narrative, the first Pharaoh is the one who brings all of Egypt into economic submission; but is also the instrument of salvation for the family of Israel, allowing them to settle in the fertile plains of Goshen during the famine. The second Pharaoh is presented as paranoid, who consequently brings the Israelites into moral servitude with excessive building programs, intending to suppress their growing numbers and power in Goshen. This, then, is the state of affairs for many generations until the third mentioned Pharaoh, who is as paranoid as the second, takes the step to declare that all newly born Israelite boys shall be unceremoniously flung into the Nile to be drowned, fully instantiating Israel's status as powerless political slaves to Egypt. The fourth Pharaoh, while continuing the inimical servitude of the Israelites, is only briefly mentioned as seeking to punish Moses for murdering an Egyptian taskmaster. The fifth mentioned Pharaoh is the ruler of the Exodus narrative,

---

[166] CLV Exodus 4:14-17

personifying the same power and paranoia of his predecessors. Each successive Pharaoh amplifies the transition from Villain/Viper to Master/Lord using their power to victimize, subjugate, and oppress their subjects, both Egyptian and Israelite, for their personal and political gain.

The Pharaohs represent the authoritarian narrative of future-egocentric authority at the top of the hierarchical system of power. They also embody the conservative psychological narrative of present-egocentric authority, driven by fear to conserve an identity of privilege and control over the domain that defines their authority. The Plague narrative is an exploration of this dynamic in the Dark Night of the Soul.

Archetypally, the Heroic Dark Night of the Soul is an invitation to change—the transformation of identity from dysfunctional to functional, from inauthentic to authentic. Moses has already committed to his own transformation and is now ready to face his own Dark Night, which for him has been his relationship to power in Egypt. The Israelites and Pharaoh are two different sides or aspects of the approaching Dark Night that will confront the Israelites' submission to Matsor. Each actor will have to choose how to respond to the process that is about to unfold. The Pharaoh represents entrenchment in the old ways, a refusal to let go of the authority structure upon which the power of Egypt is built, and the gilluls upon whom meaning and safety are manifest. As such, the Pharaoh, by nature of his function, eminently refuses to let go of a coveted source of wealth, represented by the forced labor of the Israelites. Yahweh tells Moses that even with great signs and miracles Pharaoh will not yield.

> *I appoint you an elohim to Pharaoh; and Aaron, your brother, shall come to be your prophet. You yourself shall speak all that I am instructing you while Aaron, your brother, he shall speak to Pharaoh that he dismiss the sons of Israel from his land. And I Myself shall stiffen the heart of Pharaoh, and I will increase My signs and My miracles in the land of Egypt. Though Pharaoh shall not hearken to you, yet I will lay My hand on Egypt, and I will bring forth My hosts, My people, the sons of Israel, from the land of Egypt with great judgments. And all then Egyptians will know that I am Yahweh when I stretch out My hand over Egypt, and I bring forth the sons of Israel from their midst.[167]*

Archetypally, conservatism represents an investment in one's identification within the existing power structure that is nearly impossible to let go of or change. Progress, or even variation, threatens the very core of one's power

---

[167] CLV Exodus 7:1-5

and identity. It is a theme that runs deep in the later Reified Basar myth as the foundation of asymmetric religious and political power.

The Plague narrative is a lengthy exploration of this conservative investment in the existing power structure by Pharaoh and the Egyptians. Each plague represents a gillul that is a source of power and meaning to the Egyptians. As such, it is also a confrontation with the religious and moral authority of the future-idcentric institutions. Many of the initial plague episodes are duplicated by the priests of Egypt in the narrative. However, in each plague, a line is drawn between Yahweh as Savior Elohim and the Egyptian gilluls—portraying Yahweh's power over their elohim:

> *Moses and Aaron entered to Pharaoh... just as Yahweh had instructed. Aaron flung his rod before Pharaoh and before his courtiers, and it became a snake. Pharaoh, however, called for the wise men and for the enchanters. And even they, the sacred scribes of Egypt, did so with their occultisms. Each man flung his rod, and they became snakes. Then Aaron's rod swallowed up their rods. Yet the heart of Pharaoh was steadfast, and he did not hearken to them, just as Yahweh had spoken.*[168]

From the perspective of Egypt, Moses is enrolled as Apep, the nachash that challenges the institutional authority of Egypt. As the embodiment of hierarchical power given to him by Re, Pharaoh is morally obligated to defeat the forces that challenge the moral construct of the present affairs. In the Dark Night of the Soul, the monster is the agent of change, or else the justification to prevent change, re-entrenching oneself in the current system. This is the heart of Pharaoh's dilemma. In all of Moses' challenges to the existing system, Pharaoh is unyielding to Moses' demand to let the sons of Israel go. It is impossible for Pharaoh to let go without letting go of his own identity as ruler of Matsor, the supreme power in Egypt, and as master over the Israelites.

❖Messenger of Death

The final episode of the Plague narrative is the killing of the firstborn of Matsor/Egypt by Yahweh. It is the final challenge to the asymmetric power structure of Matsor representing the archetypal Kingdom of Cain, which is invested in the authority of the firstborn son to preserve the identity and power of the father in perennial succession going back to Cain, the firstborn of Adam. Yahweh thusly declares:

> *About midnight I am going forth in the midst of Egypt. And every firstborn in the land of Egypt will die, from the firstborn of Pharaoh, sitting on his*

---

[168] CLV Exodus 7:10-11

throne, unto the firstborn of the maidservant who is behind the millstones and every firstborn of beast. There will come to be a great cry in all the land of Egypt, such as has not occurred, and such as shall not occur again. Yet against any of the sons of Israel, not a cur shall point his tongue against a man or even a beast, so that you may know that Yahweh is distinguishing between Egypt and Israel.[169]

As with the previous nine plagues of the gillul, Yahweh draws a final distinction between the asymmetric power of the political firstborn of Adam, and the newly anointed lineage of Israel as the firstborn of the Parent/Savior Elohim, representing the symmetric power of the Kingdom of Elohim.

Yahweh, then, gives special instructions to the Israelites to prepare themselves for this Dark Night when the Savior Elohim will pass over at midnight, bringing death to the firstborn of all households that are not marked by the blood of a ritually prepared lamb.

A flawless flockling, a year-old male, shall you come to have [and will slay it] ...every assembly of the congregation of the sons of Israel, between the evening hours. And they will take some of the blood and put it on the two jambs and on the lintel, on the houses in which they are eating it.

Then they will eat the flesh on this night, roasted with fire, and with unleavened bread; over bitter herbs shall they eat it... And what is left of it until the morning you shall burn with fire. And thus shall you eat it, with your waist girded, your sandals on your feet and your stave in your hand. You will eat it in urgent haste.

It is the passover to Yahweh. For I will pass through the land of Egypt in this night and smite every firstborn in the land of Egypt, from human even unto beast, and in all the elohim of Egypt I shall execute judgments; I am Yahweh.

Then the blood will become a sign for you on the houses where you are. When I see the blood I will pass over on you. And there shall not come to be a stroke on you to cause ruin when I smite in the land of Egypt.[170]

The night unfolds as Yahweh has forewarned. In dismay, Pharaoh subsequently relents and lets the Israelites go from slavery in Matsor/Egypt.

In the Passover ritual, the Israelites are given a new identity as the ones marked by the blood of the Passover lamb, symbolizing the protection of Yahweh as he brings them out of servitude in Egypt; renewing his moral obligation to Abraham, to make a great nation of them in the land of Canaan as his anointed firstborn sons under the familial kingship of Yahweh. This is the beginning of the national Kingdom of Yahweh in Israel, which will last

---

[169] CLV Exodus 11:4-7
[170] CLV Exodus 12:5-13

some four hundred years until Israel rejects this kingship under the Judge Samuel.

❖The Exodus

The book of Exodus describes the first two years of the Israelites' journey from Egypt into the Wilderness, concluding with the creation of the Tabernacle at the foot of the Mount of Elohim. However, in terms of the Israelites' exit from the land of Egypt, it is distinctly demarcated by their miraculous crossing of the eastern Sea of Reeds into the Desert of Arabia. Historically, the Kingdom of Matsor/Egypt extended from the Mediterranean Sea in the north to Nubia in the South. On the east, it historically remained, at a minimum, bounded by the edge of the Wilderness of Egypt (modern-day Sinai Peninsula[171]) along the shores of the upper eastern Sea of Reeds (the Gulf of Aqaba), and northwards up to the Negev border with Philistia on the Mediterranean Sea. This defines the mythological topography of the Exodus narrative.

After the Midnight Passover, Pharaoh relents and the Israelites gathered their belongings, including a multitude of sheep and cattle. They also gathered unleavened bread for their travels and the bones of Joseph, which they were obligated to take back to Canaan to be buried. As they leave Goshen, the Egyptians gave them a great sum of gold and silver and clothing as tribute. As the Israelites' journey begins, Yahweh becomes a visible presence to guide them on their exodus out of Matsor/Egypt and beyond, "going before them by day in a column of cloud to guide them along the way, and by night in a column of fire."[172] The Cloud of Elohim guides them across the Wilderness of Egypt to its eastern border on the shores of the Sea of Reeds, south of the Negev, specifically to avoid war with Philistia in the north. This is the nadir of the Dark Night, which sets up a final confrontation with the Pharaoh at the outside border of Egypt.

In the Dark Night of the Soul, the primary trait of the authoritarian/conservatist narrative is their "hardness of heart"—an indomitable commitment to the conservation of the traditional power structure—to prevent the change that is being called for in the Dark Night.

---

[171] The modern Sinai Peninsula has nothing to do with the Sinai in the narrative other than a misguided belief by later Christians that it was the same place. In the narrative Horeb/Sinai is described as being in Midian which is on the other side of the Sea of Reeds. Other than that, it is not certain which mountain in the Arabian Desert was identified as Sinai.
[172] CLV Exodus 13:21

Throughout the Unified Basar and Torah mythology, this same indomitable allegiance to power is represented by the moral guardians of traditional power—the Religionists and Moralists. So likewise, this is true of Pharaoh, who, after a short period of manumission, repossesses his resolve to humiliate the Israelites, musters his armies, and pursues them across the full breadth of the Wilderness of Egypt.

The Cloud of Elohim has led the Israelites into what appears to be a dead-end at the outside border of Egypt with their backs against the Sea of Reeds and boxed in on both sides by the terrain. The situation appears hopeless as Pharaoh's chariots close in on the Israelite tribes, who, in despair, cry out to Moses:

> Is it for lack of no tombs in Egypt that you have taken us to die in the wilderness? What is this you have done to us in bringing us forth from Egypt? Is not this the word which we spoke to you in Egypt, saying: "Leave off from us and do let us serve the Egyptians, for it is better for us to serve the Egyptians than for us to die in the wilderness?"[173]

There is nothing the Israelites can do to escape the power of Pharaoh and his chariots that are descending upon them to reclaim or destroy them.

The exodus from Egypt began by marking the doorway of the household with the protective blood of the lamb, identifying the firstborn of the family therein as one whom the messenger of death should pass over. This initial doorway to freedom is instantiated by a willful act of the household, to ritually prepare the meal inside and mark the outside with blood. In the morning, the Israelites walk through this bloodstained doorway to freedom. As they reach the border, with their backs to the sea, it appears their journey has culminated prematurely, clouded in apparent failure and hopelessness. The Israelites are faced with certain annihilation having nowhere to escape. Then an unforeseen second doorway is opened that is not in their control. Yahweh speaks to Moses saying:

> Raise high your rod and stretch out your hand over the sea and split it, that the sons of Israel may enter into the midst of the sea on dry ground. And I, behold Me making the heart of the Egyptians steadfast that they may enter after them; for I shall indeed be glorified over Pharaoh and over all his army, over his chariots and over his horsemen. Then the Egyptians will know that I am Yahweh when I am glorified over Pharaoh, over his chariots and over his horsemen. Hence the messenger of the One, Elohim, who was going before the camp of Israel, journeyed and went behind them. Also the column of cloud journeyed from before them and stood behind them.[174]

---

[173] CLV Exodus 14:11-12
[174] CLV Exodus 14:16-19

Yahweh unexpectedly opens a doorway through the Sea of Reeds, leading to safety beyond the borders of Egypt, into the Wilderness of Shur in Arabia. He then closes that door behind them, wiping out the pursuing armies of Pharaoh, drowning them in the sea. The power that has humiliated and enslaved the Israelites finally has been destroyed. They are now beyond the borders of the Fortress of Matsor/Egypt, free from the oppressive power of the Pharaoh.

❖ Valley of Death

The passage through the Dark Night is founded on the act of letting go of the broken or inauthentic identity that holds us to the past, which is represented by an overpowering dark force that enslaves us to our fear, vulnerability, and missingness. The Dark Night begins with a rational act, an engagement of purpose and willfulness, to descend ritually into the darkness, the face of death, through the first doorway into an uncertain destiny. It is here that our identity is initially, and often painfully, deconstructed. We pass into the wilderness with no way out, where we must finally face the monster. Here is the final test, one last pull to return to the past, to return to the place of servitude, or else to succumb to our defeat, to die in the wilderness. With no options left, our back to the wall, and nothing left to defend ourselves against an overwhelming force, we must let go of our need to control the outcome in order that a second door may open behind us to move forward. It is here that we experience the death of our former selves and the powers that held us. It is here we encounter the non-rational evocation to authenticity on the other side.

This counter-intuitive narrative challenges the rational path of domination over our foes, of conquering our fears cloaked as the egoic Victor/Hero. On the contrary, the metamorphic Hero faces the ultimate terror of losing control in the face of their worst nightmare, only then, after letting go, to find freedom on the other side.

❖ Deceitful Gift

In moralistic mythologies, false identity is sometimes a trick of the gods to punish humankind, or else portrayed as the source of all human suffering. The Greek myth of Pandora, whose name means "all-gifted," is archetypally about the consequences of false identity within the dynamics of Jealousy and Conflict. In Hesiod's version of the story, the Titan Prometheus/Forethought creates Man in the image of the Great Overseers, and the Olympian Father Zeus breathes life into him. But Zeus is distrustful, constantly maneuvering to maintain his preeminence amongst the Great Overseers. As such, he withholds benefits to Man out of spite for the subversive Titan Prometheus, who he does not trust. However, when Zeus withholds fire from Man, Prometheus, steals fire and gives it to him. In response, Zeus devises a plan to punish both Prometheus and Man, declaring:

> [Prometheus] surpassing all in cunning, you are glad that you have outwitted me and stolen fire—a great plague to you yourself and to men that shall be. But I will give men as the price for fire an evil thing in which they may all be glad of heart while they embrace their own destruction.[175]

Then, it is said, Zeus, the father of men and gods, in the true fashion of all villains, laughed aloud at his dastardly plan to create the ultimate evil. The plot continues:

> And [Zeus] bade... Hephaestus [Fire] make haste and mix earth with water and to put in it the voice and strength of human kind, and fashion a sweet, lovely maiden-shape, like to the immortal goddesses in face; and Athena [Wisdom] to teach her needlework and the weaving of the varied web; and golden Aphrodite [Sexuality] to shed grace upon her head and cruel longing and cares that weary the limbs. And he charged Hermes [Herald]... to put in her a shameless mind and a deceitful nature... And they obeyed the lord Zeus... Forthwith the famous Lame God [Hephaestus] moulded clay in the likeness of a modest maid... And the goddess bright-eyed Athena girded and clothed her, and the divine Graces and queenly Persuasion put necklaces of gold upon her, and the rich-haired Hours crowned her head with spring flowers. And Pallas Athena bedecked her form with all manner of finery. Also [Hermes] contrived within her lies and crafty words and a deceitful nature at the will of loud thundering Zeus, and the Herald of the gods put speech in her. And he called this woman Pandora [All-Gifted], because all they who dwelt on Olympus gave each a gift, a plague to men.[176]

According to this patriarchal myth, Pandora, the first Woman, is thus a punishment for challenging the power of Zeus. She is as beautiful as she is deceitful—the ultimate evil to be perpetrated on Man.

> But when he had finished the sheer, hopeless snare, the Father [Zeus] sent [Hermes], the swift messenger of the gods, to take it to Epimetheus [Afterthought] as a gift. And Epimetheus did not think on what Prometheus [Forethought] had said to him, bidding him never take a gift of Olympian Zeus, but to send it back for fear it might prove to be something harmful to men. But he took the gift, and afterwards, when the evil thing was already his, he understood. For ere this the tribes of men lived on earth remote and free from ills and hard toil and heavy sicknesses which bring the Fates upon men; for in misery men grow old quickly.

> But the woman took off the great lid of the jar with her hands and scattered, all these and her thought caused sorrow and mischief to men.

---

[175] Hesiod (2018) p.16
[176] Hesiod (2018) p.16

Only Hope remained there in an unbreakable home within under the rim of the great jar, and did not fly out at the door; for ere that, the lid of the jar stopped her, by the will of... Zeus who gathers the clouds. But the rest, countless plagues, wander amongst men; for earth is full of evils, and the sea is full. Of themselves diseases come upon men continually by day and by night, bringing mischief to mortals silently; for wise Zeus took away speech from them. So is there no way to escape the will of Zeus.[177]

All evil and suffering known to Man are initiated by the deceitful identity of Pandora. Before Pandora, in parallel with the moralized Genesis Exile myth, Man lived in the safety and comfort of an Edenic paradise "free from ills and hard toil and heavy sicknesses."

In this Olympic myth, the power of Fire is the domain of the Overseers that is encroached on by the humans, similar to the domain of the Knowledge of Goodness and Badness in the Genesis Exile myth. Zeus, acting as both Overseer and Adversary to humankind, creates the false identity of Pandora. Archetypally, she is a synthesis of Eve and the Adversarial Serpent from the moralized Christian creation myth in which the moralized Serpent deceives Eve and thereby humankind with the promise of great power and wisdom apart from the Christian-God. Pandora is the deceit of the Overseers visited upon Mankind through her great gifts and beauty bringing "sorrow and mischief to men." The Greeks' mythological declaration that *Women by their creation are not to be trusted* is an expanded version of Adam's moral deflection to Yahweh, stating, "The woman whom You gave, withal, she gave to me from the tree and I am eating."

The Pandora myth declares that it is according to the deceit of the Great Overseers to create the deceitful Woman through whom all the suffering and ills beset humankind. Her great beauty and gifts come with a great price so that men "may all be glad of heart while they embrace their own destruction." As such, the juvenile morality of the Pandora myth, in parallel with the moralized Genesis Exile myth, functions historically as a justification for the patriarchal misogynists in both Greek and Christian moralism. The first Woman in both myths is subsequently blamed by men for all the evils which beset Mankind. This is actually forewarned within the archetypal Genesis Exile myth wherein Yahweh cautions Eve that a consequence of eating the immature Fruit of Morality would instantiate a new asymmetric power dynamic between her and her husband. Adam would now treat her as a thing

---

[177] Hesiod (2018) p.16

to *rule over*, rather than a person to *relate to*, stating: "In grief shall you bear children; Yet by your husband is your [longing]. And he shall rule over you."[178]

At the heart of each myth is either Pandora's Jar, or similarly, in the moralized Christian myth, the fruit of the Knowledge of Good and Evil. In all moralized mythology, *evil* is the absence or opposite of *good*, or simply *immorality*. Olympic moralism is conceived of as a typical moral binary of good versus evil, and within the Pandora story, Man versus Woman. In the moralized Judeo-Christian interpretation, Eve eating the fruit of the Knowledge of Good and Evil becomes the moral equivalent of Pandora opening the Jar. Pandora is predestined by her false or deceitful identity to bring evil upon Man—it is in her nature. Zeus, the central authority, is both Father and Adversary. Jealousy and conflict define his relationship with humankind and sets the pattern for all relationships in this moralized context.

Ultimately, all forms of evil and suffering are a deceitful gift wrapped in a shiny package, given as a punishment for stealing the power of the gods. This is the central premise of Olympic moralism, and, for that matter, most forms of moralism, which are intrinsically based on conformity to a code of behavior in service to a hierarchical asymmetric authority. It is an explanation of why suffering is necessary to compensate for a moral imbalance in the natural order of things. Underlying all good things is a shiny evil that the gods do not want Man to enjoy. According to moralist dogma, the morally weak continually return to these deceits that seem pleasant for the moment, but ultimately lead to destruction.

The false identity symbolized by Pandora is the downfall of humankind. Psychologically, it represents the personas we create to face the world, to hide our brokenness and vulnerability, our *missingness* based on fear. These personas embody our prejudices and deceit with a veneer of civility. They make us appear beautiful while inside we are a wretched mess of suffering and pain. The way to freedom is Hope—the last thing left in Pandora's Jar. It is what drives the experience of the Dark Night when everything appears to be out of control. Hope is the unexpected doorway that in the end opens up to our freedom.

❖Lose Meaning/Identity

The prelusive chapter proem is a stanza from the song "Born in Chains"[179] by Leonard Cohen, wherein Cohen takes us on a personal journey into the emotional depths of the Dark Night symbolized by the Exodus from

---

[178] CLV Genesis 3:16
[179] Cohen (2014)

the perils of Egypt. He elicits the struggle to be free from the chains of sorrow and adversity, to find renewal on the outside of "a cruel and dark regime." But in the midst of the Dark Night, Leonard reflects on the power of the darkness to succor the longing of the suffering spirit: "I've heard the soul unfolds in the chambers of its longing... but all the ladders of the night have fallen, just darkness now, to lift the longing up."

Psychologically, adolescent morality continues to develop in response to the progressive failure of the externalized authority of our juvenile morality. The false identity inculcated from the authoritarian establishment is challenged by elemental forces within the psyche, and either engaged or rejected in the Dark Night. Fear of letting go of the societal ways entrenches us into a dysfunctional juvenile morality.

Adolescent moral development evolves as we let go of juvenile meaning and identity—the immature understanding of who we are in the world around us, and what entities influence us. It develops as we continue to recognize our own authority to engage the world and transform it. Whereas in juvenile development, our identity is founded on our relationship with our parental Guardian-Caretakers, in adolescent development it evolves in relationship to the societal systems that guide and aid us. At this stage of development, the conscience is still founded on external authorities but is beginning to move inward, to find a deeper calling.

Archetypally, the relational dynamic begins to change as our identity and role are challenged within our tribal and familial groups. We find new social groups that better define our developing value systems. Some individuals will identify the world as a place of scarcity, joining in asymmetric groups out of selfishness and greed that reinforce hierarchal values designed to conserve the authority of those already in power. Other individuals will identify the world as a place of sufficiency, joining in symmetric groups that reinforce empathy and altruism, building community and sharing resources for mutual benefit.

Model 12 - Lose Meaning/Identity (A2.2.2)

CHAPTER [3/II]

MOURNING AFTER

> And you know it's time to go… across the
> fields of mourning, light in the distance.
> And you hunger for the time—time to
> heal, desire time. And your earth moves
> beneath your own dream landscape.
> —*U2, "A Sort Of Homecoming"*

The Torah of Obligation is completed in the Wilderness of Sinai before the Mount of Elohim in the land of Midian. The descent into the Dark Night of the Soul has reached its nadir with the destruction of their former captors on the edge of the Wilderness of Egypt. The Hero's Journey begins its ascent back into the quotidian world. The Cloud of Elohim has led the Israelites beyond the boundary of the Sea of Reeds separating the Israelites from their former identity as the Slaves of Matsor. Their previous life, rooted in subjugation and humiliation, has been left behind, at least circumstantially. While it no longer has dominion over their destiny, after generations of invasive abuse and oppressive devaluation, the normalization of their victimhood is still active in their reactive impulses. Faced with the loss of identity, an overwhelming sense of scarcity, fear of the unknown path set before them, and anxiety from the unpredictability and lack of boundaries in their new situation, the Israelites yearn to return to the meager state of subsistence with which they were familiar. In principle, there is no returning through the passageway from which they have emerged. But the wilderness of unknowing beyond the Dark Night is terrifying. Once the former ways have passed, there is no road map. It will take time to let go of the old ways. It will require the reformation of new boundaries and relationships as they journey towards Canaan, the land of hope promised to their forefathers.

The last forty-year Act of the story of Moses chronicles how the Israelites engage the loss of their juvenile values and boundaries. The Israelites have been powerless for so long that they must now develop a fundamentally new moral framework—learning what is mutual freedom and what it means to be in an equal and inclusive relationship with one another and with the Savior Elohim.

In context to the Israelites' adolescent development, Yahweh evolves from the parental Guardian and Caretaker to the salvational Guide and Aide. In their journey towards a healthy and whole understanding of love, they must develop a mature responsibility towards one another. They will wander in the desert for forty years, while they establish a new identity based on their new relationship with one another and the Savior Elohim. They must mourn the past, let it go, and then build new boundaries that will enable them to move forward into the Promised Land, free from the taskmaster that still inhabits their operative memories. Moses, as the Nachash of Elohim, has fulfilled his calling to deliver the Israelites from servitude. His role has now metamorphosed into the Judge and Revealer of the Torah, the Law of Elohim. This now fully instantiates the Kingdom of Yahweh in Israel.

❖Former Slaves

Over the course of some four hundred years in Egypt, the Israelites have gone from initially being a favored tribe in Goshen under Joseph to becoming the moral servants of the archetypal Kingdom of Cain under the next Pharaoh, conscripted to build his cities. And then, by the end of this period, the Israelites have become exploited slave laborers, a subjugated people that have completely lost their freedom and societal value. With each passing generation, the Israelites fell into more severe oppression and abuse before the all-encompassing, and ever so severe, might of Matsor, until, finally, Yahweh responds to their suffering by calling on Moses to deliver the Israelites from slavery in Egypt.

Over the next four hundred years, Yahweh will become the Israelites' authority and guide, operating as Servant King through his appointed Judges, beginning with Moses. The Kingdom of Yahweh in Israel is more than just the story of how Yahweh saved the Israelites from slavery in Egypt. It is a profound story of moral development. It is the Israelite's journey to become moral and relational servants of one another under the guidance of the Savior Elohim.

Throughout the Exodus journey, the Israelites are a broken people— grumbling, doubtful, disobedient, untrustworthy, juvenile, and dysfunctional. Having been exploited by the kingdom of Matsor/Egypt and perpetually powerless to meet their own needs, they are characterized as the epitome of psychological nakedness, the primal dysfunction at the core of the Adamite Exile narrative. They are vulnerable, fearful, isolated, and terrified amidst the scarcity of Midbar-Nod. When they arrive at the Mount of Elohim and evasively bow down to worship the Golden Calf, Yahweh comes close to wiping them out and starting over with just Moses' family. But Moses intervenes, beseeching Yahweh to be merciful to his chosen people under the covenant he made with Abraham. Yahweh relents and declares:

Yahweh El, Who is compassionate and gracious, slow to anger and abundant with [kindness] and truth, preserving [kindness] to thousands, bearing with depravity, transgression and [failure], yet He is not holding innocent... but visiting the depravity of the fathers on the sons and on the sons' sons, on the third and on the fourth generation.[180]

While there are consequences for the Israelite's actions, Yahweh affirms that his character as Savior Elohim is fundamentally one of compassion and grace, working to aide and guide his anointed servants. Thus, his judgment "on the fourth generation" foreshadows that over the next forty years they will wander in the desert until a new generation that has completely let go of their collective slave mentality will then be allowed to enter the land promised to their forefather Abraham. Only then will the nation be ready to embrace their new freedom in Canaan. Archetypally, the Third Act is the story of the Adamites' adolescence, wandering querulously around the wilderness of Arabia in the shadow of hope on their way to a promised land of peace and abundance.

❖**New Relationship**

Upon passing through the eastern Sea of Reeds into the Wilderness of Shur in Arabia, Moses proceeds to lead the Israelites on a journey to the Mount of Elohim in Midian in accordance with his prior commission by Yahweh, which ordained:

When you bring the people forth from Egypt you shall serve the One, Elohim, on this mountain."[181]

On this initial journey from the Sea of Reeds to the Mount of Elohim, the newly established Servant-Savior relationship between the Israelites and Yahweh deepens and evolves into a functional alliance in which the Savior Elohim is both Guide and Aide.

Amidst the circumstantial deprivation of the wilderness, the Savior Elohim provides for the Israelites basic subsistence and health. Shortly after entering the Wilderness of Shur, having traveled just a few days, they fail to find any water. Finally, they encounter a spring, which, to their dismay, is bitter and undrinkable. Yahweh thus directs Moses to a particular tree and instructs him to throw its branches into the bitter spring, and subsequently, the water becomes drinkable. Here Yahweh pronounces his first commitment

---

[180] CLV Exodus 34:6-7
[181] CLV Exodus 3:12

to the nation of Israel, declaring that if they will heed his relational statutes to care for and love one another, he will be their Healer:

> *If you shall hearken... to the voice of Yahweh your Elohim and do what is upright in His eyes, and you give ear to His instructions and observe all His statutes, then all the illnesses which I placed on the Egyptians I shall not place on you, for I am Yahweh your Healer.*[182]

Thus Yahweh your Healer, or Yahweh-Rapha in Hebrew, becomes the foundation of this new Servant-Savior relationship between Yahweh and the tribes of Israel.

As the Israelites travel further into the wilderness, they begin to experience the scarcity of their desert asylum more profoundly, fearing that they will eventually starve to death in this sparse, arid wilderness. Some complain to Moses that at least in their previous life in Egypt as slaves they still "ate bread to satisfaction," fretting that now he has "brought us forth to this wilderness to put this entire assembly to death with famine."[183] In response to their anxious grumbling, Yahweh generously addresses their substantive need for nourishment by bestowing a daily provision of bread and meat for them to eat, identified as *manna* and quail. The *manna* is an edible substance that fortuitously appears each morning on the ground. They are told that they should collect only enough manna for their daily provision; any more than that will spoil by the next day. Thusly, the Savior Elohim provides for his Servant's essential needs for the entire nomadic journey through the deserts of Arabia and the Negev until they are settled in the land of Canaan.

Next, Yahweh addresses their need for safety and security. The Israelites soon encounter their first hostile tribe, the Amalekites, who attack them at Rephidim. As the battle begins, Moses stations himself on a hill overlooking the battle, holding up the Rod of Elohim in his hand. As long as the Rod of Elohim is raised up, the battle goes in Israel's favor, foreshadowing the raised Serpent in the later narrative. However, if Moses lowers his arm to rest, the Amalekites gain ground against the Israelites. So, Moses' attendants prop up his arm until the battle is won.

As the *Torah of Obligation* unfolds, a new trust relationship develops in the archetypal wilderness of Midbar-Nod, allowing the Israelites to put their confidence in the symmetric power dynamic of the Savior Elohim as provider, protector, and supporter in the midst of circumstantial scarcity. With each new situation they encounter, the earlier guardian and caretaker roles of the

---

[182] CLV Exodus 15:26
[183] CLV Exodus 16:3

Child-Parent dependency are supplanted by the guide and aide roles of the *Servant-Savior* relationship.

❖Intimate Encounters

The Kingdom of Elohim in Israel is founded on the direct numinous presence of the Savior Elohim who supports the independence of his children. This symmetric power dynamic is the basis for the development of the adolescent relationship within the Unified Basar and Torah mythology.

At the start of the Exodus myth, the direct intimacy between parent and child Elohim that was established in the primordial Eden narrative is reprised. Beginning with Moses' initial encounter with Yahweh on the Mount of Elohim through the burning thornbush, an ongoing intimate conversation with Yahweh is established, which then continues upon Moses' return to the Mount. The Israelites are briefly included in this direct encounter at the fiery Mount of Elohim until they abruptly reject it as being too frightening.

During the Plague narrative, Yahweh commissions Moses and Aaron as his prophets, promising to give them the words to speak before Pharaoh and the Israelites. Yahweh is then the direct power behind the Plagues as Moses confronts Pharaoh to release the Israelites. Yahweh then becomes the messenger of death in the Passover narrative.

As the Israelites leave Egypt, the direct presence of Yahweh Elohim becomes a cloud by day and a pillar of fire by night to guide the Israelites through the Wilderness of Egypt, then through the Sea of Reeds, and on to the Mount of Elohim. Most of the first two years after the exodus from Egypt occur at the foot of the Mount of Elohim. The book of Exodus ends with the building of the Tabernacle tent. As the Israelites' encampment at the Mount of Elohim comes to a close, the Cloud of Elohim descends upon the newly built Tabernacle tent, which then becomes the mobile presence of Yahweh in the midst of each new encampment as they continue their journey through the wilderness of Arabia in the subsequent books of the Pentateuch.

❖The Tabernacle of Elohim

The Tabernacle of Elohim, which Yahweh describes in detail at the end of the book of Exodus, embodies the integral Torah myth. In the Tabernacle, the newly minted Levite priests' role is limited to bringing that myth to life and preserving it, in contrast to the elaborate role of the Egyptian priests that act as oracles and authorities of the ritualized cult on behalf of the gods. The Levites are essentially ritual storytellers and caretakers of the Torah artifacts and obligations.

The prescribed layout of the Tabernacle of Elohim is fundamentally designed as a compass with ritual objects specifically placed in different directions. The entrance to the main compound is on the east side where the main sacrificial altar is placed along with a washbasin. This is where the priests enact the ritual drama of the blood sacrifices for the people as prescribed by the Levitical Laws of Moses to demonstrate the harm caused by careless actions and the value that is taken from the one that is offended. The washbasin is for the priests to cleanse themselves before entering the western inner sanctum. The inner sanctum is divided into two areas: the Holy and the Holy of Holies. The entrance into the Holy is from the east, the direction of the rising sun. On the north are the seven loaves of showbread, which are refreshed weekly, representing the continual sufficiency of daily bread provided by Yahweh as their Savior and Parent. On the south is the Menorah lamp, in the form of an almond tree with seven branches reaching skywards, topped with seven lamps that illuminate the Holy sanctuary, representing the seven days of creation. In the center of the Holy sanctum is the incense altar, which ritually purifies the air surrounding the inner sanctum with a pleasing aroma. On the west, behind a heavy curtain separating it from the other ritual objects, is the Holy of Holies containing the Ark of the Covenant. In the Ark are placed the two tablets of the Decalogue, the central moral code given to Moses on the Mount of Elohim in Sinai. The cover of the ark is beset by two Cherubim, reprising the Guardians that were placed as gatekeepers to the Tree of Life in Eden after the Genesis Exile. In composite, the narrative symbolism of the Ark represents the Tree of Life as the internalization of the Obligation of *Ahav* founded on the Mosaic Law—thus it depicts the integration of Goodness that leads to wholeness and well-being as the development of a mature conscience within the individual.

❖The Guidance

At the Mount of Elohim, Yahweh gives the Israelites a new guidance, a value template, on how to love one another—the Mosaic Law. It is composed of several sections identifying obligations for different groups of people in different roles, and for different occasions. It outlines specific obligations for social conduct and welfare, for priestly purification rituals, and for the commemoration of the Sabbath and holy days. At the root of this guidance is the Decalogue, commonly referred to as the Ten Commandments, which Yahweh himself writes on a pair of stone tablets.

The Mosaic Law is a direct manifestation of the Knowledge of Goodness and Badness from the Tree at the center of the Garden of Eden. As such, it can be viewed through the juvenile conscience of Eve as a code of morality apart from any relational understanding, without love, or it can be viewed as an instrument of the adult Elohim, a mature moral code of love. History is replete with both interpretations. The Mosaic Law has most often been viewed by the moralistic institutional religions as a loveless moral code that must be followed perfectly before an obsessive-compulsive deity that is incapable of imperfection and thus demands perfect obedience from his subservient creation. In this moralized framework, it is a list of things that one must not do, to avoid the wrath of the Christian, Jewish, or Islamic god.

However, in the Reified Basar myth, Rabbi Jeshua invokes the adult Knowledge of Goodness and Badness when he summarizes the Mosaic Law as *ahav* or act-love—inferring it to be an instruction manual on the value of others and ourselves, in relationship to one another and to the Parent Elohim. The obligations that are outlined build a value system within our conscience—developing an awareness of the healing that must take place when we harm another and inspiring us to take action to restore what value has been taken—in other words, how to continually love one another.

❖The Decalogue

The Decalogue is a set of ten core obligations requested of the Israelites as the basis for their relationship to one another—seven obligations are personal in nature and three obligations are related to property matters. Each group can be categorized according to bond, identity, and boundary. They are typically identified in the order written on the tablets in the narrative but are arguably more instructive when grouped as a product of our psychological disposition towards respectfulness, truthfulness, trustworthiness, and generosity.

At the heart of each obligation is respect for the sanctity of personhood, without which there can be no relationship, no "us." This initially is demonstrated in the sacred boundaries around the Mount of Elohim, and then the Holy of Holies in the Tabernacle. However, it is not a function educed by the Supreme Elohim as a matter of defining a Master-Servant relationship; rather it is a primary relational operative that is intrinsic to all relationships, which must be founded on the recognition of the value of another's sacred identity and boundaries. The failure of an obligation in the Torah is always a failure to recognize this intrinsic value and sacredness of the Other.

Value	Subject	Orientation	Domain	Obligation	Failure
Respectfulness	Relationship	Bond	Spiritual	I *Respect Bond with Ideal Parent*	Pride
Respectfulness	Relationship	Bond	Familial	V *Respect Bond with Family*	Arrogance
Truthfulness	Relationship	Identity	Spiritual	III *Don't Misrepresent the Ideal Parent*	Slander
Truthfulness	Relationship	Identity	Familial	IX *Don't Misrepresent An Associate*	Libel/ Lie
Trustworthiness	Relationship	Boundary	Spiritual	II *Don't Devalue the Sanctity of the Ideal Parent*	Idolatry
Trustworthiness	Relationship	Boundary	Familial	VI/ *Don't Devalue the* VII *Sanctity of Another*	Murder/ Adultery
Generosity	Property	Bond	Spiritual	IV *Appreciate what you have*	Greed
Generosity	Property	Identity	Familial	VIII *Don't Usurp Another's Domain*	Exploitation
Generosity	Property	Boundary	Familial	X *Don't Devalue Another's Domain*	Selfishness

Table 7 - Values of the Decalogue

Respectfulness. The first group of obligations focuses on *respectfulness*—value and respect for one's primary *bond* to one's parents, both spiritual and familial. In relation to the spiritual, the *first* obligation (**I**) of the Decalogue proscribes that one should have respect for one's intimate bond with their Ideal Parent, stating:

> *I, Yahweh, am your Elohim Who brought you forth from the land of Egypt, from the house of servants. There shall not come to be other elohim for you in preference to Me.*[184]

Yahweh, as Parent Elohim, is the primary source of power, identity, and life. Archetypally, the ideal Parent image sets the pattern for all other relationships. If that primary transcendent relationship based on love and respect is replaced by a transferent relationship based on chaos, fear, or strife, it diminishes one's foundation and capability for a healthy relationship.

Likewise, in relation to the Universal Family, the *fifth* obligation (**V**) of the Decalogue proscribes that one should have respect for one's intimate bond with one's ancestral parents, stating:

> *Glorify your father and your mother, that your days may be prolonged on the ground which Yahweh your Elohim is giving to you.*[185]

While our parents themselves may not meet the ideal parent image, how we respond to that relationship affects how we value others. As a core archetype

---

[184] CLV Exodus 20:2
[185] CLV Exodus 20:12

of our identity, our parents define our relationship to the world, including how we engage the inevitable imperfections of others in an intimate relationship. The prescription to honor one's parents is not based on their adequacy or performance in meeting our needs; it is based on their mutual value as Elohim, "flesh of my flesh."

There are a myriad of behavioral issues that are wrapped up in familial relationships, including abuse and neglect; and it is crucial to recognize, engage, and work through the impact those behaviors have had on us. It also may be that there are ongoing issues for which one may need to protect oneself—honor is not the same as trust. However, for the same reason that there are no exceptions to the prescription to love one another, there are no exceptions to honoring one's parents. It is the foundation of all other relationships in the Universal Family.

Truthfulness. The second group of obligations focuses on *truthfulness*— value and respect for the *identity* of those with whom one is in relationship, protecting their reputation and integrity. It is a prohibition against slander, vilification, and false accusations. In relation to the spiritual, the *third* obligation (**III**) of the Decalogue proscribes that one should not misrepresent the character or intentions of the Ideal Parent, stating:

> You shall not take up the Name of Yahweh your Elohim for futility, for
> Yahweh shall not hold innocent him who takes up His Name for futility.[186]

In the cultural milieu, one's name is one's identity, and one's reputation is sacred; it is one's most sacred possession. The name of *Yahweh*, as we have discussed previously, identifies him as the one who loves, blows, and falls— indicating his primary characteristics as a loving parent, the creator of life, and provider. He also introduces his name as indicating that he is self-existent, one who does not owe his breath to another. As such, any attempt to projectively redefine his identity based on presumption or ideology is *futility*. Any attempt to attribute a motivation or consequence that is not a product of this identity is *futility*.

And therein lies the conundrum of theology and religion, which have had a long history of ascribing thoughts and intentions to the Supreme Elohim that are contrary to his name. While powerfully stated as a spiritual prohibition with respect to the Parent/Savior Elohim, it is no less true for the

---

[186] CLV Exodus 20:7

person sitting across the table. Their identity is sacred as well—assumptions and attributions are profane.

Thusly, in relation to the Universal Family, the *ninth* obligation (**IX**) of the Decalogue proscribes that one should not misrepresent the character or intentions of an associate, stating:

> You shall not answer against your associate with false testimony.[187]

Slander is a failure to respect the value and sacredness of an associate's essential reputation—to steal or destroy their sacred identity. It is fundamentally sacrilegious, harming one's relationship, but also may cause harm to life and limb in a social or judicial situation.

Trustworthiness. The third group of obligations focuses on *trustworthiness*—value and respect for the *boundary* of another. It is a recognition that we each exist within our own sacred domain, requiring permission and trust to enter into the intimate bounds of another, the Sacred Midst of mutual relationship. In relation to the spiritual, the *second* obligation (**II**) of the Decalogue proscribes that one should not devalue the sanctity of the Ideal Parent, stating:

> You shall not make for yourself a carving nor any physical representation of that in the heavens above or that on the earth beneath, or that in the waters beneath the earth. You shall not bow yourself down to them, nor be made to serve them, for I, Yahweh your Elohim, am a jealous El.[188]

Yahweh defines his sacred domain as an intimate encounter with his children. Fidelity is the foundation of intimacy. It is a violation of that trust to seek out and serve a gillul, an inferior representation of power based on fear or missingness. It is a betrayal of trust, an act that is compared to adultery in later passages.

Likewise, in relation to the Universal Family, the sixth and seventh obligations (**VI/VII**) of the Decalogue proscribes that one should not devalue the sanctity of an associate, stating: "You shall not murder"[189] and "You shall not commit adultery."[190] Each of these proscriptions addresses the safety and sacredness of one's intimate boundaries, both physical and relational. Failure of these obligations is a failure at the most fundamental level of trust and intimacy, devaluing and destroying the Sacred Midst in between.

---

[187] CLV Exodus 20:16
[188] CLV Exodus 20:4-5
[189] CLV Exodus 20:13
[190] CLV Exodus 20:14

While at face value, it is universally accepted that murder is immoral, in practice, it is not uncommon for some to feel justified in taking another's life to satisfy an egocentric or moralistic urge. In reality, there is no foundation for this perspective, which results from a devaluation of the life of another, whether in fantasy or fact. In the social mandates of the Mosaic Law, you are not justified in killing someone for stealing or harming you in some way, other than in a few rare, but very traumatic situations. The Law limits what you can require in recompense. Thus, the antithesis of this prohibition is represented in the egocentric morality of modern religious gun culture, which lionizes the taking of another's life as an incidental justification for protecting one's honor or property, or otherwise, to assuage one's cowardice or fear of another, slanderously claiming it to be a "Biblical Mandate."

Generosity. The fourth group of obligations focuses on generosity—our intimate relationship to property, and thus, our response to scarcity. The *fourth* obligation (**IV**) of the Decalogue addresses the fear of scarcity, which drives greed and the compulsive accumulation of, and perverse bonding to, one's possessions. It obligates the Israelites to recognize an inherent sufficiency in their weekly wanderings; to cease to strive and to rest for one day of the week to appreciate what they have, stating:

> *You are to remember the sabbath day to hallow it. Six days shall you serve and do all your work, yet the seventh day is a sabbath to Yahweh your Elohim. You shall not do any work, you, your son or your daughter, your manservant or your maidservant, your bull, your donkey or your beast, or your sojourner who is within your gates. For in six days Yahweh dealt with the heavens and the earth, the sea and all that is in them, and He stopped on the seventh day. Therefore, Yahweh blessed the sabbath day and hallowed it.[191]*

This is illustrated by the earlier proscription in the Exodus myth to not collect more manna and quail than is required for one day or else it will spoil. Ironically, this becomes one of the more degenerated obligations in later moralistic enterprises as it has inherent economic consequences, leading to long discussions about what entails "work," and thus, what is allowable to do on the sabbath. Rather than a day of rest, in the moralistic traditions, it often becomes more of a day of stress and avoidance.

Rabbi Jeshua addresses this later in the Reified Basar narrative when the Pharisees attack his students for "doing on the sabbaths what is not allowed"

---

[191] CLV Exodus 20:8-11

by gleaning grain to eat while walking through a field on the sabbath. In response, Rabbi Jeshua states:

> *Did you never read what David does, when he had need and hungers, he and those with him? How he entered into the house of God under Abiathar the chief priest, and ate the show bread, which is not allowed to be eaten except by the priests, and he gives also to those who are with him? …The sabbath came because of mankind, and not mankind because of the sabbath, so that the Son of Mankind is Lord, also, of the sabbath.[192]*

The attitude of compassion and generosity is what actually motivates the Sabbath obligation.

The *eighth* obligation (**VIII**) of the Decalogue addresses the identity or ownership of one's possessions, proscribing that one should not usurp an associate's personal domain, simply stating: "You shall not steal."[193] Whereas generosity is a fundamental value within the Unified Basar and Torah myth, forcing someone to be *generous* with their property was not. The exploitation of the personal domain of another fundamentally injures their household well-being and continuity.

The *tenth* and last obligation (**X**) of the Decalogue addresses the boundary or sanctity of another's household and property, proscribing that one should not devalue an associate's personal domain, stating:

> *You shall not covet the house of your associate. You shall not covet the wife of your associate, his field, his manservant or his maidservant, his bull, his donkey or anything which is your associate's.[194]*

While coveting is an attitude and not a direct action, it violates the integrity of one's relationship with one's neighbor. It devalues the sacredness of their household, insinuating one's egocentric needs as a higher obligation than the safety and well-being of their home and family. It is a product of disrespect, selfishness, and greed; a failure of attitude that prevents generosity of spirit and the primacy of *ahav*, or act-love. It fundamentally leads to the death of the Sacred Midst within community.

❖Waters of Meribah

In the Torah mythology, the Goodness of the Israelites' circuitous march to freedom is contrasted with the Badness of their continual complaining and distrust of Moses and Yahweh. As the Israelites entered the wilderness of Zin and dwelt at Kadesh, they assembled against Moses and Aaron contending:

---

[192] CLV Mark 2:24-28
[193] CLV Exodus 20:15
[194] CLV Exodus 20:17

O that we had deceased when our brothers deceased before Yahweh! Why did you bring the assembly of Yahweh to this wilderness to die there, we and our livestock? And why did you lead us up from Egypt to bring us to this evil place? This is not a place of seed, fig, vine or pomegranate, and there is not even water to drink.[195]

In each of these recurring episodes of desperation, Yahweh responds as their Guide-Aide to provide what was essential for life and well-being. Thusly, Yahweh tells Moses and Aaron:

Take the rod and assemble the congregation, you and Aaron your brother; and you will speak to the crag before their eyes, and it will give its water. Thus you will bring forth water for them from the crag and will give drink to the congregation and their livestock.[196]

However, this time, Moses' patience is exhausted, and he is personally upset with the Israelites. He abuses his position as the Oracle of Elohim to express his own frustration and anger, thus slandering/misrepresenting Yahweh's good intentions. As such, Moses takes the Rod of Elohim before the crag and retorts, "Hear, I pray, you rebels! From this crag shall we bring forth water for you?"[197] Then, he raised up his hand and struck the crag with his rod twice in anger, instead of just speaking to it, as Yahweh had commanded him. Regardless, water springs forth for the congregation and their livestock to drink. However, Yahweh is displeased, admonishing Moses and Aaron:

Because you did not believe in Me to sanctify Me before the eyes of the sons of Israel, therefore you shall not bring this assembly into the land which I will give to them.[198]

Moses and Aaron, having misrepresented the integrity of Yahweh's character, are punished by Yahweh. The narrator states that the waters were called *Meribah* because "the sons of Israel contended with Yahweh, and He showed Himself holy among them."[199]

Soon after, Aaron goes up Mount Hor, transfers his priestly mantle to his son Eleazar, and dies, never having seen the Promised Land. Moses continues his anointing as the Judge and Leader of the Israelites through to the end of their wilderness wandering, but when they are finally ready to enter the Promised Land, his journey is ended as well. Ascending from the plains of

---

[195] CLV Numbers 20:3-5
[196] CLV Numbers 20:8
[197] CLV Numbers 20:10
[198] CLV Numbers 20:12
[199] CLV Numbers 20:13

Moab to Mount Nebo overlooking Jericho, Yahweh shows Moses all the Promised Land from afar, stating:

This is the land about which I had sworn to Abraham, to Isaac and to Jacob, saying, "To your seed shall I give it." I have let you see it with your eyes, yet you shall not cross over there.[200]

Moses, the servant of Yahweh, then dies there in the land of Moab at the age of 120 in accordance with the decree of Yahweh at Meribah.

❖**The Raised Serpent**

Shortly after the calamity at Meribah, the Israelites, having journeyed from Mount Hor by way of the Sea of Reeds to get around the land of Edom, become impatient again, speaking against both Yahweh and Moses. However, this time, it is the Israelites who profane the goodwill of Yahweh as their Savior, saying:

Why did you bring us up from Egypt to die in the wilderness? For there is no bread and there is no water, and our soul, it is irritated by the lightly esteemed bread.[201]

In response to their "light esteem," Yahweh, this time, does indeed become angry, deeming their accusations as slanderous to his generous intent and actions as their Savior. So, he sends vipers amongst the Israelites, embodying the toxic effect of their slander. The vipers bite many people, and many die. The people come to Moses and repent of their slander, imploring:

We have [failed], for we have spoken against Yahweh and against you. Pray to Yahweh that He may take the serpents away from on us.[202]

Yahweh, then, responds to Moses stating:

Make for yourself a burning serpent, and place it on a banner pole; and it will come to be that anyone bitten, when he sees it, he will live.[203]

Moses complies, making a serpent of copper as instructed, and placing it on a banner pole. Thus, anyone who was bitten by a viper that looked upon the raised serpent was restored to life.

❖**Heart of Darkness**

In moralistic mythologies, the disintegration of the boundary between Goodness and Badness is the prerogative of the gods. In moralism, the fruit of the Knowledge of Goodness and Badness—Growth and Decay, Life and

---

[200] CLV Deuteronomy 34: 4
[201] CLV Numbers 21:5
[202] CLV Numbers 21:7
[203] CLV Numbers 21:8

Death, Vitality and Vulnerability, Wholeness and Missingness, Home and Wandering, Health and Disease—are all subject to the forces moving us towards Order and Control and away from Disorder and Chaos. Yet there are consequences to every action, even amongst the gods. The Greek myth of Demeter and Persephone is archetypally about the consequences of failed boundaries in response to the gods' drive towards satisfaction of power.

Persephone is the daughter of the Sky-God Zeus and the Earth-Goddess Demeter. She will become the goddess of spring, known in the Eleusis Cult as Kore, or Young Maiden, but following her abduction by Hades, the Unseen ruler of the underworld, she also becomes the queen of the underworld, which causes Demeter to bring upon the earth the death of winter. Subsequently, Persephone's matronymic identity in the later enrollment becomes "one who brings or causes death."[204] In Homer's *Hymn to Demeter*, Persephone is initially just a young girl with no particular identity or responsibilities except to be an accompaniment to her mother.

> *[Persephone] was having a good time, along with the daughters of Okeanos... She was picking flowers... up and down the soft meadow... And the narcissus [flower]... was a wondrous thing in its splendor... [Persephone] was filled with a sense of wonder, and she reached out... to take hold of the pretty plaything. And the earth, full of roads leading every which way, opened up under her... [Hades] made his lunge... seized her against her will, put her on his golden chariot, and drove away as she... cried with a piercing voice...*
>
> *And the Lady Mother [Demeter] heard her... She sped off like a bird, soaring over land and sea, looking... [she] came to Helios, the seeing-eye of gods and men... "Tell me... who has taken [my child] away from me by force?" ...And [Helios] answered her "...Zeus himself, who gave her to Hades as his beautiful wife... But I urge you, goddess: stop your loud cry of lamentation... It is not unseemly to have... such a son-in-law as Hades..."*
>
> *But blond-haired Demeter sat down... shunning the company of all the blessed ones... She made that year the most terrible one for mortals, all over the Earth... She said that she would never... send up the harvest of the earth, until she saw... her daughter[205]*

Zeus sacrifices his own child, Persephone, to Hades, coldly treating her as a mere child-pawn of the patriarchy in a political transaction. Her abduction is an act of brutal force—the Earth opens up and rapaciously devours Persephone as she reaches for a narcissus flower, symbolizing the pride and selfishness of the powers that force her into the bowels of the underworld. In sorrow and anguish, Demeter responds by bringing famine upon the whole of

---

[204] Smith (1861) "Persephone" p.204
[205] Nagy (2020) Hymn to Demeter p. 590-607

the earth. Zeus, concerned that the Great Overseers will no longer be given their ritual sacrifices if the mortals are destroyed, variously attempts to quell Demeter's sorrow and anguish, but finally relents and sends Hermes down to Hades to bring Persephone back up to her mother, Demeter. Hades reticently complies, turning to Persephone, he entreats:

> Go now, Persephone, to your dark-robed mother, go, and feel kindly in your heart towards me: be not so exceedingly cast down; for I shall be no unfitting husband for you among the deathless gods... And while you are here, you shall rule all that lives and moves and shall have the greatest rights among the deathless gods: those who defraud you and do not appease your power with offerings, reverently performing rites and paying fit gifts, shall be punished for evermore.[206]

But before she leaves, Hades entices Persephone to eat some pomegranate seeds which, unbeknownst to her, will obligate her to return back to the realm of darkness and gloom as his wife, the Queen of Death. Soon after Persephone's joyous return, Demeter becomes uneasy, fearing that Hades may have tricked her:

> My child, tell me, surely you have not tasted any food while you were below? ...if you have tasted food, you must go back again beneath the secret places of the earth, there to dwell a third part of the seasons every year: yet for the two parts you shall be with me and the other deathless gods. But when the earth shall bloom with the fragrant flowers of spring in every kind, then from the realm of darkness and gloom thou shalt come up once more to be a wonder for gods and mortal men.[207]

Demeter, the Earth Mother, does finally rejoin the "family of the gods" along with Persephone. But for four months of every year, Persephone descends to Hades as the Queen of Death. In sorrow, the earth becomes barren in the bitter embrace of winter, in accordance with her name as the *one who brings death*. When her time below is complete, Persephone is released from the place of darkness and gloom and is ushered back to Olympus and her dear mother Demeter, and the earth springs back to life in accordance with her dual role as the goddess of spring and death. Collectively, Persephone is associated with the natural cycle of life-death-renewal. She operates as the gatekeeper at the seasonal boundary points—the initiation into winter's embrace, toward death, and the transformation of spring, back to life.

But as a young maiden abducted into Death's domain, there is an unnatural or unconstitutional quality to her story, as the joy of youth is forcibly overshadowed by the premature loss of innocence and the sorrow of an unseasonable demise. She is a youthful victim, her boundaries

---

[206] Hesiod (1920) p.315
[207] Hesiod (1920) p.317

unscrupulously violated by her uncaring Father, held captive by her uncle's selfish desires, with only her Heroic Mother to champion her. It is only the threat of the collapse of the natural order itself, caused by Demeter's anger and sorrow, that provokes Zeus to relent his decree. But in the end, the patriarchy is reaffirmed as Persephone is tricked by Hades into contracting to stay with him as his wife, if only for a portion of the year, by eating the seeds of a Pomegranate while she is in the realm of the Dead.

As the Queen of Death, Persephone is given "the greatest rights among the deathless gods"—the power to eternally punish those that do not appease her with offerings. The natural order must be maintained by sacrifices to the Great Overseers. Thus, Zeus only relents to Demeter because, if Earth were destroyed, Man would have nothing to sacrifice to the Great Overseers; and if Man were destroyed, there would be no one to worship the Great Overseers.

In Olympic moralism, the obligatory relationship between Man and Overseer as worshiper and benefactor, servant and master, is essential to maintaining the order of the cosmos. The benefit of the Overseer is essentially invoked by the obligatory offerings made by the worshiper. It is from this same moralist model that the ancient German term "god" is derived as "the one invoked or worshiped." As a fundamental religious archetype, the offering may be manifested overtly, or else made internally in the form of the ritual obligations of belief, behavior, and devotion. The failure of this obligation incites the gillul as Master Overseer to be angry and vengeful, not only withholding the benefit of their power but also punishing the derelict Servant Worshiper for their insolence.

The story of Persephone is paralleled by the myth of the Norse goddess of the underworld, Hel, daughter of Loki, who also is abducted by the gods as a child and cast into the underworld to rule over its many realms. She has a dual nature as well, symbolized by having a body that is half the color of living flesh and half the color of rotting gangrenous flesh. Her name means "hider" similar to Hades, which means "unseen." Hel is given power over the nine worlds that comprise the Norse cosmos to appoint a place for those that die of sickness or old age, as well as a place for the punishment of the very wicked.[208]

As we previously noted, the early Christian translators of the English Bible transposed the fundamental morality of the Norse Hel mythology onto

---

[208] Sturluson (2010) p.32

the original Unified Basar and Torah mythology to substantiate a syncretized version of a place where the dead are punished, which they likewise called "Hell." This derivative mythology overlays several different mythological elements in the Judeo-Christian text—Sheol, Hades, and Gehenna. In the original Jewish mythology, *Sheol* is intrinsically the place where the soul goes to sleep in silence. And in Greek mythology, *Hades* is essentially a benign place where the disembodied soul comes to rest in the afterlife. And, of course, in Jewish geography, Gehenna is the fiery desecrated garbage dump in the Valley of Ben Hinnom foreshadowing the destruction of Jerusalem. As previously discussed, Christians reimagine these mysterial vicinings as an eternal repository of unrepentant sinners, which they reinterpret as the Norse "Hell" but with fire instead of ice, reinforcing the essential boundary between those who are pleasing to the moralistic gods and those who are not.

❖Lose Value/Boundary

The chapter proem is a stanza from the song "A Sort of Homecoming"[209] by the Irish rock band U2. The song evolves from a sense of loss and disconnection, of being "dislocated" and "suffocated," desiring healing and distance from the past. Then, it continues through the liminal borderlands, where there is no looking back. And, finally finds hope in an approaching denouement, "for tonight, at last, I am coming home." Beneath this imagery of the song is the poem, "Homecoming," by the poet, Paul Celan, who famously compared poetry to "a kind of homecoming" upon the "paths on which language becomes voice... outlines for existence... for projecting ourselves into the search for ourselves."[210]

Psychologically, adolescent moral development is a response to the loss of one's juvenile value system and boundaries as the larger world of influences and ideas deconstruct one's familial ethos. Social standards challenge familial standards, allowing for greater freedom while putting more responsibility on the individual to participate in the cultural ethos. Customs and laws supersede juvenile morality—punishment becomes a function of the legal system rather than the parent.

The adolescent value system establishes a need to participate in social activity within a peer relationship, requiring empathy and trust to succeed. In the juvenile value system, there was an implicit power differential between the Child and the Parent that was either a function of the Good Parent who

---

[209] U2 (1990)
[210] Celan (2003) p.53

generously guards and cares for the Child to build moral character or else a function of the Bad Parent, the Villain-Victor, who exploits and abuses the less powerful for their own egotistic satisfaction. In the adolescent value system, the power differential is much less as the supervising adult guides and aides the adolescent, rather than catering to their infantile needs. The exploitation and abuse of the individual within the dysfunctional juvenile Victim-Villain-Victor relationship becomes more systemic in the societal Slave-Master relationship as the culture develops asymmetric systems to institutionalize the advantage of some over others.

Archetypally, as we reevaluate the asymmetric dynamics of our juvenile boundaries, our operative value system is challenged. Correspondingly, our relationships may move towards mutuality within a community or away from it. Our evaluation of our own self-worth and the worth of others actualize as we move further into the world encountering new situations and foreign ideologies. Our adolescent boundaries and associations will reflect what values we incorporate into our developing internal value narrative.

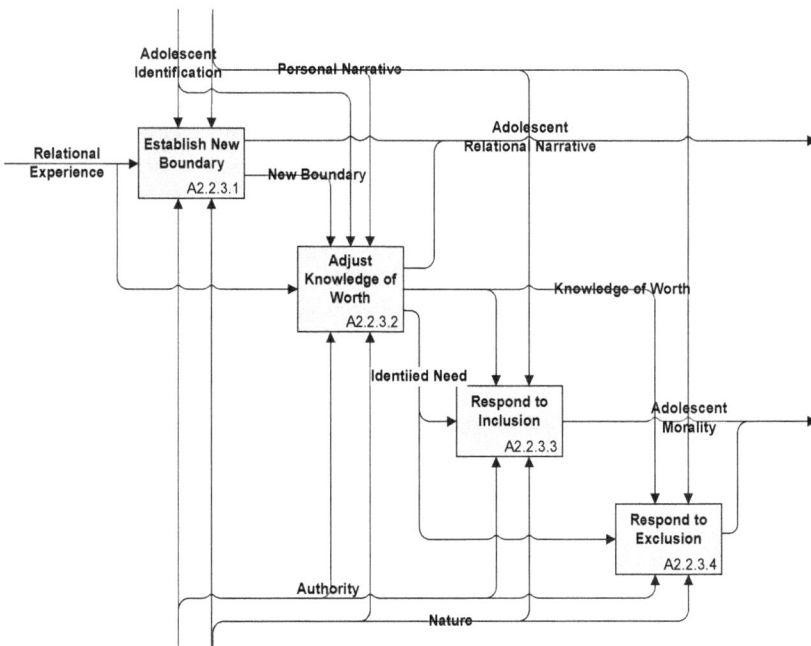

Model 13 - Lose Value/Boundary (A2.2.3)

PART III

BASAR – THE TORAH OF RESTORATION

Notre Dame Spire, Guillaume Levrier, Photo, 2019.

His hands reached deep into my chest cavity gripping my heart crushing the life force from inside out—I had come to know this villain by name, "that which isn't there." I experienced his pressing handprint as pervasive, deadly, and very real. I had always felt his presence throughout my life as darkness, anxiety, and depression, but it wasn't until a few months ago that I learned his name. Little did I know I was about to meet him face to face.

My introduction came quite surprisingly early in my work with my dramatherapist (which I was also in training to be) in the simple task of drawing a self-portrait. More often, this is an intuitive process, begun without any precursors, exploring the projective constructs of one's inner world. I cheated. I had been working on an art piece I had pretentiously and surreptitiously entitled, "A Self-Portrait of Humanity," borrowing midcentury icons that I admired to represent aspects of my interiority—a rationalization of passion, emotion, intellect, and embodiment. Over the first few weeks, the therapeutic exercise was pretty academic, introspecting the archetypal dimensions of my dubious claim to be part of humanity, until my therapist pointed to a squiggly dark mass at the center of the drawing that I hadn't really thought much about, asking "what is that?"— to which I replied, "that which isn't there"—perceiving it to be basically a placeholder for something unknown, or so I thought.

After another fruitful month or so in dialogue with this newly recognized creature, getting to know the nature of his presence and narration, and in the process connecting him to that dark crushing sensation in my chest that seemed to want to destroy me, I came to this aforementioned moment of reckoning. I had just finished a projective exploration, facing my nemesis in the form of a life-size doll—as one does on occasion in the mysterious world of dramatherapy, often filled with dolls and puppets, figurines and fabrics, musical instruments and art supplies, giving voice to the voiceless inner drama of the human soul. I was then asked to reverse roles.

In the same way that the dreamscape unfolds at the right time, given the right approach, the ritual space that had developed over several months had reached its maturity, and the unexpected transformation happens—"that which isn't there" suddenly was there, not in the form of the expected monster as I switched roles to become it, rather it unexpectedly collapsed into a terrified child grasping for dear life. No longer the menacing creature crushing my heart, it cowered in a corner alone and afraid with a death grip on my heart holding on in existential terror. What this primordial subpersonal child needed from my adult self, I was to discover after further exploration, was acceptance and assurance that it was safe. This deep vulnerability had now transformed and become a part of my wakened self—it was now after all "there."

The healing of the human soul is a process of engaging our dysfunctional narratives, created in response to trauma and immature strategies to protect our perceived vulnerabilities. These powerful narratives constellate our behavior and choices, often taking on tremendous privilege in the same way that an injured knee causes us to change how we walk, devising a gait that favors our dysfunction to avert the deepness of our pain and suffering. In our internal subrational world we may come to favor these narratives as normal, and even the source of our power, not recognizing the limitations that they inflict upon us, masking our weakness and vulnerability. We become slaves to our suffering, paradoxically unable to free ourselves from the vicious cycle of suffering caused by avoiding suffering. They inspirit the gillul we serve to pacify our fear and want.

The Reified Basar intrinsically defines the *Torah of Restoration* as a path to wholeness and healing founded, not in an egocentric drive to individuate or emancipate ourselves from the world, but in our innate relationship to one another. It invites us to courageously engage our own nakedness and vulnerability with authenticity and truth, tearing down the walls that insulate and protect us from one another; to boldly enter a world covered elementally in the vestige of love, to thusly become a healing agent to others. Accordingly, in the prophecy of Third Isaiah, the Anointed One offers comfort, freedom, and restoration to those who suffer as a pattern for all in community to emulate.[211] The Reified Basar is a model for mature human

---

[211] CLV Isaiah 61:1-3

behavior in the face of suffering. Initially, it is a definitive proclamation of the mission of the anointed firstborn of Elohim to bring the healing power of the Tree of Life into the darkest reaches of human suffering. It evolves into the central driving force that Rabbi Jeshua claims to be the purpose of the Reified Basar mission in the Universal Family.

❖**The Journey**

Our developmental journey towards mature awareness and power begins as a child exploring the universe under the supervision of our parent as Guardian-Caretaker to understand what is *good* and what is *bad*; discovering our own innate psychological nakedness and vulnerability in the shadow of scarcity and want. It continues with the adolescent awareness of our capacity to serve others beyond our egocentric needs under the guidance and aid of some supervising authority as we come to understand the value of, and our obligation towards, others. And then, ideally, if we come to terms with those stages of development, we find our own power as mature moral agents that respond to one another from an internalized value system, instantiated by an awareness of the Ideal Parent as a vanguard, leading us towards wholeness and healing, and a paragon of active compassion and empathy—to intrinsically become lovers of our fellow creatures, human and otherwise.

Purpose	Objective	Stage	Subject	Object	Object Function
Da'ath-Knowledge	Awakening	Juvenile	Child / Victim	Parent / Villain-Victor	Guardian-Caretaker / Perpetrator-Preserver
Ahav-Love	Obligation	Adolescent	Servant / Slave	Savior / Master	Guide-Aide / Abuser
Basar-Goodness	Restoration	Mature	Lover / Rival	Beloved / Adversary	Vanguard-Paragon / Competitor

Table 8 - Stages of Moral Development

At each stage of development, the Transcendent relationship of symmetric power may disintegrate into the Transferent relationship of asymmetric power as a function of how one is oriented to the archetypal topography of scarcity or sufficiency. The Child-Parent relationship disintegrates into the Victim-Villain-Victor relationship. The Servant-Savior relationship disintegrates into the Slave-Master relationship. And the Lover-Beloved relationship disintegrates into the Rival-Adversary relationship.

Initially, in the Transcendent relationship, the egoic perspective is associated with the subjective roles of Child/Servant/Lover and the non-egoic perspective is associated with the objective roles of Parent/Savior/Beloved. As a person matures, internalizing the ideal Parent, they may then come to embody the objective role in some relationships with others. However, in the Transferent relationship, there is more fluidity—the egoic perspective may become associated with either the subjective or objective roles depending on personality and opportunity manifest within the personal and cultural narratives.

❖Path to Restoration

The Reified Basar myth begins at the adolescent developmental stage, instantiated in the *Torah of Obligation,* founded on the *Servant-Savior* relationship between Rabbi Jeshua and his students. Over the course of the narrative, the relationship matures, until, at the end of his ministry, Jeshua declares:

> This is My precept, that you be loving one another, according as I love you. Greater love than this has no one, that anyone may be laying down his soul for his friends. You are My friends, if you should be doing whatever I am directing you. No longer am I terming you [servants], for the [servant] is not aware what his lord is doing. Yet I have declared you friends, for all that I hear from My Father I make known to you... In these things I am directing you, that you may be loving one another.[212]

Thus, their relationship is transformed from the adolescent *Servant-Savior* to the maturity of the *Lover-Beloved*. As the Anointed Firstborn of creation, Jeshua's mission is to invite all humanity into this symmetric relationship of the *Lover-Beloved*.

Throughout most of the Reified Basar myth, Rabbi Jeshua is the Middle Nachash, the Anointed Son who represents and speaks for the Father. Then in the crucifixion narrative, Jeshua is raised up to become the *Higher Nachash*, the fullness of adult moral power. By *laying down his soul for his friends*, Jeshua brings symmetric power to life, fulfilling the developmental journey through an act of love and compassion. He embodies *ahav* as a giving of one's breath, or life, for the benefit of others, to mercifully let go of his entitlement to restorative justice in order to free the Universal Family from the dominion of the asymmetric power system embodied by the adversarial religious and political authorities that have rejected him.

❖Archetypal Topography of Basar

At its onset, the initial archetypal topography of the Reified Basar is established as a reprisal of the Kingdom of Ahab from the Book of Kings in which the prophet Elijah was anointed by Yahweh as his oracle, the Nachash of Elohim. It is, in turn, the same asymmetric topography of the Exodus mythology. King Ahab embodies the same disintegrated power dynamics of

---

[212] CLV John 15:12-17

the Pharaoh in the Exodus narrative. Elijah embodies the same integrative power dynamic of Moses as the Nachash of Elohim, the prophet and oracle called to deliver the Israelites from the hands of the gillul, as well as those who oppress the powerless and ignore the plight of the poor and suffering.

In the Reified Basar narrative, Herod reprises the adversarial King Ahab, Johanan the Baptist reprises the prophet Elijah, and Herodias reprises Jezebel as the archenemy of the prophets of Elohim. The religious authorities represented by the Pharisees and Sadducees reembody the false prophets of Elohim that ushered in the downfall of Ahab's Kingdom.

Later, in the narrative of the *transfiguration* of Rabbi Jeshua, Moses and Elijah both appear, to counsel Jeshua, and reaffirm that he is the anointed firstborn son of Elohim. The Unified Basar and Torah narrative ultimately is a set of recursive stories, stories repeating within stories, representing a fractal projection of archetypal themes from one generation to the next.

❖ Kingdom of Ahab

The reign of King Ahab is the epitome of destructive asymmetric power in the monarchical period of the Kingdom of Israel in Samaria. Ahab is the seventh king to rule Israel after the unified Kingdom of David and Solomon separates into the northern Kingdom of Israel and the southern Kingdom of Judah. Ahab is introduced in the Book of Kings as worse than all the kings that had been before.

> As for Ahab son of Omri, he became king over Israel... [He] did what was [harmful] in the eyes of Yahweh, worse than all who had been before him. So it came to pass... that he took as wife Jezebel daughter of Ethbaal king of the Sidonians. Then he went to serve Baal and worshiped him. He set up an altar for Baal in the house of Baal that he built in Samaria. Ahab also made an Asherah pole. Thus Ahab proceeded to do more to provoke Yahweh Elohim of Israel to vexation than all the kings of Israel who had been before him.[213]

Politically, Ahab is a shrewd and powerful ruler, building alliances with the neighboring Phoenician Kingdom of Sidon through marriage and the adoption of their gilluls. He establishes peace with the southern Kingdom of Judah. Like Pharaoh before him, he is remarkable for his building programs. His territories are in a constant state of expansion and contraction due to his successes and failures in battle with other neighboring kingdoms—in particular, the Aramite Kingdom of Damascus in Syria. He eventually dies of a

---

[213] CLV 1Kings 16:29-33

mortal wound, suffered in an ill-advised military venture with Syria, under the auspices of a false prophecy by his spiritual counsel.

Ahab's Phoenician wife Jezebel is the queen of Israel and high priestess of *Baal-Karmelos*. She is ruthless and conniving. She murders the prophets of Yahweh and destroys his altars. She arranges for the judicial killing of Naboth the Jezreelite by giving false testimony in order to steal his lands for the king's vineyard. Under the assent of her husband, King Ahab, Jezebel establishes a new principal gillul in Israel, Baal-Karmelos, who is worshiped on Mount Karmel directly west of Samaria and south of her homeland of Phoenicia, overlooking the Mediterranean Sea.

❖Power of Gillul

Baal-Karmelos, the Lord of Karmel, is one of many gillul that share the title *baal* or lord/master in the Ancient Near East, and areas where the Phoenicians settled throughout the Mediterranean. In the earliest recorded mythology of the region, the Lord of Ugarit is the god of storms—the son of El the Supreme-God and Asherah the Queen-Mother (or Consort). The association of the title *Baal* with the function of Weather-God stays consistent throughout the dominant myths that evolve from this older myth, although other traits varied. *A Dictionary of the Ancient Near Eastern Mythology* states:

> As a weather-god, Baal is one of the most important deities for the western parts of the Near East. As... 'the rider of the clouds', he is manifest in the storms which herald the autumn season with thunder and lightning, the rain-swollen clouds and the coastal breeze. He symbolizes the life-giving principle of fertility in crops, animals and people. Baal battles valiantly against the unruly waters of the sea and the scorching heat of summer.[214]

The worship of Baal as the Lord of storms and fertility is founded on a deep psychological need for safety and survival. Unlike the Great River cultures of the Nile and Tigris-Euphrates, the inhabitants of the Levant did not have a source, or the technology, for irrigation in the arid hill country characteristic of the region. They are dependent upon the rains to water their grain fields that are harvested to make bread and feed their herds. They project their fear of drought and famine outward to the god of storms as a *Transferent Elohim*, offering up sacrifices to transact his favor. At the root of the Baal cult practice is the literal translation of the title as the lord/master, eliciting the

---

[214] Leick (2002) p.18-19, "Baal"

asymmetric power dynamic of subjugation, the domination of the servant under the authority of the lord/master.

The Asherah poles that Ahab makes are either a grove of living trees or a cluster of constructed poles that are used in the worship of the archetypal Mother-Goddess, Asherah. The practice is adopted from the Phoenician cult of Asherah by Jezebel as a Sidonian priestess and queen of Israel. In the older Ugaritic pantheon, Asherah is the mother of all the gods and chief consort of the supreme authority El. She is worshipped as a Fertility-Goddess associated with motherhood. It is noteworthy that the root of the term *gillul* is the image of a *log*, conjuring the act of carving one's god out of wood in order to serve them. The association of Asherah as a grove of logs only magnifies this characterization. They evince a sterile fabrication of the Tree of the Knowledge of Goodness and Badness, a juvenile morality devoid of love or relationship, projecting only one's fears and need for control.

These asymmetric symbols of fear and subjugation are the heart of the myth's journey, which will eventually lead to their transformation into the symmetric power dynamic of the *Lover-Beloved*. It is the beginning topography of the Reified Basar myth, founded on the story of Elijah and King Ahab.

❖Nachash Unwinds

Elijah, as Moses was before him, is the agent of challenge and change, functioning as the Nachash of Elohim. In the opening salvo, Elijah directly challenges the sacred domain of Baal as the Lord of the Storms by proclaiming to Ahab, "As Yahweh Elohim of Israel lives, before Whom I stand, there shall not come in these years night mist or rain, except at the bidding of my word."[215]

As the Nachash of Elohim, Elijah demonstrates similar characteristics to his predecessor Moses as oracle and judge. Many of these themes also will be reprised in the Reified Basar narrative. Elijah is introduced as being from Tishbe in Gilead, east of Samaria, across the Jordan River, and after his initial proclamation to King Ahab, he will return there to sojourn in the Wadi Cherith, adjoining the Jordan for a period. In the later narrative of the Reified Basar, this will become the domain of Johanan the Baptist. As the drought settles upon the land, the Wadi dries up and Elijah is instructed to go north to the Sidonian city of Zarephath in Phoenicia where he is told he will find a widow that, although she is destitute, will take care of him throughout the

---

215 CLV 1Kings 17:1

drought. Elijah blesses her household in the name of Yahweh and declares that the jar of meal and cruse of oil will miraculously be filled until the end of the drought. When the widow's son falls ill and dies, in support of the widow, and so as to not cast aspersions on the name of Yahweh, Elijah raises him from death.

After three years of drought and famine in Samaria, Yahweh tells Elijah to return to Samaria where he summons King Ahab to Mount Karmel along with the prophets of Baal. Then Elijah spoke to all the people saying:

> How long will you go on skipping to and fro between the two opinions? If Yahweh is the One, Elohim, go after Him. If Baal is, go after him... I am left as a prophet of Yahweh, I by myself alone, while the prophets of Baal are 450 men. Now let them give us two young bulls; and let them choose for themselves one young bull, cut it in pieces and place it on the sticks; but they should not apply fire. I myself shall prepare the other young bull; I will put it on the sticks; but I shall not apply fire. Then you will call your elohim by name, and I myself shall call Yahweh by name. And it will come to be: The One, Elohim Who shall respond with fire, He is the One, Elohim.[216]

The prophets of Baal make an altar placing a bull on it, and then proceed to call upon Baal to consume the sacrifice with fire. After hours of crying out, cutting their flesh with swords, pleading with their elohim, "there was no voice, there was no one answering, and there was no attention."[217] Then Elijah mended the demolished altar of Yahweh with twelve large stones, representing the tribes of Israel, and placed the sacrificial bull upon it. He then had his attendants soak the altar, the wood, the sacrifice, and the surrounding trench with many jars of water. Then Elijah makes his request of Yahweh, without any dramatic gestures:

> O Yahweh Elohim of Abraham, Isaac and Israel, let it be known today that You are Elohim in Israel and I am Your servant and that by Your words I have done all these things. Answer me, O Yahweh, answer me! Thus this people may know that You, Yahweh, are the One, Elohim, and that You Yourself will turn their heart around back again.[218]

Then it states that upon Elijah's request:

> The fire of Yahweh fell and devoured the ascent offering and the sticks, the stones and the soil, and it licked up the water that was in the trench. When all the people saw this, they fell on their faces and said, "Yahweh, He is the One, Elohim."[219]

---

[216] CLV 1Kings 18:21-24
[217] CLV 1Kings 18:29
[218] CLV 1Kings 18:36-37
[219] CLV 1Kings 18:38-39

The people "turn their heart around back again," fulfilling the central mission of the Prophets of Elohim in the post-Torah narrative, which is then reemphasized in the later Third Prophet of Isaiah. Subsequently, Elijah has the Prophets of Baal killed, and then, he ascends to the top of Mount Karmel to bring about the end of the drought, sending a rainstorm to drench the land.

❖Viper Redux

Shortly thereafter, upon hearing the fate of her prophets, Jezebel, in the tradition of evil villains who reveal their plans to their victims just before they attempt to kill them, sends a messenger to Elijah declaring that by the next day she shall have her revenge upon him. Elijah escapes south to Judah, and then journeys further south for another forty days to the Mount of Elohim at Horeb/Sinai, to the place where Yahweh spoke openly with Moses through the burning thornbush. Elijah stands on the mount before Yahweh, expressing his doubt and despair that he alone is left in Israel who serves Yahweh, and now he is under the threat of death by Jezebel:

> And behold, Yahweh was passing by, and a great and steadfast wind was ripping apart the mountains and was breaking up the crags before Yahweh; yet Yahweh was not in the wind. After the wind was an earthquake; yet Yahweh was not in the earthquake. After the earthquake was a fire; yet Yahweh was not in the fire. After the fire was the sound of a gentle stillness. It came to pass as Elijah heard it, he wrapped his face in his mantle and went forth and stood at the opening of the cave. And behold, a voice came to him and said, "What have you to do here, Elijah?"[220]

In revealing himself to Elijah, the numinous voice of Yahweh is not in the awesomeness of a powerful wind, or a terrible earthquake, or a mighty fire, but rather in the "sound of a gentle stillness." Yahweh responds to Elijah's despair, declaring that he will no longer be alone. He will anoint new Kings in both Syria and Israel, to purge the land, and, then he will anoint a new prophet, Elisha, who will be Elijah's close companion, eventually taking his place.

❖Intermission

After all this transpires, there comes the appointed day on which Elijah is told he will be taken up to the heavens by Yahweh. Elisha and he travel to the other side of the Jordan River, where, in the manner of Moses, Elijah casts his mantle on the waters and it divides, and they cross on dry land. As they continued walking and speaking:

---

[220] CLV 1Kings 19:11-13

> *Behold, a fiery chariot with fiery horses appeared; they caused the two of them to part, and Elijah ascended in a tempest to the heavens. Elisha… saw him no more.[221]*

Later in the book of the prophet Malachi, Elijah's return is prophesied, declaring that he would come to restore the relational statutes of Moses, to bring together father and sons.

> *Remember the law of Moses, My servant, which I instructed him in Horeb for all Israel, the statutes and ordinances. Behold, I will send to you Elijah, the prophet, before the coming of the great and advent day of Yahweh. And he will restore the heart of the fathers onto the sons and the heart of the sons onto their fathers, lest I come and smite the earth to its doom.[222]*

This prophecy of Elijah's return becomes widely accepted by those looking forward to him ushering in the apocalyptic era of the Messiah. It becomes a central tenant in Pharisaic Judaism who look forward to a Political Messiah that will restore the political Kingdom of David. The Messianist Jews of the Reified Basar, however, identify Johanan the son of Zechariah as the embodiment of Elijah, the one who prepared the way for Rabbi Jeshua as the Anointed Son of Yahweh, the Familial Messiah. These two Jewish mythologies existed side by side in synagogues throughout the first century Diaspora until the Pharisees, who dominated the synagogue leadership, pushed the Messianist Jews out of the community at the end of the first century by identifying the synagogue with those that were still waiting for Elijah and the Political Messiah to come.

❖Mission Restored

The Reified Basar myth begins with the birth narrative of Johanan the son of Zechariah as a fulfillment of the prophesied return of Elijah. The name *Johanan* in Hebrew means "Yahweh is gracious/shows favor," which portrays his mission as the one who points towards the favor of the Parent/Savior Elohim, manifested in his anointed son. As the starting point of the Reified Basar, Johanan's mission is a continuation of the Adolescent/Young Adult developmental arc of Moses and Elijah, to turn the hearts of the sons of Israel back to the relational values of the Father, in accordance with the Mosaic Law.

At the beginning of the Reified Basar myth, Zechariah the priest is tending the incense altar in the Holy of Holies of the Temple when a messenger appears to him saying:

---

[221] CLV 2Kings 2:11-12
[222] CLV Malachi 4:4-6

> *Your wife Elizabeth shall be bearing you a son, and you shall be calling his*
> *name [Johanan]... He shall be great in the sight of the Lord... and with holy*
> *spirit [ruach hakodesh] shall he be filled while still of his mother's womb.*
> *And many of the sons of Israel shall he be turning back onto the Lord their*
> *God. And he shall be coming before in His sight in the spirit and power of*
> *Elijah, to turn back the hearts of the fathers onto the children, and the*
> *stubborn to the prudence of the just, to make ready a people formed for*
> *the Lord.*[223]

Then upon Johanan's birth, his father, alluding to a passage in the book of
Isaiah, declares:

> *Now you, also, little boy, a prophet of the Most High shall be called, For*
> *you shall be going before in the sight of the Lord To make ready His roads,*
> *To give the knowledge of salvation to His people In the [release/let go] of*
> *their [moral failures], Because of the merciful compassion of our [Elohim],*
> *In which the Dayspring from on high visits us, To make Its advent to those*
> *sitting in darkness and the shadow of death, To direct our feet into the*
> *path of peace.*[224]

Johanan grows up to be a man, beginning his ministry in the wilderness
surrounding the river Jordan, likened to the prophet Elijah, "heralding a
baptism of repentance for the [release/let go] of [moral failures]."[225] He
directly calls out the contemporary religious authorities, the Pharisees and
Sadducees, as slanderous vipers—false prophets who undermine the love of
the Father, laying heavy burdens on the people. In the developing narrative of
the *Lover-Beloved*, they are portrayed as having a disintegrated *Rival-
Adversary* relationship with Father Yahweh, standing against the generous
spirit of the *Beloved Elohim.*

> *Progeny of vipers! Who intimates to you to be fleeing from the impending*
> *indignation? Produce, then, fruit worthy of repentance. And you should not*
> *be presuming to be saying among yourselves, "For a father we have*
> *Abraham," for I am saying to you that able is [Elohim], out of these stones*
> *to rouse children to Abraham. Yet already the ax is lying at the root of the*
> *trees. Every tree, then, which is not producing ideal fruit is hewn down and*
> *cast into the fire. For I, indeed, am baptizing you in water for repentance,*
> *yet He Who is coming after me is stronger than I, Whose sandals I am not*
> *competent to bear. He will be baptizing you in holy spirit [ruach hakodesh]*
> *and fire, Whose winnowing shovel is in His hand, and He will be scouring*
> *His threshing floor, and will be gathering His grain into His barn, yet the*
> *chaff will He be burning up with unextinguished fire.*[226]

Johanan's ministry is founded on the Adolescent/Young Adult moral
development of Elijah and the Mosaic Law, the externalized narrative of

---

[223] CLV Luke 1:13-17
[224] CLV Luke 1:76-79 ref. Isaiah 40:3
[225] CLV Mark 1:4
[226] CLV Matthew 3:7-12

values and obligations. It is the starting point for the maturation of the internalized Adult morality that Rabbi Jeshua will progressively demonstrate as the fulfillment of the Law. Thus, the foundation and purpose for the Reified Basar are set, developing from the *Servant-Savior* relationship of independent Adolescent morality into the interdependent Adult morality of the *Lover-Beloved*, fulfilled by the *Higher Nachash* raised up on the cross.

❖Inclusionary Authority

In the Reified Basar, inclusionary spiritual authority is founded on the *noscentric* perspective of the Lover-Beloved relationship within the Universal Family. It is a manifestation of the *Transcendent Elohim* as the ideal Parent Image. In contrast, exclusionary spiritual authority, as previously examined, is a construct of the *Transferent Elohim*, a product of our survival strategies. The Sacred Midst is the *noscentric* domain of relationship in the myth, beginning with the proclamation that the fulfillment of the law is to love Yahweh with all your heart, mind, and soul; and to love your neighbor as yourself. In his role as the Familial Messiah, Jeshua expands on this, declaring, "I am the Way and the Truth and the Life. No one is coming to the Father except through Me,"[227] invoking the prior injunction as being fulfilled in relationship with the Universal Family through the Anointed Firstborn Son. As such, Jeshua represents the Father as Guardian-Caretaker, Guide -Aide, and Vanguard-Paragon.

	Inclusionary
	Nos/Us *(N)*
FUTURE *(F)* *{Volitional, Passion, Bond}*	*NF* Love Altruism {Way}
PRESENT *(P)* *{Rational, Belief, Identity}*	*NP* Understanding Mutualism {Truth}
PAST *(X)* *{Emotional, Feeling, Boundary}*	*NX* Peace Relationalism {Life}

Table 9 - Inclusionary Spiritual Authority

The model of Inclusionary Spiritual Authority breaks down the dynamics of the various inclusive authority scripts, defining a context for their expression. In unity, the scripts build the narrative of our restoration to the Tree of Life through the internalization of the adult morality of the Tree of Knowledge of Goodness and Badness, motivated by love, founded on mutual relationship, and circumscribed by peace—the way, the truth, and the life.

---

[227] CLV John 14:6

❖**Restoration to Adult Morality**

Our restoration to peace and safety in relationship with one another is the fulfillment of mature moral development. However, rather than an event that perfects oneself or one's environment, it is a continuous process. Relationships are a series of interactions between complex individuals with varying needs and ideas, which will inevitably create conflict and missteps between them. Restoration is the process of adjustment and letting go of failure, in the moment, to maintain the relationship between one another. It is the recognition of the value of the relationship that drives the individuals to reconcile and develop peace and safety in the Sacred Midst.

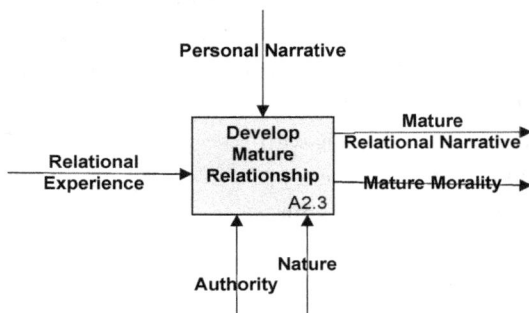

Model 14 - Develop Mature Relationship (A2.3 Context)

Our developmental journey takes us from adolescent awareness in the group mythology of Ahav/Love to adult restoration in the universal mythology of Basar/Goodness grounded in the Lover-Beloved relationship. The Beloved is a transcendent presence in the symmetric dynamic of the adult cosmos functioning as Vanguard, leading us towards true relationship, and as Paragon, the embodiment of love and value in relationship, in support of the interdependent growth of the adult.

The adult stage of moral development, the Torah of Restoration, is the revival of purpose, meaning, and value in the context of relationship. The mythology of *Basar*, the experience of goodness, brings the Reunified Family together in the exploration of the archetypal topography of scarcity and sufficiency as a supportive community that shares its aggregate strength and power amid the issues and problems one encounters in life. In the Reunified Family of the Basar, each member in the community extends themself where another falls short. It builds on the mythology of Da'ath/Knowledge by bringing the personal experience of *family* into the shared experience of the Universal Family. It builds on the mythology of Ahav/Love by drawing it together as a communal act rather than merely an individual act. Our deep-seated awareness of our vulnerability in the face of scarcity and *missingness* becomes a fact, rather than a judgment—an acknowledgment that we need one another.

Adult morality, in a real-world experience, is a struggle between the underdeveloped conscience of the juvenile *Ground Nachash* and the actualized potential of the adult *Higher Nachash*. Both narratives still exist within an individual, with the potential to integrate towards, or disintegrate from, the ideal of goodness. At this stage, as we become more aware of our own power, we realize the guidance and aide of the Savior Elohim is as much our own responsibility, in the moment, as it is a transcendent function. Once one has solved the mystery of tying one's shoelaces, it would be infantilizing of oneself and insulting to an aide, to continue to rely on another to tie one's shoelaces every morning. As we grow in awareness of our power and the knowledge of our capacity to do good, it becomes our responsibility to use that power to do good.

However, as some develop an understanding of their power, that realization will turn inward, perceiving it to be an exclusive advantage in the personal or tribal domains, developing a Rival-Adversary relationship over the less advantaged and those outside their group. "Doing good" may become a moralistic strawman to conflate one's power and advantage over others. The mere appearance of *goodness* hides the pride and avarice of the Adversary, leading one's followers to consider them ideal, while the less advantaged suffer under the weight of their failure and missingness.

On the sociological level, the *Torah of Restoration* describes our engagement with the realm of great power as full participants. The value system is no longer motivated by social customs or norms but rather is derived from an internal narrative of value for one, and for all. The Adult does not look to the Parent or the Savior, or any other social benefit construct, to take action, to do good, but rather takes the responsibility for action on themselves, to generously give to another in need.

On the psychological level, the *Torah of Restoration* describes the mature state of moral development, not a perfect formation of behavior and intent, but rather a dynamic capacity to engage and respond to the consequence of our actions in the moment. Whenever we cause harm, intentionally or not, we uphold our obligation to restore what has been taken. And when we are injured, rather than *forgiveness* for those we have judged guilty, we find the strength to endure the harm done to us, to let go of our entitlement even to judge another, to let go of any claim of repayment for what has been taken, as an act of compassion and generosity, founded on the value instantiated in the Sacred Midst that one seeks to maintain at any cost.

Archetypally, the restoration to adult morality is the revival of purpose and connection, meaning and identity, and value and boundaries within the Sacred Midst. The focus is no longer on either individual in relationship but rather on the relationship between one another. Love is the action we take to feed and restore the Life in the Between. It is not construed as a perfect path but rather embodies the determination to stay engaged with one another until we can fix what has been broken in a relationship; there is no avoiding or running away, just the absolute imperative to listen and to struggle together until the hard work of restoration is finished.

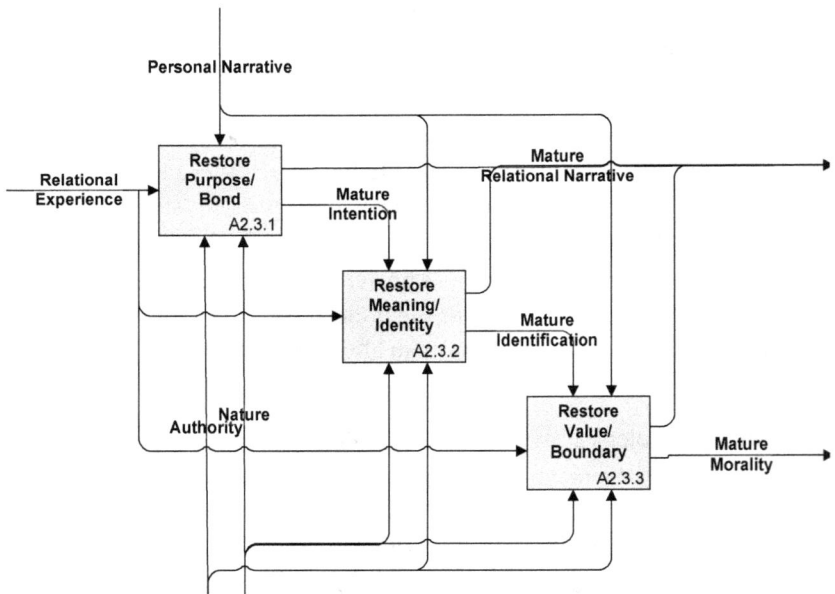

Model 15 - Develop Mature Relationship (A2.3)

Chapter [1/III]

WAY OF THE LOVER

> Out of the huts of history's shame, I rise. Up from a past that's rooted in pain, I rise. I'm a black ocean, leaping and wide, Welling and swelling, I bear in the tide. Leaving behind nights of terror and fear, I rise. Into a daybreak that's wondrously clear, I rise. Bringing the gifts that my ancestors gave, I am the dream and the hope of the slave. I rise.
> —*Maya Angelou*, "Still I Rise"

The first revelation of the Edenic Nachash is that our eyes will be unclosed as a result of the Fruit of Morality, knowing goodness and badness, realized in the experience of purposefulness and missingness. With eyes wide open, we engage the ordeals of life, yielding to the moment as it authentically is in joy and sorrow; or else, with eyes averted in habituated ignorance, we surrender to our fears of what is not, becoming enslaved to our insecurities and vulnerabilities, hoping in a lie. At the heart of human experience is our capacity to enter into the midst of the possibilities within and between one another and bring them to life. It is our unknowing that is the possibility of truly knowing. A search for a knowledge that leads to domination and control is not truly knowing. The sacred moment in meeting another is the openness to what is, what we do not know in each other—each holding the possibility and the intrinsic value of the other. When we let go of our expectations, truth and value emerge from the relationship in the Between. Only then do we discover our true power as elohim, the power that comes from reaching out to another—listening, responding, and supporting each other—to authentically love one another. Our weakness as individuals is our strength when we come together and support one another—this is the way of Love.

The egocentric search for moral perfection and dominion leads us on the false path to asymmetric power—our belief that our dominance brings satisfaction by overcoming the obstacles set before us through force and superiority. We are all broken in some way but not because we are powerless. Our salvation does not lie in the *unbreaking*, but rather, by finding empathy and strength through it in our common humanity. It is the strength to meet another who is broken and patiently hold their brokenness in recognition of our own; holding them, not as their rescuer, but as their friend and beloved, to become the wounded healer who offers healing out of one's own scars, as a consecrated balm of wholeness, truth, and authenticity.

❖ Vulnerability Versus Invincibility

The path of the Anointed Son, the Familial Messiah, is not the path of perfection and control by a superior force, but rather the path of the Beloved as Vanguard and Paragon, an inspiration and model for all Adamites in relationship to one another in the Universal Family. The Basar, the good news of Isaiah, is our gift of healing and life to one another—to raise up those who are humiliated, to bind up the brokenhearted, to liberate the captives, give sight to those that have none, to release those in bondage, and to comfort those in mourning.

In idolatry, we seek salvation from some superpower, some gillul, outside of ourselves, transacting safety by giving up our sanctity. We become infantilized victims in a world of victimizers, searching for a superhero that will do what we feel desperately needs to be done. In the Reified Basar, on the other hand, we are the ones responsible for saving one another. Love is not something done to us, it is what we do for one another, what we do to lessen, to eliminate, or to embrace the suffering of another. Sometimes we are the ones in need, reaching out for support; and sometimes we are the ones who must reach out, in fulfillment of our giftedness as elohim, to support another who suffers—this is family, this is community, this is the way of Life.

At the heart of the Reified Basar is the crucifixion of the Familial Messiah. It is intrinsically a story about willfully reaching into our vulnerability and rejecting the path of force and domination. Love is not a weakness, but rather a powerful choice to enter into our own vulnerability, manifest in the Between, even in the face of abject rejection. It is a narrative of transcending the ignorance and frailty of those that fight against us, to find the power of service to others, to be the Suffering Servant, despite our egoic drive for justice and retribution.

❖ Way of Fear

In the Genesis Exile myth, the Edenic Nachash opens the Adamite's eyes to their nakedness, their deeply felt vulnerability within an adverse world that envelopes them in a fog of fear and terror in which they subsequently hide. It is the beginning of an egoic awakening to their innate missingness in the death of the Sacred Midst, evoking a struggle to reconcile their imminent separateness with their essential connectedness to one another and to the Parent Elohim.

In the waking world, our search for purpose and connectedness within the Juvenile framework of our familial and tribal affiliation eventually reaches its limits. As we move out into the world, we lose our initial purpose and connectedness, finding ourselves in a larger world of responsibility. As we enter Adolescent moral development, we are taught our obligations to community and society. In turn, we learn what our value is in relation to other members of our community and the greater society. In this journey, some find their way to safety and others become enslaved by their fears, and yet, others will find their security in the exploitation and abuse of others whom they seek to master as a way to grapple with their own insecurity. There is a fundamental tension between the realities of the Kingdom of Cain, an asymmetric world of scarcity and competition, and the Kingdom of Elohim, an ideal symmetric world of sufficiency and community that Rabbi Jeshua claims to restore.

❖Kingdom of Fear

In the Kingdom of Elohim narrative of the Reified Basar, those who are identified with the asymmetric dynamic of exploitation, accumulation, and control of wealth and power do not belong to the Kingdom of Elohim. Those who rule the Kingdom of Cain through scarcity and fear stand in opposition to Yahweh. Rabbi Jeshua proclaims:

> No [servant] can be [serving] two lords, for either he will be hating one and loving the other, or he will be upholding one and despising the other. You cannot [serve Elohim] and [Mammon/Wealth].

> Now the Pharisees also, inherently fond of money, heard all these things, and they [scoffed at] Him. And He said to them, "You are those who are justifying yourselves in the sight of men, yet [Elohim] knows your hearts, for what is high among men is an abomination in the sight of [Elohim].[228]

The loan word *mammonas* from the Aramaic/Chaldean into Greek is used in the Jeshuaic text above to describe the worship of wealth, which mythically is rooted in the Syro-Phoenician god of riches, Mammona, who is similar to Plutus, the Greek god of wealth. Jeshua is chastising those who worship wealth as a gillul to serve and guide their path and actions, and to circumscribe their fear of scarcity. He invokes *Mammon* to personify their avarice and misuse of power. In the Kingdom of Elohim narrative, little hope is given for those that abuse their power to exploit or misuse others, who ignore the plight of the poor and weak. The wealthy and powerful are not excluded from the Kingdom, but their orientation and propensity to try to

---

[228] CLV Luke 16:13-15

conserve their advantage over others as masters of the asymmetric hierarchy leads Rabbi Jeshua to proclaim:

> The rich [with difficulty] will be entering into the kingdom of the heavens...
> it is easier for a camel to be entering through the eye of a needle than for a
> rich man to be entering into the kingdom of [Elohim].[229]

It is in this context that the central conflict of the Reified Basar is constructed between Rabbi Jeshua and the social and religious authorities, referred to therein as the Sadducees and the Pharisees.

It should be noted that the mythological lens of the Reified Basar is out of sync with the social realities of first-century Palestine. As Jeshua states, "what is high among men is an abomination in the sight of Elohim." Whereas the prophets portrayed these social and religious elites as failures before the Mosaic Law, in society, and by their own assertion, these elites were seen as the embodiment of success within the Mosaic tradition, which is why the students of Rabbi Jeshua reply to the aforementioned dromedary admonition with astonishment, stating, "Who, consequently, can be saved?"[230]

The *Sadducees* were the political conservatives, the wealthy and powerful economic leaders who were invested in the status quo. They were pragmatic in their dealings with their Roman overlords, seeking ways to preserve their power and wealth by maintaining a stable social structure as the ruling class. Politics and religion have historically been two sides of the same coin. As such, the High Priest that headed the Temple cult typically came from the ruling class of Sadducees. Their economic advantage was seen as a blessing from the Jewish-God, signifying their deservedness to hold such power and influence in society.

The *Pharisees* were the social conservatives, the zealous moralists, typically from the upper-middle class, which insulated them from the social and economic repercussions of their puritanical ideology. They portrayed themselves as meticulously following the Mosaic tradition, even extending their ritual adherence beyond the social regulations of the Mosaic Law by keeping the priestly Levitical purity laws in their daily lives as well. In particular, the Pharisees saw the dinner table as a sacred representation of the Temple, requiring one to enact the same cleansing rituals and abstinence prohibitions required of the priests in the Temple, with every meal. Many also believed that if everyone in Israel were to follow meticulously their interpretation of the Law for a single day that it would immediately bring the

---

[229] CLV Matthew 19:23-24
[230] CLV Matthew 19:25

advent of the Political Messiah, who would liberate them from Rome, cleanse the moral impurity from Israel, and restore the ancestral Davidic Kingdom. So, they took it quite personally when they saw someone fail to meet their standards, or as they saw it, the standards of Moses.

In addition to these mainstream conservative groups, there were two other significant ideological communities at this time—the Essenes and the Zealots. The *Essenes* were also social conservatives; however, they had lost faith in society, Pharisees and Sadducees be-damned, and ran off to the desert to wait for it all to blow up—the original survivalists. Their apocalyptic vision entailed waiting for the Political Messiah to come and wipe out both the Romans and the corrupt social hierarchy of the Jewish ruling class. They spent their time hunkered down in caves and fortresses in the desert studying and copying sacred text—which is where we eventually get the now-famous cache of Dead Sea Scrolls. Some scholars see similarities in the teachings and behavior of Johanan the Baptist.

The last group is the *Zealots*, a progressive movement of men who were not waiting for change to happen; they believed in becoming the change. While they still were looking for a political leader, a Messiah, to lead them into a final glorious battle, they were prone to needle away at the current political establishment, which they saw as corrupt collaborators with their Roman overlords. And by needle, I mean they were known for their sharp pointy daggers that they would use when they stealthily bumped into a known collaborator in a crowd, leaving a sharp pointy hole in the collaborator's abdomen, while they slipped away. They were also prone to follow any number of hopeful Messiahs in raids against the Romans, only to be shown the error of their ways by the sharp pointy spears of the Roman Legions, and the plentiful roadside exhibition of hanging Zealots on crosses. One student of Rabbi Jeshua, Judas, was surnamed Iscariot, which some scholars believe may refer to his association with the Zealots, and might explain his final actions, not as a rejection of Jeshua's Messiahship, but rather as a forceful but wrong-headed way to provoke Rabbi Joshua into using his great powers to start a revolution as the Political Messiah.

❖Political Messiah

The tradition of the Political Messiah, the Warrior King who is anointed to bring salvation to Israel through the defeat of their perpetual overlords, is developed as a response to the political turmoil of the Second Temple period, the sixth century BCE to the first century CE. Over the course of that history, the Messiah had become another gillul with competing notions of what actions, or transactions, were needed to occur for the Messiah to come to their rescue, or else, what Israel needed to become, to be deserving of his rule. The immediacy of the humiliation felt by Jews over the centuries of foreign occupation by the Persians, Greeks, and Romans was transformed into a desire for a superhero to rescue them and bring back the glory of Jewish self-rule idealized under David and Solomon. As such, they interpreted the messianic prophecies as meeting this very real political necessity of the day.

The hope and belief in a Political Messiah, the Warrior King, functioned as an obligatory gillul, which was universally held in Jewish society as an expression of their missingness and vulnerability as a nation. The Reified Basar myth indicates that Rabbi Jeshua's students were no different in their beliefs. As such, a good part of the Reified Basar myth is dedicated to reframing their understanding of "messiah" from the political to the relational; from the asymmetric dynamics of the conquering hero to the symmetric dynamic of the anointed firstborn son—from gillul to familial.

❖Familial Messiah

The Familial Messiah established in the Isaiah Basar myth is anointed to preserve and protect the Universal Family, in particular, those who are suffering and oppressed. Unlike a gillul who may cause suffering and ill fate as punishment when crossed, and whose repair of suffering is conditioned on the supplicant's deservedness, as evidenced by the quality of their offering, the Anointed Son represents the Good Father as unconditionally committed to the well-being of each of his children. The support of the children is based solely on their intrinsic value of sharing the same breath, in their identity as *elohim*, within the Family of Elohim.

In the Reified Basar, the Anointed Son embodies the love of the Good Father, and demonstrates this unconditional love through his ministry, restoring the symmetric power of the Kingdom of Elohim. There are countless healings and miraculous interventions cited in the myth, most just broadly stating "those having need of a cure, He healed."[231] These events happen without preconditions or sacrificial offerings. Expanding on the plague narrative of the Exodus myth, they draw a line between the transactional nature of the gillul and the generosity of the Good Father.

A few dozen miraculous interventions, however, are specifically mentioned. The first intervention is at a wedding feast in Cana where the host

---

[231] CLV Luke 9:11

runs out of wine and, at the behest of his mother, Jeshua gathers jars of water and turns them into wine (really good wine, I might add). It is performed as an act of generosity in support of the celebration without demands for offerings or obeisance, symbolizing the Good Father's generous support for his children's happiness. There are also two events where Jeshua feeds thousands who have followed him out into the countryside. With no food truck or fast-food joint to be found, Jeshua takes and miraculously multiplies a few fish and loaves of bread to sufficiently meet the crowd's immediate need for sustenance, purely out of concern for their well-being. In addition, there are five blind people that are specifically mentioned as being healed, two incidents of healing multiple cases of leprosy, a half dozen or so healings of individuals with paralysis in one or more limbs, various mentions of healing people with oppressive spirits, and three cases of raising victims of an untimely death.

Rather than indicating that the cause of their misery and disease was that the sufferer was being punished by an angry gillul/god, their misfortune is indicated to be an unnatural state that the Good Father cares about, and to which he desires to restore wholeness and healing. Each circumstance addresses the depths of scarcity and vulnerability in the human condition as the source of fear and suffering—hunger, oppression, disease, and death.

❖Yahweh Your Healer

In the Exodus myth, the first covenant Yahweh makes regarding his relationship to the Israelites after crossing through the Sea of Reeds, from slavery in Egypt into the freedom of the Wilderness of Shur, was to be Yahweh Rapha, Yahweh your Healer.[232] It was a promise predicated on their ardent adherence to his relational statutes, to value and care for one another, foreshadowing, or presupposing, what would become the Mosaic Law in the subsequent narration. This establishes the Adolescent association between love and healing—between the Tree of Morality and the Tree of Life in the Sacred Midst—which Rabbi Jeshua continues to invoke throughout his ministry.

This first covenant also emphasizes a mythological relationship between the outward manifestation of disability and the internal state of missingness. From our Juvenile state of Life in the Garden to our Exile into the world without the healing attributes of the Tree of Life restoring us to wholeness, we are broken creatures crippled by the ravages of age and disease, suspicion

---

[232] CLV Exodus 15:26

and doubt, fear and denial. We are dying under the deception and misfortune of Pandora's curse, the lie that gives birth to death. Contrary to the moralist credo of Original Sin as the *cause célèbre* for our guilt, justifying eternal damnation, this belief in our congenital failure and inadequacy is one of the greatest causes of our misery and defeat in asymmetric culture, convincing us that we are powerless and unworthy. It is an artifact of the Accuser, or *saw-tan*, the Ground Nachash that lives subtly within the depths of our souls, who convinces us that we are inadequate or incapable of approval; that we are inherently disappointments to our families, to our spiritual Father, and to our own hopes and dreams; that we don't deserve to be happy, or even to live or to exist; that we are helpless to resist the chaos that seeps into our souls.

In our frailty, the voice of the Adversary speaks both from within ourselves, and collectively in society and religion, to accuse us of our failures, branding our identity with missingness and vulnerability, or, as Christians are fond of decrying, our "sinfulness." As the crippled man who spends his days at the city gate begging for what meager subsistence will allow him to live another day, while suffering the scoffs and rejection of people passing to the other side of the gate, we eventually internalize our insufficiency. Implicitly, we come to believe that all we are, is that man who disgracefully begs at the city gates—"I am my disease, and I can never be anything else." The disease becomes the outward manifestation of our internal brokenness; changing our circumstances will not change the limits we feel inside.

It is in this context that Jeshua equates the inner and outer state of the sufferer during an encounter with a paralytic who has been brought to him to be healed:

> And lo! they brought to Him a paralytic, prostrate on a couch. And Jesus, perceiving their faith, said to the paralytic, "Courage, child! [released/let go] are your [missingness/failure/limitations]!"[233]

In context to this encounter, the Greek word *aphienai*[234] means "to send away or to let go." However, the translators habitually moralize the meaning as "to pardon or forgive" to coincide with a mistranslation of the Greek word *hamartia* to inaccurately mean "sin/guilt" instead of its literal translation of "missingness" or "failure." This recurs throughout the translation of the Reified Basar accounts and is fundamentally important to consider as it draws a line between the moralized theology of *forgiveness of sin/guilt* and the core psychological or spiritual guidance to let go of our *missingness, failure, or limitations* as well as the *missingness, failure, or limitations* of others that

---

[233] CLV Matthew 9:2
[234] Strongs G836

may cause us harm. Guilt implies that one has already been judged and condemned by conscience or the law. Failure, in and of itself, on the other hand, only implies brokenness and loss, which may or may not lead to judgment. Mercy and graciousness indicate letting go of judgment as an act of generosity and love towards another. It intrinsically implies a value in relationship that transcends what is owed. It is the love of a parent or comrade, who strives to retain connection and community in the face of a lapse of consideration by their beloved.

On the other hand, in the moralistic interpretation of Judaism, at least prior to the destruction of the Second Temple, sin/guilt must be paid in blood by animal sacrifice, and, similarly, in moralistic Christianity, sin/guilt must be paid for by human sacrifice, albeit of one who is also a gillul/god. Neither of these moralistic enterprises actually forgives or lets go of one's failure. After all, if one's sin/guilt is paid for, then one is not, in fact, forgiven. And, likewise, if one's failure is let go, or ignored, then there is nothing to judge and therefore nothing to be paid. These two concepts cannot logically exist in the same philosophical or theological universe except by disingenuously slurring over this fundamental contradiction. Yet, in moralism, all sins must be punished otherwise chaos ensues. And the fear of chaos is what drives moralism.

Thus, when Jeshua tells the paralytic man that his failures are let go, some of the scribes said among themselves, "This man is [slandering]" to which Jeshua, perceiving their sentiments, replied:

> Why are you brooding wickedness in your hearts? For what is easier, to be saying, '[Let go] are your [failures/limitations],' or to be saying, 'Rouse and walk'? Now, that you may be perceiving that the Son of Mankind has authority on earth to [let go of failures/limitations][235]

He turns back to the paralytic, man saying, "Being roused, pick up your couch and go into your house."[236] Jeshua equates the inner and outer state of the man's missingness. As the Anointed Son, he claims the authority to send away/let go/ignore the man's failures and limitations, restoring him to safety and wholeness both physically and emotionally.

❖**The Art of Relationalism**

In the relational paradigm of the Unified Basar and Torah mythology, one's behavior does not dictate or limit relationship—failure does not break

---

[235] CLV Matthew 9:3-6
[236] CLV Matthew 9:6

the family bonds. Rather, an action that fails to value another obligates the one who takes from another, to restore what was taken, and then, some additional gift in recompense—nothing more, nothing less. In fact, the Mosaic Law protects the lawbreaker by limiting what is owed to the one offended— one cannot kill someone who steals, trespasses, or looks menacingly at you as an egotistic act of vengeance. Nor does the offense become some black mark on a cosmic scorecard that follows one throughout their life, to be held in balance in some ultimate judgment. The only unforgivable or unreleasable failure, in the context of the Reified Basar, is to live in such a way as to misrepresent or slander the Father's generosity and mercy in drawing his children to himself, which is represented in the text as a habitual condition of the conservative social and political establishment. In regard to one's imperfect behavior towards the Good Father, failure may be disciplined as a father does his children; yet, even in this, the Father proclaims that he is merciful and slow to anger.

Once we move beyond the grand cosmic contrivance of *sin against the Holy Father* to the actual text, we are repeatedly confronted with the issue of the Children's negative beliefs and attitudes toward the Father—the distorted judgment represented by Eve's suspicions in the Garden that her limitations are caused by the Parent Elohim, and the subsequent belief that her missingness prevents her from intimacy with the Parent Elohim. Jeshua's proclamation of ignoring, or letting go, of another's obligation to restore value brings to the forefront our internal state of failure to see the generosity of the Good Father as the Ideal Parent image. The Anointed Son represents the graciousness of the Good Father, having the authority to represent to the sufferer that the Good Father habitually lets go of the judgment of one's failures as a matter of character and intrinsic value within the Universal Family. He encourages the sufferer, likewise, to move beyond their state of missingness and failure, to encounter Yahweh as their Healer.

❖Letting Go

Letting go is, in actuality, the central dynamic of transformation and healing throughout the Unified Basar and Torah mythology. Developmentally, it stands in opposition to our egocentric need to dominate and control the outcome of our story. It is what moves us back from the asymmetric power dynamic of the Victim-Villain-Victor, Slave-Master, and Rival-Adversary relationships to the symmetric power dynamic of Child-Parent, Servant-Savior, and Lover-Beloved relationships. It is the transformative moment in the metamorphic Hero's encounter with the Dark Force that deconstructs the inauthentic path, the death of Control in the Dark Night, which allows for the reconstruction of the new life beyond death. It is the *letting go* of the old world in the cataclysmic Flood and *letting go* of the old life as death passes over in the dark of night. It comes at the moment we realize we are not in control of others, let alone our own lives, and there are no options left, but to *let go*.

As such, *letting go* is the essential salutary agency at the heart of psychological healing. Throughout our lives, our dysfunctional narratives develop out of our resistance to authentically face our vulnerabilities, which wildly exaggerates the power of the neurotic eidolon that haunts our unintegrated shadow narrative. This regressive orientation to the nemetic power of the Transferential Elohim vainly compels us to try to control others, our emotions, or our circumstances, perilously disconnecting us from our authentic identity as truth-tellers of our own story. In this context, we don't really heal anything; we simply let go of our compulsive need to control the narrative to protect some perceived vulnerability, what Rabbi Jeshua variously portrays as slavery to our missingness or vulnerability.

However, *letting go* is not another moralistic rule that governs relationship. It is a fundamental choice—a choice to be used with wisdom. There is a difference between, on one hand, *letting go* of our judgment and need for vengeance, and then, on the other hand, *letting go* of consequences. Consequences help us to build healthy boundaries. There are times that *letting go* of consequence does not serve the greater good. The countervailing decision to hold one accountable before the law or a moral code is not a sign of weakness or bad judgment, any more than forgiveness or letting go. Discipline is a reasonable choice in a healthy relationship. What is asked of the one offended is to judge what is beneficial to all involved, including the victim, the perpetrator, and the community at large. Appropriate punishment may be the loving choice to enforce boundaries that are habitually broken or are of no concern to the perpetrator. It may be the loving choice to protect one's family or community by allowing the judicial process to remove a continual threat posed by a perpetrator. In particular, it may be necessary to protect the vulnerable or the powerless from one whose conscience has no issue in continuing to harm another. What is asked of the one offended is to let go of one's entitlement to avenge, but also to seek a greater good, which may or may not include the enforcement of one's boundaries.

Letting go, ultimately, is the foundation of love in relationship. It is the primary characteristic that defines the character of the Good Parent as merciful, compassionate, and generous. It becomes the example and pattern that his children are called to emulate. This is outlined in a part of what is known as the Lord's Prayer, which properly translated, states:

> *And [let go] our debts [obligation], as we also [let go] our debtors. And mayest Thou not be bringing us into trial, but rescue us from [hardship]. For if you should be [letting go] men their [faults/limitations], your heavenly Father also will be [letting go] you. Yet if you should not be [letting go] men their [faults/limitations], neither will your Father be [letting go] your [faults/limitations].[237]*

As a reciprocal principle, healthy relationships can only exist within the boundaries of compassion and trust. The moralist who refuses to let go of perceived harm, or the imperfections of others, as a matter of control, cannot substantially be in a functional relationship. There is a give-and-take in empathy and sociability that motivates us to *let go* of failure for the benefit of a relationship. A healthy relationship is not born out of perfect behavior but rather is nurtured through the inevitable imperfections that arise, motivated by the value of the other. A parent or friend that disowns a child or comrade the first or next time they falter is fundamentally incapable of being in a relationship. Our capacity to *let go* of imperfection, and move towards the imperfect, is the way of love.

❖Liber Pater

Greek mythology, on the other hand, is fundamentally about order and control in a world founded on Chaos—each god jealously exercises control over their domain with force and intensity. The Greeks meticulously outlined the natural and psychological powers of the universe, developing narratives that instructed the civilized Greeks on how to live their lives wisely and properly. But then, on the other hand, there is Dionysus, the god of wine, embodying freedom from oppressive social constructs, letting go of misery and pain, joining others in festive communal celebrations of ecstasy and madness—known in some traditions as *Liber Pater*, the *Father of Freedom*. He is the antithesis of Greek moralism and is generally believed to predate it.

Dionysus is born of the Sky-God Zeus and one of various earth-born mortal or immortal mothers—Semele, Demeter, or Persephone. He exists in between these worlds, neither fully above nor below, perpetually wandering the earth, without a specific home. He has no temple, but rather he is worshiped out in the open woodlands. He is the only Greek god that is believed to inhabit his worshipers in an intimate embrace of joyful reverence. Over time, his worship becomes more chaotic—from the joyous release of modestly drinking the fruit of the vine, to becoming wild festivals of drunken

---

[237] CLV Matthew 6:12-15

orgies and excess in some corners of his worship, in particular, as a practice in the Roman Bacchanal festivities.

Archetypally, Dionysus represents joyous freedom from oppression and disease. However, this does not exist outside of our value systems. When present within an egocentric morality of scarcity and vulnerability, it becomes the freedom to live a self-centered life without rules or social constraints. When present within a value system of empathy and mutuality, it becomes the freedom to live authentically, unrestrained by the shackles of a social system anchored in fear and disability. Moralism, on the other hand, thrives on control structures—there is no greater fear for those so predisposed than to remove the social and religious constraints, to fully let go.

❖Restore Purpose/Bond

The alchemical proem at the start of the chapter is from, "Still I Rise,"[238] a poem by the phenomenal Maya Angelou. It is a journey of transformation from slavery to freedom, transcending "nights of terror and fear," to find hope and redemption lost to generations in suffering and pain. In the first stanza, Maya challenges those who "may write me down in history with your bitter, twisted lies... trod me in the very dirt, but still, like dust, I'll rise." It is a proud proclamation of personal worth and purpose for existence in the face of an adversarial establishment that has continually abused and exploited oneself and one's kindred over generations out of pure hatred and corrupt selfish desire. And yet with each debasement, Maya transcends the voice of suppression and degradation, to find love for herself, to resurrect dignity and honor in the heroic declaration, "Still I rise." She reminds us that love for one another arises out of personal power, as a manifestation of love and respect for oneself.

Psychologically, mature moral development begins as the power of our adolescent morality becomes more symmetric in the emerging Lover-Beloved relationship, restoring an inclusive purpose and connection to the Sacred Midst of the relationship. The codified obligations of adolescent morality, to love one another, become our core internal value system upon which we instinctually respond. As mature moral actors in the social milieu, we actively seek to influence the well-being of others in our community, rather than waiting for some superhero to save us from the ills that befall us.

At the heart of mature morality is letting go of the idea of moral perfection and our sense of entitlement to judge others. Human relationships

---

[238] Angelou (1994) p.163-164

are prone to conflict as the varying streams of expectations and responsibilities converge in the arena of social engagement. More often than not, there is no right or wrong answer to the pressing questions that plague us—what to eat tonight, whose turn is it to do the dishes, why doesn't he just say what's on his mind, should we pull the plug on grandma's life support machine—no easy solutions to resolve our differences. Either we can force our perspective on another, or we can work out the difficult problems by letting go of our absolutist urges, to find some middle ground, while still holding on to the essential principles of love and respect. Mature engagement is a process, not an end-result—it is a way of life, a way to love one another.

Archetypally, our restoration to mature morality is the revival of purpose and connection within the Sacred Midst. The inclusive value system of love and mutuality becomes internalized. Our belief in the intrinsic value of those in our community leads us to respond to the needs of others, to support others, to love one another using our strengths to strengthen others and to aid those who are broken. The developmental journey of cultivating our humanity has taken us from the juvenile framework of the parent-child relationship in search of goodness and mutual support to the adult framework of mutual relationship founded on our intrinsic power to build the bonds of goodness and mutual support within the Universal Family through altruistic action.

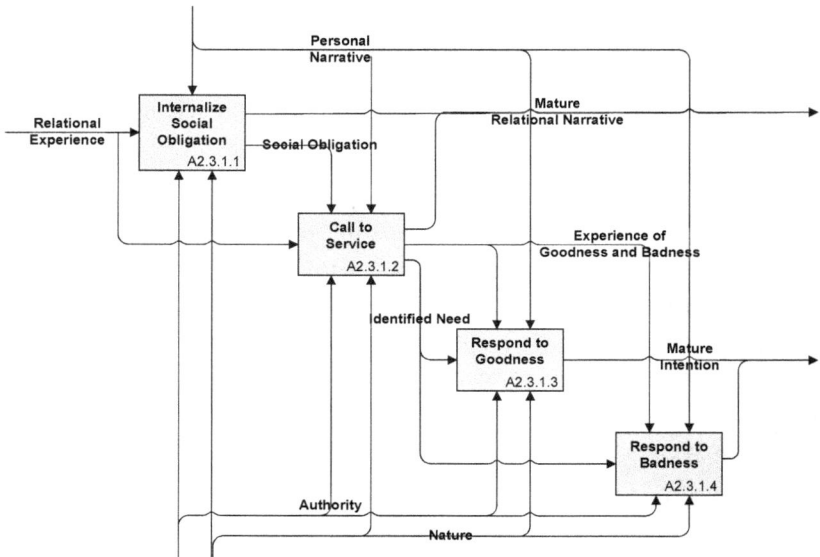

Model 16 - Restore Purpose/Bond (A2.3.1)

CHAPTER [2/III]

TRUTH SHALL SET YOU FREE

> Humankind is being led along an evolving course, through this migration of intelligences, and though we seem to be sleeping, there is an inner wakefulness that directs the dream, and that will eventually startle us back to the truth of who we are.
> —*Rumi*, "The Dream That Must be Interpreted"

The second revelation of the Edenic Nachash is that we will become like the Imago Elohim as a direct result of the Fruit of Morality. From the beginning, we are identified as Child Elohim within a Universal Family of Elohim, in relationship to the Parent Elohim. The mature moral development of the Imago Elohim is represented by, and through, the Anointed Son as our big brother, which is restored in humanity through the call to action in the Reified Basar.

In the Basar account of John, this revelation of love as the path towards mature relationship within the Universal Family is identified and elaborated on as the essential Truth of the mythology. Upon his arrest by the Jewish authorities on charges of blasphemy and sedition, Rabbi Jeshua is brought before the Roman governor, Pontius Pilate, and questioned as to what he has done, and whether he has, in fact, claimed to be a *king* in opposition to the Roman emperor. In response, Rabbi Jeshua testifies to the *Truth* of his mission and authority:

> My kingdom is not of this world. If My kingdom were of this world, My deputies, also, would have contended, lest I should be given up to the Jews. Yet now is My kingdom not hence... You are saying that I am a king. For this also have I been born, and for this have I come into the world, that I should be testifying to the truth. Everyone who is of the truth is hearing My voice.[239]

Pilate, then, dismissively ripostes, "What is truth?"[240] And yet this is the central question underlying Jeshua's declaration.

❖Quid Est Veritas

The mythology of *Truth* in the first-century Greco-Roman world is founded predominantly on classic Greek philosophy and its ideological

---

[239] CLV John 18:36-37
[240] CLV John 18:38 (from the presumed Latin phrase *"Quid Est Veritas"*)

descendants, in particular, the Middle Platonists of the day. In Plato's *Laws*, he identifies *Truth* as a moral principle, stating:

> Truth is the beginning of every good thing, both to Gods and men; and he who would be blessed and happy, should be from the first a partaker of the truth, that he may live a true man... for then he can be trusted.[241]

The Basar account of John, more so than the three synoptic Basar accounts, is in direct conversation with the Hellenistic philosophical ideas of Logos, Ethics, and Truth; however, putting the Messiah of the Reified Basar at the center of these broadly debated topics. The Basar of John begins:

> In the beginning was the [Logos/Word], and the [Logos/Word] was toward [theos/god], and [theos/god] was the [Logos/Word]. This was in the beginning toward [theos/god]. All came into being through it, and apart from it not even one thing came into being which has come into being.[242]

This first part of John's Basar account is a straightforward Middle Platonist rendition of the "arche logos"—also found in contemporary Jewish philosophy as *memra* (Aramaic for "word")—specifying an original thought or intention as the ultimate expression from, and representation of, the theos/god, which intrinsically brings all things into existence. Then John elaborates:

> And the [Logos/Word] became flesh and [camps] among us, and we gaze at His glory, a glory as of an only-begotten from the Father, full of [generosity] and truth. [Johanan] is testifying concerning Him and has cried, saying, "This was He of Whom I said, `He Who is coming after me, has come to be in front of me,' for He was first, before me," for of that which fills Him we all obtained, and [graciousness] for [generosity]. For the law through Moses was given; [generosity] and truth came through [Jeshua the Anointed Son].[243]

This second paragraph deviates from the initial philosophical construct and expands on it as a relational dynamic, identifying Jeshua as the embodiment of the Logos "full of generosity and truth," bringing the original intent into the moral realm. As a psychological experience of Goodness and Badness founded on the Tree of Morality, the Logos instantiates the Truth of *ahav* as the Law within humankind—the conscience that moves us towards act-love, which has existed from the beginning. It summarizes the ultimate intent of creation as love.

---

[241] Plato (2013) p. 92, The Law Book V
[242] CLV John 1:1-3
[243] CLV John 1:14-17

❖Truth and Consequence

In context to moral development, the conscience is a consistent moral operator within each of us that evaluates the truth or value of a stimulus. It operates independently of any external value narratives or social mandates. Rather its function is to search for truth based on the internal narrative fabric that has already been inculcated as one's subjective truth. Any consequent action is a product of our conscience. As the core psychic function that evaluates the truthfulness and value of what potential is set before us, we are geared to operate on what we perceive to be "truth," prompting us to act in support of that "truth." However, the commitment and behavior of a person who *believes* in an empirical fallacy are no different than one who believes in an empirical fact. An immature conscience will act upon an egocentric morality as its own "truth" with no less commitment to its fulfillment than one whose conscience is founded on a mature wisdom of the Law of Love. The focus and outcome of our conscientious engagement are intrinsically a product of an internal aesthetic that underlies the conscience.

Given the complexity of many situations and the saturation of propagandistic messaging by those vying to control the narrative, a moral concern may be entangled with conflicting values from which to discern a course of action. Ultimately, the process of interpreting the truth and value of a moral concern is a product of education, experience, and one's developed capacity for critical thinking. A subjective *truth* may, in fact, be an objective lie. The failure to test an observation may lead to a dangerous or unfounded conclusion being incorporated into one's identity. As such, the search for authentic truth requires investment in one's beliefs, evaluating each proposition and its source.

Much of the mythology of the Reified Basar is a testament to its *truth*, constructed out of the presage of the earlier prophets, and the narrative of the Torah, in context to the actions of Rabbi Jeshua recorded in the Reified Basar accounts. As indicated earlier, the metaphysics of these claims is outside of the purview of this exploration. However, internal to the mythscape it is important to annotate the self-referential fulfillment of the claims, according to the criteria that it sets for itself as Truth. The myth does not ask the student to blindly believe what authority tells them that they should believe. It is built on the testament of those who are eyewitnesses within the mythology and then asks the listener to test for themselves. Authentic truth exists outside of the bias of an individual's or a group's rational belief system. It exists on a deeper empirical level of a shared truth of a verified holomorphic narrative built over generations.

❖Kingdom of Truth

In the Unified Basar and Torah mythology, Truth is a fundamental quality identifying the Imago Elohim, an essential aspect of moral character. The Parent Elohim describes his own character as "compassionate and gracious, slow to anger and abundant with [kindness] and truth."[244] A central aspect of this truth within the mythology is the promise Yahweh Elohim makes to the patriarch Abraham of a promised land of peace and prosperity for his many descendants. It is an evocation to a place of sufficiency—a return to a mythic Eden. The prophet of Third Isaiah invokes the truthfulness of the Parent/Savior Elohim who keeps his promises, describing a future kingdom founded on symmetric power, in an ideal harmony of nature and experience nurtured by the Tree of Life:

> *He who is blessing himself in the land, he shall bless himself by the Elohim of truth, And he who is swearing in the land, he shall swear by the Elohim of truth; For the former distresses are forgotten, And indeed they are concealed from My eyes.*
>
> *For behold Me creating new heavens and a new earth, And the former shall not be remembered, Nor shall they come up on the heart. But rather be elated and exult in the futures of the future which I shall be creating, For behold Me creating Jerusalem an exultation, And her people an elation.*
>
> *I exult in Jerusalem, And I am elated in My people; And the sound of lamentation shall not be heard in her any longer, Or the sound of outcry. No longer shall there be thence an infant of few days, Or an old man who shall not fill his days; For a youth shall die at a hundred years old, And he who misses a hundred years old shall be lightly esteemed.*
>
> *They will build houses and dwell in them, And they will plant vineyards and eat their fruit; They shall not build, and another dwell there; They shall not plant, and another eat, For like the days of the tree of life will be the days of My people, And the work of their hands shall My chosen use to the full.*
>
> *They shall not labor for nought, Nor shall they give birth in vain, For the seed of Yahweh's blessed are they, And their offspring with them. And it will be that ere they are calling, I Myself shall answer; While they are still speaking, I Myself shall hearken.*
>
> *The wolf and the lambkin shall graze alike, And the lion shall eat crushed straw like the ox, And the serpent shall have soil as its bread. They shall not do [harm], Nor shall they bring ruin in all My holy mountain, says Yahweh.[245]*

The holy mountain is Zion upon which the city of Jerusalem is built. Jerusalem is an ancient city that predates the Israelite occupation of the Canaanite

---

[244] CLV Exodus 34:6
[245] CLV Isaiah 65:16-25

lands. In the Torah mythology, it is introduced as *Salem*, the kingdom of Melchizedek in the Abraham narrative, stating:

> Then Melchizedek king of Salem, he brought forth bread and wine, for he was a priest for El Supreme; he blessed him and said: "Blessed be Abram by El Supreme, Owner of the heavens and the earth. And blessed be El Supreme, Who has awarded your foes into your hand." And Abram gave him a tenth of all the booty.[246]

Melchizedek, meaning the "king of righteousness," is introduced as the priest of El Supreme in the city of *Salem*, meaning "peace/safety." Salem will later be referred to as *Yeruwshalem*[247] prefacing *shalem* with *yarah* indicating "to flow as water"—thus symbolizing the place from which peace/safety flows. It is a mountaintop city comprised of two heights, Mount Zion, which becomes the upper city, and Mount Moriah, which becomes the temple mount. From its introduction as Salem, through the later Jewish mythologies, it fundamentally represents the dwelling place of Yahweh, similar to Mount Horeb/Sinai in the wilderness of Midian. In this passage, Isaiah invokes a new Jerusalem as the foundation of peace, and the intimate place of Yahweh's dwelling on earth in the midst of his people—a reprisal of the intimacy of the Garden of Eden.

However, this narrative of the future kingdom of peace is prefaced in the text by a proclamation scorning those sons of Israel who choose a path "after their own devisings," resulting in their being disinherited as the firstborn of nations. Yahweh subsequently blesses a people that had not sought him or called his name, thus restoring the Universal Family:

> I let Myself be inquired of by those who did not ask for Me, I am found by those who did not seek Me; I say... Behold Me! to a nation that has not called on My Name; I spread out My hands the whole day to a stubborn and rebellious people, Who are walking in the way that is not good, after their own devisings... Who are saying, "Keep near to yourself! You must not come close to me, for I am holy to you!" ...I called, yet you did not `answer, I spoke, yet you did not hearken, And you are doing [harm] in My eyes, And you choose that in which I take not delight. Therefore... My servants, they shall eat, yet you shall famish! ...My servants, they shall drink, yet you shall thirst! ...My servants, they shall rejoice, yet you shall be ashamed! ...My servants, they shall be jubilant from a good heart, yet you shall cry from pain of heart, And from brokenness of spirit shall you howl![248]

The "stubborn and rebellious people" are dispossessed from their place of honor in the kingdom. Their adversarial relationship with the Parent Elohim

---

[246] CLV Genesis 14:18-20
[247] Strongs H3389
[248] CLV Isaiah 65:1-2, 5, 12-14

results in them being removed from the blessing of the firstborn to become a broken people.

Likewise, in the Basar of John, Rabbi Jeshua while discussing his mission and relationship with the Father Elohim is confronted by some pious Jews who defiantly proclaim, "Our father is Abraham," to which Jeshua retorts:

If you are children of Abraham, did you ever do the works of Abraham? Yet now you are seeking to kill Me, a Man Who has spoken to you the truth which I hear from [Elohim]. This Abraham does not do. Yet you are doing the works of your father. If [Elohim] were your Father, you would have loved Me. For out of [Elohim] I came forth and am arriving. For neither have I come of Myself, but He commissions [anoints] Me...

Seeing that you can not hear My word. You are of your father, the Adversary, and the desires of your father you are wanting to do. He was a man-killer from the beginning, and does not stand in the truth, for truth is not in him. Whenever he may be speaking a lie, he is speaking of his own, for he is a liar, and the father of it... If I am telling the truth, wherefore are you not believing Me?[249]

Rabbi Jeshua associates the pious Jews with the Kingdom of Cain, the original adversary and man-killer, and the archetype of human civilization. Those Jews who insist that their birthright is founded on being a descendant of Abraham without loving service to the Parent Elohim and the Universal Family are consequently identified as children of the Adversary, the father of murderers and liars. As such, they will not inherit the Kingdom of Elohim.

Later in the Reified Basar, the inhabitants of the Kingdom of Elohim are identified as those who serve one another and the Parent Elohim with loving-kindness; thus reflecting the Father's character in his children who are similarly "compassionate and gracious, slow to anger and abundant with kindness and truth." Archetypally, the kingdom of truth is not a destination, but rather a representation of the Logos, the original intention of creation, a restoration of Eden that is established by a community founded on the symmetric power dynamic of act-love. On the other hand, the Adversary fundamentally represents the asymmetric power dynamic that destroys the community through deception and abuse.

❖The Anointed Son

The narrative of the Reified Basar is founded on Rabbi Jeshua's identity as the anointed firstborn son of Yahweh who represents the character and will of the Father to the family. In the Basar of John, the pious Jews ask Rabbi Jeshua, "Who are you?" to which he replies:

---

[249] CLV John 8:42-47

Much have I to be speaking and judging concerning you, but [the Father] Who sends Me is true, and what I hear from Him, these things I am speaking to the world... Whenever you should be exalting [raising up] the Son of Mankind, then you will know that I am, and from Myself I am doing nothing, but, according as My Father teaches Me, these things I am speaking. And He Who sends Me is with Me. He does not leave Me alone, for what is pleasing to Him am I doing always... If ever you should be remaining in My word, you are truly My [students], and you will know the truth, and the truth will be making you free.[250]

Jeshua, as the Anointed Son, represents the Father's generosity towards his Family. As such, he embodies the Nachash of Elohim that does not speak on his own, but as an oracle, speaks the truth of the Father.

In the slavery narrative of the Exodus myth, Yahweh reveals the truth of his power and identity in the lead-up to the Dark Night. As he prepares to bring the Israelites out of slavery, he affirms his relationship to the children of Israel as his anointed firstborn of Nations and demonstrates his power over the Egyptian gilluls. Moses, as the anointed Nachash of Elohim and Savior, is appointed to deliver the Israelites from slavery to freedom. Likewise, when Jeshua states, "the truth will be making you free," he claims to bring humankind out of slavery into freedom. However, the pious Jews rebut this claim, stating:

The seed of Abraham are we, and we have never been slaves of anyone. How are you saying that `You shall be becoming free'?[251]

Rabbi Jeshua responds that fundamentally their actions to protect their missingness and vulnerability enslave them to their fear, tying this narrative back to both the Genesis Exile and the Exodus Dark Night.

Everyone who is [failing to love], is a slave of [missingness]. Now the slave is not remaining in the house for the [eon/age]. The son is remaining for the [eon/age]. If ever, then, the Son should be making you free, you will be really free.[252]

In the Reified Basar, Jeshua represents the Savior/Beloved Elohim that has come to deliver Adamkind from their missingness, making them truly free from the bondage of their fears, the terror of their vulnerability that resulted from partaking of the immature fruit of Morality in the Exile myth. He then restores them to their true identity as Servant/Lover Elohim through the power of act-love.

---

[250] CLV John 8:25-32
[251] CLV John 8:33
[252] CLV John 8:34-36

256

Similarly, as the Anointed Son, Rabbi Jeshua has the moral authority to represent the generosity and truth of the Father. In the bonds of that familial relationship, Jeshua proclaims that in truth you will find peace.

> All was given up to Me by My Father. And no one is recognizing the Son except the Father; neither is anyone recognizing the Father except the Son and he to whom if the Son should be intending to unveil Him. Hither to Me, all who are toiling and laden, and I will be giving you rest. Lift My yoke upon you and be learning from Me, for meek am I and humble in heart, and you shall be finding rest in your souls, for My yoke is kindly and My load is light.[253]

Jeshua's moral authority is established in continuity with the prior revelation of the Mosaic Law as the basis for loving relationships within the Universal Family. His ministry is a fulfillment of the values instantiated within this Law:

> You should not infer that I came to demolish the law or the prophets. I came not to demolish, but to fulfill. For verily, I am saying to you, Till heaven and earth should be passing by, one iota or one serif may by no means be passing by from the law till all should be occurring. Whosoever, then, should be annulling one of the least of these precepts, and should be teaching men thus, the least in the kingdom of the heavens shall he be called. Yet whoever should be doing and teaching them, he shall be called great in the kingdom of the heavens.[254]

Befittingly, the Anointed Son, as the embodiment of the Mosaic Law, is empowered by the Father to judge the Family with respect to the Law:

> For neither is the Father judging anyone, but has given all judging to the Son, that all may be honoring the Son, according as they are honoring the Father. He who is not honoring the Son is not honoring the Father Who sends Him.[255]

This sets up the ultimate dilemma for Rabbi Jeshua in the crucifixion narrative, whether to pursue justice and punish those that have slandered and abused him, condemning him to death, or else, to walk a different path of mercy and love.

❖Crux of the Dark Night

The Dark Night of the Reified Basar myth is the trial and execution of Rabbi Jeshua, provoked ex-cathedra by the conservative religious establishment based on false accusations of religious slander and political sedition. Rabbi Jeshua's claim to be the Familial Messiah challenges the conservative canon of Jewish Nationalism and Traditional Moralism, which

---

[253] CLV Matthew 11:27-30
[254] CLV Matthew 5:17-19
[255] CLV John 5:22-23

was rooted in the class privilege of the Pharisees and Sadducees in Roman Palestine.

The Pharisees and Sadducees reject the Familial Messiah as a matter of principle—the principle being that not all people are deserving of protection or salvation from suffering, a central trait of political conservatism and religious moralism. People who do not measure up to their standards must be marginalized and destroyed. The moralized world order is divided up into those that belong to the favored group and those that do not. This is the exclusionary principle of most political "isms" by definition, adding the criteria before the "ism" to indicate what is the focus of exclusion from the favored domain—racism, tribalism, nationalism, sexism, conservatism, individualism, egotism. The -ism defines one's identity for which one will fight to maintain superiority—hierarchical asymmetric power is inherent in the bias.

While the *truth* may set you free, the *lie* invariably enslaves, or worse, kills. Deliberative *slander* is the art of destroying one's opponent by damaging the integrity of their reputation through vilification and false accusations. Non-deliberative *slander* is a product of one's immersion in the asymmetric power dynamic of the Victim-Villain-Victor, subconsciously devaluing one's perceived opponent as exclusively and unidimensionally embodying the Villain/Monster role, thus making anything they do or say a threat deserving of the most violent response. As the Monster, they are valueless and must be destroyed. In a social setting, *slander* is intended to debilitate the power and authority of a person within one's community. In a legal setting, *slander* is intended to harm one's fundamental right to life and property as protected by the state. In the Mosaic Law, the prohibition against slander enforces an essential right, protecting the truth of the reputation and identity of both the individual within their community, and with regard to the spiritual Father, as the basis for intimacy and love in a relationship.

❖False Identity

As we have seen in the Exodus narrative, the Dark Night is fundamentally the process of deconstructing false identity. In the Reified Basar narrative, the false identity is specifically the *Political Messiah*, the heroic Warrior King who dominates and destroys the opposition; in the parlance of first-century Judaism, he is the one who frees the nation from foreign rule. Archetypally, this false identity invoked by the narrative is the embodiment of the asymmetric power dynamic of the Villain-Victor, Master, and Adversary. It is the inverse companion to the false identity in the Exodus narrative of Victim and Slave.

Initially, Rabbi Jeshua confronts this false identity at the beginning of his ministry in the Wilderness trial when the Adversary gives him the opportunity to use his power selfishly to reach his inherent needs and desires for sustenance, safety, and prestige. In the *Passion* narrative leading up to his crucifixion, Rabbi Jeshua is faced with the eventuality of his unjust murder by the conservative religious and political elites, thus ending his life and ministry. He again is confronted with the allure of becoming this false messiah, using his power to save himself and punish his enemies.

❖**Unleavened Body**

The Dark Night of the Reified Basar begins with the final Passover Feast of Unleavened Bread. In the Mosaic tradition, the Passover Feast of Unleavened Bread commemorates the foundation of the national identity of Israel as the anointed firstborn of nations brought forth out of slavery to the land promised to the patriarch Abraham. The blood of the Passover lamb and the unleavened bread are the central symbols of the ritual feast, commemorating a new beginning for Israel, inaugurated by the passing over of the Messenger of Death in Egypt to bring them out of slavery.

In the Passover myth, *leavened* bread is the symbol of civilization under the authority of Matsor/Egypt, representing the archetypal kingdom of Cain, the firstborn of Adam. *Leaven* is the yeast that makes bread rise. Traditionally, the yeast culture was transferred from one batch of dough to the next by reserving a small portion of leavened dough from one batch and mixing it in with the fresh dough. The yeast culture epitomizes human culture in the manner in which the firstborn son represented the continuation of the culture of the forefathers going back through the generations. The firstborn of Egypt in the Dark Night of Exodus represents the continuity of generations going back to Cain as the father of human civilization—the asymmetric culture of hierarchy and scarcity.

Thus, *unleavened* bread represents a fresh start—a break from the past and an opportunity for a new beginning. In the Exodus myth, it represents *freedom*, leaving behind the culture of scarcity and slavery to discover a promised land of provision and mutuality. As the events of the Dark Night of Exodus unfold, Yahweh ordains that the Israelites should observe an annual Feast of Unleavened Bread to commemorate the Passover of Yahweh as the Messenger of Death, breaking from their previous cultural identification as slaves in Egypt, specifying as follows:

They shall take for themselves, each man a flockling according to their fathers' house... Then they will slay it... And they will take some of the blood and put it on the two jambs and on the lintel, on the houses in which they are eating it. Then they will eat the flesh on this night, roasted with fire, and with unleavened bread; over bitter herbs shall they eat it... with your waist girded, your sandals on your feet and your stave in your hand.

You will eat it in urgent haste. It is the passover to Yahweh. For I will pass through the land of Egypt in this night and smite every firstborn in the land of Egypt, from human even unto beast, and on all the elohim of Egypt I shall execute judgments; I am Yahweh. Then the blood will become a sign for you on the houses where you are. When I see the blood I will pass over on you. And there shall not come to be a stroke on you to cause ruin when I smite in the land of Egypt.

Hence this day will become for you a memorial, and you will celebrate it as a festival to Yahweh. Throughout your generations shall you celebrate it as [a perpetual] statute. Seven days shall you eat unleavened bread... for anyone eating what is leavened... that soul will be cut off from Israel. On the first day you shall come to have a holy meeting, also on the seventh day a holy meeting. No work at all shall be done on them; only what is eaten by every soul, that alone may be prepared by you. You will observe the instruction, for on this very day I will bring forth your hosts from the land of Egypt. And you will observe this day throughout your generations as [a perpetual] statute.[256]

The first door in the Dark Night of Exodus is marked by the blood of the ritually prepared Lamb. Inside, it provided protection from the Messenger of Death that roamed outside. Then, in the morning, it marked the doorway to freedom. Later, a second door is unexpectedly opened, providing a path through the Sea of Reeds, completing the Israelites' exodus, beyond the borders of Egypt.

In the Dark Night of the Reified Basar, Rabbi Jeshua celebrates the Passover Feast of Unleavened Bread with his students establishing a "new covenant" founded on act-love:

Now near drew the festival of unleavened bread, termed the Passover.... And He dispatches Peter and John, saying, "Go and make ready for us the passover, that we may be eating."

...And when the hour came, He leans back at table, and the twelve apostles with Him. And He said to them, "...I yearn to be eating this passover with you before My suffering. For I am saying to you that under no circumstances may I be eating of it till it may be fulfilled in the kingdom of [Elohim]."

And, receiving the cup, giving thanks, He said, "Take this and divide it among yourselves. For I am saying to you that under no circumstances may

[256] CLV Exodus 12:3-17

> *I be drinking, from now on, of the product of the grapevine till the kingdom of [Elohim] may be coming."*
>
> *And, taking bread, giving thanks, He breaks it and gives to them, saying, "Take. This is My body, given for your sakes. This do for a recollection of Me."*
>
> *Similarly, the cup also, after the dinner, saying, "This cup is the new covenant in My blood, which is shed for your sakes."*[257]

In this narrative, Rabbi Jeshua proclaims that his body is the ritual unleavened bread, and his blood is the ritual lamb's blood represented by the cup of wine in the Passover meal. This establishes a new covenant of restoration and protection in the Adult moral development of the Lover-Beloved relationship, ushering in the Reunified Family of the Universal Kingdom of Elohim founded on act-love.

❖Angel of Mercy

At the heart of the Dark Night of the Reified Basar is the trial and execution of Rabbi Jeshua under the authority of the adversarial conservative elites, the Pharisees and Sadducees, with the support of their followers. It is the last salvo in the battle between the asymmetric power culture of the Political Messiah and the symmetric dynamic of the Familial Messiah. A clear line is drawn within the narrative of the trial before the Roman governor, Pilate, who indicates that it is a custom during the festival to release one prisoner and he offers to release Jeshua:

> *Yet they cried out, all as one multitude, saying, "Away with this one! Yet release for us Bar-Abbas"—who was, because of a certain insurrection occurring in the city, and a murder, cast into jail. Now again Pilate shouts to them, willing to release [Jeshua]. Yet they retorted, saying, "Crucify, crucify him!" Now for the third time he said to them, "for What evil does this man? Not one cause of death did I find in him. Disciplining him then, I will release him." Yet they importuned with loud voices, requesting that He be crucified. And their voices and the chief priests' prevailed.*
>
> *Now Pilate adjudges that it occur as they request. Now he releases him who because of insurrection and murder had been cast into jail, whom they requested. Yet [Jeshua] he gives up to their will.*[258]

The religious authorities and their followers reject Jeshua as a Familial Messiah in favor of Bar-Abbas, a Zealot in the fight against Roman occupation who was in jail for sedition and murder. The choice for Bar-abbas and against Rabbi Jeshua represents a choice in favor of a Political Messiah who would lead them in fighting the Roman occupiers.

---

[257] CLV Luke 22:1-20
[258] CLV Luke 23:18-25

The Dark Night unfolds as a deeper representation of the symmetric dynamic of love within the narrative. As the Anointed Son, Jeshua has the authority to judge those in the Family according to the Mosaic Law, which states that those who slander or misrepresent the character of another are to suffer that same judgment to which the one they have slandered would have suffered:

> In case a malicious witness should rise against a man asserting his defection, then the two men who have the dispute must stand before Yahweh and before the priests and the judges who shall come to be in those days. The judges will inquire diligently, and if the false witness asserts false testimony against his brother, then you must do to him just as he schemed to do to his brother. Thus you will take out the evil from among you. The remainder, they shall hearken and fear, and they shall no longer continue to do anything like this evil matter among you.[259]

According to the Law, the Pharisees and Sadducees who are seeking to put Rabbi Jeshua to death through false and malicious testimony should lose their lives. This would be the just outcome of the Dark Night of the Basar. Yet Jeshua does not judge those who falsely accuse him. He does not use his power to fight the injustice, to crush his enemies, or to force a Kingdom of Jeshua on Israel or the world. Rather, while hanging on the cross, Jeshua lets go of his rightful judgment:

> And when they came away onto the place called "Skull," there they crucify Him... Now [Jeshua] said, "Father, [forgive/let go of] them, for they are not aware what they are doing." ...And it was already about the sixth hour, and darkness came over the whole land till the ninth hour, at the defaulting of the sun. Now rent is the curtain of the temple in the middle. And shouting with a loud voice, [Jeshua] said, "Father, into Thy hands am I committing My spirit." Now, saying this, He expires.[260]

Jeshua lets go of their slander and treachery, instead, turning towards the Father and *commits his spirit*, invoking David's Psalm in his time of despair:

> In You, O Yahweh, have I taken refuge; Do not let me be ashamed for the [eon/age]; In Your righteousness deliver me. Stretch out Your ear to me; Rescue me quickly, O Yahweh! Become mine for a Rock, a Stronghold, For a house of fastness to save me. For my Crag and my Fastness are You, And on account of Your Name, O Yahweh, You shall guide me, And You shall conduct me. You shall bring me forth from the net That they have buried for me; For You are my Stronghold. Into Your hand am I committing my spirit; You have [let go/unbound] me, O Yahweh, El of [truth].[261]

---

[259] CLV Deuteronomy 19:16-20
[260] CLV Luke 23:27-46 excerpted
[261] CLV Psalm 31:1-5

The meaning and purpose of the crucifixion can be summarized as letting go—letting go of the judgment that is rightfully Jeshua's, against those that have slandered him, whilst Yahweh, as the Power of Truth, lets go of the bonds that hold him to his suffering—and thus, the truth of El sets him free.

❖Serpent on the Cross

As the central dynamic of the crucifixion myth, Rabbi Jeshua is represented as the Raised Nachash of the Exodus myth. In that story, the Israelites slander Yahweh and Moses accusing them of malicious intent in bringing them out of Egypt. Yahweh responds by sending venomous Vipers into their midst, embodying the destructive effect of their slander. Many die and, subsequently, many others repent, pleading with Moses to bring them again to safety. Yahweh instructs Moses to craft a fiery nachash and to raise it up on the upper stretch of a pole, setting it prominently in the camp, stating whoever should look upon the fiery nachash will be saved from the venomous Ground Nachash. As the Higher Nachash, Jeshua is the embodiment of a conscience motivated by truth and love. Although Jeshua is given the authority to judge his adversaries for their slander, that is not his purpose. The Basar of John states:

> And, according as Moses [lifts up] the serpent in the wilderness, thus must the Son of Mankind be [lifted up], that everyone [believing/trusting] on Him should not be perishing, but may be having life [perpetually]. For thus [Elohim] loves the world, so that He gives His only-begotten Son, that everyone who is [believing/trusting] in Him should not be perishing, but may be having life [perpetually].[262]

Rabbi Jeshua is slandered and subsequently murdered by the conservative religious and political authorities with the intent to conserve their existing power within Jewish society and to preserve their belief in a coming Political Messiah who would conquer the Romans, which, of course, as a pretext, would enhance their existing social and political advantage, giving them even greater power and authority over Israel. The authorities have no value, need, or desire to be saved from their lust for power or their lack of love—they are wholly and completely identified with their egocentric drive for power and control.

Archetypally, the adversarial Ground Nachash/Viper symbolizes the limited perspective of an egocentric morality that causes suffering, division, and death. The fiery Nachash raised to the sky represents the mature conscience that looks beyond one's egoistic morality to the ideal of the loving Parent Elohim and the needs of the Universal Family. Safety and healing are

---

262 CLV John 3:14-16

instantiated by looking beyond our egoistic concerns. As the Higher Nachash, Rabbi Jeshua represents the healing power of a mature conscience that looks upward and outward, embodying the value of act-love.

Psychologically, those that look to Jeshua's act of mercy and love are made safe from the asymmetric system of power. When that narrative of love takes root in us, it becomes a part of our own personal narrative, and we are empowered by the same generosity and truth in letting go of our own adversarial drives, to be able to fully love one another.

❖**Destruction of the Temple**

The Temple in Jerusalem is a fancier institutional version of the humble Tabernacle tent that Moses is instructed to construct in the Exodus myth. The original Tabernacle is the symbolic dwelling place of Yahweh in the midst of his firstborn Nation throughout the four-hundred-year period of the Kingdom of Elohim in Israel under his Judges. It represents Yahweh's relationship with Israel as their king/elohim. In the Exodus myth, the Tabernacle is a temporary structure, a tent that is periodically taken down, dismantled, and brought along with the Israelites from one encampment in the wilderness to another. Once Israel settles into the Promised Land, the central cult object of the Ark of the Covenant continues to be housed in various improvised tents and buildings.

Then, at the height of the era of political kings, Solomon, the third and last king of the unified political kingdom of Israel, builds an elaborate stone structure to replicate the Tabernacle tent on a much grander scale. This first institutional Temple built by Solomon represents Israel's relationship to their Elohim over the next four-hundred-year period of the political kingdoms of Israel and Judah. At the end of this period, in 586 BCE, the Neo-Babylonians conquered Judah destroying Jerusalem and the Temple of Solomon. Then, after the Persians conquered the Neo-Babylonians and released the Judahites from captivity, the Judahites returned to Jerusalem as vassals of the Persian King Cyrus to rebuild Jerusalem and a new Temple. This Second Temple then represents Israel's relationship to their Elohim over the six-hundred-year period of the Vassal Kingdom of Judah, which lasts from around 516 BCE to 70 CE. Then, at the end of this period, it, similarly, is destroyed by the Romans during the First Jewish-Roman War.

At the end of the Vassal Kingdom Era, Judah's perpetual struggle for political autonomy tragically ends in the three Jewish-Roman wars. The first war from 66 to 73 CE resulted in the destruction of Jerusalem and the Second Temple in 70 CE. The second war from 115 to 117 CE was less dramatic but resulted in furthering the belief by the Romans that the cult of Judaism was the source of unrest in the Jewish population and that it needed to be stamped out; inspiring the Roman emperor Hadrian's decision in 130 CE to build a new Roman colony, Aelia Capitolina, on the site of Jerusalem. This directly contributed to the third and final Jewish war from 132 to 136 CE, led by the acclaimed political messiah, Simon bar Kokhba, which did, in fact, lead to two years of self-rule over parts of Judea, before being decisively crushed by six Roman legions. Subsequently, the Romans barred Jews from Palestine, ending any political presence in what remained of Jerusalem or Judea for some eighteen centuries, with the minor exception of a few months in 614 CE due to a short-lived occupation of the city during the Byzantine–Sasanian War of 602–628 CE. For all practical and political purposes, the Nation of Israel/Judah ceased to exist in 136 CE becoming a loosely organized ethnic community in exile spread throughout Europe and the Middle East.

From the Jewish perspective, the destruction of the Temple and banishment from Judea is the end of the world and becomes a part of apocalyptic literature throughout this period. This is an important subject in the Reified Basar, which describes the event as the end of an eon and the beginning of a new one; symbolically, as a new heaven and earth. The event also is referred to in several non-Basar writings in the Christian New Testament, including the apocalyptic myth known as John's Revelation in which the Christian Jesus returns as the Political Messiah to wipe out his enemies and establish a new kingdom, unironically contradicting the entire premise of the Reified Basar myth.

In the Reified Basar account, the apocalyptic destruction of the Second Temple closes the National Age of Yahweh Elohim. Jeshua proclaims that, in the succeeding Universal Kingdom, an external ceremonial dwelling place for Yahweh is no longer necessary or relevant. Instead, the Realm of Great Power will exist within each Child Elohim. As such, the Basar of Luke states concerning the Temple:

> And at some saying concerning the [Temple] sanctuary, that it is adorned with ideal stones and votive offerings, [Jeshua] said, "These which you are beholding—there will be coming days in which not a stone will be left here on a stone, which will not be demolished... Now whenever you may be perceiving Jerusalem surrounded by encampments, then know that her desolation is near. Then let those in Judea flee into the mountains, and let those in her midst be coming out into the country, and let not those in the country be entering into her, for days of vengeance are these, to fulfill all that is written... Thus you also, whenever you may be perceiving these things occurring, know that near is the kingdom of [Elohim]. Verily, I am

saying to you that by no means may this generation be passing by till all should be occurring.[263]

Elsewhere, when Rabbi Jeshua drives the merchants and moneychangers out of the Temple, indicating that their presence was a defilement of the temple's purpose and sanctity, he is asked for an explanation:

The Jews... said to [Jeshua], "What sign are you showing us, seeing that you are doing these things?" [Jeshua] answered and said to them, "Raze this temple, and in three days I will raise it up." The Jews, then, said, "In forty and six years was this temple built, and you will be raising it up in three days!" Yet He said it concerning the temple of His body. When, then, He was roused from among the dead, His [students] are reminded that He said this, and they believe the scripture and the word which [Jeshua] said.[264]

Finally, in the Crucifixion myth, at the moment when Jeshua dies, the curtain in the Temple that separates the Holy of Holies from the Holy sanctum is torn in two, symbolizing the restoration of intimacy in the Sacred Midst between Yahweh and his Children as Lover and Beloved, and correspondingly decommissioning the Temple as an institutional dwelling place of Yahweh, foreshadowing the apocalyptic end of the National Age.

❖Baptism of Fire

Johanan the Baptist indicates that Rabbi Jeshua not only will baptize in the holy spirit/breath but also will baptize by *fire*. The element of fire is often used to describe anger or judgment, as it does here. From the beginning of the era of Political Kings, through the prophets, and then, in Rabbi Jeshua's teachings, Yahweh's anger at the Israelites is palpable as Israel is progressively deconstructed from their status as his favored nation under his kingship to what is described in Third Isaiah as the apocalyptic end of the National Age of Israel. In the end, there is no more nation, the Jewish people are broadly dispersed as a fragmented ethnic group throughout the Roman world, forbidden from returning to Palestine by the Roman Emperor.

Much of Rabbi Jeshua's teaching discusses the judgment of the conservative political and religious elites, stating that they will be cast out into either outer darkness or fire. According to the judge Samuel, the judgment was set in motion when the Israelites rejected Yahweh as their Servant King, and instead, chose to serve another elohim, a Political King, at the beginning of the Political Era. It is highlighted in the struggle between those that hope in a Political Messiah who will restore control to the political

---

[263] CLV Luke 21:5-6, 20-22, 31-32
[264] CLV John 2:18-20

elites, versus those that embrace the Familial Messiah who will restore relational intimacy in the bond of the Universal Family founded on love. The rejection of the Familial Messiah is just a repetition of a theme going back to Eve and Adam's rejection of Yahweh as Parent Elohim in the Garden, and later the newly freed Israelites' rejection of Yahweh as Savior Elohim at Mount Sinai by constructing the Golden Calf, and finally, colonial Israel's rejection of Yahweh as Servant King in the story of Samuel at the end of the Kingdom of Elohim in Israel.

The end of the National Age begins with the destruction of Jerusalem and the Second Temple. From a Jewish perspective, it is the end of the world, an apocalyptic travesty beyond imagination. The ancient Jewish historian Josephus describes the horror of the event in his codex on the *War of the Jews*, where he indicates that up to a million inhabitants of the city perished. The siege of Jerusalem began when the legions of the Roman commander Titus surrounded the city and cut off all supplies while he set about building ramparts to breach the massive walls. Strategically, as the siege commenced during the Feast of Unleavened Bread, Titus first allowed hordes of religious observers to enter the city before closing it off; thus, causing the city's supplies to dwindle much faster. This resulted in a debilitating famine within the city walls. Chaos ensued inside the city as desperation set in, the wasted dead were strewn unceremoniously about, robbers roamed the streets stealing the possessions of the dead and dying, while opposing militant factions fought each other more than the Romans, who for the most part, merely waited. Eventually, those barely surviving, overwhelmed by the magnitude of death, would just dispose of the bodies over the walls into the valley below. Josephus recounts:

> Now every sort of death was thought more tolerable than the famine, insomuch that, though the Jews despaired now of mercy... Nor was there any place in the city that had no dead bodies in it, but what was entirely covered with those that were killed either by the famine or the rebellion;[265]

In the final battle, much of the city burned including the Temple itself; the fire was everywhere, the blood of the slain drenched the streets, and the cries of anguish, weeping and gnashing of teeth, echoed throughout the city. Josephus expounds:

> While the holy house was on fire, everything was plundered that came to hand, and ten thousand of those that were caught were slain; nor was there a commiseration of any age, or any reverence of gravity; but children and old men, and profane persons, and priests, were all slain in the same

---

[265] Josephus (1981), p. 585 (The War of the Jews Book 6 Chapter 7)

manner; so that this war went round all sorts of men, and brought them to destruction...

The flame was also carried a long way, and made an echo, together with the groans of those that were slain; and because this hill was high, and the works at the temple were very great, one would have thought the whole city had been on fire. Nor can one imagine anything either greater or more terrible than this noise; for there was at once a shout of the Roman legions, who were marching all together, and a sad clamor of the seditious, who were now surrounded with fire and sword. The people also that were left above were beaten back upon the enemy, and under a great consternation, and made sad moans at the calamity they were under; the multitude also that was in the city joined in this outcry with those that were upon the hill; and besides, many of those that were worn away by the famine, and their mouths almost closed, when they saw the fire of the holy house, they exerted their utmost strength, and broke out into groans and outcries again...

Yet was the misery itself more terrible than this disorder; for one would have thought that the hill itself, on which the temple stood, was seething hot, as full of fire on every part of it, that the blood was larger in quantity than the fire, and those that were slain more in number than those that slew them; for the ground did nowhere appear visible, for the dead bodies that lay on it; but the soldiers went over heaps of these bodies, as they ran upon such as fled from them.[266]

As the first Jewish-Roman War concluded, the destruction of Jerusalem and the Temple annihilated the sacred heart of the Jewish culture. However, the Jews would continue their struggle through two more insurrections over the next sixty-five years, before being decisively defeated and subsequently exiled from the land. Mythologically, the fire of Yahweh's judgment, ignited by their rejection of the Servant King at the beginning of the Political Kingdom Era, was concluded by laying waste to Jerusalem (for the second time), according to the presage of the Jewish prophets.

❖Resurrection of Hope

The end of the Dark Night of the Basar is the resurrection of Jeshua from the grave. In the same way that Pharaoh perceived himself to have all power over the people and was humbled before the might of Yahweh in the Exodus myth, the Jewish leaders, the chief priests and religious authorities, are humbled in the Reified Basar as their judgment of Jeshua is abrogated, rendered powerless by Yahweh overturning their illicit death sentence. Yahweh demonstrates the symmetric power of the Anointed Son, as Familial Messiah, over the asymmetric power of the religious authorities and their belief in a Political Messiah. As the Viper/Ground Nachash represents the

---

[266] Josephus (1981), p. 581 (The War of the Jews Book 6 Chapter 5)

system of hierarchical power and submission, the resurrection represents the disempowerment of this abusive system and, subsequently, the empowerment of Love within the Reunified Family of the Universal Kingdom of Elohim.

The resurrection is the second door of the Dark Night, the unexpected pathway that leads to freedom in the face of apparent defeat. It corresponds to the parting of the Sea of Reeds in the Exodus narrative that leads the Israelites out of Egypt, destroying the power of their former masters, once and for all, creating a new path to freedom and a restored life. It begins the transitional period that ushers in the Kingdom of Elohim upon the destruction of Jerusalem and the Temple.

❖Prometheus Chained

In Greek mythology, Zeus reigns supreme, by the might of his Lightning Bolt, over all the Cosmos. His rule is capricious and self-centered, demanding all to submit to his authority, while at the same time, he habitually indulges his own appetites and desires, even when it disrupts the order of the Cosmos. The identity of humankind within the mythology is to be servants of the gods. Humans have no sentimental value or worth to Olympus—they merely exist to be controlled, according to the purpose and power of the gods. The gods embody the asymmetric power dynamic of a hierarchically ordered universe.

An important exception to this orientation to power and subjugation was Prometheus/Forethought, who formed Man in the image of the gods, and once Zeus breathed life into Man, continued to show favor to Man, even defying Zeus by giving fire to Man. The story of Zeus and Prometheus is a struggle between the way of hierarchical authority and the way of relationship. In the moralistic framework, authority over the ordered Cosmos is inviolable. Yet Prometheus risks his own well-being by caring for the well-being of Man—symbolizing love standing against oppressive political authority. In moralism, love cannot possibly prevail because it threatens the order of the power structure. There must always be consequences for those in servitude who would seek for betterment in the face of the hierarchy. If those in servitude no longer serve their masters as ordained by the mastery, the system fails—control is essential and inviolable.

Prometheus threatens the political hierarchy by disobeying Zeus for the benefit of Man. Not only does Zeus punish Man by creating the first Woman, Pandora, as a deception, which originates all suffering, but he also casts Prometheus into Tartarus/Pit, where he is chained to a rock to be eternally tormented by having his heart or liver eaten out by birds. And since he is immortal the heart/liver then grows back so that it can happen all over again the next day. Thus, the moralistic authority of the ruling hierarchy is reaffirmed by the suffering of those who would challenge its inherent injustice.

❖**Restore Meaning/Identity**

The inductive chapter proem is a stanza from "The Dream That Must be Interpreted,"[267] a poem by the 13th-century philosopher, poet, and Sufi mystic, Rumi. The poem begins, "This place is a dream. Only a sleeper considers it real. Then death comes like dawn, and you wake up laughing at what you thought was your grief." Rumi invites us to reinterpret the significance of our grief in our somnific journey through life—to gain a mature perspective on our suffering and loss, by bravely facing our vulnerability, which will inevitably, "startle us back to the truth of who we are."

Psychologically, mature moral development continues as an understanding of our adolescent morality becomes more inclusive in the emerging Lover-Beloved relationship, restoring meaning and identity to the Sacred Midst of relationship. Authentic identity becomes the foundation of relationship, both in clarification and presentation of one's own identity and in one's openness to listen to, and learn of, another's—to truly see and be seen. The unforgivable failure in a relationship is to slander or misattribute false ideas to another, which intrinsically undermines value and intimacy in the Between.

The great truth of the myth is that we are *elohim*, the image and embodiment of an ideal great power. As such, we have the responsibility to use that great power justly and generously, and the obligation to use our power for good, for the benefit of those that need our support. However, that same great power can also be used egocentrically to benefit oneself at the expense of others, to devalue and exploit others, causing great harm. We each have an essential choice between love and selfishness. The corollary to "I am elohim, a great power," is "*you* also are an elohim, a great power"—the recognition of the power and worth of another, accompanied by the responsibility to protect that power and worth. The truth of who we are in relationship sets us free to love one another.

---

[267] Rumi (1995) p.112-113

Archetypally, our restoration to mature morality is the revival of meaning and identity within the Sacred Midst. It is built on our mutual identification as members of a Universal Family of Elohim. As we recognize ourselves as having great power, we must then choose how to use that power. It becomes our responsibility to use that power appropriately to benefit others who suffer, to bring restoration to the Reunified Family. The developmental journey of cultivating our humanity has taken us from the juvenile framework of the limited power of the child in search of sufficiency and authenticity to the adult framework of authentic relationship founded on our intrinsic power to build the bonds of sufficiency and authenticity within the Universal Family as the foundation of truth.

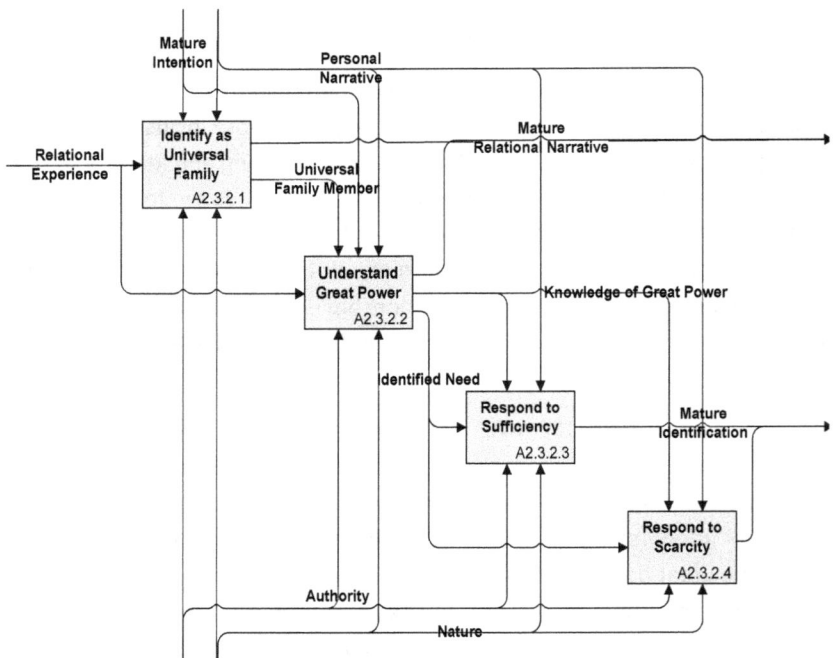

Model 17 - Restore Meaning/Identity (A2.3.2)

CHAPTER [3/III]

LIFE FOREVER AFTER

> In spite of the difficulties and frustrations of the moment,
> I still have a dream…. when we allow freedom to ring…
> from every village and every hamlet… we will be able to
> speed up that day when all of God's children, black men
> and white men, Jews and Gentiles, Protestants and
> Catholics, will be able to join hands and sing in the words
> of the old Negro spiritual: "Free at last! Free at last! thank
> God Almighty, we are free at last!"
> —*Martin Luther King Jr, "*I Have a Dream Speech"

The last revelation of the Edenic Nachash is that we will not die as a result of the Fruit of Morality, neither will we be struck down or destroyed by the Elohim in satisfaction of some holy urge for vengeance. In the Genesis Exile myth, the cardinal consequence of eating the Fruit is the dying of the Sacred Midst, the death of intimacy between the Adamites and the Parent Elohim, which is felt immediately as nakedness, vulnerability, and existential terror. Likewise, the resulting exile from the Garden is not stated to be a punishment but rather a protective measure to prevent the Adamites from reaching out and eating the fruit of the Tree of Life, implying that it was essential to put a limit on a life outside of the Sacred Midst, without intimacy and love. Ultimately, in fulfilment of the Reified Basar, Rabbi Jeshua identifies himself as the restoration of the Tree of Life, the embodiment of the Sacred Midst, declaring, " I am the Resurrection and the Life."[268]

Thus, the resurrection of Jeshua from the steely grip of Hades moves us beyond the nadir of the Hero's Journey, out of the Dark Night. It is an essential fulfillment of the Torah of Restoration as the rebirth of the Sacred Midst, which ushers in the Reunified Family of the Universal Kingdom of Elohim as a fulfillment of the Law of Love.

❖Rebirth of Sacred Midst

The Kingdom of Elohim is fundamentally the fulfillment of the relational obligations of the Mosaic Law. It is embodied in the four core values of the Decalogue—respectfulness, truthfulness, trustworthiness, and generosity.[269] The Basar of Isaiah represents the failure of these values as brokenness,

---

[268] CLV John 11:25
[269] See Table 7 - Values of the Decalogue

darkness, sadness, and scarcity. Rabbi Jeshua declares that his mission is to bring the lovingkindness of the Good Father into the missingness of his children's lives as a fulfillment of the relational Law of Moses and the Prophet's call to restoration. Jeshua thusly states:

> You should not infer that I came to demolish the law or the prophets. I came not to demolish, but to fulfill.[270]

The rebirth of the Sacred Midst is a journey beyond the wilderness of missingness, devaluation, and exclusion into the safety of the Reunified Family, restoring the relationship between the Parent Elohim and his children in the Universal Kingdom of Elohim.

Thus, the Reified Basar mythology is essentially defined by how the Parent/Savior Elohim brings us to safety in the renewed Sacred Midst as a fulfillment of Jeshua's name, which means "Yahweh brings us to safety." The path to peace and safety is brought to life in the ministry of Rabbi Jeshua as the reification of the Basar of Isaiah, which states:

> The spirit of My Lord Yahweh is on Me Because Yahweh anoints Me to bear tidings [basar] to the humble [weak]; He sends Me to bind up the broken of heart, To herald to captives, liberty, And to the sightless, unclosed eyes, And to the bound, emancipation, To herald an acceptable year for Yahweh, And a day of [vengeance/ justice] for our Elohim; To comfort all mourners, To establish rejoicing for Zion's mourners, To give them beauty instead of ashes, The oil of elation instead of mourning, The muffler of praise instead of a spirit of languor;[271]

As such, to understand the path to safety one must first understand what is the danger that makes us unsafe, devalued, or excluded.

In the moralistic Christian theologies, the danger is most often the Christian-God himself who determines one's eternal fate, assigning value to some lives and taking value from others, judging whether one should be allowed to enter "paradise" or "heaven," or rather, should be sent to eternal damnation, to suffer in "Hell." The actual formula required to transact safety from these moralistic versions of the Christian-God is a matter of debate and varies between sects. However, it is usually founded in some theological apologetic that gaslights their followers into believing it is their own fault that the all-knowing and all-powerful god must brutally torture them for eternity in order to satisfy his holy urges. Quite to the contrary, within the mythology, this moralized objectification of humanity is quintessentially the slanderous voice of the saw-tan, the Accuser speaking as an institutional authority to

---

270 CLV Matthew 5:17
271 CLV Isaiah 61:1-3

misrepresent the Parent Elohim as a vengeful adversary to humankind, which, of course, is in direct opposition to the Yahweh in the myth identified as the Good Father who loves his children, blows life into them, and provides for their needs.

From the very beginning of the Unified Basar and Torah myth, the dangers that humankind faces are identified as the *badness* manifest in the world, the elements in our wilderness environment that feed on our vulnerability—death, disease, brokenness, strife, slavery, exploitation, abuse, injustice, hunger, poverty, darkness, and loss. Our path to safety, to *goodness*, necessitates moving beyond the gilluls that we serve to pacify our fear of the *badness*, to find authentic love in community. Each person develops their own gillul as a reaction to their vulnerability, which is ultimately a function of one's history, traits, and personality. Rabbi Jeshua never answers the question the same when asked or inferred, "how must I be saved?" His answers always come from his insight into the vulnerability of the one who asks the question—what causes them to fear their vulnerability, to feel powerless, valueless, and unsafe.

Danger	Condition	Reaction	Response	Value	Focus	Notes
Missingness	humble/poor	bear tidings	*Empower*	Love	Relation-ship	Good News
Brokenness	broken of heart	bind up	*Heal*	Respect	Bond	relational
Brokenness	spirit of languor/ dimmed spirit	give them muffler of praise	*Encourage*	Respect	Bond	personal
Darkness	sightless	unclosed eyes	*Enlighten*	Truth	Identity	light/ knowledge
Sadness	mourning	comfort	*Support*	Trust	Boundary	comfort/ life
Sadness	mourning/ashes	give them beauty	*Restore*	Trust	Boundary	beauty
Sadness	mourning	give them oil of elation	*Restore*	Trust	Boundary	elation
Scarcity	captives	herald liberty	*Release*	Generosity	Property	political servitude
Scarcity	bound	emancipation	*Release*	Generosity	Property	economic servitude

Table 10 - Conditions in the Basar of Isaiah

Missingness. The path to letting go of our fear of *missingness* encompasses all the conditions in the Basar of Isaiah. Missingness is founded on our vulnerability and inadequacy that we uncover throughout our lives as the experience of goodness and badness, which inspires our search for power and control. In the myth, it begins with the juvenile Eve and Adam's fear and distrust of the Parent Elohim, representing the distortion of the ideal Parent Image that we inculcate in childhood. The authority of the Bad Parent disintegrates into the hunger of the Villain who seeks to feed off the weakness of his Victim. The child becomes the prey in a tale of devaluation and exclusion. *Love* then becomes the transformative element that restores wholeness and freedom based on a renewed trust in the goodness and loving-kindness of the ideal Parent in the Reunified Family that incarnates the Imago Elohim.

In the Basar of Isaiah, the Anointed Son brings tidings/good news to the humble, the poor, and the powerless. The Basar/Good-News that defines the Reunified Family of the Kingdom of Elohim is the beneficent love of the Father expressed through his anointed firstborn son to the Family. Trust in that love restores the relationship to the ideal Parent, reestablishing intimacy with the Good Father in the Between of the Sacred Midst, which is then reflected in our own ability to represent that love to others.

This is a theme that is reinforced repeatedly in the ministry of Rabbi Jeshua. When the students of Jeshua fail to heal an epileptic child, the child's father comes to Jeshua for help. Jeshua heals the child, and afterward, his students approach him privately to inquire why they were not able to heal the child—to which Jeshua replies:

> Because of your scant faith. For verily I am saying to you, If you should have faith as a kernel of mustard, you shall be declaring to this mountain, "Proceed hence—there!" and it will be proceeding. And nothing will be impossible for you.[272]

The religiousized term *faith* is an attempt to translate the Greek word *pistis*[273], which describes one's conviction or belief in the truth of a matter. Psychologically, *pistis* describes the incorporation of a valid or invalid narrative assertion into the belief system that defines the integrity of one's identity. In the Kingdom of Elohim narrative, the assertion that is posited is the Parent Elohim's love for his children as the ultimate goodness, which Rabbi Jeshua declares, if accepted as truth, brings one into the fullness or wholeness of great power inherent in their identity as Child Elohim—"I am Elohim, a great power, the child of my loving parent Elohim." The child may then embody the mature power of the ideal parent as a fulfillment of their identity—the belief in their own power and goodness to love and support others.

Brokenness. The path to letting go of our fear of *brokenness* is a journey beyond the asymmetric domain of the wilderness, to find our intrinsic value in a deeper truth of our identity, to find wholeness in the personal and

---

[272] CLV Matthew 17:20
[273] Strongs G4102

relational dynamics of our brokenness within community. The condition of broken-heartedness, devaluation, and depression is described as languor or dimness of spirit. It is conceived in the perceived state of social and psychological valuelessness, the indomitable state of ultimate victimhood. It is the utmost subversion of the child's worth, destroying any sense of value in relation to the ideal Parent. It is the elemental deconstruction of identity in response to the death of the Sacred Midst—the abandoned child lost in a dangerous world.

In the Basar of Isaiah, the Anointed Son binds up the broken of heart and gives praise to those with a spirit of languor. It is the process of healing our relational brokenness and encouraging our personal sense of self-worth. restoring us to wholeness in the Between of the Sacred Midst by encouraging us to see ourselves in the loving eyes of the ideal Parent.

The myth of Photini, a Samaritan woman from Sychar, as she is described in later traditions, is one of the most intimate and well-described narratives in the Basar accounts. She typically is referred to as the unnamed woman at the well, which underlines her status as barely noticeable in the social schema. Her marginalized value is emphasized several times in the myth. Initially, when Rabbi Jeshua asks her to draw him water to drink, she is astonished, "How are you, being a Jew, requesting a drink from me, being a Samaritan woman?"[274] And then, the narrator explains, "For Jews are not beholden to Samaritans."[275] Later, the Rabbi's students "marveled that He spoke with a woman."[276] Then, in dialogue with Photini, Jeshua gives prophetic insight into her relational history, stating, "five husbands have you had, and now he whom you have is not your husband."[277] In any, and every measure, Photini is at the bottom of the asymmetric schema, lacking any social worth: first, as a woman in a deeply patriarchal society; second, as a Samaritan whom the Jews considered ignoble half-breeds, the remnant of the tribes of Israel that intermarried with the local Canaanite tribes after the desolation of the Northern Kingdom; and then, third, as a divorced and abandoned woman, not just once but five times over, living in a situation that would have been considered improper in the social narrative of her local community with a man that is not her husband. She is a broken woman, barely surviving in the social milieu, relegated psychologically to the distant

---

[274] CLV John 4:9
[275] CLV John 4:9
[276] CLV John 4:27
[277] CLV John 4:18

margins of indecency and worthlessness, cutting deep into the framework of her identity.

It is in this context that Rabbi Jeshua opens up a dialogue with her, discussing enigmatic philosophical and theological matters, affirming her intelligence and insights. Most profoundly, Jeshua recognizes her existence, transcending her social disparagement. Knowing full well her social status and personal history, he addresses the scarcity of her life story and the desertification of her psychological needs by promising that she will be satisfied with "living water" that "will become... a spring of water, welling up into life eonian."[278] In the final scene, Photini calls to her neighbors, stating, "Hither! Perceive a Man Who told me all whatever I do. Is not this the [Messiah]?"[279] For once in her life, she is seen, and respected for who she authentically is—Jeshua's response to her is to restore her self-worth as a beloved child in the loving eyes of the ideal Parent, the Good Father.

Darkness. The path to letting go of our fear of *darkness*, the inability to see and comprehend what lurks in the shadows before and within us, both physically and spiritually, is founded on a deep sense of helplessness that must be recognized and compassionately engaged through our trust in the community. Ultimately, life is unknown. While we may construct ideological edifices to control and predict what tomorrow may bring, in reality, we are merely leaves floating in the stream of time; we cannot control or predict what happens in the future. We can only prepare for the possibilities.

As such, *community* is a function of our need to trust in others for what may happen. The truth of who we are is founded in our shared responsibility for one another's well-being, to be our brother's keeper. If tomorrow brings calamity or disease, there are those who make themselves available to help us find safety—doctors, social workers, and friends who are dedicated to supporting each other in times of need. There are shopkeepers and merchants who make available food for tomorrow's meal, and factory workers who manufacture the tools and materials we need to build each day's subsistence. What I may be helpless to do on my own is aided by this social network of community members. Humanity is built on a shared reality, a shared sense of responsibility to one another as the moral foundation of goodness.

In the Basar of Isaiah, the Anointed Son gives unclosed eyes to the sightless. The "unclosed eyes" is an invocation to the power and truth of the

---

[278] CLV John 4:14
[279] CLV John 4:29

Tree of Knowledge of Goodness and Badness, the fruit that awakens the juvenile Adamite's awareness of their nakedness, their vulnerability in adversity. In their juvenile state of distrust, they fear the danger of exposure due to their imperfection and weakness. Subsequently, as they mature in their awareness of their intrinsic power, they are able to see the potential of trusting others and the efficacy of being trustworthy—to love and give to others in need.

In the Reified Basar, Rabbi Jeshua heals a man, blind from birth, on the Sabbath. The moralistic Pharisees, absurdly look past the good that was done for this poor wretch of a man and seek to condemn Jeshua for not *following the rules*, stating, "This man [Jeshua] is not from [Elohim], for he is not keeping the sabbath."[280] To which Jeshua responds:

> For [judgment/separation] came I into this world, that those who are not [observing/seeing] may be observing, and those observing may be becoming blind.[281]

Blindness symbolizes sight turned inward, our inability to see beyond ourselves due to our closed boundaries, both real and imagined. Elsewhere in the Basar of Matthew, Rabbi Jeshua quotes the first prophet of the Book of Isaiah, concerning the inability of those committed to conserving the asymmetric establishment to perceive the truth of the Parent Elohim:

> In hearing, you will be hearing, and may by no means be understanding, And observing, you will be observing, and may by no means be perceiving. For stoutened is the heart of this people, And with their ears heavily they hear, And with their eyes they squint, Lest at some time they may be perceiving with their eyes, And with their ears should be hearing, And with their heart may be understanding, And should be turning about, And I shall be healing them.[282]

Jeshua expands on this proclamation of truth as an enlightenment of the heart, stating:

> Still a little time the light is among you. Be walking while you have the light, lest the darkness may be overtaking you. And he who is walking in the darkness is not aware whither he is going. As you have the light, be believing in the light, that you may be becoming sons of light... I have come into the world a Light, that everyone who is believing in Me should not be remaining in darkness.[283]

---

[280] CLV John 9:16
[281] CLV John 9:39
[282] CLV Matthew 13:14-15 referencing Isaiah 6:9-10
[283] CLV John 12:35-46 excerpted

The psychological or spiritual path out of inner darkness is developed as the belief or trust in the truth of the prescribed path to love within the Reunified Family, founded on the actions and directives of the Anointed Son in restoring the Sacred Midst between the ideal Parent and one's Adamic siblings. In this context, a Chief Pharisee by the name of Nicodemus comes to Rabbi Jeshua under the cover of darkness to inquire about the nature of Jeshua's power and authority. Jeshua replies that the Kingdom of Elohim, the realm of great power, cannot be perceived unless one is "begotten anew" of the *water* of renewed relationship and the *spirit* of love:

> If anyone should not be begotten of water and of spirit, he cannot be entering into the kingdom of [Elohim]. That which is begotten by the flesh is flesh, and that which is begotten by the spirit is spirit. You should not be marveling that I said to you, "You must be begotten anew." The [wind/breath] is blowing where it wills, and the sound of it you are hearing, but you are not aware whence it is coming and where it is going. Thus is everyone who is begotten by the water and the spirit... that which we have perceived are we speaking, and to that which we have seen are we testifying, and our testimony you are not getting...

> And, according as Moses [lifts up] the serpent in the wilderness, thus must the Son of Mankind be [lifted up], that everyone [believing/trusting] on Him should not be perishing, but may be having life [perpetually/beyond the age]. For thus [Elohim] loves the world, so that He gives His only-begotten Son, that everyone who is [believing/trusting] in Him should not be perishing, but may be having life [perpetually/beyond the age].

> For [Elohim] does not [dispatch/set apart] His Son into the world that He should be [judging/separating] the world, but that the world may be [made safe] through Him. He who is [believing/trusting] in Him is not being [judged/separated]; yet he who is not [believing/trusting] has been [judged/separated] already, for he has not [believed/trusted] in the name ["Yahweh brings us to safety"] of the only-begotten Son of [Elohim].

> Now this is the [judging/separating]: that the light has come into the world, and men love the darkness rather than the light, for their acts were [hurtful]. For everyone who is committing bad things is hating the light and is not coming to the light, lest his acts may be exposed. Now he who is doing the truth is coming to the light that his acts may be made manifest, for they have been wrought in [Elohim/Great Power].[284]

Nicodemus is a man who is deeply committed to the Mosaic Law and the tribal affinity of the Abrahamic covenant. However, Rabbi Jeshua cuts to the heart of the ethnocentric foundations of Jewish identity as children of Abraham, stating that one cannot be entering into the Kingdom of Elohim if he has only been begotten of the flesh, as a child of Abraham. Instead, one must be begotten anew of the water and spirit of a loving relationship to

[284] CLV John 3:5-21 excerpted

enter the Kingdom. The baptismal identification of *water* symbolizes a renewed identification with the relational Law of Moses, the Law of Love, and the baptismal identification of the *spirit* symbolizes the experience of Love inspired by the Sacred Breath.

To the contrary, those that do hurtful and destructive acts demonstrate that they are not of the enlightenment of the water of renewed relationship and the spirit of love. They are separated from the symmetric dynamic of the Reunified Family by their selfishness and greed, seeking to preserve their advantage in the doomed asymmetric political and economic hierarchies from which they derive their power. To enter the realm of great power, one must let go of their fear of darkness born of ignorance, egocentrism, and greed, to come into the light of the community.

Sadness. The path to letting go of our fear of *sadness* in the face of existential trauma is founded on a renewed purpose and hope in the possibility of transcending the perceived limitations of life and the loss of what we value. Death, both physically and relationally, is the ultimate devaluation of one's relationship. Construed as separation from purpose and value, it arouses desperation, distress, and purposelessness as we mourn the privation of an intimate bond. In the Genesis Exile myth, the death of the Sacred Midst between child and parent invokes a deep sense of vulnerability and existential terror.

In the Basar of Isaiah, *dying* is not portrayed as some ultimate trauma for the one who passes to the land of the dead. In the myth, the focus, rather, is on the one that loses their beloved, stating that the Anointed One brings comfort to those that mourn, restoring beauty and elation to winter's pale. It represents the Anointed Son's power to restore hope and purpose in the face of great loss and despair.

In the parable of Lazarus the Beggar, Rabbi Jeshua describes the death of the Sacred Midst of the tribal affiliation represented as Abraham's Bosom. Lazarus, whose name means "helpless," is a poor man afflicted with ulcers who begs at the portal of an unnamed rich man, indicating that the rich man ignores the suffering at his doorpost while enjoying his wealth, "daily making merry splendidly."[285] Both men die, and their conditions are reversed. The rich man now suffers in scarcity and deprivation, while the poor man is

---

[285] CLV Luke 16:19

comforted in Abraham's Bosom. The rich man begs for some comforting, to which Abraham replies:

> *Child, be reminded that you got your good things in your life, and Lazarus likewise [hurtful] things. Yet now here he is being consoled, yet you are in pain. And in all this, between us and you a great chasm has been established, so that those wanting to cross hence to you may not be able, nor yet those thence may be ferrying to us.*[286]

Abraham is the patriarchal founder of the tribe of Israel. Jews identified themselves as the children of Abraham upon whom a special covenant was dispensed as the foundation of their tribal identity. In the story of Lazarus, Rabbi Jeshua again strikes at the heart of this ethnocentric identity, arguing that Abraham, rather than the founder of some privileged tribal association, is the father of compassion and love for his family. Those claiming to be children of Abraham while disregarding this obligation to care for the tribal family as obligated under the relational mandates of the Mosaic Law are cut off from Abraham's Bosom, symbolized by a great impenetrable chasm. Lazarus represents those that have suffered rejection and deprivation due to the neglect of the tribal mandates. Ultimately, Lazarus is restored to the purpose and bond of intimacy within the Abrahamic family, a renewed life within the Sacred Midst of Abraham's Bosom.

In another story involving a different Lazarus who falls gravely ill and dies, Jeshua identifies himself as the restoration of the Tree of Life in the Sacred Midst of the Reunified Family. Lazarus of Bethany is a close friend of Rabbi Jeshua and the brother of two close female students, Mary and Martha. As the story goes, the sisters summon Rabbi Jeshua to come and attend to Lazarus in Bethany when he becomes seriously ill. By the time Rabbi Jeshua arrives, having traveled several days from Samaria to Bethany in Judea, amidst a deliberate delay of two days before setting out, Lazarus has been dead for four days. His grieving sisters firmly believe that Jeshua could have saved their brother from his illness and are deeply disappointed in Jeshua's inability to have gotten there in time, each one decrying "Lord, if [you were] here, my brother would not have died."[287] Rabbi Jeshua responds to Martha, promising, "Your brother will be rising."[288] Martha, considering this to be an apocalyptic statement of things to come, disappointedly responds, "I am aware that he will be rising in the resurrection [rising up] in

---

[286] CLV Luke 16:25-26
[287] CLV John 11:21,32
[288] CLV John 11:23-24

the last day." In response, Jeshua's reframes the final precaution of the Genesis Exile narrative in which the Parent Elohim states:

> *Behold, man has become like one of Us in knowing good and [bad]. Now lest he should stretch out his hand and take also of the tree of life and eat and live for the eon [he should be separated from it].[289]*

Identifying himself as the restoration of the Tree of Life from which the Adamites were separated, Jeshua declares to Martha:

> *I am the Resurrection and the Life. He who is believing in Me, even if he should be dying, shall be living. And everyone who is living and believing in Me, should by no means be dying for the eon.[290]*

Rabbi Jeshua then demonstrates this proclamation by proceeding to the tomb of Lazarus and, having unsealed the entrance, calls the deceased Lazarus to come out. Lazarus rises from the tomb, wrapped in his grave clothes, and is restored back to the living.

Jeshua identifies himself as the restoration of the Tree of Life in the midst of the Garden that resurrects the Sacred Midst between the Parent Elohim and his children. As a manifestation of the Experience of Goodness and Badness, *Living* represents a fulfillment of purpose, whereas *Dying* represents a loss of purpose. Thus, the restoration of the Tree of Life symbolizes the renewal of trust, value, and purpose founded in act-love, the giving of life to one another in the Universal Family. Archetypally, both Lazarus' in the mythology are restored to a life of purpose and value, giving hope to those who have suffered separation and loss.

Scarcity. The path to letting go of our fear of *scarcity*, our deep-felt sense of vulnerability, deprivation, and weakness in the face of perceived deficiencies in the resources we wish for, or desire to possess, is founded on the power of mutuality, sharing with one another, and supporting one another in community. Scarcity drives fear. It foments hierarchal systems of asymmetric power based on exploitation, selfishness, and greed. The fear of scarcity incites the prolific accumulation of wealth and resources to the exclusion and detriment of others, far beyond one's actual needs. It is what Rabbi Jeshua describes as service to Mammon, the gillul/idol god of wealth and materialistic power.

In the Basar of Isaiah, the Anointed Son invokes the Torah tradition of Jubilee, heralding liberty for the captives and emancipation for those bound

---

[289] CLV Genesis 3:22
[290] CLV John 11:25

in servitude, as well as a day of judgment for those who abuse the poor and powerless—ignoring Yahweh's mandate to care for all within the community. The asymmetric institutions in Judah, as well as in all societies, exist for the purpose of conserving the wealth and advantage of the powerful over the poor and powerless. This provokes the judgment on Sodom and Gomorrah by Yahweh, then the judgment of Israel and Judah according to the prophets, and finally, the judgment of the Goats in the gathering of nations by Rabbi Jeshua.

In the Reified Basar, the conservative political and religious establishment is identified locally with the Sadducees and Pharisees, and more broadly with the Herodian dynasty and the Roman Empire. The local representatives of the political ruling class were the Tax Collectors— deputized Jewish citizens who were given carte blanche to collect the Roman taxes, earning their way by adding an extra fee for themselves. With the full resources of the Roman Empire behind them, they could add whatever amount to their neighbor's tax bill that they felt they could get away with. As long as it did not create social unrest, the ruling class did not care how they did their job. This opportunistic arrangement made the Tax Collectors very wealthy. In turn, it provoked a great deal of animosity towards them. They were seen by the Jewish populace as collaborators with their Roman overlords and as extortionists who preyed upon the oppressed. The Tax Collectors are so thoroughly demonized by contemporary society that they are often singled out among those who fail the Mosaic Law according to the oft-used phrase, "tax collectors and other law-breakers" sometimes adding prostitutes as a second category of exceptional disreputation.

And yet, in the Reified Basar, the Tax Collectors are often the first to repent of their abusive ways, exemplifying Jeshua's mission to seek and save those who are lost, which is then, in turn, contrasted with the self-righteousness of the Pharisees who did not see a need to repent. In the Basar of Luke, Johanan the Baptist pronounces Yahweh's judgment on Judah for ignoring the relational mandate of the Law of Moses. In response, the crowd asks him[291], "What, then, should we be doing?" Johanan answers by invoking the third prophet of Isaiah: "He who has two tunics, let him be sharing with him who has none, and let him who has food be doing likewise." Then the Tax Collectors who have come to be baptized by Johanan ask the same question, to which he replies: "Impose nothing more than has been prescribed to you." Later, Rabbi Jeshua, in discussing the ministry of Johanan, states:

---

[291] CLV Luke 3:10-11

A greater prophet, among those born of women, than [Johanan] the baptist, there is not one. Yet the smaller, in the kingdom of [Elohim] is greater than he. And hearing, the entire people, even the [tax] collectors, justify [Elohim], being baptized with the baptism of [Johanan]. Yet the Pharisees and those learned in the law repudiate the counsel of [Elohim] for themselves, not being baptized by him.[292]

While the social stigma of the Tax Collectors as traitors to the Jewish struggle was a devastating reputation, Rabbi Jeshua puts the Pharisees beneath them—by comparison, even the Tax Collectors responded to Johanan's message of the Kingdom of Elohim. Rabbi Jeshua even calls one Tax Collector, Matthew/Levi son of Alphaeus, to be one of his primary twelve students.

In another story of the Chief Tax Collector, Zaccheus of Jericho, Rabbi Jeshua recognizes him as a man who has lost his way. As such, the story begins with Zaccheus, a man of small stature, climbing a mulberry tree in order to see over the crowd that had gathered as Rabbi Jeshua passed through that way:

And as [Jeshua] came onto the place, looking up, [he] perceived him and said to him, "Zaccheus! Hurry! Descend, for today I must remain in your house."

And hurrying, he descended, and entertains Him with rejoicing. And perceiving it, all grumbled, saying that with a man who is a [moral failure] He entered to put up for the night.

Now standing, Zaccheus said to the Lord, "Lo! the half of my possessions, Lord, I am giving to the poor! And if from anyone I get anything by blackmail, I am giving back fourfold."

Now [Jeshua] said to him that "Today salvation came to this home, forasmuch as he also is a son of Abraham. For the Son of Mankind came to seek and to save the lost."[293]

The moralistic Pharisees, who believed that the dinner table was a sacred representation of the Temple, were incensed that a Rabbi would see fit to share a dinner table with "tax collectors and law-breakers." In response, Rabbi Jeshua tells a story regarding "some who have confidence in themselves that they are just, and are scorning the rest," proclaiming:

Two men went up into the sanctuary to pray, the one a Pharisee, and the other a [tax] collector. The Pharisee, standing, prayed this to himself: "[Elohim], I am thanking you that I am not even as the rest of men, rapacious, unjust, adulterers, or even as this [tax] collector. I am fasting twice of a sabbath. I am taking tithes from all whatever I am acquiring."

---

[292] CLV Luke 7:28-30
[293] CLV Luke 19:5-10

Now the [tax] collector, standing afar off, would not even lift up his eyes to heaven, but beat his chest, saying, "[Elohim], make a [propitiatory/conciliatory] shelter for me, [a moral failure]!"

I am saying to you, this man descended to his home justified, rather than that one, for everyone who is exalting himself shall be humbled, yet he who is humbling himself shall be exalted.[294]

In Rabbi Jeshua's proclamation of the Kingdom of Elohim, it is the attitude of the heart rather than perfect behavior that justifies a human in his relationship to his community and to the Parent/Savior Elohim.

These narrative threads come together in Rabbi Jeshua's encounter with a wealthy young ruler of the Jews, who comes to him inquiring about what he must do to have perpetual life. In the Basar of Mark (with similar stories in Matthew and Luke), Rabbi Jeshua initially replies that he should be keeping the relational precepts in the Law of Moses. The wealthy man responds that he has done so all his life. Then the narrator states that Jeshua, "looking at him, loves him, and said to him," in response:

Still one thing you are wanting. Go. Whatever you have, sell, and be giving to the poor, and you will be having treasure in heaven. And hither! Follow Me, picking up [your stake].[295]

The Greek word *stauros* literally means "an upright stake," but in the common vernacular can sometimes refer to the stake used by the Romans upon which they crucified criminals. Religious translators tend to favor the vernacular term "cross" because of its later usage in Rabbi Jeshua's crucifixion. However, in the text, there is no reason to infer that Rabbi Jeshua is asking the man to submit to judicial punishment. In context, the term references a stake that must be picked up in order to move, such as a tent stake, a more consistent and literal interpretation, pointing to the impoverishment of Rabbi Jeshua's itinerant lifestyle that relies on the generosity of his hosts, rather than bringing along bags of money to stay at the local luxury hotel and spa. Such an impoverished lifestyle was unthinkable to the wealthy inquisitor, such that he "came away sorrowing, for he was one who has many acquisitions."[296] Jeshua turns to his students and states to their astonishment:

How squeamishly shall those who have money be entering into the kingdom of [Elohim]! Easier is it for a camel to pass through the eye of a needle than for a rich man to be entering into the kingdom of [Elohim]...

---

[294] CLV Luke 18:9-14
[295] CLV Mark 10:21
[296] CLV Mark 10:22

[Although] with men it is impossible, but not with [Elohim], for all is possible with [Elohim].[297]

The fear of weakness, poverty, and want keeps the wealthy inquisitor from finding a deeper freedom and purpose. Unless he lets go, he will always be held in bondage to this fear.

Conspectus. The path to safety begins with a person's own life story, rather than some grand cosmic narrative of danger caused by some hungry or angry gillul requiring some propitiatory transaction to pacify them. With each encounter throughout his ministry, Rabbi Jeshua looks into the life of the one inquiring of him and challenges the gillul/idol that motivates the inquisitor's livelihood, pacifying their greatest fears and inspiring the rebirth of the Sacred Midst. To a broken woman, he offers respect, healing, and empowerment. To a blind leader of the people, he offers enlightenment to the truth of love in relationship. To a mourning sister, he offers hope, trust, life, and restoration. To a wealthy tax collector and a ruler, he offers a genuine freedom and deeper purpose out of a generous spirit, apart from the false security of material possessions and power.

As the mythologist Joseph Campbell points out, on our journey to discover our own purpose and safety:

Where there is a way or path, it is someone else's path. You are not on your own path. If you follow someone else's way, you are not going to realize your potential.[298]

The myth provides the map—the path taken is your own, led by the motiving spirit, or higher conscience, of love, inspiring us to value one another and open our boundaries to those in need, in support of the Reunified Family of Elohim.

❖First Kingdom of Elohim

The story of the restoration of the Kingdom of Elohim begins with the rejection of the first Kingdom of Elohim in Israel at the beginning of the Political Kingdom Era. This conspicuously echoes the rejection of the parental authority of Yahweh in the Genesis Exile myth. And which, in turn, reflects the rejection of the direct agency of Yahweh before Mount Sinai in the Exodus myth, wherein the Israelites push Moses to go up the mount alone to return with Yahweh's guidance; followed closely, thereafter, by them creating a Golden Calf to represent Yahweh's guidance. The Adamites' direct numinous

---

[297] CLV Mark 10:24-27
[298] Campbell (1991) p.16

encounter with the Elohim as Parent, Judge, and Servant King is only realized halfheartedly—each time, they eventually invoke some intermediary elohim or gillul to take his place.

In the Exodus myth, Moses, as the Nachash of Elohim, reveals the Law/Guidance of Elohim and then becomes its first mediary judge. Over the next four hundred years, Israel is ruled by Yahweh Elohim as their Servant King, directed through more than a dozen intermediaries acting as judges. This is the first Kingdom of Elohim in Israel. Eventually, the Israelites come before the last judge, Samuel, saying, "Behold, you are old, and your sons do not walk in your ways. Now do appoint for us a king, to judge us like all the other nations." Samuel disappointedly brings this before Yahweh, who replies:

> Hearken to the voice of the people, to all that they are saying to you; for it is not you they have rejected; it is Me Whom they have rejected from being King over them. According to all the deeds that they have done to Me from the day I brought them up from Egypt until this day, in that they have forsaken Me and have served other elohim, so also they are doing to you. And now hearken to their voice. Only you should... testify to them and tell them the customary rights of the king who shall reign over them.[299]

So, Samuel goes before the Israelites as Yahweh has instructed and warns them what will happen once they establish the asymmetric authority of a kingship, portending:

> He shall take your sons for himself and he will make them serve with his chariots and with his horsemen; and they will run before his chariot. Some he will appoint for himself as chiefs of thousands and chiefs of fifties; others will plow his plowland, reap his harvest, make his implements of war and the equipment of his chariotry. He shall take your daughters for perfumers, for cooks and for bakers. He shall take your fields, your vineyards, your olive groves, the best ones, and he will give them to his courtiers. He shall take the tenth of your seeds and your vineyards, and he will give it to his court officials and to his courtiers. He shall take your menservants, your maidservants and your choice young men, the best ones, and your donkeys, and he will use them for his work. He shall take the tenth of your flock; and you shall become slaves for him. You will cry out on that day because of your king whom you have chosen for yourselves; yet Yahweh shall not answer you on that day.[300]

The people reject the warning, and Samuel proceeds as Yahweh has directed to anoint Saul as their first Political King. At the onset of the appointment process, Yahweh decries:

---

[299] CLV 1 Samuel 8:7-9
[300] CLV 1 Samuel 8:11-18

I brought Israel up out of Egypt and rescued you from the hand of Pharaoh
king of Egypt and from the hand of all the kingdoms that were oppressing
you. Yet you have today rejected your Elohim Who has been bringing
salvation to you from all your evils and your distresses.[301]

Thus ends the first Kingdom of Elohim in Israel as the struggle between the symmetric power of Yahweh Elohim as Servant King, the one who watches over his people, and the asymmetric power of a Political King, the one who rules over the people. After four hundred years of slavery, then four hundred years of the Kingdom of Elohim in Israel, there will now be four hundred years of the formal political kingdom of Israel, which will last until its destruction by the Babylonians in the sixth century BCE. Thereafter, a vassal kingdom is established under the control of the Persians. Judah will remain under foreign rule by the Persians, Greeks, and Romans until the nation is completely destroyed by the Romans in the second century CE.

❖Restored Kingdom of Elohim

The restored Kingdom of Elohim is eponymically expressed as the *"realm of great power"* which Rabbi Jeshua characterizes as *ahav* or act-love. It is what inspires the Sacred Midst, the relationship between the Lover and Beloved, representing a mature adult morality based on trust and intimacy.

The restored Kingdom is described as both present and future. There is a lower Kingdom realm of Yahweh's love that is present, here and now, as the embodiment of the Law of Love in the daily lives of humanity. Then, there is an upper Kingdom realm of Yahweh's love that is presented as being a future reconciliation to intimacy with the Father; a full restoration to Eden, to a New Jerusalem from which peace flows directly to the Family, filling the people's lives.

In the Basar of Matthew, the Kingdom of Elohim is alternately described as the Kingdom of the Sky or Heavens. This was traditionally done to avoid using a direct reference to Yahweh Elohim in Hebrew text due to the religious belief that to utter or even write his name would be to take his name in vain as a violation of the Second Commandment of the Decalogue. However, this heavenly epithet also underscores the broad, undefinable spiritual presence of the Parent/Savior Elohim in relationship to the Earth and Humanity. Archetypally, it reinforces the image of the Higher Nachash raised towards the sky or heavens as representing the restorative power of the Imago

---

[301] CLV 1 Samuel 10:18-19

Elohim. However, for the most part, the Kingdom of Elohim and the Kingdom of the Sky/Heavens are synonymous.

It should also be pointed out that the text of the Basar accounts is written in Greek but are describing people who primarily speak Aramaic and Hebrew. So, the Greek translation of *Kingdom of Elohim* in the existing Basar accounts uses the word *theos* indicating deity, which holds the moralistic baggage of Hellenistic culture and its views on hierarchies and control, whereas in the native language the term that would be used is *elohim* meaning a *great power*, which does not inherently have such a political connotation. This Hellenistic bias in the translation is carried over into the renewed politicization of the Messiah as a Warrior King in the non-Gospel portion of the New Testament canon. The English translation, of course, retains the earlier moralistic connotations borrowing the Germanic word *god*, characteristically meaning a *gillul* or idol with whom one transacts benefit.

In the Reified Basar, the Father gives the Anointed Son the authority to judge the Kingdom of Elohim—the realm of great power. However, the narrative deliberately reforms the political language of asymmetric power associated with Kings and Kingdoms into the familial language of the symmetric power of service to others, contrasting the political Warrior King with the Anointed Son as the Servant King, the guardian and caretaker of the family. When a rivalry breaks out amongst his students as to "which of them is seeming to be greatest," Rabbi Jeshua reproves them, stating:

> The kings of the nations are lording it over them, and those exercising authority over them are called benefactors. Yet you are not thus, but let the greatest among you become as the youngest, and he who is leading as he who is serving. For who is greater, the one lying back at table or the one serving? Is it not the one lying back? Yet I am in your midst as the One Who is serving.[302]

In another case, Rabbi Jeshua is asked more generally, "Who... is greatest in the kingdom of the heavens?" To which he responds by calling a little child to him, standing in their midst, he proclaims:

> Verily, I am saying to you, If you should not be turning and becoming as little children, you may by no means be entering into the kingdom of the heavens. Who, then, will be humbling himself as this little child, he is the greatest in the kingdom of the heavens.[303]

Elsewhere Rabbi Jeshua demonstrates the *realm of great power* in loving service to others by performing the humblest of tasks for his students, the

---

[302] CLV Luke 22:25-27
[303] CLV Matthew 18:1-4

customary washing of feet upon entering the household, which was usually performed by the least of the household servants:

> [Rabbi Jeshua] is rising from dinner and is laying down His garments, and, getting a cloth, He girds Himself. Thereafter He is draining water into the basin, and begins washing the feet of the [students] and wiping them off with the cloth with which He was girded...
>
> When, then, He washes their feet, and took His garments and leans back again, He said to them, "Do you know what I have done to you? You are shouting to Me 'Teacher!' and 'Lord!' and you are saying ideally, for I am. If, then, I, the Lord and the Teacher, wash your feet, you also ought to be washing one another's feet. For an example have I given you, that, according as I do to you, you also may be doing.
>
> Verily, verily, I am saying to you, A [servant] is not greater than his lord, neither is an apostle greater than He Who sends him. If you are aware of these things, happy are you if you should be doing them![304]

In the lead up to the Sermon on the Mount, the Reified Basar is described as the fulfillment of the Kingdom of Elohim:

> And Jesus led them about in the whole of Galilee, teaching in their synagogues and heralding the [good news/basar] of the kingdom, and curing every disease and every debility among the people. And forth came the [good news/basar] of Him into the whole of Syria. And they bring to Him all who have an illness, those with various diseases and pressing torments, also demoniacs and epileptics and paralytics, and He cures them.[305]

And then, Rabbi Jeshua begins the Sermon on the Mount by describing the power of the Kingdom as finding happiness in the humblest of circumstances:

> Happy, in spirit, are the poor [weak], for theirs is the kingdom of the [sky/heavens].
> Happy are those who mourn now, for they shall be consoled.
> Happy are the meek, for they shall be enjoying the allotment of the land.
> Happy are those who are hungering and thirsting for righteousness, for they shall be satisfied.
> Happy are the merciful, for they shall be shown mercy.
> Happy are the clean in heart, for they shall see [Elohim].
> Happy are the peacemakers, for they shall be called sons of [Elohim].
> Happy are those persecuted on account of righteousness, for theirs is the kingdom of the [sky/heavens].
> Happy are you whenever they should be reproaching and persecuting you and, falsifying, saying every wicked thing against you, on My account.

---

[304] CLV John 13:4-17
[305] CLV Matthew 4:23-24

> *Rejoice and exult, for your wages are vast in the [sky/heavens]. For thus*
> *they persecute the prophets before you.*[306]

The Kingdom, rather than a place of domination and control, is a place of humility and service to others, represented as the Reunified Family. The King, rather than being one who is served, is one who serves others, harkening back to the original idea of the chief patriarch/anointed son whose responsibility was to care for the family. All are servants to one another as Mature Elohim. All are to love one another—offering comfort to the poor and humble, freedom to the captives and oppressed, and restoration to the blind and brokenhearted in service to the Reunified Family.

❖Sacred Breath of Elohim

The Sacred Breath, or *ruach hakodesh*, is the *arche logos*—the original intention of act-love, the Higher Nachash or conscience that inspires the Kingdom of Elohim. The Hebrew *ruach*[307] and Greek *pneuma*[308] mean *breath* referring to the animating principle that gives us life and directs or motivates our actions. Thus, in the sense of inspiriting speech, forming words, it is characterized as an expression of our motivation and desire. In the Genesis myth, the ruach/breath of the Imago Elohim is the *logos* or word that inspires the creation of all things:

> *In a beginning Elohim created the heavens and the earth. As for the earth,*
> *it came to be a chaos and vacant, and darkness was over the surface of the*
> *abyss. And the [spirit/breath/ruach] of Elohim was vibrating over the*
> *surface of the waters. And Elohim said: "Let light come to be! And light*
> *came to be."*[309]

Yahweh Elohim then creates the Adamites from the clay of the ground and the breath of life:

> *And Elohim said: "Let Us make humanity in Our image and according to*
> *Our likeness" ...male and female He created them... Yahweh Elohim formed*
> *the human out of soil from the ground [adamah], and He blew into his*
> *nostrils the breath of life; and the human became a living soul.*[310]

The *breath of life* is a compound of two words that are rooted in breathing. The Hebrew word *khaw-yaw*[311] translated as *life* is derived from an image of breathing as the indication of life. The word *nesh-aw-maw*[312], translated as

---

[306] CLV Matthew 5:3-12
[307] Strongs H7307
[308] Strongs G4151
[309] CLV Genesis 1:2-3
[310] CLV Genesis 1:26-27, 2:7
[311] Strongs H2421
[312] Strongs H5397

breath, is similar to *ruach* but is rooted in an image of a woman panting in labor. Both *nesh-aw-maw'* and *ruach* are used throughout the Hebrew text to describe the essence of life as breathing, often translated into English as *spirit*.

The ruach/breath expresses the motivation and intent of an elohim. Its formation is an outgrowth of the moral character and maturity of the elohim's conscience. Thus, the breath can be characterized as sacred/clean (*hakodesh*[313]) or unclean (*tam'ah*[314]). The unclean breath (*ruach tam'ah*) is an expression of an immature conscience. In the book of the prophet Zechariah, it is characterized as the motivating inspiration of the false prophet when Yahweh proclaims:

> I shall cut off the names of [idol fetishes] from the land, and they shall no
> longer be remembered. And, moreover, I shall cause the prophets and the
> unclean spirit [ruach tam'ah] to pass from the land... In case a man is
> prophesying still, then... those giving him birth [his parents], will say to
> him, "You shall not live, for you speak falsehood in the Name of Yahweh."
> ...And it will come to be in that day that the prophets shall be ashamed,
> each because of his vision, when he prophesies... And he will say, "I am not
> a prophet. I am a man serving the ground, for human service, it has owned
> me from my youth."[315]

In the Reified Basar account, the term *unclean spirit/breath* is used to describe the *ruach ta'mah* as a tormenting or accusative spirit that inspires deceit and suffering in the life of the oppressed:

> And at [Jeshua's] coming... straightway there meets Him a man... with an
> unclean spirit, who had a dwelling among the tombs. And not even with
> chains was anyone able any longer to bind him... And continually, night
> and day, among the tombs and in the mountains was he, crying and
> gashing himself with stones. And perceiving [Jeshua] from afar, he ran and
> worships Him, and, crying with a loud voice, he is saying, "...Son of [Elohim]
> Most High! I am adjuring Thee... Not me shouldst Thou be tormenting!"
> For [Jeshua] said to it, "Come out, unclean spirit, out of the man!"[316]

On the other hand, the sacred or clean breath (*ruach hakodesh*) is an expression of a mature conscience. The prophet Isaiah invokes the sacred or clean spirit/breath of the Elohim as guiding the Israelites in the days of Moses towards peace and rest, and then, subsequently, grieving over the Israelites' rebelliousness:

---

[313] Strongs H2932
[314] Strongs H2392
[315] CLV Zechariah 13:2-5
[316] CLV Mark 5:1-8

The [kindness] of Yahweh I shall bring to remembrance, The praises of Yahweh, According to all that Yahweh has dealt out to us... His compassions, And... His many [kindnesses]... In His love and in His sparing He Himself redeems them, And He lifts them up and carries them all the days of the [eon/age]. Yet they rebelled and grieved His holy spirit [ruach hakodesh], So that He was turned to be their Enemy...

Yet He remembers the days of the [eon/age], of Moses and His people. Where is He Who brought them up from the sea with the shepherd of His flock? Where is He Who placed among them His holy spirit [ruach hakodesh], Who conducted them by the right hand of Moses, His beauteous arm rending the water before them, To make for Him a Name [in perpetuity]... That like a domestic beast which is descending into a valley, The [spirit/breath/ruach] of Yahweh should give them rest? [317]

And then, in the Reified Basar account, the sacred or clean spirit/breath of the Elohim is a central theme throughout the narrative. It is portrayed as the mature conscience of the Higher Nachash, with whom the Anointed Son baptizes or identifies the Reunified Family. At the beginning of the Basar of Luke, Johanan baptizes those seeking to reconcile their hearts with the Father by the waters of the Jordan River. But when questioned whether he is the Anointed One, the Messiah, he points to Rabbi Jeshua as the one who will baptize them in the Sacred Breath of the Elohim, to become fully identified with the Parent Elohim's love for his children, separating out those authorities who falsely and abusively claim to represent or identify with the Father, stating:

I, indeed, in water am baptizing you. Yet coming is One stronger than I... He will be baptizing you in holy spirit [ruach hakodesh] and fire, Whose winnowing shovel is in His hand, and He will be scouring His threshing floor and be gathering the grain into His barn, yet the chaff shall He burn up with unextinguished fire." [318]

Later in the Basar of Luke, the Sacred Breath is identified as a hallmark of the Family that is generously given by the Good Father to whomsoever requests it:

Now of some father of you a son will be requesting bread. No stone will he be handing him! Or a fish, also. Not, instead of a fish, a serpent will he be handing him! Or he will also be requesting an egg. He will not be handing him a scorpion! If you, then, being inherently [hurtful], are aware how to give good gifts to your children, how much rather will the Father Who is out of heaven, be giving holy spirit [ruach hakodesh] to those requesting Him! [319]

---

[317] CLV Isaiah 63:7-14
[318] CLV Luke 3:16-17
[319] CLV Luke 11:11-13

However, those who reject or vilify the generosity and loving-kindness inspired by the Sacred Breath are held accountable for their unclean spirit/breath [*ruach ta'mah*] characterized as slander:

> *And everyone who shall be declaring a word against the Son of Mankind [that is, Jeshua], it shall be [let go of] him, yet the one who [vilifies/slanders] the holy spirit [ruach hakodesh] shall not be [let go].*
>
> *Now whenever they may be bringing you before the synagogues and the chiefs and the authorities, you should not be worrying about how or what your defense should be or what you may say, for the holy spirit [ruach hakodesh] will be teaching you in the same hour what you must be saying.*[320]

In the Basar of John, the Sacred Breath of Elohim becomes a key construct in the Reunified Family of the Kingdom of Elohim as a guide and teacher. Rabbi Jeshua refers to the Sacred Breath [*ruach hakodesh*] as the consoler/helper represented by the Greek word, *parakletos*[321], meaning the one who comes alongside, which is given to his students as the spirit/breath of truth to guide them once Jeshua has gone away:

> *If you should be loving Me, you will be keeping My precepts. And I shall be asking the Father, and He will be giving you another consoler, that it, indeed, may be with you for the [eon/age]—the spirit of truth, which the world can not get, for it is not beholding it, neither is knowing it. Yet you know it, for it is remaining with you and will be in you...*
>
> *Now the consoler, the holy spirit [ruach hakodesh], which the Father will be sending in My name, that will be teaching you all, and reminding you of all that I said to you...*
>
> *Now, whenever the consoler which I shall be sending you from the Father may be coming, the spirit of truth which is going out from the Father, that will be testifying concerning Me. Now you also are testifying, seeing that, from the beginning, you are with Me.*[322]

In the absence of Rabbi Jeshua's direct teaching regarding love and relationship, the Sacred Breath of Elohim becomes the mature conscience of the Reunified Family of the Kingdom of Elohim, the anchor point concerning healing, morality, and judgment:

> *But I am telling you the truth. It is expedient for you that I may be coming away, for if I should not be coming away, the consoler will not be coming to you. Now if I should be gone, I will send him to you. And, coming, that will be exposing the world concerning [missingness] and concerning righteousness and concerning judging: concerning [missingness], indeed,*

---

[320] CLV Luke 12:10-12
[321] Strongs G3875
[322] CLV John 14:15-15:27 excerpted

seeing that they are not [trusting] in Me; yet concerning righteousness, seeing that I am going away to My Father, and no longer are you beholding Me; yet concerning judging, seeing that the Chief of this world has been judged.

Still much have I to say to you, but you are not able to bear it at present. Yet whenever that may be coming—the spirit of truth—it will be guiding you into all the truth, for it will not be speaking from itself, but whatsoever it should be hearing will it be speaking, and of what is coming will it be informing you. That will be glorifying Me, seeing that of Mine will it be getting, and informing you. All, whatever the Father has, is Mine. Therefore I said to you that of Mine is it getting, and will be informing you.[323]

The Sacred Breath of Elohim, *ruach hakodesh*, is the intimate guide, the mature conscience, that leads the Reunified Family into *ahav*, the giving of breath to one another, or act-love. It is the inspiration and foundation for the restored Kingdom of Elohim. It also sets the moral boundaries against those who would harm the Family by trying to subjugate them under hierarchical asymmetric institutions.

❖**Tree of Breath**

The Tree of Life/Breath is the impetus for wholeness and healing. In the Genesis Creation myth, the Tree of Life is the complement of the Tree of Morality in the Sacred Midst of the Garden. It is the essential domain of the Sacred Breath of the Elohim as the mature conscience that inspires love and the generative force of life and healing. The Sacred Breath is the realization of the Sacred Midst, unifying the Tree of Morality and the Tree of Life through Love and Healing.

The path of the Anointed Son is to embody the Tree of Morality in his life, embracing the Higher Nachash as the mature conscience founded on the value of the Family. By letting go of his own authority to judge the harmful actions against him in response to the injustice of the crucifixion, Jeshua fulfills the challenge he gave his students:

Love your enemies. Be doing ideally to those who are hating you. Bless those who are cursing you. Pray concerning those who are [insulting/abusing] you. To him who is beating you on the cheek, be tendering the other also. And you should not be preventing him who is taking away your cloak from taking your tunic also. Now you, be giving to everyone who is requesting, and from him who is taking away what is yours be not demanding it. And, according as you are wanting that men may be doing to you, you also be doing to them likewise.

[323] CLV John 16:7-13

And if you are loving those loving you, what thanks is it to you? For [the morally immature] also are loving those loving them. And if you should be doing good to those doing good to you, what thanks is it to you? For [the morally immature] also are doing the same. And if you should ever be lending to those from whom you are expecting to get back, what thanks is it to you? For [the morally immature] also are lending to [the morally immature], that they may get back the equivalent. Moreover, be loving your enemies, and be doing good, and be lending, expecting nothing from them, and your wages will be vast in the heavens, and you will be sons of the Most High, for He is kind onto the ungrateful and [hurtful].[324]

By acting in love instead of revenge, Jeshua fulfills his obligation to the Family, even to those that harm him; reifying the relationship of the Lover-Beloved in his earlier proclamation, "Greater love than this has no one, that anyone may be laying down his soul for his friends."[325]

By embodying love through mature moral action, the Anointed Son breathes life back into the Sacred Midst of the Lover-Beloved relationship that died with the insult of the immature Fruit of Morality. Archetypally, as the deconstructive urge for egoistic judgment is let go, the mature morality of act-love restores the life in Between. The path is completed in the restoration of the Tree of Life by fulfilling the life-supporting intent and character of the Sacred Breath as the Higher Nachash that brings love and healing, inspiring new life in relationship with one another.

❖Kingdom Within

The Kingdom of Elohim is the *realm of great power* founded on *ahav*, act-love. The realm is motivated by the Sacred Breath as the higher conscience, which integrates and inspires the value of all within the Reunified Family. It is not a goal, nor an act, nor is it a thing. It is the development of a mature conscience that responds from the gut, not the head. It does not perform acts of compassion to be seen, to be praised and highly esteemed by others, or some imagined gillul that will reward them. It does what is beneficial because the one in need has intrinsic value and is worthy to be protected and nurtured for their own sake.

If a precious vase tips over and rolls towards the edge of a table, it is an instinctual response to protect the object of value. One does not deliberate while the vase rolls towards the edge because there is no question to be asked. There is a stirring in one's being to urgently act as a consequence of one's internal value system. On the contrary, if a used napkin is blown by the

---

[324] CLV Luke 6:27-35
[325] CLV John 15:13

wind towards the edge of a table, one might deliberate whether to disrupt one's current preoccupation, a conversation or a meal. While one might be reminded of an ethical responsibility to not litter taught to them by some past authority, they might delay their response to finish a current action, a bite of food or a word to a companion, before chasing the napkin to the edge of the table to try to retrieve it. But, in the end, if the wind is too strong, perhaps, the chase will come to an abrupt impasse with a dismissive sigh, "Oh well, I'll do better next time," and then, quickly return to one's meal or conversation undaunted as the unseen napkin now floats under a bush and beyond—out of sight, out of mind.

The Sacred Breath acting as the Higher Nachash inspires the Lover to respond to the Beloved with the same instinctual reactivity as described in this example of the precious vase. Rabbi Jeshua, likewise, states:

> Like is the kingdom of the heavens to a treasure hidden in the field, finding which, a man hides it, and, in his joy, is going away, and is selling all, whatever he has, and is buying that field.
>
> Again, like is the kingdom of the heavens to a man, a merchant, seeking ideal pearls. Now, finding one very precious pearl, he comes away, having disposed of all whatever he had, and buys it.[326]

The Kingdom of Elohim, the realm of great power, reveals the tremendous value of that which it contains. It is inherently a relational value system that recognizes how precious each person is, regardless of, or despite, their political or social stature.

Rabbi Jeshua explains that the realm of great power is within us, not some destination, or some acquired future state to which we must strive to learn or possess:

> Now, being inquired of by the Pharisees as to when the kingdom of [Elohim] is coming, He answered them and said, "The kingdom of [Elohim] is not coming with scrutiny. Neither shall they be declaring `Lo! here!' or `Lo! there!' for lo! the kingdom of [Elohim] is inside of you."[327]

The experiential nature of the Kingdom of Elohim is a product of the myth, the Good Story. If you test the truth of the Good Story and find its value, then it becomes a truth rooted within you. We operate instinctually on what we believe and trust to be true. If you trust in a Bad Story, a lie, then your life will be founded on that lie. If you trust in something from a deeper well of truth, founded on the Holomorphic mythological universe that has developed through generations of storytellers, and/or by some deeper numinous

---

[326] CLV Matthew 13:44-46
[327] CLV Luke 17:20-21

revelation of wisdom, then the truth will set you free from your missingness, your vulnerability and fear. Whatever value system you accept as truth will produce the fruit of that "accepted truth":

> *All, then, whatever you should be wanting that men should be doing to you, thus you, also, be doing to them, for this is the law and the prophets... Take heed of those false prophets who are coming to you in the apparel of sheep, yet inside they are rapacious wolves. From their fruits you shall be recognizing them... Thus every good tree ideal fruit is producing, yet the rotten tree noxious fruit is producing. A good tree can not bear noxious fruit, neither is a rotten tree producing ideal fruit.*
>
> *Every tree not producing ideal fruit is hewn down and cast into the fire... Not everyone saying to Me "Lord! Lord!" will be entering into the kingdom of the heavens, but he who is doing the will of My Father Who is in the heavens. Many will be declaring to Me in that day, "Lord! Lord! Was it not in Your name that we prophesy, and in Your name cast out demons, and in Your name do many powerful deeds?" And then shall I be [saying] to them that "I never knew you! Depart from Me, workers of lawlessness!"[328]*

The fruit does not choose what it is but instead is a product of the nature of the tree itself and that which nurtures its well-being.

Likewise, a tree does not become a tree by reasoning that it is a tree one day. The tree begins as a seed, which then must establish its life as a seedling, growing roots in the soil, and reaching higher to the sunlight, to become a sprightly stalk. It then, over time, grows a trunk and an abundance of leaves, and finally, it will grow fruit that can reproduce itself, and also nurture those around it. However, it must suffer through the heat of summer and the cold of winter over many seasons. There may be fires and insects that challenge its well-being. It may have to twist its way around the forest to find the light it needs in between the sprawling chaos surrounding it.

There is a developmental path that we all must journey. The Reified Basar mythology provides a map toward a mature conscience founded on act-love, but it does not specify a path along the many routes available. This ultimately is one's calling, to find one's unique path, to listen to the guiding pull of the psychogenetic imprint of the Imago Elohim in each of us, the Sacred Breath passed on from one generation to the next from the beginning of time. We must recognize our own implicit power to impact the world, and then, choose whether to use that power for goodness or badness, for love or control. Over many seasons, through many trials and tribulations, once we let

---

[328] CLV Matthew 7:12-23

go of our fears and feeble attempts to control the world around us, like the tree, we will reach skyward into the heavens.

❖Morality of Death

In Greek mythology, Man's purpose is to submit to the order and control of the gods and to serve them; otherwise, we are left to fend for ourselves against the weavers of our fate—this is the order of things. However, there are a few gods that challenge that order, showing compassion to those who are suffering, and offering relief, despite the impersonal mandate of Olympic moralism. Two we have already discussed. Dionysus challenges the moral order of the gods by liberating humankind from suffering and oppression, showing us the way to freedom in a world of control, and helping us to find goodness in life. Prometheus challenges the moral order of the gods by leading humankind on the path of sacrifice in support of the needs of those we care about, bringing fire to those in need of warmth, even when we know we may suffer consequences from the authority structure that stands against us. Prometheus shows us the truth of the great power we each possess and identify with as elohim—the power of forethought, to empathically anticipate what goodness we can bring to another, and to act upon it.

The last moral challenger is Asclepius who shows us the way to wholeness and healing, life in abundance. We began this literary journey sitting at the doorstep of Asclepius in Epidaurus, Greece, finding inspiration and healing in the numinosity of his power in myth and dream. In the Orphic Hymns, Asclepius is honored as a blessed savior who defends human life:

> Great [Asclepius], skill'd to heal mankind,
> All-ruling Pæan, and physician kind;
> Whose arts medic'nal, can alone assuage
> Diseases dire, and stop their dreadful rage:
> Strong lenient God, regard my suppliant pray'r,
> Bring gentle Health, adorn'd with lovely hair;
> Convey the means of mitigating pain,
> And raging, deadly pestilence restrain.
> O pow'r all-flourishing, abundant, bright,
> Apollo's honor'd offspring, God of light;
> Husband of blameless Health [Hygeia], the constant foe
> Of dread Disease the minister of woe:
> Come, blessed saviour, human health defend,
> And to the mortal life afford a prosp'rous end.[329]

It is Asclepius who dares to challenge death itself. His skill at preventing death from injury and disease, and then eventually, developing the skills to bring

---

[329] Orpheus (1896) p.130-131

the dead back to life, does not go unnoticed by the gods. In particular, Hades notices that his daily headcount starts to drop, calling into question his entire business model. In short order, Hades complains to the Chief Executive God, Zeus, who in turn fires Asclepius. And by fire, I mean strikes him dead with a thunderbolt. But then, after a tiff with Asclepius' father, Apollo, he relents and elevates Asclepius to the constellation Opiuchus, the Serpent-Holder, as explained by the first-century scholar Hyginus in his work on Poetic Astronomy:

> *Ophiuchus, who is called Anguitenens ["serpent-holder"] by our writers, is located above Scorpio; in his hands he holds a serpent which winds around his body... Many astronomers, however, think this is Asclepius, whom Jupiter [Zeus] placed among the stars for Apollo's sake. For when Asclepius was on earth, he excelled in the medical arts to such a degree that he was not content with alleviating human pain, but aspired to restore the dead to life. And he was said, most recently, to have resuscitated Hippolytus, who was killed because of the inequity of his stepmother and the ignorance of his father, as Eratosthenes relates. Some say that Glaucus, the son of Minos, was brought back to life by Asclepius's skill. On account of this transgression, Jupiter [Zeus] destroyed Asclepius's house with a thunderbolt, but placed him, because of his skill and for the sake of his father Apollo, among the stars, holding a serpent.[330]*

The morality of death is the sovereign domain of the moralistic gods, defining their ultimate control over humankind, separating the mortal from the immortal. Asclepius, out of compassion for mortal Man, challenges the natural order invested in Hades, the god of death. As an immortal god, or demigod, son of Apollo, Asclepius is then killed, which challenges the supernatural order, causing a battle between Apollo and Zeus. Apollo, in retribution for the death of his son, kills the Cyclopes, who is the maker of Zeus' thunderbolts. Eventually, order is restored when Zeus raises Asclepius from the dead to become a divine constellation and then punishes Apollo by humbling him to be the servant of a human king for a while.

In the Reified Basar, the Anointed Son also challenges the morality of death by bringing some who have suffered a premature death back to life. However, rather than a violation of the gods' power and domain, it is portrayed as an act of mercy and goodness, a letting go of their missingness as a fulfillment of the realm of great power, the Kingdom of Elohim. And then, in the death of the Messiah, the Anointed Son, the morality of death is ultimately changed by an act of love. Rather than retribution—an apocalyptic sweeping away of humankind at the hands of a vengeful gillul/god, righting

---

[330] Condos (1997) p.106 Hyginus, Poetic Astronomy 2.14 "Ophiuchus"

the balance of justice for the death of righteous man, the favored firstborn son of Elohim, love stands in the midst of destruction. The lover affirms the essential value and worth of his beloved, despite his failure.

In the mythology, the political kingdom of Israel/Judah is ultimately judged, but not for the murder of Jeshua. As forewarned by the judge Samuel and the subsequent Prophets, Israel is scorned as the favored nation for continually rejecting Yahweh as their elohim. At the end of the first Kingdom of Elohim in Israel, they turn to serve a political gillul as elohim/king in place of Yahweh. In the political kingdoms of Israel, the first and second temples are both symbolic of the institutionalization of this political theology. And thus, their destruction represents the deconstruction of the asymmetric political system that has rejected Yahweh as their elohim.

Mythologically, the path to the final destruction of Jerusalem and the Temple by the Romans occurs over many centuries, through various exiles and apocalyptic events, including the previous destruction of Jerusalem and the Temple by the Babylonians. Israel, and then Judah, progressively lose all their coveted political power, and yet, at each stage, try all the harder to reestablish it. According to Rabbi Jeshua, the destruction and exile of the Judahites as scorned firstborn scions, initiates a new eon/age, a new Kingdom of Elohim, of Yahweh's direct universal rule in the Reunified Family, including the Jews, through his anointed firstborn son, as a Kingdom Within, leading humankind to love one another. The morality of death is transformed into life in the Between, the Sacred Midst, as humanity is reunited in intimacy with the spiritual Father, the ideal Parent within, through the Sacred Breath of love.

❖Restore Value/Boundary

The final chapter proem is excerpted from the famous "I Have A Dream"[331] speech made by Martin Luther King, Jr. in 1963, which invites the audience to consider a world community based in equality, acceptance, and love. It is a dream of renewed value for all humanity that transcends ideological and tribal boundaries, to free ourselves from racism, religious bigotry, and cultural dysfunction, to join together in one voice, to speak the truth of one universal human family that is once and for all free—"free at last."

Psychologically, mature moral development is fulfilled as the dynamic of our adolescent morality becomes more symmetric in the Lover-Beloved

---

[331] King (2009) p.232-234

relationship, restoring value and boundaries to the Sacred Midst of the relationship. The morality of *ahav*, instantiated in the Mosaic Law, becomes internalized as the Tree of Morality merges with the Tree of Life to become a Kingdom Within, breathing new life into the relationship Between the Reunified Family, restoring us to intimacy and love. Love reaches past our need for justice, to find the humanity, the intrinsic value, of even those that seek to do us harm; to let go, to have compassion and mercy, even in our suffering. The true gospel/basar does not establish a community based on agreement or acceptance of a creed, but rather one of value that extends to each and every person, regardless of belief or behavior. Religious tribalism and political patrimony are the antitheses of the Reunified Family of the Kingdom of Elohim, despite the claims of the asymmetric institutions that promulgate such ideologies in the name of that Kingdom.

Archetypally, our restoration to mature morality is the revival of value and boundaries within the Sacred Midst. Authentic relational experience in community is founded on an honest acceptance of our missingness—facing our terror of exposure to one another and the Beloved Elohim. The Kingdom requires us to deconstruct our boundaries, opening them up to the world, making them permeable, and responsive to the truth of ourselves and one another. Such bravery does not come easily, just as a tree does not grow fruit as a sapling. Moral development is a process; our growth is a consequence of our commitment to responsibly engage in conflict and build deeper bonds through the hard work of relationship, facing our fears, to find a trust that transcends moral perfection. The developmental journey of cultivating our humanity has taken us from the juvenile framework of the limited boundaries of the immediate tribe or family in search of inclusion and worth to the adult framework of open relationships founded on our shared identity to build the boundaries of inclusion and worth within the Universal Family, founding our responsibility and obligation to love one another.

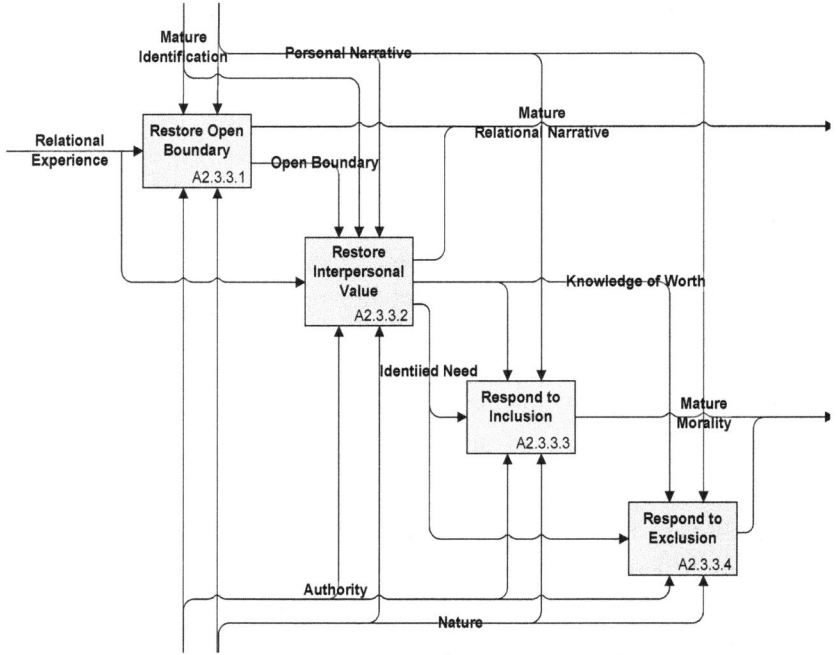

Model 18 - Restore Value/Boundary (A2.3.3)

The Reified Basar is a map to a restored life in the Sacred Midst of the Reunified Family, the path we take is our own. Either we live it openly, or we die avoiding it, circling the walls that we have built to protect ourselves from what we fear in the depths of our souls. The way to the fullness of life is the way of truth and love beyond these walls.

THE AND

The glow of an unseen morning sun begins to dull the crisp dark night sky as we gather at the ocean's edge, the tropical night air still cool but comfortable. Dressed only in my bathing suit, I step gently along the volcanic rock until my foot reaches the shallow of the bay. As I join a sacred chorus of my fellow students in chanting a traditional Hawaiian greeting to the morning sun, I continue my steps until I am fully baptized in the warm ocean waters along with them. The fiery sunrise peeks over the horizon, echoing back our chant in

Sunrise Hilo Bay. Hugo A. Fisher, Oil Painting, 1896.

glorious red, yellow, and orange across the eastern horizon, and an island rainbow emerges in front of us, and then, a second one behind us. I am in awe before the wonder that now cradles my body and soul in warmth and splendor.

It is our first morning in Hilo on the Big Island of Hawaii as guests in the Halau of a local community of Hawaiian elders. We are here to learn about the culture and traditional healing practices of the Hawaiian people. Bound in all directions by a vast eternity of ocean, island culture evolved for the most part on its own. Originating in the Polynesian culture of the South Pacific, some three thousand miles away, the Hawaiians were able to continue some minimal contact over the centuries with their ancestral home by periodically navigating the boundless expanse of ocean via oral maps passed down through chants. However, for the most part, the Hawaiians existed in isolation, learning to live harmoniously with one another in an oft turbulent volcanic island environment.

Rather than an absence of conflict, the Hawaiians had to learn how to deal with conflict. Unlike the Western ethos of "screw up and move west," the vast oceans surrounding Hawaii did not allow for such stubborn irresolution by the island's inhabitants; there was simply nowhere to run and hide from one's problems. In Western lore, the unbounded frontier never led to any *permanent boundary, there was always a new frontier to follow.* Manifest Destiny *conspicuously never arrived anywhere, never calmed the unrest that provoked the Western European's incessant need to wander west towards the setting sun to escape the problems of the past. In contrast, island culture grew around the necessity of doing whatever it takes to resolve conflict as it is exposed, giving rise to the tradition of* Ho'oponopono, *a way of bringing the entire community together to ensure that those in conflict stay engaged until an issue is resolved.*

The heart of Ho'oponopono, and for Hawaiian culture throughout, is aloha. The Hawaiian principium of aloha is a sacred presence, sometimes translated into English as love. It is invoked as a blessing, often in greetings or as a farewell. Literally, aloha means "the presence of breath." It is very similar in intent to the Hebrew word ahav, which we have already explored, meaning, "to breath after," indicating the giving of life to another. The Hawaiian word is centered on being present in life, to be-love, to be at peace with one another, whereas the Hebrew word inspires act-love, action in giving to another—both are necessary for life, for healing, and for relationship to flourish.

Humanity, in the modern era, has reached the proverbial end of its *westward* expansion. Western Europeans dominated the colonial era setting the foundations of the modern transnational commercial culture worldwide. From Western Europe, they brought Western Culture to the Americas, moving west across the continent, subjugating land and indigenous peoples, to the edge of the Pacific Ocean; and then, finally moving further west, to the mythical ends of the earth, where *"thar* be dragons," to a remote string of islands in the very middle of that ocean. The colonization of Hawaii in the nineteenth and twentieth centuries quite literally marked the end of the road for the meandering colonial era. Mythically, we reached our limits, and it is us.

The reality is, when all is said and done, our planet is an island—a world we all share, and from which there is no escaping or ignoring the consequences of our actions. The whole planet now faces the same dilemma that the Hawaiians faced a millennium ago—there is simply nowhere to run. We can no longer ignore our problems. The salvation of our world, both relationally and environmentally, now rests in the world's cultures and their peoples, each of us, letting go of the old ways of exploitation and missingness, to listen to the wisdom of a thousand generations of island people telling us how to live in peace, to have the presence of breath with one another and nature; to love our selves enough to listen and to resolve our underlying problems.

To love one another... or not? It is a simple choice given to each generation, built out of a million choices laid out before us, behind us, on a road that leads us here to this moment. Each choice is a thread woven into the moral fabric of who we are. Love is not a destination, but a journey—one fraught with unlovingness, a lot of missingness, and, if we choose, a lot of letting go and making things right, restoring the value of the Other. Love is not perfection, nor is it a fairy tale. It is a commitment to always strive for community, for life in the Between, the Sacred Midst that brings us together and reminds us of our intrinsic value to one another.

No man is an island—when one soul suffers, we all suffer. But then we have a choice to come together, to reach out to one another, to alleviate the suffering of the One, and the All. We are not hopelessly bound by our failures, struggling, endlessly fighting, against an adversary born of our own fear and deep-seated vulnerability. The truth of who we are in love sets us free. The Sacred Breath whispers the words of life, the Good Story, and that story may become our own story as we become lovers in a world in need of love.

GLOSSARY

adamite : [*Merriam Webster*] a descendant of Adam : a human being; of, relating to, or descended from Adam — [*Context Usage*] a member of the Universal Family of Elohim originating with the Juvenile Elohim that are created in the Garden of Eden from the adamah (red clay) and the sacred breath of the Parent Elohim; referencing Eve and Adam and their descendants; all humans.

ahav : [*Anglicized Hebrew*] אָהַב 'âhab, aw-hab'; or אָהֵב 'âhêb — [*Strongs H157*] a primitive root; to have affection — [*Gesenius' Hebrew-Chaldee Lexicon*] to love; to delight; to breath after; from Chaldee root "to produce fruit" — [*Context Usage*] act-love, to give or restore life/breath to another.

archetype : [*Merriam Webster*] the original pattern or model of which all things of the same type are representations or copies; psychology : an inherited idea or mode of thought in the psychology of Carl Gustav Jung that is derived from the experience of the race and is present in the unconscious of the individual — [*New Usage*] a proposed *mythological archetype* describing an essential narrative pattern underlying human experience across cultures and languages; theoretically, a simplification of Jung's Neo-Platonic theory of a metaphysical framework of meaning encoded in the unconscious, relying rather on actual experience than metaphysical abstractions transferred generationally through unknown and untestable means (thus neither contesting nor supporting Jung's usage of the term).

basar : [*Anglicized Hebrew*] בָּשַׂר bâsar, baw-sar' — [*Strongs H1319*] a primitive root; properly, to be fresh, that is, full (rosy, figuratively cheerful); to announce (glad news) — [*Context Usage*] a good story; invoked by Rabbi Jeshua's identification with its usage in Isaiah 61 focused on the Anointed One's mission to restore humanity to peace and safety — [*Traditional Usage*] see *gospel*.

Christianity : [*Merriam Webster*] the religion derived from Jesus Christ, based on the Bible as sacred scripture, and professed by Eastern, Roman Catholic, and Protestant bodies — [*Traditional Usage*] the secondary historical branch of the Abrahamic religious tradition based on the prophetic teachings of the neo-apostle Paul, which developed separately from the anti-religious social gospel of Rabbi Jeshua that is presented in the four Gospel accounts; derived from Paul's moralized theology as recorded in his epistles that are canonized in the New Testament, and expanded on by the Early Church Fathers, incorporating the Neo-Platonic philosophy of Augustine, and then eventually spawning some thirty thousand exclusionary sects of varied interpretations over the last two millennia — [*Context Usage*] an ideology primarily concerned with the moralized framework of sin, condemnation, heaven, and hell, which conspicuously ignores Rabbi Jeshua's claim that the social gospel/basar of Isaiah 61 is the basis for his anti-religious/anti-moralist teachings on love as the foundation of the Universal Family.

da'ath : [*Anglicized Hebrew*] דַּעַת da'ath, dah'-ath — [*Strongs H1847*] knowledge — [*Traditional Usage*] primary component of the epithet *Knowledge of Goodness and Badness* (da'ath of tov and ra) — [*Context Usage*] awareness or knowledge of goodness and badness, or morality; the foundation of the torah/guidance of the Genesis Creation myth.

decalogue : [*Merriam Webster*] ten commandments — [*Traditional Usage*] the ten primary obligations for the Tribes of Israel that were specified on two stone tablets given to Moses by Yahweh on the Mount of Elohim in Sinai — [*Context Usage*] a relational mandate summarized by Rabbi Jeshua as the obligation to love Yahweh completely and love your neighbor as yourself.

elohim : [*Anglicized Hebrew*] אֱלֹהִים 'ĕlôhîym, el-o-heem' — [*Strongs H430*] exceeding, very great, mighty; judge or ruler — [*Traditional Usage*] often translated into English as the old Germanic word "god," meaning one to whom a supplicant pours out an offering (i.e., an idol); this inaccurate translation forces the translators to insert qualifiers that are not in the text when it refers to a human being, or one that is not of an otherworldly origin — [*Context Usage*] as a plural word, it may reference many entities with great power; when used to reference a single subject, the proper translation is "a very great power" or "one with many or much power"; the term inherently describes a functional capability, but in Genesis 1:27 where Yahweh creates humanity in his/her image, it also describes an inclusive classification of a family of *elohim* extended through Eve and Adam.

egocentric : [*Merriam Webster*] concerned with the individual rather than society; taking the ego as the starting point in philosophy; limited in outlook or concern to one's own activities or needs — [*Context Usage*] a psychological bias towards, and moral preoccupation with, one's own needs and concerns to the exclusion or diminution of others; from the Latin *ego* meaning "I".

gillul : [*Anglicized Hebrew*] גִּלּוּל gillûl, ghil-lool' — [*Strongs H1544*] properly, a log (as round); by implication, an idol — [*Traditional Usage*] an object initially crafted from a wood log, but later used to describe an object crafted from any material that is served in order to transact its power — [*Context Usage*] a projection of some deficiency within one's self or environment functioning as an archetypal authority by which one gains a sense of control by allying with its power through worship and offerings to transact some benefit or to avoid punishment.

god : [*Merriam Webster*] a being or object that is worshipped as having more than natural attributes and powers; specifically, one controlling a particular aspect or part of reality — [*Origin*] from Old German conception of deity to which one pours out libations — [*Traditional Usage*] term used by biblical translators to represent the Greek word *theos* (Strongs G2316) meaning a force that moves, motivates, or oversees some domain of the cosmos, and the Hebrew word *elohim* (Strongs H430) meaning a very great power — [*Context Usage*] may be used archetypally to describe the forces of nature and psychology; or else used same as *gillul* referring to an objectified totem or ideal that one uses to manifest and control what one fears through offerings.

gospel : [*Merriam Webster*] the message concerning Christ, the kingdom of God, and salvation — [*Traditional Usage*] Middle English word used broadly in Christianity and New Testament historical studies as a derivative translation of Hebrew *bâsar* (Strongs H1319) and Greek *euangélion* (Strongs G2098) meaning a good message; may refer to any of the first four books of the Christian New Testament; alternately used in the letters of the neo-Apostle Paul as a reference to a moralized interpretation of the mission of the Christian Jesus to save humankind from "sin" that eventually becomes the foundation for the Christian religion — [*Context Usage*] a good story; originally used by Rabbi Jeshua to describe his mission to alleviate suffering based on Isaiah 61, which is then used to label the four accounts of his life by Matthew, Mark, Luke, and John that form the core mythology of the Reified Basar.

Ground Nachash : [*Label*] an archetypal representation of the degraded egocentric conscience founded on the asymmetric power dynamic of pride, selfishness, and greed; experienced as the one who reveals our vulnerabilities to attack; also symbolized as the viper and saw-tan.

Higher Nachash : [*Label*] an archetypal representation of the integrated noscentric conscience founded on the symmetric power dynamic of love; experienced as an internal dynamic that reveals our power and strength to love one another; also represented as the Sacred Spirit/Breath.

holocentric : [*New*] a psychological perspective centered on an integrative dynamic that essentially moves the narrative psyche towards wholeness and healing; from the Latin *holo* meaning "whole."

holomorphic : [*New*] a focus on the whole or complete psychoanatomy of an individual emphasizing the dynamic interplay between the rational/conscious and the non-rational/egoic-unconscious; from the Latin *holo* meaning "whole."

idcentric : [*New*] a psychological bias towards, and preoccupation with, the needs and concerns of a cultural or moral system to the exclusion or diminution of oneself and others; indicating an exclusionary focus on the impersonal and abstract authority manifest within a system or ideology such as a religion, cultural institution, or tribal ethos; from the Latin *id* meaning "it".

Imago Elohim : [*Label*] the ideal image of personal power that defines the bond, identity, and boundaries of the Family of Elohim.

Islam : [*Merriam Webster*] the religious faith of Muslims including belief in Allah as the sole deity and in Muhammad as his prophet; Arabic indicating submission (to the will of God) — [*Traditional Usage*] the tertiary historical branch of the Abrahamic religious traditions that evolves in context to Prophet Mohammed's early experience with the Nestorian and Ebionite Christian sects of Western Asia and then developing more distinct characteristics through his prophetic visions in the cave of Hira on Mount Jabal al-Nour near Mecca — [*Context Usage*] the institutional dogma of the various sects of Islam deeply rooted in a moralistic world view of rewards and punishment by a monotheistic deity.

Jeshua : [*Anglicized Hebrew*] יְהוֹשׁוּעַ Yᵉhôwshûwaʻ, yeh-ho-shoo'-ah; or יְהוֹשֻׁעַ Yᵉhôwshuʻa — [*Strongs H3091*] Yehoshua meaning "Yahweh causes to be safe or free" as a compound of the identified roots in *Strongs* H3068 meaning Yahweh/Yehova plus Strongs H3467 meaning "to be open, wide or free (by implication) to be safe; causatively, to free or succor" — [*Traditional Usage*] in the Christian tradition, the name is commonly transformed into the Anglicized derivative "Jesus" from the Greek Iesous (Strongs G2424 Ἰησοῦς Iēsoûs, ee-ay-sooce') as a part of a deliberate movement to sublimate the Jewish origins of the mythology to appeal to a broader Hellenistic public in the Early Church movement — [*Context Usage*] refers to the name given to the original Jewish rabbi in the pre-Christian Basar mythology as contained in the four Gospel/Basar accounts, as opposed to the nominally Jewish, or anti-Jewish, Christian Jesus of the Hellenized Pauline tradition and its institutional progeny.

Jew/Judahite : [*Merriam Webster*] a member of the Kingdom of Judah composed of the tribes of Judah and Benjamin; a member of a nation existing in Palestine from the sixth century BCE to the first century CE; a person belonging to a continuation through descent or conversion of the ancient Jewish people — [*Strongs H3064/ G2453*] see reference — [*Traditional Usage*] after the unified

Kingdom of Israel split into the Northern Kingdom of Israel in Samaria and the Southern Kingdom of Judah, the Northern Kingdom was eventually destroyed by the Assyrians in the eighth century BCE and only the Judahites were left to represent the original tribes of Israel. Eventually, the Judahites colonized Samaria and the term Israelite became synonymous with the term Jew, as a derivation of Judahite — [*Context Usage*] a person so described above, inclusive of the traditional Rabbinic Jews and the Messianic Jews of the Basar tradition — [*Note*] in the Gospel accounts, the term "the Jews" is sometimes used narrowly, and somewhat pejoratively, to represent a subgroup of pious Jews who opposed the Jewish Rabbi Jeshua.

Judaism : [*Merriam Webster*] a religion developed among the ancient Hebrews and characterized by belief in one transcendent God who has revealed himself to Abraham, Moses, and the Hebrew prophets and by a religious life in accordance with Scriptures and rabbinic traditions; the cultural, social, and religious beliefs and practices of the Jews; conformity to Jewish rites, ceremonies, and practices — [*Traditional Usage*] the primary historical branch of the Abrahamic religious traditions; the term is first applied in the fourteenth century CE, however, conceptually the movement originates in Hasidic revival movement during and after the Babylonian Exile of Judah in the sixth century BCE, which results in the collection and consolidation of the Hebrew canon that is used in Judaism and Christianity. As with any religious movement, it is not a singular enterprise but an aggregate of approaches and theologies that have evolved from the struggle within and between competing communities. In the first century CE, the two primary schools constellated around the more conservative Rabbi Shammai and the more liberal Rabbi Hillel. When the temple is destroyed in 70 CE, it undermined the conservative focus on the temple as the basis for Jewish religious life, thus Hillel's followers, who were focused on religious life in the synagogue, became the dominant influence thereafter into modern times. Originally, the Jews who recognized Rabbi Jeshua as the messiah were a part of the community synagogues of Hillel until they were forced out by the political messianists starting in 80 CE — [*Context Usage*] the term is used anachronistically (before it was coined in the 14th century) to define the various Jewish religious movements from the sixth century BCE onwards.

Kingdom of Cain : [*Label*] the realm of asymmetric power and influence symbolized by Cain, the firstborn of Adam, as the founder of human civilization and idolatry who builds the first city, establishes agriculture, art, and metallurgy. Archetypally stands in opposition to the symmetric dynamics of the Kingdom of Elohim. Often symbolically represented throughout the Torah by Matsor/Egypt.

Kingdom of Elohim : [*Label*] literally the "realm of great power." Refers to the intimate influence of Yahweh as Parent, Savior, and Beloved in the Universal Family, or else, more narrowly within the nation of Israel as his anointed people. Rabbi Jeshua describes it as evolving into an internal state of universal symmetric power founded on love, the "kingdom within" that is the context for the Reunified Family of Elohim.

Kingdom of Heaven/Sky : [*Label*] same as the Kingdom of Elohim

Knowledge of Goodness and Badness : [*Label*] morality; a moral system identifying the goodness and badness of an action or activity — [*Context Usage*] originates in the mythology of the Tree of the Knowledge of Goodness and Badness in the Garden of Eden.

Matsor : [*Anglicized Hebrew*] מָצוֹר mâtsôwr, maw-tsore' — [*Strongs* H4693/H4692] Egypt; something hemming in; (subjectively) a fastness:—besieged, bulwark, defense, fenced, fortress, siege, strong (hold), tower — [*Context Usage*] Egypt as a fortress, the everted image of the Garden of Eden as a protected place; archetypally identified with the Kingdom of Cain representing human civilization as the place of asymmetric hierarchal power of kings and *gilluls*, as well as agriculture, architecture, metallurgy, and the arts.

midbar : [*Anglicized Hebrew*] מִדְבָּר midbâr, mid-bawr' — [*Strongs* H4057] wilderness; a pasture (i.e., open field, whither cattle are driven); by implication, a desert; also, speech (including its organs): desert, south, speech, wilderness. — [*Context Usage*] wilderness suitable for limited habitation; symbolic of East of Eden where the Adamites are sent after they are separated from the Tree of Life; archetypally a place of scarcity, toil, and struggle associated with the groundworker in the Genesis Exile.

Middle Nachash : [*Label*] an archetypal representation of the unintegrated conscience, which is in flux between the disintegrated Lower/Ground Nachash and the integrated Upper/Higher Nachash. May also represent the projected moral conscience of an elohim by a representative messenger enrolled as a prophet or oracle.

missingness : [*Oxford*] The quality or condition of being missing; absence — [*Strongs* H2398/G266] The Hebrew *chatta'ah* (H2398) and the Greek word *hamartia* (G266) are similarly defined as missing an objective — [*Traditional Usage*] inaccurately equated with *sin/guilt* by early English Bible translators and carried forward into modern versions of the Bible — [*Context Usage*] a psychological state of nakedness and vulnerability in response to a broken relationship, evoking fear and a desire to protect one's self; initiated in the Genesis Exile myth indicating a traumatic self-awareness of separation between the Adamites and the Parent Elohim; elsewhere used to indicate a failure to love pointing to the relational mandates of the Mosaic Law.

moralism : [*Merriam Webster*] the habit or practice of moralizing; a conventional moral attitude or saying; an often-exaggerated emphasis on morality — [*Context Usage*] a psychological and moral perspective which emphasizes following the rules of a moral system without any responsibility to one's relationship with the people affected; morality without love.

myth : [*Merriam Webster*] a usually traditional story of ostensibly historical events that serves to unfold part of the world view of a people or explain a practice, belief, or natural phenomenon; a popular belief or tradition that has grown up around something or someone, especially : one embodying the ideals and institutions of a society or segment of society; (pejoratively) an unfounded or false notion, or a person or thing having only an imaginary or unverifiable existence — [*Origin*] Greek word meaning *story* — [*Context Usage*] a narrative artifact in psychology which exists, or has evolved, beyond a singular event, to represent a deeper universal or archetypal truth regarding human nature presented in a moral framework to inspire and instruct; at times it may be related to historical events as a psychological impression of experiences refined through generational retelling.

nachash : [*Anglicized Hebrew*] נָחָשׁ nâchâsh, naw-khawsh' — [*Strongs* H5175/5172] a snake (from its hiss); serpent; root meaning to hiss or whisper related to magic and oracles — [*Traditional Usage*] in moralism, refers to an evil entity that lies to the Adamites bringing sin and evil into the world, however, it is not a part of the actual Torah mythos — [*Context Usage*] a complex, multimodal archetype representing either a disintegrative force that brings destruction and death or else an integrative force that brings renewal and oracular wisdom.

Nachash of Elohim : [*Label*] a person who is enrolled as an oracle for the Elohim, to represent and reveal the Elohim's wisdom, power, and/or authority to the community.

nod : [*Anglicized Hebrew*] נֹוד Nôwd, node — [*Strongs H5113/H5112*] exile, wandering; vagrancy; Nod, the land of Cain — [*Context Usage*] missingness; exile; the place of wandering both physically and/or spiritually; a place of scarcity, often represented as a desert or a land suffering from drought.

noscentric : [*New*] a psychological bias towards, and moral preoccupation with, the needs and concerns of a relationship inclusive of all participants; indicating a comprehensive focus on the interpersonal relationship between oneself and others; from Latin *nos* meaning "us."

psyche : [*Merriam Webster*] the totality of elements forming the mind, (originally used in Freudian psychoanalytic theory to indicate) the id, ego, and superego including both conscious and unconscious components; from Greek psyche indicating soul (also a reference to butterfly) — [*Context Usage*] a narrative artifact describing the entirety of one's distinct personality and identity both conscious and unconscious to the ego.

psychoanatomy : [*New*] the psychological framework of an individual that comprises the functional capacity and orientation of their identity or truth as a product of nature and nurture; although inherently immeasurable, it is known through the implied narrative patterns revealed by human nature and behavior.

psychogenetic : [*New*] the elemental psychological disposition that emerges out of biological and archetypal patterns of behavior imprinted in human nature, which may be passed down through history and genealogy as what makes us human both collectively and individually; inclusive of Carl Jung's neo-Platonic theory of a Collective Unconscious that underlies human nature and experience.

ra : [*Anglicized Hebrew*] רַע ra', rah — [*Strongs H7451*] bad; derived from root H7489 ra'a indicating, to spoil (literally, by breaking to pieces); figuratively, to make (or be) good for nothing — [*Traditional Usage*] in moralism, it is translated as *evil* to indicate a substantial force that dominates or consumes its victim, such as a monster or villain, whose primary characteristic is their appetite for destruction — [*Context Usage*] badness, the quality of losing one's purpose or integrity.

Reified Basar : [*Label*] the reification or actualization of the Basar/Good Story of Isaiah 61 through the life and ministry of Rabbi Jeshua as recorded in the four Basar/Gospel accounts of Matthew, Mark, Luke, and John, offering comfort to the poor and humble, freedom to the captives and oppressed, and restoration to the blind and brokenhearted.

relationalism : [*New*] a psychological and moral perspective focused on the ethics of prosocial behavior in an open and inclusive community; emphasizes an individual's responsibility to foster healthy, supportive relationships with others, founded on equality and the shared value of each person within a community as a fulfillment of a moral system motivated by altruism, mutuality, and love; a morality of love

Reunified Family of Elohim : [*Label*] Humanity as a unified entity founded on the mythology of Eden as it develops from an original ideal of a Universal Family that disintegrates in the exclusionary wilderness narratives through nationalism, tribalism, religionism, and individualism, and then reintegrates over the developmental arc into a reunified Universal Family based on a morality of love and inclusivity.

Sacred Breath : [*Label*] the prime generative force of goodness in creation and relationship as an expression of the love of the Parent/Creator Elohim, identified in the Basar of John as the *arche logos*, the original word or intention that inspires life and instantiates all things in existence that is fulfilled in the Anointed Son's life and ministry in support of the Basar/Good Story; Identified with the Higher Nachash as the fulfillment of mature moral development.

Sacred Midst : [*Label*] an archetypal third presence between two individuals representing the relationship born of mutuality and nurtured in intimacy; the life and health of the relationship between two people that is dependent on the trustworthiness and commitment to the safety of each participant, and dies without it; it is symbolized in the Genesis Creation myth by the Tree of Morality and the Tree of Life, then in the Exodus myth by the Pillar of Cloud and Fire, and then by the Tabernacle; the overall arc of the Unified Basar and Torah myth establishes it as primary archetype between child and parent Elohim in the Garden, which dies in the Exile narrative. It then reemerges as a path towards restoration or resurrection in the Reified Basar; represented as the realm of great power founded on love.

saw-tan : [*Anglicized Hebrew*] שָׂטָן sâṭân, saw-tawn' — [*Strongs H7854/ H7853*] an opponent; adversary, from the root; to attack, (figuratively) accuse: (be an) adversary, resist — [*Traditional Usage*] Satan, the arch-enemy of good; the guardian archetype of pride, selfishness and greed; the antagonist in the moralist mythology of the fight between good and evil; although, it is not actually in the Unified Basar and Torah myth — [*Context Usage*] The degraded egocentric conscience manifested as a limited power within a narrow hierarchical perspective on what is good based on the needs of the individual to the exclusion of the community and others.

sin : [*Merriam Webster*] an offense against religious or moral law; transgression of the law of God; a vitiated state of human nature in which the self is estranged from God — [*Origin*] Middle English sinne, from Old English synn; Latin sont-, sons meaning guilty — [*Traditional Usage*] to be judged guilty and condemned for a violation of a religious mandate/law; although it is not in the Unified Basar and Torah mythology, it overlays and replaces the psychological concept of *missingness* in the myth represented by the Hebrew word *chatta'ah* (*Strongs* H2398) and the Greek word *hamartia* (Strongs G266) — [*Context Usage*] a moralistic concept promoted by religious institutions to describe why God is justified in punishing humankind for disappointing his perfect moral character.

torah : [*Anglicized Hebrew*] תּוֹרָה tôwrâh, to-raw'; or תֹּרָה torah — [*Strongs H8451*] a precept or statute; law; instruction — [*Traditional Usage*] Decalogue or Pentateuch — [*Context Usage*] a principal guidance in the Unified Basar and Torah myth, used to reference three primary torah/guidances: (1) Awakening (Genesis Creation), (2) Obligation (Mosaic Law), (3) Restoration (Gospel/Basar).

tov : [*Anglicized Hebrew*] טוֹב ṭôwb, tobe — [*Strongs H2896*] good — [*Context Usage*] the manifestation of the *arche logos*, or original intention/purpose of creation; also symbolic of authenticity, integrity, and truth.

Transcendent Elohim : [*Label*] the ideal Parent Image that inspires our strengths and capacity for compassion and cultivates our commitment to care for one another in the Universal Family of Elohim.

transference : [*Merriam Webster*] the redirection of feelings and desires and especially of those unconsciously retained from childhood toward a new object (such as a psychoanalyst conducting therapy) — [*Context Usage*] projection of one's psychological dynamics onto a comparable or representative object or person.

Transferent Elohim : [*Label*] the denigrated Parent Image upon which we project our fears of inadequacy and separation; may manifest as archetypal gods/idols that demand submission and service to pacify their hunger and irritability.

Unified Basar and Torah myth : [*Label*] a cohesive developmental journey from the mythic child-parent relationship of the Elohim in the Garden of Eden to the adult lover-beloved relationship in the Reunified Family of the Universal Kingdom of Elohim; presented as two parts in the religious traditions that borrow from it, but unified in and by the Reified Basar narrative.

voscentric : [*New*] a psychological bias towards, and moral preoccupation with, the needs and concerns of another to the exclusion or diminution of one's self; indicating an exclusionary focus on an external authority to define one's motivations and perspectives; may be subtly coercive as a social institution that subjugates specified members to a dominant class such as women in patriarchal societies, or may be directly coercive as in the subjugation of a race or class within the institutions of feudalism or slavery; from the Latin *vos* meaning "you".

Yahweh : [*Anglicized Hebrew*] יְהֹוָה Yᵉhôvâh, yeh-ho-vaw', yahweh — [*Strongs H3068*] (the) self-Existent or Eternal — [*Arabic*] one who loves, blows, and/or falls — [*Traditional Usage*] God; LORD; in moralism, an adversarial deity with hierarchical control over the universe, demanding all creation to submit to his authority, threatening to punish anyone who defies his supremacy and purity, but also promising to reward those who submit to his will, thus earning his "love" — [*Context Usage*] in relationalism, the parent Elohim characterized in the Torah as compassionate and gracious, slow to anger and abundant with kindness and truth; one who loves his Children, breathes life into them and generously bestows his blessings/provision upon them.

REFERENCES

_____. *Blue Letter Bible*. Online reference. http://www.blueletterbible.org/

_____. *Christian Bible. Concordant Literal Version, the Sacred Scriptures*. United States: Concordant Publishing Concern, 1926.

_____. *Christian Bible. New International Version*. Grand Rapids, MI: Zondervan, 2011.

_____. *Christian Bible. King James Version*. Royal Family Publication Society. 2020. (Original work published 1831).

_____. *Interlinear Scripture Analyzer*. The Netherlands: Scripture4All Publishing, 2015.

_____. *Lexico Dictionary*. Oxford University Press. Lexico.com. 2021.

_____. *The Merriam-Webster Dictionary*. United States: Merriam-Webster, 2004.

Adams, Douglas. "Introduction." *The Restaurant at the End of the Universe*. United States, Random House Worlds, 2008, p.1-2.

Aeschylus. *Seven Against Thebes*. United Kingdom, Oxford University Press, 1991.

Aizenstat, Stephen. *Dream Tending: Awakening to the Healing Power of Dreams*. United States, Spring Journal, 2011.

Angelou, Maya. "Still I Rise." *The Complete Collected Poems of Maya Angelou*. New York, Random House, 1994, p.163-164.

Aristophanes. *Delphi Complete Works of Aristophanes (Illustrated)*. N.p., Delphi Classics, 2013.

Bad Religion. "Sorrow." *The Process of Belief*, Epitaph, 2002, track 8. CD.

Boadt, Lawrence, et al. *Reading the Old Testament: An Introduction*. United States, Paulist Press, 2012.

Buber, Martin. *I And Thou*. United States: Charles Scribner's Sons, 1970.

Buber, Martin. *On Judaism*. United Kingdom: Schocken Books, 1995.

Campbell, Joseph. *The Joseph Campbell Companion: Reflections on the Art of Living*. United States, HarperCollins, 1991.

Celan, Paul. *Collected Prose*. United Kingdom, Routledge, 2003.

Cohen, Leonard. "Born in Chains." *Popular Problems*, Columbia, 2014, track 8. CD.

Condos, Theony. *Star Myths of the Greeks and Romans: A Sourcebook*. United States, Red Wheel Weiser, 1997.

Corbett, Lionel. *Psyche and the Sacred: Spirituality Beyond Religion*. United Kingdom, Taylor & Francis, 2019.

Cott, Jonathan. *Fellini's Language of Dreams: Rolling Stone Interview*. Rolling Stone, Issue #421, May 10, 1984. Accessed from http://scrapsfromtheloft.com/2017/12/05/fellinis-language-of-dreams-rolling-stone-interview-1984/

Dickens, Charles. "Chapter 58 Absence." *David Copperfield*. United Kingdom, Oxford University Press, 1997, p.793.

Diogenes Laertius. *The Lives and Opinions of Eminent Philosophers*. United Kingdom: H. G. Bohn, 1853.

Hannah, Barbara. *Jung, His Life and Work: A Biographical Memoir*. United Kingdom, Chiron Publications, 1997.

Hardcastle, Gary. *Monty Python and Philosophy: Nudge, Think!* Australia, ReadHowYouWant.com, Limited, 2010.

Harding, Mary Esther. *The Parental Image: Its Injury and Reconstruction: a Study in Analytical Psychology*. United States, Sigo Press, 1993.

Hesiod, *The Homeric Hymns, and Homerica*. Translated by Hugh G. Evelyn-White. United Kingdom, W. Heinemann, 1920.

Hesiod. *Theogony and Works and Days*. Ann Arbor, University of Michigan Press, 2006.

Hesiod. *Theogony, Works and Days, and the Shield of Heracles*. Translated by Hugh G. Evelyn-White. N.p., Digireads.com, 2018.

Jamieson, Robert. *Commentary Critical and Explanatory on the Whole Bible*. United States, Christian Classics Ethereal Library, 2002.

John of the Cross, Saint. *The Collected Works of Saint John of the Cross*. Translated by Kieran Kavanaugh and Otilio Rodriguez. United States, ICS Publications, 1991.

Josephus, Flavius. *The Complete Works of Josephus*. Translated by William Whiston. United States, Kregel Publications, 1973.

Jung, Carl Gustaf. *Collected Works of C.G. Jung, Volume 11: Psychology and Religion: West and East*. United States, Princeton University Press, 2014.

King, Martin Luther. "I Have a Dream Speech (1963)." From Sundquist, Eric J., *King's Dream*. New Haven, Yale University Press, 2009, p.232-234.

Kruse, Kevin. *One Nation Under God: How Corporate America Invented Christian America*. United States, Basic Books, 2015.

Larson, Gary. *The Prehistory of the Far Side*. Kiribati, Warner Books, 1992.

Lawrence Kohlberg, Em Griffin, cmglee, CC BY-SA 4.0, Public domain, via Wikimedia Commons. Illustration, 2012 from http://commons.wikimedia.org/wiki/File:Kohlberg_Model_of_Moral_Development.svg

Leick, Gwendolyn. *A Dictionary of Ancient Near Eastern Mythology*. United Kingdom: Taylor & Francis, 2002.

Morgan, David. *Monty Python Speaks! The Complete Oral History of Monty Python, as Told by the Founding Members and a Few of Their Many Friends and Collaborators*. United States, HarperCollins, 1999.

Muir, John. *John of the Mountains: The Unpublished Journals of John Muir*. United States, Houghton, Mifflin, 1938.

Nagy, Gregory. *The Ancient Greek Hero in 24 Hours: Sourcebook*. United States, Perseus Project, 2020.

Orpheus. *The Mystical Hymns of Orpheus*. Translated by Thomas Taylor. United Kingdom: Betram Dobell, Reeves and Turner, 1896.

Ovid. *The Metamorphoses*. Translated by A. S. Kline. United States, Poetry In Translation, 2000.

Plato. *Laws*. United States, Dover Publications, 2013.

Plato. *The Dialogues of Plato, Volume One*. Translated by B. Jowett. Oxford University Press, 1892.

Rand, Ayn. *The Virtue of Selfishness*. United Kingdom: Penguin Publishing Group, 1964.

Rumi, Jalal al-Din. "The Dream That Must Be Interpreted." *The Essential Rumi*. United Kingdom: HarperCollins, 1995, p. 112-113.

Sanchoniatho, *The Theology of the Phoenicians*. In Cory, I. P. *The Ancient Fragments: Containing what Remains of the Writings of Sanchoniatho, Berossus, Abydenus, Megasthenes, and Manetho Also the Hermetic Creed, the Old Chronicle, the Laterculus of Eratosthenes, the Tyrian Annals, the Oracles of Zoroaster, and the Periplus of Hanno*. United Kingdom, W. Pickering, 1828.

Shakespeare, William. "Act 3 Scene 2." *Romeo and Juliet*. United States, Yale University Press, 2004, p.111.

Siculus, Diodorus. *Delphi Ancient Classics: Complete Works of Diodorus Siculus (Delphi Classics)*. N.p., Delphi Publishing Limited, 2011.

Smith, William. *Dictionary of Greek and Roman biography and mythology*. United Kingdom, Walton and Maberly, 1861.

Stephany, Timothy. *Enuma Elish: the Babylonian Creation Epic*. United States, CreateSpace Independent Publishing Platform, 2013.

Strongs, James. *Strongs' Expanded Exhaustive Concordance of the Bible*. Nashville: Thomas Nelson, 2009.

Stroud, James Edward. *The Knights Templar & the Protestant Reformation*. N.p., Salem Author Services, 2011.

Sturluson, Snorri. *The Prose Edda: Tales from Norse Mythology*. United States, Dover Publications, 2012.

Tabor, James. *Paul and Jesus: How the Apostle Transformed Christianity*. United States, Simon & Schuster, 2013.

Toorn, Karel van der. *Dictionary of Deities and Demons in the Bible*. Germany, Eerdmans Publishing Company, 1999.

Tregelles, Samuel. *Gesenius' Hebrew-Chaldee Lexicon*. United States: Eerdmans, 1964.

U2. "A Sort of Homecoming." *The Unforgettable Fire*, Island, 1990, track 1. CD.

Yancey, Philip, Brand, Paul. *Fearfully and Wonderfully: The Marvel of Bearing God's Image*. United States: InterVarsity Press, 2019.

MEDIA

Sark stone stairs of cellar dungeon, Hannu Viitanen, Stock Photo, 2020.
Anterovium, Royalty-Free License via Colourbox.
[Source]=http://www.colourbox.com/image/sark-stone-stairs-of-cellar-dungeon-loosing-freedom-concept-image-51611656
[Use]=Front and Back Covers/Redacted and Edited

The Cathedral, Auguste Rodin, Sculpture, 1908.
Yair Haklai, CC BY-SA 4.0, via Wikimedia Commons.
[Source]=http://commons.wikimedia.org/wiki/File:Auguste_Rodin-The_Cathedral-Rodin_Museum,_Paris.jpg
[Use]=Title Page/Redacted and Filtered

Eve, Auguste Rodin, Sculpture, 1882.
Steve Cadman from London, U.K., CC BY-SA 2.0, via Wikimedia Commons.
[Source]=http://commons.wikimedia.org/wiki/File:Eve_by_Auguste_Rodin.jpg
[Use]=The Cellar/Redacted and Filtered

Café Terraces at Night, Vincent Van Gogh, Drawing, 1888.
Vincent van Gogh, Public domain, via Wikimedia Commons.
[Source]=http://commons.wikimedia.org/wiki/File:Vincent_van_Gogh._Caf%C3%A9_Terrace_at_Night._1888._Reed_pen_and_ink_over_pencil_on_laid_paper,_(65.4_x_47.1_cm)._Dallas_Museum_of_Art.jpgover_pencil_on_laid_paper,_(65.4_x_47.1_cm)._Dallas_Museum_of_Art.jpg
[Use]=Preface/Filtered

Abaton, Epidaurus. Chabe01, Photo, 2022.
Abaton Épidaure. Chabe01, CC BY-SA 4.0, via Wikimedia Commons.
[Source]=http://commons.wikimedia.org/wiki/File:Abaton_%C3%89pidaure_-_%C3%89pidaure_(GR11)_-_2022-03-24_-_16.jpg
[Use]=Initiation/Redacted and Filtered

Ptolemaic System. "Annotazione sopra la Lettione della Spera del Sacrobosco", Mauro Fiorentino, Illustration, 1550.
Mauro Fiorentino, Theosebo, Phonasco, & Philopanareto., Public domain, via Wikimedia Commons.
[Source]=http://commons.wikimedia.org/wiki/File:1550_SACROBOSCO_Tractatus_de_Sphaera_-_(16)_Ex_Libris_rare_-_Mario_Taddei.JPG
[Use]=The World As I See It/Filtered

Scenography of the Copernican World System, Andreas Cellarius, Illustration, 1661.
Andreas Cellarius, Public domain, via Wikimedia Commons.
[Source]=http://commons.wikimedia.org/wiki/File:Cellarius_Harmonia_Macrocosmica_-_Scenographia_Systematis_CopernicaniFXD.jpg
[Use]=The World As I See It/Filtered

Map showing Assyria, Babylonia, and Armenia., FlorinCB, Photo, 2021.
FlorinCB, CC0, via Wikimedia Commons.

[Source]=http://commons.wikimedia.org/wiki/File:4000BCE_map_of_the_w
orld_showing_Armeny_Ashur_Bavel_Akkad-British_Museum-
Object_Number-92687-PubDomain-details5.svg
[Use]=Imago Mundi/Filtered

Redwood Trees, Julia Rodgers, Photo, 1920.
Rogers, Julia Ellen, b. 1866, No restrictions, via Wikimedia Commons.
[Source]=http://commons.wikimedia.org/wiki/File:The_tree_book_-
_A_popular_guide_to_a_knowledge_of_the_trees_of_North_America_and_
to_their_uses_and_cultivation_(1920)_(14596581567).jpg
[Use]=Part I/Filtered

The Kiss of Death. Ferran Pestaña, Photo, 2010. Cropped and Filtered.
Ferran Pestaña, CC BY-SA 2.0, via Wikimedia Commons.
[Source]=http://commons.wikimedia.org/wiki/File:El_bes_de_la_mort_-
_The_kiss_of_death_-_El_beso_de_la_muerte.jpg
[Use]=Part II/Redacted and Filtered

Notre Dame Spire on Fire. Guillaume Levrier, Photo, 2019.
Levrier Guillaume, CC BY-SA 4.0, via Wikimedia Commons.
[Source]=http://commons.wikimedia.org/wiki/File:Fl%C3%A8che_en_feu_-
_Spire_on_Fire.png
[Use]=Part III/Filtered

Sunrise, Hilo Bay. Hugo A. Fisher, Oil on Canvas, 1896.
Hugo Anton Fisher, Public domain, via Wikimedia Commons.
[Source]=http://commons.wikimedia.org/wiki/File:Hugo_Anton_Fisher_-
_%27Sunrise,_Hilo_Bay%27,_oil_on_canvas,_1896.jpg
[Use]=The And/Filtered

Tyrannosauripus pillmorei. James St. John, Photo, 1994.
James St. John, CC BY 2.0, via Wikimedia Commons.
[Source]=http://commons.wikimedia.org/wiki/File:Tyrannosauripus_pillmor
ei_theropod_dinosaur_footprint_(Raton_Formation,_Upper_Cretaceous;_P
hilmont_Ranch_tracksite,_North_Ponil_Canyon,_northern_New_Mexico,_U
SA)_(15352953647).jpg
[Use]=Author/Redacted and Filtered

INDEX

AUTHOR

Tom Strelow is the hero in his own imaginal quest to find the mythic grail. He was last seen looking quite despondent while clumsily holding the Imago Mundi upside down at the fabled fork nigh to the very miry Slough of Despond. As a scholar and explorer, Tom has endeavored to probe the essence of human experience and relationship through the lens of depth and experiential psychologies, mythology, philosophy, history, and religious studies in an attempt to map the topography of the archetypal soul. Herein are some momentous waypoints on his journey to show that he is very serious, and smarter than he looks:

- MA in Counseling Psychology with Emphasis on Depth Tradition from Pacifica Graduate Institute, Carpinteria, CA
- Certificate in Drama Therapy from the Drama Therapy Institute of Los Angeles
- Certificate in Experiential Psychologies from Trees of Life Institute, Santa Barbara, CA
- Cofounder of PAX (Personal Art Exchange)
- Producer of Art&Soul Lecture Series
- Producer at Baytown Arts and Entertainment
- Facilitator of Xrysalis Community Group
- CEO/Principal Consultant for Ultrablue Consulting
- BS in Mathematics and Computer Science from UCLA

Let the inquisitor beware, thar be dragons afoot...

www.ingramcontent.com/pod-product-compliance
Lightning Source LLC
Chambersburg PA
CBHW062116020426
42335CB00013B/982